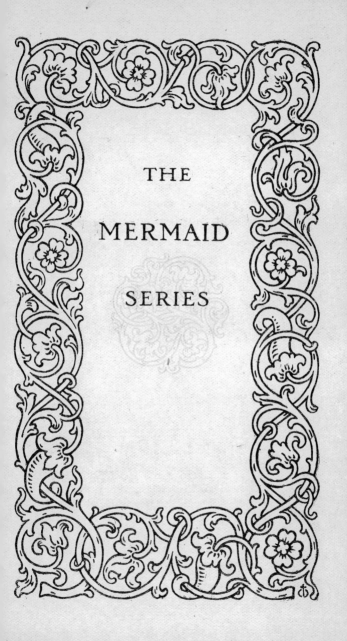

THE

MERMAID

SERIES

JAMES SHIRLEY

THE MERMAID SERIES.

Literal Reproductions of the Old Text, with etched Frontispieces.

The Best Plays of Christopher Marlowe. Edited, with Critical Memoir and Notes by HAVELOCK ELLIS; and containing a General Introduction to the Series by JOHN ADDINGTON SYMONDS.

The Best Plays of Thomas Otway. Introduction and Notes by the Hon. RODEN NOEL.

The Complete Plays of William Congreve. Edited by ALEX. C. EWALD.

The Best Plays of John Ford. Edited by HAVELOCK ELLIS.

The Best Plays of Philip Massinger. With Critical and Biographical Essay and Notes by ARTHUR SYMONS.

The Best Plays of Thomas Heywood. Edited by A. W. VERITY. With Introduction by J. A. SYMONDS.

The Complete Plays of William Wycherley. Edited, with Introduction and Notes, by W. C. WARD.

Nero and Other Plays. Edited by H. P. HORNE, ARTHUR SYMONS, A. W. VERITY, and H. ELLIS.

The Best Plays of Beaumont and Fletcher. Introduction and Notes by J. ST. LOE STRACHEY.

The Best Plays of Webster and Tourneur. With an Introduction and Notes by JOHN ADDINGTON SYMONDS.

The Best Plays of Thomas Middleton. With an Introduction by ALGERNON CHARLES SWINBURNE.

The Best Plays of James Shirley. With Introduction by EDMOND GOSSE.

The Best Plays of Thomas Dekker. Notes by ERNEST RHYS.

The Best Plays of Ben Jonson. Vols. 1, 2 & 3. Edited, with Introduction and Notes, by BRINSLEY NICHOLSON and C. H. HERFORD.

The Complete Plays of Richard Steele. Edited, with Introduction and Notes, by G. A. AITKEN.

The Best Plays of George Chapman. Edited by WILLIAM LYON PHELPS, Instructor of English Literature at Yale College.

The Select Plays of Sir John Vanbrugh. Edited, with an Introduction and Notes, by A. E. H. SWAIN.

The Best Plays of John Dryden. Edited, with an Introduction and Notes, by GEORGE SAINTSBURY. 2 vols.

The Best Plays of Thomas Shadwell. Edited, with an Introduction and Notes, by GEORGE SAINTSBURY.

Other Volumes in Preparation.

JAMES SHIRLEY.

From the Picture in the Bodleian Gallery.

JAMES SHIRLEY

N76-1666

WITH AN INTRODUCTION

BY

EDMUND GOSSE, M.A.

Clark Lecturer at Trinity College, Cambridge

" I lie and dream of your full Mermaid wine."—*Beaumont*

LONDON
T. FISHER UNWIN
NEW YORK
CHARLES SCRIBNER'S SONS

"What things have we seen
Done at the Mermaid! heard words that have been
So nimble, and so full of subtle flame,
As if that every one from whence they came
Had meant to put his whole wit in a jest,
And had resolved to live a fool the rest
Of his dull life."

Master Francis Beaumont to Ben Jonson.

———◦•◦•◦——

"Souls of Poets dead and gone,
What Elysium have ye known,
Happy field or mossy cavern,
Choicer than the Mermaid Tavern?"

Keats.

CONTENTS

PR
3142
G605
1903a

2556

JAMES SHIRLEY.

N considering the copious work of Shirley we are brought face to face with a man who was obviously a student of the printed writings of his immediate predecessors. The works of the dramatists had begun to be edited when he first came forward. Ben Jonson had collected his plays in 1616, Shakespeare was edited in 1623; Lyly followed in 1632, Marston in 1633. Shirley was, obviously, a devourer of printed plays, and he is sometimes scarcely to be distinguished from the Barry Cornwalls and George Darleys who wrote "dramatic scenes" in the Elizabethan spirit two centuries later. More than enough has been said of Shirley as a supposed representative of the decadence; he has never recovered from the unjust sneers of Dryden. Yet, in reality, to study the drama in the process of pulverisation we must turn, not to him, but to Glapthorne, Brome, and Jasper Mayne. Shirley,

an essentially literary poet, took up the drama as literature, and held it up for fifteen years in an artificial condition. Meanwhile, outside his compact and unaltering stage, it was rapidly sinking year by year. Shirley neither sinks nor rises. As a purely literary poet, although one that went down to address the public on the boards with great skill, he stood aloof from the theatre, and in the retirement of his study he was unaffected by the tempests of the times. He is one of the most uniform of writers, always graceful, fluent, and accomplished, never deviating far from a certain standard of excellence which he had put before him, entirely unaffected by the striking faults of his age, its violence, its obscurity, its prosodical licence. Shirley writes in the age of Ford, and again in the age of Ravenscroft, without any change of note, always polished, skilful, and unobtrusively adroit. He has an apparently inexhaustible vein of delicate poetry, which he has fed on the romantic parts of Shakespeare, on the masques of Ben Jonson, on the tragedies of Webster, but most of all on those pliant and luxurious dramas of Beaumont and Fletcher which he so piously edited in 1647.

Little has been gleaned concerning our poet's career since Gifford began, and Dyce so competently finished the editing of his works in six volumes, in 1833. James Shirley or Sherley, was born, according to seven entries in the tables of Merchant Taylors' School, on the

13th of September, 1596, in a house soon afterwards pulled down to make room for the Stocks Market, and therefore presumably in the parish of St. Mary Woolchurch, London. At the time of his birth Marlowe and Greene were dead, Shakespeare was opening his career, Beaumont and Ford, the youngest of the great dramatic school, were children. At the age of twelve, Shirley was sent to Merchant Taylors' School, where he did well, and remained for nearly four years. From this school he proceeded to St. John's College, Oxford, of which Laud was then President. According to Wood, Laud, although very fond of Shirley, declined to permit him to study for holy orders, on account of a large mole which disfigured the young man's left cheek. There is no sign of this defect in the existing portraits of the poet. It is supposed that Shirley soon transferred himself to Cambridge, for "he did spend some precious years at Catherine Hall," where he took his degree. While he was at Cambridge his first production, *Echo, or the Unfortunate Lovers*, was printed in London in 1618. There can be little question that this was the same poem as the reprinted (*hæc olim*) *Narcissus* of 1646; but no copy has been seen since the middle of last century, when Mr. Astle of Yoxall possessed and described the volume.

Narcissus is perhaps the most graceful of the humanistic successors of Shakespeare's popular

Venus and Adonis, published in 1593. It deals
with the familiar, long-drawn emotions of an
enamoured maiden vainly striving to awaken
passion in a cool woodland youth. This poem
lacks force and conviction, but it is full of pretty
ideas and picturesque conceits, and is composed
in smooth verses. The following stanzas give a
favourable idea of its merit :—

> " The wind, thy herald, flies about the groves,
>   Aloud proclaiming thee the wood-nymphs' king
> Snatching up odours, as he whistling roves,
>   At thy hand to unlade them from his wing ;
> The sylvans frisk about, while nymphs prepare
> A rosy garland to o'ertop thy hair.

> " Shepherds shall all the day new pastimes spring,
>   A masque of satyrs shall beguile the night ;
> The choicest birds shall to the[ir] antics sing,
>   The stars grow brighter to behold the sight ;
> Yet these but shadows of the mirth we'll prove
> If thou wilt stay and be thy Echo's love.

> " I have a cloister overlooks the sea,
>   Where every morning we, secure from fear,
> Will see the porpoise and the dolphin play,
>   And all the wonders that inhabit there ;
> While many a bark into the clouds d th leap,
> While surges caper round about the ship.

> " Lovely Narcissus, prithee stay with me ;
>   If thou do thirst, from every spring shall rise
> Divinest nectar, and thy food shall be
>   The glorious apples of Hesperides ;
> A nymph shall be thy Hebe, if thou need
> Shalt have another for thy Ganimede."

Already in this early poem we see Shirley
writing as a literary scholar of the greater and
older men. There is not merely the influence of
Shakespeare upon him, but that of Marlowe's
Hero and Leander and possibly of Beaumont's
Salmacis and Hermaphroditus as well. Yet he

is not a plagiarist, nor even a mere imitator; he goes to school to these poets, as the Fletchers went to the school of Spenser, and takes a genuine inspiration at second hand.

In 1619 he was still at Cambridge, and in 1623 he was appointed master at St. Albans Grammar School. Between these dates it would appear that Shirley took orders in the Church of England, received a living in or near the town of St. Albans, and on becoming a convert to Rome, resigned the benefice without leaving the town. It would seem from a passage in the *Grateful Servant* that he was connected, as a Catholic, with the order of Benedictines. He remained faithful to his new convictions until the end of his life. He continued to be a school-master for about two years, probably resigning his appointment, which was extremely irksome to him, soon after the success of his first play.

The comedy originally called *Love Tricks* was licensed on the 10th of February, 1625. It was not printed until 1631, when it appeared as *The School of Compliment;* it was one of Shirley's most popular pieces and was reprinted several times. In the prologue Shirley said that his Muse had never before saluted an audience, and that he himself had not made up his mind—

"To swear himself a factor for the scene."

The success of *Love Tricks* probably induced him to take up the dramatic profession in earnest. The play is not a good one; it is a series of fragments, most of them reminiscences of scenes from writers of the preceding generation. The first two acts are mainly sustained by fun about the delusions of a love-sick old man, Rufaldo, who fancies that passion has made him look young. Into the third act is abruptly introduced a mildly Aristophanic scene, possibly imitated from *The Clouds*, of a school where young men are taught to make rhetorical compliments. In the fourth and fifth acts we get a somewhat naïve imitation of Shakespeare's and Fletcher's pastoral passages. There is a brace of sisters, Felice and Selina, who pass away into the forest disguised, the former as a shepherdess, the latter as a shepherd; to them comes the melancholy and romantic Infortunio, who is in love with Selina, but does not recognise her dressed as a boy. The bucolic bewilderment reaches its climax when Selina, in the garb of a youth, dances with Antonio, who is in woman's clothes. The influence of *As You Like It* is very strongly marked in this play, but there are traces also of Ben Jonson, Fletcher, and perhaps Massinger. It is the most imitative of Shirley's works, and yet, if it were anonymous, it would at once be recognisable as his. It has his limpid fancy, cheerful tone, and easy but correct versification.

Exactly a year later, in 1626, Shirley produced his second play and earliest tragedy, *The Maid's Revenge*. He did not greatly value this piece himself; and it was not till 1639, and with many apologies, that he printed it. This Portuguese tragedy was an attempt on the part of Shirley to produce one of the blood-and-thunder melodramas which were so popular at this time; but his gentle gifts were little fitted to be strained in this violent way, and *The Maid's Revenge* is uninteresting. The only incident which dwells in the memory is the amiable kidnapping of Berinthia, which is not very ingeniously managed. The characters in the piece are singularly devoid of individualisation. Later in the same year Shirley produced another and a better tragedy, *The Brothers.* In this play he has settled down into the manner which is henceforth habitual to his measured, well-constructed, and fluent pieces. There is here an agreeable absence of violence, a recurrence of honest and wholesome fancies and reflections, and a vein of poetry that is genuine if not very deep or rich. The description Fernando gives of his love was long ago made famous by Dr. Farmer's praise. These lines are as graceful and not so well known :—

> " Yes, Felisarda, he is gone, that in
> The morning promised many years; but death
> Hath in few hours made him as stiff as though
> The winds of winter had thrown cold upon him,
> *And whispered him to marble.*"

The last scene of the fourth act of *The Brothers*, between Fernando and Felisarda, may be mentioned as the earliest satisfactory example of Shirley's tender and innocent love-passages.

The next play produced by our dramatist was, it seems probable, *The Wedding*, which I propose to attribute to the year 1627. Gifford, from whom no one would rashly differ on such a point, placed it farther on in the list of Shirley's writings, after *The Witty Fair One*. By some accident it was not entered in Sir Henry Herbert's licensing book, but it was printed in 1629. My reason for considering that it should be given to an earlier year is that the style seems to belong to a period of transition between *The Brothers* and *The Witty Fair One*. It is brisker and more skilful in construction than the former, but less easy and accomplished than the latter. *The Wedding* is a variation upon the theme of Shakespeare's *All's Well that Ends Well*. The action is overlaid with comic matter of rather a poor kind, as it appears to me, but the somewhat narrow central thread of tragi-comedy is very tenderly and humorously worked out. The distress and incredulity of Beauford when Marwood first makes his accusation, and the heroic patience of Gratiana under her agony, form some of the best scenes which the poet has left us; and there is something happy in contriving that Marwood himself should be able to make his charges in good faith, although the particular artifice by which this is effected is coarse and improbable. In *The Witty Fair One*, which is here reprinted, there are perhaps no scenes quite so brilliant as those in the second act of *The*

Wedding, but the former is the better play as a whole, and the more characteristic example of Shirley's skill as a dramatist. *The Wedding*, which was the earliest of his theatrical publications, was very popular and was several times reprinted. *The Witty Fair One*, the author tells us, "wanted no grace on the stage," when it was brought out at Drury Lane in the autumn of 1628; but it was not printed until 1633. In both these plays a sense of reality is secured by the fact that the scene is laid in the neighbourhood of London.

Shirley was now, in 1628, a recognised figure in the world of dramatic letters. He had made writing for the stage his profession, and during the next decade we must look upon him as sharing with Massinger its main profits. He now began to be encouraged by the eulogies of his great contemporaries. In 1629 Ford, who was ten years his senior, declared that "loud Fame" would "in every age renew" Shirley's name; and in 1630 Randolph very neatly defined his friend's position among the "Lycophronian buskins" of the hour. He praised, what we still acknowledge, the grace and suavity of Shirley's style. He says—

> "Thy Helicon, like a smooth stream, doth flow,
> While others with disturbèd channels go,
> And headlong, like Nile-cataracts, do fall
> With a huge noise, and yet not heard at all."

The great and excellent Massinger, too, in this same year comes asking leave to be "a modest

b

votary at the altar of thy Muse;" and Habington promises Shirley the crown of English poesy when "divinest Jonson" dies. These panegyrics, no doubt, express on the part of the poets a feeling shared by the public and by the managers, since from this time forward the pen of Shirley is exceedingly prolific. We possess no fewer than twenty of his plays brought out between 1629 and 1638, and although this is a tribute of more than two dramas a year, doubtless it by no means exhausts the sum of his actual production. It may perhaps a little take away from the impression which we are apt to receive, that Shirley belonged to a period of very late decadence, to remind ourselves that when that great Elizabethan, Ben Jonson, died, Shirley had already brought out on the boards, to our certain knowledge, twenty-four pieces, and that if he had been buried with that rare poet, we should still possess all that is most characteristic and most desirable from Shirley's pen. We should all resign without any great reluctance what our dramatist wrote during the last twenty-five years of his life.

The Grateful Servant is styled a comedy by the author; we may rather take it as a type of his skill in tragi-comedy. It was produced in 1629 and printed in 1630, being therefore, Shirley's second appeal to the reading public. In this play we meet with a character, Belinda, a lady of frolic temper, in whose mouth the poet

has placed some of his most elaborate and or-
nate language. "She is poetical," we are told,
"more than half a fury." In her extravagances the poet abandons his usual reserve, with
something of conscious humour, and his blank
verse spreads its wings to the widest. Belinda
cries—

> "I was not born to perch upon a dukedom,
>   Or some such spot of earth, which the dull eyes
>   Examine by a magnifying glass,
>   And wonder at ; the Roman eagles never
>   Did spread their wings upon so many shores ;
>   *The silver moon of Ottoman looks pale*
>   *Upon my greater empire ;* kings of Spain,
>   That now may boast their ground doth stretch as wide
>   As day, are but poor landlords of a cell
>   Compar'd to mine inheritance ; the truth is
>   I am the Devil."

This is as near as Shirley ever gets to the
audacious rapture of Webster and Marlowe, and
it is to be noted that his reasonable nature can
only concede so much as this with a purpose
that is slightly comic. Some choice poetry is
placed in the old friar's mouth, and *The Grateful
Servant*, though not a very interesting play,
shows a definite advance upon its predecessors.
It was followed by a tragedy which marks
Shirley's highest achievement as a dramatic
poet. From this point we travel over a long
tableland, and then reach a slow decline.

The tragedy of *The Traitor*, which we here
reprint, was licensed in May 1631, and published
in 1635. It was always much admired, and in
1692 a mysterious attempt was made to wrest
it from the crown of Shirley. It was revived at

the Theatre Royal, and the playwright Peter
Motteux, who perhaps was responsible for
adapting it for revival, wrote that "Shirley only
ushered it in to the Stage : the author of it was
one Mr. Rivers, a Jesuit, who wrote it in his
confinement at Newgate, where he died." Motteux was probably repeating a vague rumour
that this Rivers had in some way been connected
with *The Traitor.* It is not impossible that
Shirley may have visited his co-religionist in
prison, and may have accepted from him some
hint of the plot. No one, however, who reads
the play will doubt for a moment that it is all
written as it now stands by the author whom it
represents in so typical a manner. The versification, the arrangement of scenes, the morality,
all belong to Shirley and to Shirley only. If
other evidence were needed, it is to be found in
the poet's epistle dedicatory to the Earl of
Newcastle, in which he uses language which
would be fraudulent were the writer of the letter
not also the writer of the play. An adaptation
of *The Traitor*, by Sheil, was brought on the
stage so late as 1819.

Shirley's next contribution to the players was
The Duke, 1631, which is not now known to
exist. *Love's Cruelty*, which was acted at Drury
Lane late in the same year, was not published
until 1640. It is a tragedy, which opens with a
very beautiful scene between Bellamente and his
mistress Clariana ; the high level of these exqui-

site verses is hardly sustained throughout, and
we may consider *Love's Cruelty* as the first play
of Shirley's in which a certain languor invades
the action of the piece. At the time when it
was produced, Clariana was one of the greatest
favourites with the public among all the author's
creations. It was played, until women's parts
were taken by girls, by the actor Burt. *Love's
Cruelty* is an unpleasant piece, unusually coarse
for Shirley; it may be consulted for two fine
soliloquies, one by Hippolita, in Act ii., describing the masques which were at that time so
fashionable, and the other Bellamente's description of a virtuous wife, in Act iii. It was printed
but once.

We now reach a period during which Shirley
applied himself exclusively to comedy. From
1631 to the close of 1635, when he went to reside
in Dublin, the fertile dramatist supplied the
actors, to our knowledge, with twelve consecu-
tive comedies, and the list we possess is probably not complete. The series terminated with
what is probably Shirley's finest comic work, both
in language and in construction, *The Lady of
Pleasure*. We must briefly enumerate the individual plays, into a critical examination of which
we have no space to proceed, and the less inclination since our reprint presents the reader
with two specimens of this attractive and spark-
ling cluster of comedies. *The Changes, or Love
in a Maze*, was acted at Salisbury Court in 1632,

and printed the same year. *The Bird in the Cage*, 1632 (printed 1633), is ironically dedicated to Prynne, who was at that moment in prison, after standing " earless on high " in the pillory for having printed his insolent *Histriomastix*, 1632. This play comprises a masque, in which the female parts were taken by women, an innovation at that time very rare, and looked upon with much suspicion. In this masque ladies drew a huge cage on to the scene, with Philenzo, in disguise, as " the Bird in the Cage." *Hyde Park*, 1632 (printed 1637), which we reprint, was a very popular play. It was acted on the occasion of the opening of Hyde Park to the public by the first Earl of Holland, to whom the park belonged. During the fourth act races are proceeding ; when the play was revived in Pepys' time the horses were led across the stage itself, to the great excitement of the audience. It would not appear that this was attempted by Shirley, since the stage directions—" confused noise of betting within," and " a shout within, and crying, 'A jockey ' "—together with the fact that the personages enter to inform their friends of their luck, seem to show that the horses were kept out of sight of the audience *Hyde Park* is unusually interesting as a study of contemporary manners.

The Ball, in which Shirley enjoyed some help from the aged George Chapman, was brought out in 1632, and printed in 1639.

This play, which includes a masque of the
same name, gave great offence at its first performance, from the fact that in imitating one of
the fashionable court entertainments the actors
travestied the persons of well-known courtiers.
This does not appear to have been done in
malice, but the victims of the freedom warmly
objected, and the poet was threatened with
punishment. He was, however, high in favour
next year with the Master of the Revels, who has
made the following very interesting entry in his
office-book on registering there Shirley's comedy
of *The Young Admiral*, on the 3rd of July,
1633 :—

> "The comedy called the *Young Admiral*, being free from oaths,
> profaneness or obsceneness, hath given me much delight and
> satisfaction in the reading, and may serve for a pattern to other
> poets, not only for the bettering of manners and language, but for
> the improvement of the quality, which hath received some brushings
> of late. When Mr. Shirley hath read this approbation, I know it
> will encourage him to pursue this beneficial and cleanly way of
> poetry, and when other poets hear and see his good success, I am
> confident they will imitate the original for their own credit, and
> make such copies in this harmless way as shall speak them masters
> in their art, at the first sight, to all judicious spectators. It may be
> acted this 3rd July, 1633. I have entered this allowance for direc-
> tion to my successor, and for example to all poets that shall write
> after the date hereof."

The Young Admiral is a very graceful play,
and its language is remarkably void of offence;
but, in the face of so very unctuous a recommen-
dation of its chastity, we may notice that there
is a page in the fourth act which apparently
escaped Sir Henry Herbert's attention. The
expression "Oh, my stars!" which we regret to
find in the fifth act, is perhaps an oath; but, to

be serious, Shirley, after his scare with *The Ball*, is seen in *The Young Admiral* on his very best behaviour. *The Gamester*, 1633 (printed 1637), was acted at Court; it was written to the King's order, and his majesty deigned to supply the outline of the plot. We are therefore not surprised to be informed that "the King said it was the best play he had seen for seven years." An adaptation of *The Gamester* was acted in 1827.

The prologue to *The Example*, 1634 (printed 1637), shows that English drama was beginning to pass under the shadow of Puritanism. The author writes in vague fear and trembling; he says:—

> " We have named our play
> *The Example,* and for aught we know, it may
> Be made one ; for at no time did the laws,
> However understood, more fright the cause
> Of unbefriended poesy."

This was followed in 1634 by *The Opportunity*, printed in 1640, and in 1635 by *The Coronation* (printed 1640), and *Chabot, Admiral of France* (printed 1639), which latter was mainly a posthumous work of Chapman; by *The Royal Master*, printed in 1638, and finally by that brilliant comedy, *The Lady of Pleasure*, printed in 1637. *The Coronation* was early claimed for Fletcher, who probably had some share in it. We know that in 1633 Shirley "corrected" that writer's *Night Walker*, and he had a hand in preparing several other plays of Fletcher's for the stage. It is not quite certain when *The Royal Master* was produced; it was not licensed until 1638, but it seems to have been acted in Dublin before the occasion of Shirley's first appearance there, soon after the opening of Ogilby's Castle Theatre in 1635. The beautiful and sprightly drama of *The Lady of Pleasure*, which is certainly the jewel in this charming cluster of comedies, was licensed in October, 1635, and printed in 1637.

After the production of *The Lady of Pleasure*, Shirley proceeded to Ireland. Mr. Dyce considered that this exile was made in the year 1637. I believe that this is considerably too late a date, and that his abrupt disappearance from the books of Sir Henry Herbert, where we do not find his name between January 1636 and June 1640, shows that he had soon after the former time transferred his services to the theatre of his friend Ogilby in Dublin. If we could discover the date of the prologue in which Shirley says that "two year he has lived in Dublin" we could settle this difficulty. As it is, we may perhaps safely conjecture that he went over to Ireland to help Ogilby at the new Werburgh Street Theatre in the early part of 1636. This is borne out by the fact that in the dedication of *The Royal Master*, printed in 1638, he tells Lord Kildare that his affairs in England are hastening his departure from Ireland, so that this is probably the term of the "two year." In 1640 five plays of Shirley's were printed, perhaps on occa-

sion of his final return to England. We cannot
tell when these dramas were originally produced, but certainly some, and probably all, of
them were designed in the first instance for
Irish audiences. They are the tragi-comedy of
The Doubtful Heir, the comedies of *The Constant
Maid* and *The Humorous Courtier*, the pastoral
of Sidney's *Arcadia* dramatised, and the curious
drama called *St. Patrick for Ireland*. This latter
is an extraordinary work, to which due attention
has never been paid. The first act, describing
the arrival of the saint, is full of the most ele-
vated poetry that Shirley has written ; the
second act might have been taken from any of
its author's amatory comedies ; in the third he
stoops to buffooneries that are most unusual
with him, and then finishes off with a ghost.
The fourth act is a farrago of everything, farce
and tragedy, masque and high comedy ; while
the fifth recovers much of the spiritual dignity
of the first act. *St. Patrick for Ireland* is a
failure, but it is the failure of a man of genius ; it
is Shirley's one divergence into the region of
pure eccentricity. The last speech which St.
Patrick makes is of singular beauty. A second
part of this play was promised, but has either
been lost or was never written.

To the brief period which lay between Shirley's
return from Ireland and the first ordinance for
the suppression of stage plays, belong nine or
ten dramas, some of which have disappeared.

One, *The Country Captain*, was published at the Hague in 1649, with an attribution to the Duke of Newcastle. Mr. A. H. Bullen, who printed this play in 1883 from a MS., was the first to point out that the style of his comedy betrays it as manifestly Shirley's. The following fine poetical passage occurs at the end of the fourth act :—

> "My dream
> Was full of rapture, such as I with all
> My wakening sense would fly to meet. Methought
> I saw a thousand Cupids slide from heaven,
> And landing here made this their scene of revels,
> Clapping their golden feathers, which kept time
> While their own feet struck music to their dance,
> As they had trod and touched so many lutes ;
> This done, within a cloud formed like a throne,
> She to whom Love has consecrate this night,
> My mistress, did descend, and, coming towards me,
> My soul that ever wakes, angry to see
> My body made a prisoner and so mock'd,
> Shook off the chains of sleep, lest I should lose
> Essential pleasure for a dream. 'Tis happy !
> I will not trust myself with ease and silence,
> But walk and wait her coming that must bless me."

The recovery of this valuable play is one of many debts which the student of poetry owes to Mr. Bullen's taste and industry.

The Gentleman of Venice, The Politician, The Imposture, The Cardinal, and *The Sisters* were all first printed between 1652 and 1655, though of course they had been written before the closing of the theatres. These plays are, as a whole, less interesting than Shirley's earlier works, but perhaps only because we reach them when our attention is already somewhat fatigued by the monotony of his method of construction and the even sweetness of his verse. We have selected *The Cardinal* for the present reprint as a vigorous example of Shirley's latest style, and as perhaps the last great play produced by the giants of the Elizabethan age. When we think what English drama, from *Tamburlaine the Great* to *The Cardinal*, consists of, we may well marvel at the wealth poured out in sixty years.

Wood has described in the following terms Shirley's fate during the Rebellion. It is almost needless to say, by way of preface, that the favourite dramatist of the Court was a convinced Royalist:—

"When the Rebellion broke out, and he thereupon forced to leave London, and so consequently his wife and children (who afterwards were put to their shifts), he was invited by his most noble patron, William, Earl (afterwards Marquess and Duke) of Newcastle, to take his fortune with him in the wars; for that Count had engaged him so much by his generous liberality towards him, that he thought he could not do a worthier act, than to serve him, and so consequently his prince."

It must, therefore, be taken for granted that, with a neglect of his impoverished wife and children which we could wish better explained, Shirley retired to France, with Newcastle, after the disaster of Marston Moor. It is very singular, by the way, that the Duchess makes no mention of Shirley in her life of her husband. We further learn from Wood that upon the complete decline of the King's cause Shirley crept back quietly to England, and found entertainment with an old and wealthy friend, Thomas Stanley, the poet and Hellenist. To eke out a livelihood

he had to take up the old distasteful business of
a schoolmaster, which he practised with great
success in Whitefriars. In 1646 he issued a
volume of his *Poems*, including his masque of
The Triumph of Beauty. Copies of this book, in
good condition, with the portrait-frontispiece,
are much sought after by bibliophiles. At the
Restoration Shirley's plays were once more set
upon the stage, but they were found to be old-
fashioned. His knowledge of the profession
was, however, taken advantage of by dramatic
amateurs, such as the Duke of Newcastle and
the Hon. Edward Howard, though to what extent
we cannot now discover.[1] It is also said that
Ogilby used Shirley "as a drudge" in his heavy
translations of Homer and Virgil. Shirley's end
was melancholy in the extreme. His second
wife and he, at the great fire of London, were
driven out of their house near Fleet Street, and
died of terror and exposure on the same day in
the parish of St. Giles-in-the-Fields, where they
were buried in one grave, on the 29th of October,
1666. The poet was then aged seventy years
and three weeks. His dramatic work almost
immediately fell into a disrepute which is posi-
tively unaccountable.

---

[1] In 1853 Mr. Halliwell-Phillips printed at the end of the
catalogue of the Plymouth Public Library a very poor play called
The General. Mr. Bullen informs me that he has recently found
in the library of Worcester College another MS. of the same. But
the conjecture by which this performance has been fastened on
Shirley is certainly incorrect. *The General* has no trace of his
style.

No memoir of Shirley would be complete which did not mention his masques. In the preparation of these elaborate entertainments he is surpassed only by Ben Jonson, whom, in this department of his art, he studiously follows. We have reprinted in this volume *The Triumph of Peace*, which was presented by the Inns of Court before the King and Queen in 1633, as our typical example of these masques, in which the enchantments of motion and melody, of colour and verse, were united. Shirley's language, whether in verse or prose, is nowhere more gorgeous, more jewelled than it is in these pages. But it is another masque, *The Contention of Ajax and Ulysses*, 1659, which contains Shirley's noblest lyric, "the fine song which old Bowman used to sing to King Charles:"—

> "The glories of our blood and state
>   Are shadows, not substantial things;
> There is no armour against fate;
>   Death lays his icy hand on kings;
>   Sceptre and crown
>   Must tumble down,
> And in the dust be equal made
> With the poor crooked scythe and spade."

Almost as good is the ode beginning "Victorious man of earth," in *Cupid and Death*, 1653. As a lyrical poet Shirley attained great sweetness; his best songs have something in them of the enamoured and roseate effusion of Carew. Yet graceful as these lyrics are, it is difficult to find one which is absolutely without a flaw. The following, from *The Imposture*, is perhaps the best of Shirley's songs :—

" Ye virgins, that did late despair
    To keep your wealth from cruel men,
Tie up in silk your careless hair,
    Soft peace is come again.

" Now lovers' eyes may gently shoot
    A [modest ?] flame that will not kill ;
The drum was angry, but the lute
    Shall whisper what you will.

" Sing Iö, Iö ! for his sake,
    Who hath restored your drooping heads ;
With choice of sweetest flowers, make
    A garden where he treads :

" Whilst we whole groves of laurel bring,
    A petty triumph to his brow,
Who is the master of the spring,
    And all the bloom we owe."

In Shirley's own time his style was recognised as being " discreet," " sober," and " sweet-tempered." These qualities were particularly admirable in an age that was hurrying to decay, and attempting to recover its vitality by mere storm and excess. Shirley's style is uniform to an extraordinary degree, and the level country over which his muse reigns, with its broad flowery meadows, slow streams and rich woods, is charming rather than striking, and pleases us without creating astonishment or rapture. His comedies are polite and amusing without grossness ; his tragedies inspire pity rather than terror or indignation. He is a remarkably elegant and competent writer, whose high posi-

tion in the second rank is never likely again to
be seriously assailed.   If the experiment which
the " Dramatic Students " have been making to
restore the Elizabethan masterpieces to the stage
should succeed, we may hope to see Shirley
again successful on the boards.   His skill in
theatrical construction would probably make
him one of the easiest of the great playwrights
to present to a modern audience.

EDMUND GOSSE.

THE WITTY FAIR ONE.

 HE Comedy of *The Witty Fair One* was licensed by the Master of the Revels in October, 1628, acted by His Majesty's Servants at the Private House in Drury Lane, and published in 1633. In 1666, shortly after Shirley's death, the play was revived.

To the Truly Noble Knight,

SIR EDWARD BUSHELL.

SIR,

OUR candid censure of some unworthy poems which I have presented to the world, long since made me your servant in my thoughts, and being unwilling to rest long in the silent contemplation of your nobleness, I presumed at last to send this comedy, to kiss your hand, as the first degree to my greater happiness in your more particular knowledge of me. It wanted no grace on the stage; if it appear acceptable to you in this new trim of the press, it will improve abroad, and you oblige the author to acknowledge a favour beyond the first applause. Pardon the rudeness of my public address to you, in the number of many whom with more excuse I might have interrupted. I am bold, but your mercy will incline you not to despise these (at the worse) but errors of my devotion, and the weak expression of his service whose desires are to be known,

Your true honourer,

JAMES SHIRLEY.

DRAMATIS PERSONÆ.

SIR GEORGE RICHLEY, a rich old Knight.

WORTHY, his Brother.

AIMWELL, Lover of VIOLETTA.

FOWLER, a wild young Gentleman.

SIR NICHOLAS TREEDLE, a foolish Knight.

CLARE
MANLY } Gentlemen.

BRAINS, SIR GEORGE RICHLEY'S Servant.

WHIBBLE, WORTHY'S Servant.

TUTOR and Companion to SIR NICHOLAS.

Two Gentlemen.

Footman.

Messenger, Servants, &c.

VIOLETTA, SIR GEORGE RICHLEY'S Daughter.

PENELOPE, WORTHY'S Daughter.

SENSIBLE
WINNIFRED } Chambermaids.

SCENE—LONDON and CROYDON.

THE WITTY FAIR ONE.

ACT THE FIRST.

SCENE I.—*London. The Garden of* WORTHY'S *House.*

Enter Sir GEORGE RICHLEY, WORTHY, *and* WHIBBLE.

Wor. So soon after dinner?

    Rich. I am engaged, and must away; excuse me, brother.

    Wor. Well, make ready his horse.

    Whib. His worship's pad shall be prepared.—If your gelding be not ready in a minute, your worship shall ride me.   [*Exit.*

    Rich. I shall

Not need to urge your care upon my daughter,
On whom, next the devotion of my soul
To Heaven, all my desires and thoughts reflect
I leave her to your trust,
And, in my absence, doubt not you will be
Both uncle and a father.

    Wor. Willingly

I would depose myself from both these titles,
To serve my niec   her virtue will reward me;
I know she is your study; in your want[1]
I will put on your jealousy.

    Rich. It would not

                [1] *i.e.* Absence.

Become me to confine your entertainments
Of friends and visitants ; but, remember, brother,
She's now my sole heir, and by the late death
Of her twin sister, she derives the right
Of all my wealth to her.   Gallants, I fear,
I' the town hold too fruitful intelligence
In these affairs ; and if they be not watched,
They'll with their wit charm all the dragons guard
These golden apples.

   Wor. There are such, indeed.

   Rich. Oh, sir, there are too many ; not a virgin,
Left by her friends heir to a noble fortune,
But she's in danger of a marriage
To some puffed title.   What are these enter the garden ?

   Enter AIMWELL, *followed by* FOWLER *and* CLARE.

   Wor. The gentlemen that dined with us.

   Fow. Why, how now Frank ? grown musty on a sud-
       den ?
Head hung, and playing the thief thus with your friends,
To steal your person from us !   What's the matter ?

   Aim. Nothing, nothing, gentlemen.

   Clare. Very like,
And yet you leave our company for this nothing !

   Fow. Let's in again to the ladies.

          [*Exeunt* AIMWELL, FOWLER, *and* CLARE.

   Rich. What is he ?

   Wor. One Master Fowler, a reputed wit
I' the town, affected by young gentlemen
For his converse, yet lives upon no pension
But his own fortune, and a fair one.
The other, Master Clare,
A friend to Master Aimwell, whom they both
Seem to solicit.

   Rich. Master Aimwell !

   Wor. A hopeful gentleman.

   Rich. Brother, did you not observe at dinner

His eyes shoot beams upon my daughter, more
Than I was pleased with?   Aimwell call you him?
I may suspect unjustly, but such looks
Are often loose conveyers.

  Wor. Make no part
Of him your fear.

  Rich. I do not, when I call
To mind my daughter's virtue and obedience.
She knows my purpose to dispose her to
Sir Nicholas Treedle.

  Wor. And how do you find
Her inclination?

  Rich. As I would direct it.

  Wor. She will maintain it to your comfort, sir.
However, with what vigilance becomes me,
I will preserve 't, while she remains within
My custody.

  Rich. I'll leave a servant to wait upon her.

  Wor. Brains?

  Rich. The same.

  Wor. He is a cunning fellow.

  Rich. He has a sconce
Carries some subtilty, which he employs
Still honestly in discharge of any trust
Committed to him.

  Wor. Good.

  Rich. And 'tis his pride,
He was ne'er o'er-reached in any action.

  Wor. He knows his charge?

  Rich. Perfectly; but I lose time; Sir Nicholas
Treedle expects me this night in the country.

  Wor. When do you return?

  Rich. Within these three days at most.
Trouble yourself no further.

  Wor. I'll wait on you to your horse, sir.   [*Exeunt.*

SCENE II.—*Another part of the same.*

Enter AIMWELL.

Aim. She has shot a fire into my bosom from
Her eye, or I have drawn in at mine own
Love poison.   Oh, my stars were too ungentle
To point her out the mistress of my thoughts,
Who is so much, like them, above the hope
Of ever climbing to.   I see a fatal
Impossibility divide us ; yet,
The more I would discharge this new guest, it
Strengthens itself within me, and renews
Vigour to keep possession.   She's above me,
And her great fortune makes my expectation
So dull and painful ; a great heir——Her uncle !

Enter WORTHY.

Wor. Master Aimwell, what, alone ! come, let's
To cards ; where be the gentlemen ?
Aim. Within, sir.
Has Sir George Richley left us ?
Wor. Some affairs
Importuned his departure.
Aim. When shall we expect him ?
Wor. Three days hence.   This your inquiry
Doth promise you have business with him.
Aim. Little—
But you did motion cards ; I'll choose my partner,
And for a set or two I'm at your service.
Wor. Make your own election.
Aim. Why do you mock me ?[1]
Wor. How ! mock you ?
Aim. Yes.
Wor. You do n t mean in earnest.
Aim. I shall betray my passion.   [*Aside.*

[1] Aimwell affects to understand Worthy as permitting him to
make choice of his niece as a *partner for life.—Gifford.*

Enter VIOLETTA.

Wor. I find him.

Aim. You may, for I am lost.   [*Aside.*

Vio. He's here.—Good uncle, is my father gone?

Wor. Yes, gentle niece.

Vio. Delight to both your walks ! I'll take this arbour.
    [*Retires.*

Aim. So breaks the day, and hides itself again
Among the western shades ! Were she to dwell
Within your garden, it should need no sun ;
Her smiles were powerful to infuse a warmth
Into the flowers, her breath perfume your arbours.
The trees grow rich in blossom and bear fruit
At the same instant, as 'twere ever spring
And ever summer : when she seats herself
Within some bower, the feathered quiristers
Shall play their music to her, and take pride
To warble aëry notes till she be weary,
Which, when she shall but with one accent of
Her own express, an hundred nightingales
Shall fall down dead from the soft boughs before her,
For grief to be o'erchanted.

Wor. Here's pretty madness !

Aim. 'Tis so ; you have done my passion justice, sir ;
For love is but a straggling from our reason.

Wor. If you do love my niece, let you and I
Talk out of metaphor.

Aim. You knew my father?

Wor. He was my noble friend.

Aim. For his sake, give me your free answer to
One question.

Wor. What is't ? promise yourself,
What I can do or say is at your service.

Aim. Is there a possibility, admit
I loved your niece, she might be won at last
To be my wife ?

Wor. I'll not dispute the extent

Of what is possible, yet my answer may
Be satisfactory.

    Aim. You were ever generous.

    Wor. I were uncivil not to reply to
A question ; you shall find my love more fruitful,
You shall have both my answer and my counsel.

    Aim. Let me embrace a perfect friend.

    Wor. Do you know what
Fortune my young niece may bring her husband ?

    Aim. I guess a great one ; but I set more value
Upon her person ; my affection springs
Not from her wealth.

    Wor. But yet her portion
Is worth your taking notice, Master Aimwell ;
Her father is a man who, though he write
Himself but knight, keeps a warm house i' the country,
Amongst his tenants ; takes no lordly pride
To travel with a footman and a page
To London ; humbly rides in the old fashion,
With half a dozen wholesome liveries,
To whom he gives Christian wages, and not countenance
Alone, to live on ; can spend by the year
Eight hundred pounds, and put up five ; sleeps quietly
Without dreaming on mortgages or statutes,
Or such like curses on his land ; can number,
May be, ten thousand pound in ready coin
Of his own, yet never bought an office for't ;
Has plate, no question, and jewels too,
In his old lady's cabinet, beside
Other things worth an inventory, and all this
His daughter is an heir to.   Now, pray tell me
What's your revenue ?

    Aim. Some three hundred pounds—

    Wor. Per annum ?   Grant it ; what expectation
Have you abroad ?

    Aim. None.

    Wor. That's quickly summed.
You have not made your love known to my niece yet ?

Aim. No; my intention was to pre-acquaint you.

Wor. You have done wisely; do not think on her
When you're at prayers, she will but puzzle
Your devotion; there's no hope of her.

Aim. Ha!

Wor. I mean for you to arrive at her, your own
Disparity in fortune.

Aim. I do find it.

Wor. Excuse my plainness, sir; her father looks
A great deal higher; and, to take away
Your least encouragement to prosecute,
Within my knowledge she's designed already
To a wealthy gentleman, and within few days
'Twill be a marriage; you shall but procure
Your own affliction to employ your hope
Where things remain so desperate.

Aim. I thank you.

Wor. You do yourself more right.

Aim. If such affairs
Have past, it were not noble to continue
This path; you have done me gentle office, sir;
I must believe you are generous: this new flame
My reason shall suppress, before it grow
Too mighty for me.

Wor. It becomes you well.
Love, like to sin, inveterate is strong;
He prevents danger that destroys it young.—
Come, to your friends. [*Exeunt.*

SCENE III.—*The same.*

Enter FOWLER, PENELOPE, *and* CLARE.

Fow. Your soft stars will not let you be so cruel, lady,
to give repulse to a lover.

Clare. Do not believe him; he does but compliment;
I have known him court a hundred, with as much for-

mality, wooed them in the nuptial cut, made verses on their hair, set lilies and roses, a whole garden, in their cheeks, cherries in their lips, stellify their eyes, and yet in a twinkling—

Pen. Sure you do him wrong, sir?

Clare. Wrong!

Fow. He measures my affection by the length of his own : prithee, Satire, choose another walk, and leave us to enjoy this ; thou knowest not my intent.

Clare. Thou mayst be honest with one, and that's a miracle, and will ask a strong faith to believe it. I hope she has more wit than to trust your voluble courtship. I'll seek out my friend Aimwell.

[VIOLETTA *comes from the arbour.*

Viol. [*Aside to* CLARE.] Sir, if your engagement require no haste. [*They walk aside.*

Pen. I do wonder a gentleman of your knowledge should so deceive himself.

Fow. Express yourself, fairest.

Pen. Fair sir, I am not taken with your flatteries ; I can see through you.

Fow. If you have so active an eye, lady, you may see a throng of passions flaming at my heart, set on fire by your beauty, I protest to you ; come, shame not your wisdom to believe report or opinion of the world ; 'tis a malicious age we live in ; if your ears have been abused with any ill noise of me, you shall tell yourself, if you love me, the world is a shameless and miserable detractor : you do not despise me, lady?—

Pen. No, I pity so handsome a gentleman, and of so fair a fortune, should want his eyes.

Fow. How! blind?

Pen. To your own follies, sir.

Fow. Shall I swear I love you as I am a gentleman?

Pen. As you are a gentleman, I know you can swear anything, 'tis a fashion you are most constant in, to be religiously wicked ; an oath in your mouth, and a reservation in your heart, is a common courtship! Do not swear as you are a gentleman.

Fow. As I am an honest man?

Pen. Out upon't! that's a worse; my tailor cozened me t'other day with the same oath. Save your credit, and let swearing alone; I dare take your word—

Fow. Well said.

Pen. For a greater matter, but not for this. You and I have not eaten a bushel of salt yet; in time I may be converted, and think your tongue and heart keep house together, for, at this time, I presume they are very far asunder.

Fow. Would you have my tongue in my heart, lady?

Pen. No, by my troth, I would rather find your heart in your tongue; but you are valiant, and 'tis only fear, they say, brings a man's heart up to his mouth.

Fow. Why, your wit is a tyrant; now, pray tell me, do not you love me mightily above potatoes?[1] come I see the little blind boy in your eyes already.

Pen. Love you, sir?

Fow. Yes, I know by your bitterness you wish me well, and think there is some hope I may be won too, you take pains to whip me so handsomely; come, I'll be a good child, and kiss the rod.

Clare. [*To* VIOLETTA.]—You oblige my service to
you; I am one
Aimwell called friend, and shall be happy to
Convey him any knowledge may concern him.

Vio. Then briefly thus: I understand he loves me.
Pray you, do him the true office of a friend,
And counsel him desist; I am disposed of
Already in my father's thoughts, and must

---

[1] Gifford remarks: "I have no great confidence in the genuineness of this expression: if, however, it came from the author, it would seem to mean, above the power of philtres or provocatives. Potatoes, long after their introduction into this country, were not considered as an article of food; but were either used as conserves, or brought to table highly seasoned with spices, ambergrise, &c."

Shew my obedience ; he shall beget
But his own trouble, if he move
My uncle or my father, and perhaps
Draw their suspicion and displeasure
On me too, by so indiscreet proceeding.
I would not have a gentleman of his worth
Do himself so great injury to run
A course of so much hazard ; if you please
To bear the burden of my thanks for his,
On my part, undeserved opinion,
And make him sensible, in time he may
Place his affection where he may expect
Better return, you shall discharge a friendship
To him, and with it make my thoughts your debtor.

Clare. You have expressed a nobleness in this ;
Were all of your mind, lady, there would be
Less willow worn.

Fow. You would have me praise you, now ; I could
ramble in your commendation.

Pen. I think so.

Fow. Do you but think so ? why, you shall hear me :
Your hairs are Cupid's nets, your forehead like
The fairest coast of Heaven without a cloud,
Your eyebrow is Love's brow, while either eye
Are arrows drawn to wound ; your lips the temple
Or sacred fane of kisses, often as they meet, exchanging
        roses ;
Your tongue Love's lightning, neck the milky path
Or throne where sit the Graces.—
Do not I know that I have abused you all this while, or
do you think I love you a thought the better, or, with all
my poetical daubings, can alter the complexion of a hair,
now ?

Pen. I would not have you, sir.

Fow. No dispraise to you,
I have seen as handsome a woman ride upon a sack to
market, that never knew the impulsion of a coat or the

price of a stammel[1] petticoat ; and I have seen a worse
face in a countess ; what o' that ? Must you be proud
because men call you handsome ? and yet, though we
are so foolish to tell you so, you might have more wit
than to believe it ; your eyes may be matched, I hope ;
for your nose, there be richer in our sex ; 'tis true that
you have colour for your hair, we grant it, and for your
cheeks, but what do your teeth stand you in, lady ? your
lips are pretty, but you lay them too open, and men
breathe too much upon them ; for your tongue, we all
leave you, there's no contesting : your hand is fine, but
your gloves whiter, and for your leg, if the commendation
or goodness of it be in the small, there be bad enow in
gentlemen's stockings to compare with it ; come, remember you are imperfect creatures without a man ; be
not you a goddess ; I know you are mortal, and had
rather make you my companion than my idol : this is no
flattery now.

Enter WORTHY, AIMWELL, *and* BRAINS.

Wor. Where be these gentlemen ?

Fow. How now, Frank !

Wor. You look well to your charge, Brains. [*Aside.*

Bra. A question, sir ; pray you, are you married, sir ?

Clare. Why dost thou ask ?

Bra. Because you should answer me ;
I cannot see it in your forehead, sir.

Clare. How now, my officious trencher-squire ?

Wor. Excuse him, Master Clare, 'tis his blunt zeal
To do his master service, who enjoined his
Best care and vigilance upon this gentlewoman.

Clare. I am married, sir.

Bra. Then I hope you have met with your match
already.
I have nothing to say to you—

Clare. This fellow's mad.

---

[1] A kind of fine worsted.

Bra. Nor my master neither, though he left his brains behind him. I hope a man may ask a question, sir?

Wor. Come hither, Brains.

Fow. On my life thou art in love.

Clare. You are not.

Fow. Do not mistake yourself, for I am.

Clare. Caught?   I am glad on't.

Fow. No, indeed, not caught neither, therefore be not overjoyed, good morality? why, dost thou think it possible a woman's face, or anything without her, can enchant me?

Bra. [*To* WORTHY.]—Let me alone. [*Exit* WORTHY.

Clare. Why dost thou court them, then?

Fow. Why, to try their wits, with which I sharpen my own. Dost think I am so mad to marry? sacrifice my liberty to a woman; sell my patrimony to buy them feathers and new fashions, and maintain a gentleman-usher to ride in my saddle when I am knighted and pointed at, with Pythagoras for my tame sufferance; have my wardrobe laid forth and my holiday breeches, when my lady pleases I shall take the air in a coach with her, together with her dog that is costive; be appointed my table, what I shall eat, according as her ladyship finds her own body inclined; fed upon this or that melancholy dish by prescription, guarded with officious salads, like a prisoner in a throng;[1] praise her bountiful allowance of coarse mutton, that have the world of dainty flesh before me? 'twere a sin to discretion, and my own freedom.

Bra. Young mistress, I observe you.   [*Aside.*

Clare. You do not mean to die in this faith?

Fow. Prithee, do not talk of dying; a pox on the bellman and his *Omnia benes!*[2] but that I think I know thy father, I should hardly believe thou wert a gentle-

---

[1] I do not understand this, unless a ridiculous pun be intended between salads, vegetables, and sallet, a helmet.—*Gifford.*

[2] From the manner in which this expression "*All's well*" is introduced; it would seem to have some reference to the times of "the sickness," always dreaded, and always fatal.—*Gifford.*

man; however, thy Aristotle's Ethics will make thee
uncapable of their company shortly; if you catechise
thus you shall have few gentlemen your disciples that
have any blood or spirit about them. There is no discourse so becoming your gallants now, as a horse race,
or Hyde-park,—what ladies' lips are softest, what fashion
is most terse and courtly, what news abroad, which is
the best vaulting-house,[1] where shall we taste canary and
be drunk to-night? talk of morality!—here be ladies
still, you shall hear me court one of them; I hope you
will not report abroad among my friends that I love
her; it is the love of mounting into her maidenhead, I
vow, Jack, and nothing else.

Clare. You are a mad lover.

[*As* AIMWELL *comes towards* VIOLETTA *she
turns, and exit.*

Bra. That was cunningly cast about.

Fow. Whither is't, lady?

Pen. I am walking in, sir.

Fow. I'll wait on you, and after that abroad; 'tis an
inviting day, are you for the coach?

Pen. No.

Fow. Or for the couch? Take me a companion for
Pen. Neither. [either.

Fow. How! neither? blame yourself if you be idle;
howsoever, you shall not be alone: make use of my arm,
fairest; you will to your lute, I heard you could touch it
cunningly; pray bless my ears a little.

Pen. My lute's broke, sir.

Fow. A string, you mean; but it is no matter, your
voice is not; ravish a little with that, if you please, I can
help you to an heir:—by this black eye, which nature
hath given you, I'll not leave you, I'll follow you.

[*Exeunt* FOWLER *and* PENELOPE.

Aim. All this from her?

Clare. You may believe me, sir.

Aim. Why this to him? Could she not give me

---

[1] Brothel.

repulse, but she must thus proclaim it? I never moved it to her; her uncle hath had no opportunity to acquaint her. What's the mystery?—[*Aside.*]—Prithee, repeat again the substance of what she said.

Clare. With my best memory her words were: she wished you not proceed, for she was already "disposed of in her father's thoughts."

Aim. "In her father's thoughts"? Haply not in her own.

Clare. "It would be fruitless to move her uncle or her father in it."

Aim. Ha! "not move her uncle or her father"?— This may beget encouragement there's hope I may propound my affection to her, and be happy in't.   Proceed.

Clare. "She would be sorry a gentleman of your worth should run a course of so much hazard."

Aim. Hazard! that word does yet imply there is a possibility.

Clare. So, with compliment of her thanks for your fair opinion of her, she'd wish me "make you sensible in time to place your love where you might expect better return."

Aim. Ah, that's wormwood; let me see; better return; this last return hath spoiled the whole term, and undone my suit; umph! No, it doth admit a fair construction; "She would have me sensible in time to plant my love where I may expect better return." Why—that I may from her, for ought I know.

Clare. *Amantes sibi somnia fingunt;* how apt are lovers to conster[1] all to their desires!

Aim. I will not let my action fall.

Clare. Do not build castles.

Aim. I'll smooth it with her uncle; if it hit, O my blest stars!

Clare. He's a-bed already!

Aim. Venus assist one to thy altar flies, And I'll proclaim thy son hath found his eyes   [*Exeunt.*

---

[1] Construe.

ACT THE SECOND.

SCENE I.—*Croydon. A Room in* Sir NICHOLAS TREEDLE'S *House.*

Enter Sir NICHOLAS TREEDLE *and a* Servant.

REED. Where's Martext, my chaplain?

Ser. He is newly walked out of his meditation in the kitchen into the garden.

Treed. Bid him read prayers in the dining-room.

Ser. Before your worship come?

Treed. I will not pray to-day.—Dost hear? Bid my tutor come down to me.

Ser. Which of them?

Treed. Why, he that reads travel to me; the wit that I took up in Paul's[1] in a tiffany[2] cloak without a hatband; now I have put him into a doublet of satin——Stay, he's here.

Enter Tutor.

'Morrow, tutor; what hour take you it?

Tutor. It is no hour at all, sir.

Treed. How?

Tutor. Not directly any hour, for it is between eight and nine, sir.

Treed. Very learnedly; then I was ready between six and seven to-day.

Tutor. Are you disposed for lecture?

---

[1] St. Paul's was a general rendezvous for those who sought employment.   [2] Very thin silk.

Treed. Yes, sir, yes.

Tutor. You remember my last preliction of the division of the earth into parts real and imaginary? The parts real into continent and island, ... [1] the subdivision of the continent, into peninsula, isthmus, and promontory?

Treed. In troth, sir, I remember some such things; but I have forgotten them.

Tutor. What is an isthmus?

Treed. Why, an isthmus is an elbow of land.

Tutor. A neck, a neck.

Treed. A neck? Why, I was near it; if you had let me alone, I should have come up to it.

Tutor. 'Twas well guessed. What is an island?

Treed. An island is an high mountain, which shooteth itself into the sea.

Tutor. That is a promontory.

Treed. Is it so? An island then is—no matter, let it go; it is not the first island we have lost.

Tutor. How are you perfect in your circles, great and less, mutable and immutable, tropical and polar?

Treed. As perfect in them as I am in these; faith, I shall never con these things handsomely? may not a man study travel without these circles, degrees, and altilatitudes you speak of?

Tutor. Yes, you may.

Treed. I do not care for the nearest way; I have time enough to go about.

Tutor. Very well, you shall lay aside your globe then.

Treed. Ay, and if't please you, I will have it stand in my hall to make my tenants wonder, instead of the Book of Martyrs.[2]

---

[1] There is probably an omission here.

[2] This custom is now worn out: but I have seen the *Book of Martyrs*, and Sir Richard Baker and Stow in the window seat of more than one old hall, where, when books were not so common as at present, they found many readers among the tenants and casual visitors of the family.—*Gifford.*

Tutor. It will do well; now name what kingdom or province you have most mind to.

Treed. What say you to England?

Tutor. By no means; it is not in fashion with gentlemen to study their own nation; you will discover a dull easiness if you admire not, and with admiration prefer not the weeds of other regions, before the most pleasant flowers of your own garden; let your judgment reflect, upon a serious consideration, who teaches you the mimic posture of your body, the punctuality of your beard, the formality of your pace, the elbows of your cloak, the heel of your boot? do not other nations? Are not Italian heads, Spanish shoulders, Dutch bellies, and French legs, the only notions of your reformed English gentlemen?

Treed. I am resolved to be ignorant of my own country; say no more on it. What think you if I went over to France, the first thing I did?

Tutor. By sea!

Treed. Do you think I have no more wit than to venture myself i'the salt water; I had rather be pickled and powdered at home by half, that I had.

Tutor. I apprehend — you are cautious; it is safe travelling in your study; but I will not read France to you.

Treed. No!

Tutor. *Pardonnez-moi*, it is unnecessary; all the French fashions are here already, or rather your French cuts.

Treed. Cuts!

Tutor. Understand me; there are divers French cuts.

Treed. We have had too many French cuts already.

Tutor. First, there is your cut of the head.

Treed. That is dangerous.

Tutor. Pshaw! a hair, a hair, a periwig is your French cut, and in fashion with your most courtly gallants; your own hair will naturally forsake you.

Treed. A bald reason.

Tutor. Right: observe their prudent and weighty

policy who have brought up this artificial head-piece, because no man should appear light-headed.

Treed. He had no sound head that invented it!

Tutor. Then there is the new cut of your doublet or slash, the fashion of your apparel, a quaint cut.

Treed. Upon taffeta.

Tutor. Or what you please; the slash is the emblem of your valour, and, besides declareth that you are open breasted.

Treed. Open, as much as you will, but no valour.

Tutor. Then, sir, there is the cut of your leg.

Treed. That is when a man is drunk, is it not?

Tutor. Do not stagger in your judgment, for this cut is the grace of your body: I mean dancing o' the French cut in the leg is most fashionable, believe it, pupil, a genteel carriage.

Treed. But it is fain to be supported sometime with a bottom.

Enter Servant.

Ser. Here is Sir George Richley, sir, newly alighted.

Treed. Oh, my father-in-law that shall be.

Tutor. Then we are cut off.

Treed. There is a match concluded between his daughter and me, and now he comes for my answer. Conduct him to the gallery.

Tutor. Rather, sir, meet him.

Treed. Let him go before, and tell him we are coming, and we'll be there as soon as he.   [*Exeunt.*

SCENE II.—*London.   A Room in* WORTHY'S *House.*

BRAINS *and* WHIBBLE *at table.*

Whib. Brains!

Bra. What is the matter?

Whib. Let's rifle the other bottle of wine.

Bra. Do not endanger thy sconce.

Whib. How?

Bra. I'll drink no more.

Whib. Why?

Bra. Because I will not be drunk for any man's pleasure.

Whib. Drunk!

Bra. It is good English now: it was Dutch.[1] May be you have some conspiracy upon me.

Whib. I?—Who has betrayed me? his mistress procured the key of the wine-cellar, and bade me try if I could wind up his brains handsomely, he knows on 't—[*Aside.*] —Not one health more?

Bra. Not one, good Whibble; if you urge again I shall suspect.

Whib. Suspect me?

Bra. And beat you, Whibble, if you be not satisfied.

Whib. I am; but in friendship—

Bra. Dost tempt me?

Whib. I will drink your health and be drunk alone.

[*Exit.*

Bra. This whelp has some plot upon me, I smell powder; my young mistress would have blown up my brains! this peter-gunner[2] should have given fire: it is not the first time she hath conspired so, but it will not do, I was never yet cozened in my life, and if I pawn my brains for a bottle of sack or claret, may my nose, as a brand for my negligence, carry everlasting malmsey in it, and be studded with rubies and carbuncles!—Mistress, you must pardon my officiousness; be as angry as a tiger, I must play the dragon, and watch your golden fleece: my master has put me in trust, and I am not so easily corrupted. I have but two eyes, Argus had a hundred, but he must be a cunning Mercury must pipe them both asleep, I can tell you. And now I talk of sleep, my

[1] Meaning that we derived the term as well as the vice from the Germans. This was not strictly the case; but the belief was pretty general in Shirley's time, and the dissoluteness of those who had served in the Low Countries was some support to it.—*Gifford.*

[2] A derisive nickname given to gunners and sportsmen.

lodging is next to her chambers; it is a confidence in my master to let his livery lie so near her; servingmen have ere now proved themselves no eunuchs, with their masters' daughters; if I were so lusty as some of my own tribe, it were no great labour to commit a burglary upon a maidenhead; but all my nourishment runs upward into brains, and I am glad on 't; a temperate blood is sign of a good liver; I am past tilting.—Here she is, with the second part of her to the same tune, another maid that has a grudging of the green sickness, and wants a man to recover her.

Enter VIOLETTA *and* PENELOPE.

Pen. Be this enough between us, to bind each to help the other's designs.

Vio. Here is Brains; he has not yet been drenched.

Pen. He is too subtle.

Vio. How now, Brains?

Bra. As you see, forsooth.

Pen. Thou art very sad.

Bra. But I am in sober sadness, I thank my stars.

Vio. Witty!

Bra. As much wit as will keep Brains from melting this hot weather.

Pen. A dry whoreson, not thus to be wrought upon.
                                                    [*Aside.*

Bra. Very good sack and claret in the house.

Pen. Thou hast not tasted?

Bra. O yes, O yes, my brains swim in canary, exceeding excellent sack; I thank you, ladies, I know it is your pleasure I should not want the best blood of the grape, in hope there might be a stone in my cup to mar my drinking afterwards:—

Enter SENSIBLE *with a letter.*

Mistress Sensible! what jig's in the wind, she moves so nimbly?

Pen. From whom?

Sens. Master Fowler.

Bra. A letter! whence flew that paper kite?

Pen. What is this?

Bra. Another enclosed, without direction; happily observed.

Pen. [*Reads.*] "If you can love, I will study to deserve, and be happy to give you proof of my service; in the mean time it shall be a testimony of your favour to deliver this inclosed paper to your cousin, from her servant Aimwell. Farewell, and remember Fowler."
Look you, cousin, what Master Fowler writes; I dare trust you with the secret. At your opportunity peruse this paper.

Bra. Conveyances! I read juggling in that paper already; and though you put it up I will not. Oh, for so much magic to conjure that paper out of her bosom into my pocket! now I do long to know what pitiful lover, for it can be no other, is doing penance in that white sheet already.—[*Aside.*]—Mistress Sensible, hark ye; whence came that letter?

Sens. From Master Fowler to my mistress.

Bra. It is a she letter, it seems.

Sens. A she letter; why so?

Bra. Because it had a young one in the belly of it, or I am much mistaken.

Pen. Does he not write like a bold gamester?

Bra. And a bowling-gamester, too, for his bias was towards my mistress; but I may chance to cast a rub in his way, to keep him from kissing.[1] [*Aside.*]

Vio. He hath very good parts in him, questionless; but do you love him?

Bra. O the cunning of these gipsies! how, when they list, they can talk in a distinguishable dialect; they call men foxes, but they make tame geese of some of us; and

[1] These are all bowling terms; the mistress was the stationary bowl at which the players aimed.

yet, like one of those in Rome, I may prove so happy to
preserve your distressed capitol.—What news brings this
kickshaw?   [*Aside.*

Enter WINNIFRED.

Win. Master Fowler desires to speak with you.

Brd. Already! he might have delivered his own letter.
                                                 [*Aside.*

Vio. I'll to my chamber.

Bra. It will do very well.   [*Aside.*

Vio. I hope you will be careful that I am not troubled
with any visit of gentlemen; it will become your officiousness, good Dametas, to have a care of your charge Pamela.[1]

Bra. So I can suffer this jest.   [*Exit.*

Vio. Ha! is he gone? I am glad of it, I will take
this opportunity to read the paper Master Aimwell sent
me. No superscription!

Re-enter BRAINS, *behind.*

Bra. She is at it already; thus far off I can read her
countenance, if she spare her voice.

Vio. [*Reads.*]

"I do not court your fortune, but your love
    If my wild apprehension of it prove
    My error, punish gently, since the fire
    Comes from yourself, that kindled my desire.
    So my poor heart, full of expectance, lies
    To be your servant, or your sacrifice."

It shall be answered.   [*Exit.*

Bra. It shall! the game's afoot: were I best to discover thus much, or reserve it to welcome home the old
knight withal? I will be more familiar with this juggling,
first: the scrivener has a name, and if he be worth his
own ears, he shall be worth my discovery.

Re-enter PENELOPE *with* FOWLER.

Here come the gallant and the t'other toy, now.

---

[1] Dametas is the foolish shepherd. in Sir P. Sidney's *Arcadia*, in
whose charge Pamela was placed by the king her father.

Pen. I received your letter, sir.

Fow. In good time.

Pen. You might have spared your hand a labour if you had resolved to put your feet upon this expedition.

Bra. Good.

Fow. I confess I wrote something in my own cause; but the chief cause was to convey my friend's affection to his mistress.

Bra. And I will convey your affection to somebody else. [*Exit.*

Pen. Then you made me a property?

Fow. It is for your honour, if you help any way to advance an honest business; and yet, mistake me not; though the rack should enforce it from me—without a second reason I had not wrote to you; yet, for so much as concerned myself, by this kiss, my pen hath but set down the resolution of my heart to serve you.

Pen. To serve me! how?

Fow. How! why, any way: give me your livery, I will wear it, or a coat with a cognizance,[1] by this light, I fear you are an heretic still, and do not believe as you should do; come, let me rectify your faith, serve you.

Pen. Since the compliment of service came up, gentlemen have had excuse for their love. I would not have you serve me, sir.

Fow. Not serve you! Why, do you think a man cannot love and serve too?

Pen. Not one serve two, well.

Fow. You are two literal; and yet in the strict sense I have known a woman has served half a dozen gentlemen handsomely; so, so; and yet the last had enough of her too: why should not one man serve two gentlewomen? it argues against your sex, that you are more insatiable of the two. But I have a simple affection, I protest, and individual; I'll ne'er serve but one.

Pen. But one at once!

---

[1] A badge bearing the arms or crest of the family.

Fow. But one at once, and but one always, by this diamond.

Pen. Nay, keep your oath, sir.

Fow. I am forsworn if I do not; for I vowed, before I came, to bestow it; come, wear it in your bosom, it shall be an earnest of more precious jewels, though not of so bright a lustre, that will follow.

Pen. I pray, sir, resolve me one thing, and be plain.— Do you love me?

Fow. Love you!

Pen. It is my question.

Fow. It is a very foolish one; to what purpose have I been talking all this while, that you make it a question? has not it been the theme of all my discourse hitherto, that I do love you?

Pen. In what sense?

Fow. In what sense? Why, in any sense, at your own choice, or in all the senses together, an you doubt me: I do love to see your face, hear your voice, smell your breath, touch your tree, and taste your golden apples.

Pen. But this does not satisfy me.

Fow. You do not doubt my sufficiency, do you?

Pen. Now you are immodest; I only ask if you love me.

Fow. And have I not told you? Pray teach me a better way to express it. Does a wise man love fools' fortune, and a nobleman another beside my lady? Does the devil love an usurer, a great man his flatterer, the lawyer a full term, or the physician a dead time to thrive in?

Pen. Spare yourself; this is but coarse love.

Fow. I'll spin it finer and finer every day, sweet; to be plain with thee, what dost thou think of me for a husband? I love thee that way.

Pen. Would you did else.   [*Aside.*

Fow. Is there anything in me would commend itself, that I may spare my other commendations? for I am

resolved to be yours at any rate of my own praise, or
what I can purchase from my friends.

Pen. Sir, if your meaning be no stranger to your language, although I cannot promise myself, you bind me to
be thankful for it.

Fow. She nibbles already. [*Aside.*

Pen. But pardon me if I suspect you still; you are too
wild and airy to be constant to that affection.

Enter BRAINS *and* WORTHY.

Bra. There be the pigeons.

Wor. An't be no worse I care not.—Master Fowler,
A most welcome friend.

Fow. I would be to your daughter,

Bra. Let her use to entertain him so, and he will bid
himself welcome.—[*Aside.*]—Hark you, sir, you do like
his company.

Wor. Yes.

Bra. So I say, but if I were worthy to give your
daughter counsel, she should have a special care how she
treads, for if this gentleman be not a whoremaster, he is
very like one, and if she chance any way to crack her
Venice glass, it will be not so easily soldered.

Wor. Meddle with your charge, sir, and let her alone.

Bra. I have done; here is a fresh gamester.

Enter MANLY.

Man. By your noble leave.

Wor. You are welcome, sir.

Man. I was directed hither to find a gentleman.

Fow. Manly, how is't?

Man. I was to inquire for you at your lodging.

Fow. Pray know this gentleman, lady; — Master
Worthy, he'll deserve your acquaintance.

Man. You oblige my services.—But what make you
here, my woman-errant?

Wor. Come hither, Penelope.

Fow. Soliciting a cause of Venus.

Man. I suspect as much; but with her? is she a whore?

Fow. No, but I'll do the best to make her one; she loves me already, that's some engagement; I dare trust thee with my sins.—Who's here? Aimwell and Clare!

Enter AIMWELL, CLARE, *and* BRAINS.

Wor. Withdraw yourself.

Fow. Frank!

Aim. Master Worthy.

Wor. A knot of friends.

Aim. What of my letter?   [*Aside to Fowler.*

Fow. 'Tis delivered; you must expect.

Wor. What news, gentlemen?

Aim. We hear none; you visit the Exchange, sir; pray furnish us.

Bra. What do all these butterflies here? I do not like it.   [*Aside.*

Aim. I hope your daughter is in health?

Wor. Perfect, I thank Heaven.

Aim. And your niece, at whose naming I am bold to tender my thanks for your last friendship; I might have plunged by this time into passion, had not you nobly, just as I was falling, prevented my unhappiness.

Wor. Your opinion of what I did gives value to the action; however, 'twas a duty I was bound to.

Bra. This is the youth, I'll pawn my brains;—[*Aside.*] —Hark you, sir, what do you call this gentleman?

Clare. Master Aimwell.

Bra. He may shoot short for all his aiming; he wears bachelors' buttons, does he not?

Clare. Yes, old truepenny and loops, too; thou art jealous, now.

Bra. One word more.

Fow. I have a plot, and thou must help me.

Man. Let it be a safe one.

Aim. May we not see her?

Wor. Brains, where's thy mistress?

Bra. She's a little busy.

Fow. Who's that?

Wor. My niece.

Fow. An she be but a little busy she's more than half at leisure.

Bra. Do not you know that a woman is more troubled with a little business, than some men with managing the troubles of a whole commonwealth? it has been a proverb, "as busy as a hen with one chicken;" marry, an she had twenty, twenty to one she would not be so fond of them.

Wor. He says right.—Gentlemen, we are friends; it is my brother's pleasure, who is her father, to deny frequent access to her, till he hath finished a design; for my part, I am not of his mind, nor shall my daughter be a prisoner to his fancy:—you see, sir, I do not seclude her; if she choose within any limits of reason, I move in her.

Aim. You speak nobly.

Enter WHIBBLE.

Whib. Sir George Richley, sir, and Sir Nicholas Treedle, are newly arrived.

Wor. My brother! acquaint my niece.

Bra. 'Tis my office, I'll do it.   [*Exit.*

Man. Shall's stay?

Aim. By all means; let's see the doughty knight that must free the lady from her enchanted castle.

Clare. Didst ever see him?

Aim. No; but I've heard his character.

Man. Prithee let's have it.

Aim. They say he's one, was wise before he was a man, for then his folly was excusable; but since he came to be of age, which had been a question till his death, had not the law given him his father's lands, he is grown wicked enough to be a landlord: he does pray but once a year, and that's for fair weather in harvest; his inward senses are sound, for none comes from him; he speaks words, but no matter, and therefore is in election to be of the peace and quorum, which his tenants think him fit for, and his tutor's judgment allows, whom he maintains to make him legs and speeches. He feeds well himself, but, in obedience to government, he allows his servants fasting days; he loves law, because it killed his father, whom the parson overthrew in a case of tithes; and, in memory, wears nothing suitable; for his apparel is a cento, or the ruins of ten fashions. He does not much care for Heaven, for he's doubtful of any such place; only hell he's sure of, for the devil sticks to his conscience: therefore, he does purpose, when he dies, to turn his sins into alms-houses, that posterity may praise him for his bountiful ordination of hot pottage; but he's here already: you may read the rest as he comes towards you.

Enter Sir GEORGE RICHLEY, Sir NICHOLAS TREEDLE, *and* Tutor.

Wor. Brother!

Rich. Let your kindest respects meet this gentleman.

Wor. Sir Nicholas Treedle, I desire you would write me in the number of your servants.

Treed. 'Tis granted.—Gentlemen, I have an ambition to be your eternal slave.

Fow. 'Tis granted.

Tut. And I to be your everlasting servant.

Aim. 'Tis granted.

Clare. A couple of cockloches.[1]

Enter PENELOPE, VIOLETTA, WINNIFRED, SENSIBLE, *and* BRAINS.

Rich. Here comes my daughter.

Treed. [*To* PENELOPE.]—Lady, and mistress of my heart, which hath long melted for you,—

---

[1] Silly coxcombs. Fr. *Coqueluche.*

Rich. This is my daughter.

Treed. Then it melted for you, lady.

Fow. His heart is whole again.

Treed. Vouchsafe to entertain a servant, that shall study to command—

Tut. Well said!

Treed. His extremest possibilities—in your business.

Aim. Abominable courtship!

Sens. [*Aside to* AIMWELL.] Sir, I am servant to Mistress Violetta, who commends this paper to you.

Aim. O, my best angel!

Bra. As the devil would have it! are you there, Sensible?

Fow. Master Worthy, I take my leave.

Wor. Will you not stay supper?

Man. We are engaged.

Aim. My service shall wait on you, gentlemen.

Clare. And mine.

Treed. Come on, my queen of diamonds.

Rich. Brother, lead the way.　　　　　[*Exeunt.*

Bra. If she carry away this letter so, call me shallow-brains: I was never yet cozened in my life :—this night? it shall be so; I will not come with bare relation of your plots,

　　I'll bring active intelligence that shall tell

　　Your secret aims, so crush them in the shell.

　　　　　　　　　　　　　　　[*Exit.*

ACT THE THIRD.

SCENE I.—Sir GEORGE RICHLEY'S *House.* VIOLETTA'S
Bedchamber.

BRAINS *is discovered with a paper in his hand.*

RA. Sure this is it, my mistress and her
maid are both fast still; I have watched
under the bed all night, to rob her
pocket of this paper, and I have done
it. Some fellow, at this opportunity,
would have wriggled himself into one
of their flesh.

Vio. Who's there? Sensible?

Bra. Death! her tongue is awake already.

Vio. Who's in the chamber?

Bra. Help me, brains, before she wakes the t'other.—
'Tis I, forsooth, but looking for the chamber-pot.

[*Counterfeits* SENSIBLE'S *voice.*

Vio. Beshrew you for your noise.

Bra. Where's the door?   [*Stumbles.*

Sens. Who's there?

Bra. The t'other spirit is raised in the trundle-bed.[1]
What will become of me now?

[SENSIBLE *comes forward.*

Sens. Here's nobody.

---

[1] In the trundle-bed. A low bed occupied by the servants that
ran on castors, and was only drawn out at night from beneath the
other bed.

Vio. Make an end, and get thee to bed.

Sens. An end of what? Does she talk in her sleep? she was not wont.

Bra. So, so!   [*Exit.*

Sens. [*Going to the door.*]—Ha! the spring is open,
I might forget to make it fast last night;
'Tis so; and happily some cur or cat
Has been in the chamber, for I hear a noise
About the door; I'll make it fast,
And so to bed again; I think it is day already. [*Retires.*

SCENE II.—*Another Room in the same.*

Enter Tutor *in his gown, with a paper.*

Tutor. So; this fancy, wrote for Sir Nicholas, like a
forked arrow, points two ways; wenches are caught with
such conceits : they will imagine it none of his invention,
then,—whose but mine? my person does invite more
acceptation, but the father aims at the estate; no matter,
if I can insinuate myself into her opinion; 'tis no impos-
sibility; her portion will be enough for both.
Shall I live still dependent, and not seek
Ways to advance myself? busy my brains
In ballads to the giddy chambermaids?
Beggar myself with purse and pincushion?
When she that is the mistress may be mine?
'Twill be a masterpiece if I can gull him.—
But he's here already.

Enter Sir NICHOLAS TREEDLE *with a paper.*

Treed. Noble Tutor! 'morrow to you! have you
finished the whimsey for my mistress already?

Tutor. I have done it; this paper carries the love-
powder.

Treed. For fear you had forgotten me, I have made a

quibbling in praise of her myself; such a one as will fetch up her heart, Tutor.

Tutor. That were a dangerous vomit, sir; take heed of that.

Treed. Ay, but I will not hurt her, I warrant thee; an she die within a twelvemonth and a day, I'll be hanged for her.

Tutor. Will you, sir?

Treed. Marry will I. Look you, sir.—But first let me see yours.—Can you not write it in my own hand? I shall hardly read it.

Tutor. I'll read it to you.

Treed. Sir George!—Give me it!

Enter Sir GEORGE RICHLEY *and* WORTHY.

Rich. See, they are at it.

Treed. And how do you like it?

Wor. 'Morrow, noble Sir Nicholas.

Rich. 'Morrow, gentlemen!

Treed. 'Morrow to you both.—Sir George, I have been making poetry this morning.

Tutor. He has a subtle fancy.

Rich. What's the subject?

Tutor. No subject, but the queen of his affections.

Treed. I scorn subjects; 'tis my empress your daughter's merit[1] hath set my Muse on fire.

Tutor. Read, sir.

Treed. No, you shall read them for me.

Tutor. 'Tis a hue and cry, sir.

Rich. A hue and cry! for what?

Treed. For what! why, for somewhat, I'll warrant you.

Tutor. You may call it "Love's hue and cry."

Treed. Call it what you will, I know what it is.

Wor. Are you so poetical?

Treed. I have been dabbling in Helicon; next to travel, 'tis all my study.—Mark the invention.

[1] Old copy, "muse." Gifford suggested "merit."

Tutor. [*Reads.*] "In Love's name you are charged hereby
    To make a speedy hue and cry,
    After a face, who t' other day
    Came and stole my heart away ;
    For your directions in brief
    These are best marks to know the thief:
    Her hair a net of beams would prove,
    Strong enough to captive Jove,
    Playing the eagle : her clear brow
    Is a comely field of snow.
    A sparkling eye, so pure a gray
    As when it shines it needs no day.
    Ivory dwelleth on her nose ;
    Lilies, married to the rose,
    Have made her cheek the nuptial bed ;
    Her lips betray their virgin red,
    As they only blushed for this,
    That they one another kiss ;
    But observe, beside the rest,
    You shall know this felon best
    By her tongue ; for if your ear
    Shall once a heavenly music hear,
    Such as neither gods nor men
    But from that voice shall hear again,
    That, that is she, oh, take her t'ye,
    None can rock Heaven asleep but she."

Treed. How do you like my pippin of Parnassus,
gentlemen ?

Rich. Wor. Very handsome.

Treed. Nay, I'll warrant you, my Tutor has good furniture in him.

Wor. I do not think he made them.   [*Aside to* RICH.

Treed. Now you shall hear some verses of my own
making.

Rich. Your own ! did you not make these ?

Tutor. He betrays himself.   [*Aside.*

Treed. Hum : yes, I made them too, my Tutor knows.

Tutor. I'll take my oath who made them.

Treed. But I wrote them for another gentleman that had a mistress.

Rich. My daughter, you said.

Treed. I may say so ; but, that their faces are nothing alike, you would hardly know one from t' other. For your better understanding, I will read them myself.— " Her foot—"

Wor. Do you begin there ?

Treed. Oh, I will rise by degrees.

[*Reads.*] " Her foot is feat [1] with diamond toes,
          But she with legs of ruby goes :
          Thighs loadstones, and do draw unto her
          The iron pin of any wooer."

Wor. Precious conceit !

Treed. " Her head—"

Rich. Her head !

Wor. You were between her thighs but now.

Treed. 'Tis my conceit : I do now mean to go downwards again, and meet where I left, in the middle—

[*Reads.*] " Her head is opal, neck of sapphire,
          Breast carbuncles, shine like a fire ;
          And the naked truth to tell ye,
          The very mother of pearl her belly.
          How can she choose but hear my groans,
          That is composed of precious stones ? "

Wor. Ay, marry, sir.

Treed. Now, " If you lik't you may." [2]

Wor. A word with you, sir : pray what do you think of your pupil ?

Tutor. I think nothing, sir.

Wor. But deal ingenuously ; your opinion ?

Tutor. Shall I tell you ?

Wor. Pray, sir.

Tutor. Nothing.

[1] Fashioned.
[2] This is from the prologue to Ben Jonson's *Cynthia's Revels*, and was popular as a playful defiance.

Wor. I think so too. What doth my brother mean, to make this fond election?

Tutor. For my own part, you hear me say nothing; but the good parts and qualities of men are to be valued.

Wor. This fellow's a knave; I smell him.

Tutor. Something has some savour.

Treed. When you please; name your own time; I'm ready to be married at midnight.

Rich. About a seven-night hence.

Treed. Let it be three or four, I care not how soon. Is breakfast ready?

Rich. It waits upon you.

Treed. I do love to eat and drink in a morning, though I fast all day after.

Rich. I'll follow, brother.

Wor. We'll both attend. [*Exeunt.*

SCENE III.—AIMWELL'S *Lodgings.*

Enter AIMWELL *with a letter.*

Aim. This opportunity let my covetous eye
Take to enrich itself; but first prepare
With reverence, as to an altar, bring
No careless but religious beams along
With you to this new object; this small paper
Carries the volume of my human fate,
I hold my destiny betwixt two fingers,
And thus am I wrapt up without a name,
Being, or expectation of world's joy
More than this table (when the curtain's drawn)
Presents in character to my thirsty eyesight.—
Hail, thou ambassador from thine and my
Mistress, bringing peace, or unkind war,
Thou emblem of her whiteness, which I kiss,
And thus again salute.

Enter Boy *and* CLARE.

Boy. There he is, alone.

Clare. So, leave us.   [*Exit* Boy.

Aim. Coming from her,
Can it be guilty of defiance to me?
Had she not meant me happy, she had given
My letter to the flame, and with it I,
In those thin ashes had been buri`ed,
Nor had she deigned this answer, which the circum-
        stance
Of my receiving prompts me to believe
Gracious; the gentle messenger commended it,
Not as a thing she would have public, but
With eyes full of suspicion, (which had been
Needless, had she contemned my services;)
So, smilingly, departed.   Thus I sent my paper,
Which what but love taught her to imitate?
Without a superscription.—[*Seeing* CLARE.]—Oh, Clare,
        welcome,
welcome to that shall make thy heart dance in thy bosom
if thou beest a friend, and canst rejoice to know me
happy.   You thought me ridiculous, and that I did with
too much flattery of myself, expound your story.   Had I
been, like thee, of frosty apprehension, and cold, phlegmatic judgment, I had missed a blessing that wanton
Jove would have been rival for.   Dost see this paper?

Clare. Nothing on the outside?

Aim. 'Tis inly precious.

Clare. You have not searched the lining, that you promise so.

Aim. I see through it; hast thou not heard the perfect
        magnet
Will, though inclosed within an ivory box,
Through the white wall shoot forth embracing virtue
To the loved needle?   I can read it, Clare,
And read a joy in't that transports me; this

Came from my mistress; having touched her hand,
Whence it received a whiteness, hath it not
Brought incense too? dispersing a rich breath,
Sweeter than all Arabian spicery,
About the room, in which, while it remains,
We suck in perfumed air. It came from her,
My honest Clare, from her, whose rare wit taught,
When in thy dull opinion I was lost,
My apprehension a new hope to thrive
In my ambitious love.—Excellent woman!
The top of all creation, I shall be
At once too happy.—Unrip thou the seal,
Read it, and let thy voice convey it gently,
Lest I be surfeited. But why should any
Be honoured to receive her loving letter [1]
But I, to whom she hath directed it?
By thy leave, silent paper;—confident
Of bliss, I open my Elysium,
And let my soul into it.—Ha!—   [*Reads.*
Laden with mighty hopes, how desperately
Have I launched forth, and find a storm!

   Clare. What's this? Your own letter returned!
Can it be otherwise than in scorn?

   Aim. In scorn!

   Clare. Have you not now cause of triumph? who is
now the truer prophet? You would nourish hope in spite
of reason; now you feel a punishment in her derision.

   Aim. Is this credible?

   Clare. Credible! 'Tis no wonder in a woman;
Though she had promised, vowed, affection to you,
It had not been a miracle to find
A change in her affection; yet you cannot
Accuse her much.

   Aim. Appeared I so unworthy,
That 'mong so many ways she had to express
At what poor value she esteemed my proffered

---

[1] The words "loving letter" were supplied by Gifford.

Service, her pride could find out none but this,
To send me mine own again !

   Clare. Do but imagine
You sent a servant with a message to her,
She not within, he is returned again
Without an answer.

   Aim. Incivility !
She might have thanked me, and subscribed her name?
I was not bound to her observance.

   Clare. Come, be free again.

   Aim. I will be so ; with this
That I could cancel my affection !

                            [*Tears the letter in pieces.*

   Clare. What do you mean ? it "having touched her
Is full of incense and Arabian spicery;"   [hand,
You are too prodigal of your perfume.

   Aim. Do not thou mock me, too.

   Clare. Well, I have done.

   Aim. Would I had so !   I cannot empty all
My torment ! wherefore should a man love woman?
Such airy mockeries ; nothing but mere echos,
That owe their being to our opinion,
And in reward of honouring them, send back
As scornfully the language we bestowed,
Out of our too much dotage.

   Clare. If they send
All they receive from us, accuse them not,
We have our hearts again.

   Aim. And I'll have mine.
I will, I have not yet : here wants a guest,
Invite him home again.   Why should not I
Be as coy as she, and with as much neglect
Throw her behind my thoughts ?   Instruct me with
Witty revenge, and thou shalt see me toss
This shuttlecock with as much pride ; and when
I'm sated with this sport, let fall this vanity
Into as low disdain ; psha !

Clare. Nobly resolved!

Aim. Come, to a tavern ; drench the memory
Of these poor thoughts.

Clare. Let's seek out Master Fowler and Manly.

Aim. And warmed with sack, we'll try
Who can make satires best.

Clare. A match! let's to them.   [*Exeunt.*

SCENE IV.—FOWLER'S *Lodgings.*

FOWLER, *as if sick, upon a couch ; and* MANLY *disguised as
a* Physician *attending him : phials, &c. on a table.*

Fow. An thou dost not play the doctor handsomely,
I'll set the College of Physicians upon thee, for practising
without a license.

Man. Can you be sick ?

Fow. I would but counterfeit.

Man. So must I the physician.

Fow. I have known a spruce en.piric hath given his
patient two or three stools with the bare repetition of
crude words and knotty sentences, which have come
from him like a phlegm, which, besides the operation
in the hearers, who admire him for it ; while he beats
like a drum, at their barrel head, and turns their brains
like beer, does him the benefit to scour his own dirty
maw, whose dregs else would putrify ; and infest his
cheeks worse than a gangrene.

Man. Are you sure she will visit you ?

Fow. As sure as I am well ; for, an I were sick and
would sleep, I would rather take a nap on the ridge of
Etna, and the fall of deafening Nilus, than endure the
visitation of any of their tribe.—[*Knocking within.*—
One knocks ; my pillow, and lay my head in the aching
posture.

Enter AIMWELL *and* CLARE.

Man. 'Tis Aimwell and Clare.

Aim. Where's my witty bacchanalian?—How now? what means this apothecary's shop about thee? art physical?

Fow. Sick, sick.

Aim. Didst not look in a glass to-day? how scurvily this nightcap shows upon thee!

Clare. What's the disease?

Man. A fever, sir.

Aim. Hang fevers! let's to the tavern, and inflame ourselves with lusty wine; suck in the spirit of sack, till we be delphic, and prophesy, my bully-rook.

Fow. Alas!

Aim. A lass! is that the disease! Drench her, drench her in sack: sick for a lass! do not fool thyself beyond the cure of Bedlam; be wise and well again.

Fow. You are merry; it seems you have won the lady.

Aim. What lady? the lady i' the lobster? I was half sick for a foolish thing called a woman; a toy took me in the head, and had like to have taken away my heart too; but I have recovered. Do not trust thy body with a physician, he'll make thy foolish bones go without flesh in a fortnight, and thy soul walk without a body a seven-night after.

Man. These are no doctors.

Aim. Doctor! art a Parisian, a Paduan, or a Leyden [1] doctor? How many, and be true to us, hast thou killed the last spring? will it puzzle thy arithmetic, my precious rectifier of nature the wrong way?—Faith, thou must excuse me, Jack, that I cannot condole with thee; by this whey beard of Esculapius, I dare not endanger myself with so much melancholy, lest I fall into a relapse. —Whom have we here?

[1] The old copy reads, "Le den"—perhaps the author intended to be witty; if so, there is a pun spoiled.—*Gifford,*

Enter WHIBBLE *and* PENELOPE *disguised.*

Whib. 'Tis reported that Master Fowler is sick, and keeps his chamber ; I hope he is within ?

Pen. Noble sir.

Aim. Fair lady.

Pen. How fare you, sir?

Fow. The better to see you here.

Man. Upon the entrance of this gentlewoman, I find your grief much altered.

Pen. Upon mine ?

Man. Yes, and by that I dare presume to say, you are the cause of his distemper?

Pen. I, sir?

Fow. A cunning doctor!

Man. For I observed, so soon as his searching eye had fastened on her, his labouring pulse, that, through his fever, did before stick hard, and frequent, now exceeds in both these differences ; and this Galen himself found true upon a woman that had doted upon a fencer.

Clare. Ay !

Whib. She did long for t'other bout then ?   [*Aside.*

Pen. Give us leave, pray.

[AIMWELL *and the others walk aside.*

Aim. A very pretty fellow.

Clare. Well skilled i' the pulse.

Aim. You know my disease too, do you not ? will not my complexion give you the hint on't ?

Man. You are not very well.

Aim. How, sir ?

Man. By your favour, you will come to't.

Aim. To what?

Man. To a burning fever.—Is there not one woman in the world ?—

Aim. I think there is, and too much of that ; what then ? what conclude you?

Man. Nothing but syrup of violet would comfort you, going to bed.

Aim. Violet!

Clare. He has given it you.

Fow. It does me good, lady, to feel you by the hand.

Pen. Would it were in my power to recover you.

Fow. The doctor, I thank him, has taken pains with me ; but he says—nothing will do me good—

Pen. Nothing?

Fow. But that which is another sickness to reveal.

Pen. Pray, sir, acquaint me.

Fow. I know you love me. I have a great mind, an 'twere but for two or three minutes, to have a maid warm my bed—

Pen. That may be done.

Fow. With her body—else 'twill do me no good, the doctor says—to put life in some of my limbs, a little virgin warmth would do it.

Pen. You have a burning fever.

Fow. But now and then I have such cold fits again— and 'tis the doctor's opinion—a very learned man.

Pen. A learned pander.   [*Aside.*

Man. He's at it.

Fow. Doctor!

Clare. [*To* AIMWELL.] Again passionate!

Aim. Why, I may love her name without offence to you. Why did he waken my remembrance? I had for-gotten her.

Clare. Think upon her scorn, then.

Aim. I have done : and till I hear her name again, I will throw this dulness off.

Clare. Let's choose another subject.
How closely they consult! the doctor is in a fit of coun-sel; I suspect some juggling—he comes off; I'll gage a limb this fellow's an impostor.

Aim. Is there not much danger in him?

Man. Within two minutes, gentlemen, I have discovered happier symptoms.

Aim. So, sir.

Man. The redundant choleric matter—

Aim. 'Tis no matter, sir.

Man. I think you do not love him.

Clare. Pursue it.

Aim. What shall I give you to poison him?

Man. How?

Aim. Would he were in Heaven! do you like well of this complexion?   [*Shows him money.*

Man. It shall hire me to kill your father.

Pen. To show how much I value, sir, your life,
For I believe you do not mock, soon as
Your strength will give you leave to visit me
At my father's house, where I can command
An opportunity, my true love shall
Present you with your wishes; my maid only
Shall be of counsel to admit you; but
You'll make me satisfaction by marriage?

Fow. At a minute's warning.

Pen. One thing more; ere I give up my honour, I will have your oath no other woman hath enjoyed your person.

Fow. Willingly; alas! I could ne'er be tempted, and but that there is a kind of necessity—

Pen. Be confident of my best love.

Fow. Seal it now;   [*Kisses her.*
I feel my spirits gather force already,
My blood shake off the corrupt humour; ha?
What an I go home with you, lady?

Pen. You are pretty well already, then! you may excuse our meeting.

Fow. O, no, no; we are all apt to flatter ourselves. Farewell, sweet lady,—if I live, I'll see you; if I die—

Pen. Whibble.—

Whib. At hand and foot to do you service.

                    [*Exeunt* PEN. *and* WHIB.

Aim. You will poison him?

Man. He is dead; as you find me in this, let me have your custom.

Aim. You quicksalving rogue! [*Beats him.*

Man. Do; be valiant. [*Discovers himself.*

Fow. A stratagem, my noble Tully, a stratagem; she's my own, the castle of comfort is yielding up; I see it prostrate already, my valiant engineer.

Clare. The old humour; now has he the promise of some maidenhead.

Fow. The believing creature could not hold out.

Aim. If you thrive so well in your wench, I am no company for you.

Fow. Not for me! I'll worry thee, Frank, to death, if thou flinchest. To the Oracle,[1] boys, thou shouldst hunt, as I do, these wanton rabbit-suckers. Come, we'll have thy story in Apollo, now my own tale is over. I'll busy my brains to set thy wheals in a handsome motion again. Bold as I am, let no denial make thee remove thy siege; they must come to parly, make but wise conditions, and the fort's thine own, I warrant thee. Come, to the Oracle! [*Exeunt.*

SCENE V.—*A Room in* Sir GEORGE RICHLEY'S *House.*

Enter BRAINS *with a letter.*

Bra. Crack, my sides, with laughter: here's a purchase happier than I expected; her own letter to Aimwell! his (which was the most I could hope for) would have been but presumption, this is evidence against the world; to this have I added seal and superscription to the old knight my master. Oh, how I could hug myself

---

[1] J nson's club-room at the Devil tavern. The allusion is to the line over the door, "To the Oracle of Apollo."—*Gifford.*

with the thought on't! they may talk of women's wit, 'tis as slender as their apron-strings, from whence they fetch it; they have no reaches in them. Here comes my mistress's moveable,—

Enter SENSIBLE.

she shall do the feat.—Mistress Sensible, here's a letter to my master; I am going in some haste to dispatch some business; when he comes, at opportunity do so much as deliver it, wilt?

Sens. A greater courtesy than this for you.

Bra. Oh, that I were a youth of one and twenty again!—

Sens. What then?

Bra. Hear my wish out,—and ten thousand pounds in a musty coffer, a house well furnished, acres enough of my own about it, fifty ploughs a going, twenty horse in the stable, beside a caroch and six Flanders mares; ten tall knaves in livery, eight velvet pages, six footmen in cadis;[1] I would marry thee, love thee, lie with thee, and get so many Brains without sage, as should furnish any nation in Christendom with politicians, girl. Farewell, sweet, kind Sensible! [*Exit.*

Sens. What crotchets be these? the fellow's mad, I think.

Enter VIOLETTA, *hastily.*

Vio. Oh, look, Sensible, seek everywhere about the chamber; I have lost the letter Aimwell sent me. If we should be discovered, we are quite undone. What's that in thy hand?

Sens. A letter.

Vio. Whence?

Sens. I know not; 'twas left here, and Brains, having some business to dispatch, requested me to deliver it.

Vio. Let me see't. "To the right worshipful Sir George Richley." I see him coming; lose no time;

---

[1] The cheap worsted fringe or lace with which the liveries of servants were trimmed.

employ thy diligence to search for mine; I will deliver this.

Sens. I shall, mistress.   [*Exit.*

Vio. My father presses me to marry Treedle: short time's allowed for the prevention.

Enter Sir GEORGE RICHLEY.

My good angel assist me.—Here's a letter, sir.

Rich. Whence?

Vio. I know not; your servant Brains received it.

        [RICHLEY *opens the letter and reads.*

Rich. What's here?—Daughter, do not you know whence this letter came?

Vio. Not I, sir.

Rich. You cannot be so ignorant.

Vio. What means my father?

Rich. You are familiar with the contents?

Vio. I beseech you, sir, have no suspicion.

Rich. I'll read it to you.—[*Reads.*] "Master Aimwell, I received your letter, and praise your apprehension; upon the first view of your person, I conceived opinions of your merit, the flame is now too great to be suppressed: it is no time to protract your hopes, nor dishonour in me to yield upon noble conditions at the first summon; I accept your love, and require your industry to prevent my father's purpose. My servant Sensible you may trust; I will use some invention to delay my expected marriage.   Farewell."

Vio. My harsh fate!   [*Aside.*

Rich. Do you know this character?   Where's my man Brains?

Vio. Your man devil.   [*Aside.*

Re-enter BRAINS.

Bra. Did your worship call?

Rich. Oh, my best servant.—
Does not thy very soul blush to deceive me?

Bra. What's the matter, mistress?

Vio. Hear me, I beseech you.

Rich. In the height and puzzle of my care to make
Thee happy, to conspire thy overthrow!
I will not hear.

Bra. Good sir.

Vio. This was your work, you can read.

Bra. And write, too, the superscription of a letter
or so.

Rich. Where's Sensible?

Re-enter SENSIBLE.

For your good service to your mistress, housewife,
Pack up your trinkets, I here discharge you.

Bra. I hope you are Sensible?

Vio. Oh, wench, my father hath my letter.

Sens. Yours!

Vio. And I, mistaking, sealed and returned Aimwell
that which he sent.

Sens. How came he by it?

Vio. Talk not of that. Oh, for some heart to help us!
                                        [*They converse aside.*

Bra. Let me counsel you not to express any violence
in your passions, lest you mar the possibility of reclaim-
ing her; it seems Aimwell has missed the intelligence.
Where shame is enforced too much upon the delinquent,
it begets rather an audacious defence of the sin, than
repentance. Soft rain slides to the root, and nourishes,
where great storms make a noise, wet but the skin i' the
earth, and run away in a channel.

Sens. A most rare project!

Vio. It will appear the same; both made together,
Which, since my sister's death, I have not worn.

Rich. Which of my cares reward'st thou with this
folly?

Vio. Sir, can you pardon?

Rich. I love you but too well; go to your chamber.

Vio. But must we part?

Rich. Dispute it not.

Bra. 'Bye, sweet Mistress Sensible! I hope we shall meet again as merry as we part.

Sens. 'Tis very violent, but we obey your pleasure; I have only apparel, and some few trifles—

Rich. Take them all with you, and be gone.

Vio. Beside my own misfortune, I have cause to pity thine; my father is displeased, and not unjustly.—Happy genius!—   [*Exeunt* VIOLETTA *and* SENSIBLE.

Rich. So, things must be managed wisely; I will hasten the marriage.

Bra. By all means let it be sudden.

Rich. Within two days—to-morrow.

Bra. I would not sleep till she be married—but carry things smooth; let not the knight suspect you are troubled; your daughter will be fetched about with a bias again.

Rich. How thou deserv'st me! let us in.

Bra. Hereafter, for my sake, and subtle pains,
Whoe'er is wise, let the world call him Brains.

        [*Exeunt.*

ACT THE FOURTH.

SCENE I.—AIMWELL'S *Lodgings*.

Enter AIMWELL *and* SENSIBLE.

Aim. Can this be true?

    Sens. As I have faith to Heaven.

    Aim. Take this, and this, and this, for
        thy sweet story.   [*Gives her money.*
        Thou hast entranced me with thy lan-
        guage : laden
With my despairs, like a distressèd bark
I gave myself up lost in the imagined
Tempest ; but at point of striking
Upon a rock, what a celestial gale
Makes my sails swell with comfort ! and enforcing
My ship into the channel, I do feel it
Bound on the waves, discretion at the helm,
Which passion had forsaken ; I now bless
The minute I weighed anchor; oh, my destiny,
Dwell longer on this thread, and make it firm ;
Upon it hangs the weight of such a fortune,
That, if it crack, will, swifter than Jove's flaming
Arrow, dig my grave in the earth's centre.
Forgive me, sacred sex of women, that
In thought or syllable, I have declaimed
Against your goodness, I will redeem it
With such religious honouring your names,
That when I die, some ne'er thought-stained virgin
Shall make a relic of my dust, and throw

My ashes, like a charm, upon those men
Whose faiths they hold suspected.   To what pitch
Of blessedness are my thoughts mounted!

Sens. Sir,
This is an opportunity for action;
Time will run fast upon the minute.

Aim. Pardon
The trespass of my joy, it makes me wild;
I am too well rewarded for my suffering,
Promise thyself a noble recompense.

Enter MANLY *and* CLARE.

Man. Come, have you finished your discourse yet?

Aim. You are my friends;   [*Exit* SENSIBLE.
I was deceived in my Violetta,
She 'oves, she has sent me proof; but a mistake
Sent back my letter, and detained her answer,
Wh'ch was betrayed to her father.   But keep your
          wonder
To honour her rare wit, which, if the stars
Show themselves not malicious, will assure
All my desires in her; a divine project;
She is the master-engine; you must work too,
Will you not, friends?

Clare. Man. You know you may command us.

Aim. Then spread your bosoms; you shall straight
          procure
A caroch [1] be ready on the back side of my lodging;
Do not lose time in questioning; my fate
Depends upon your haste.

Man. Promise it done.   [*Exit.*

Aim. You shall disguise yourself; I must employ you
In rougher action.

Clare. I refuse no office
To advance your hopes.

Aim. My certainties: on thee

[1] Coach.

The frame of our whole building leans   Come on.
Move slowly, time, until our work be done.   [*Exeunt.*

SCENE II.—*A Room in* Sir GEORGE RICHLEY's *House.*

Enter VIOLETTA *and* Tutor.

Vio. I was not blind to your deserts,
Nor can be so ungrateful now, as not
To give encouragement to your affection;
My father may command my person, never
My love, to marry Treedle

Tutor. He is an ass; I made his best verses for him.

Vio. I thought his fancy could not reach them.

Tutor. His sconce is drier than a pumice.

Vio. There be ways to prevent marriage, for I'm
already changed.

Tutor. You are wise; let us run away together.

Vio. But how shall I be sure your love is firm?

Tutor. Try me, and trust me after.

Vio. And I will, for it shall be a hard task I will
impose on you; dare you fight?

Tutor. If I like my enemy.

Vio. It is a poor old fellow.

Tutor. Then I will kill him; his name?

Vio. My father's servant, Brains.

Tutor. He is dead
By this lime.

Vio. Stay, there is a circumstance
To be observed: by some means I'll procure
He waits on me to the Strand this afternoon——

Enter Sir NICHOLAS TREEDLE, *and* WHIBBLE, *who is
busied in adjusting the knight's dress.*

Sir Nicholas!——your ear for the rest.   [*Whispers him.*

Tutor. He will suspect nothing by our privacy;

He bade me take occasion to urge
His good parts to you : should he ask, I'd swear
I did but press his commendations.

Treed. Is thy name Whibble?

Whib. Yes, an't please your worship.

Treed. I like thee the better for that; my name's

Whib. I thank your worship.   [*Treedle.*

Treed. Hast done hooking o' me?

Whib. Every eye hath his object already.

Treed. A witty knave! what place dost thou occupy under thy master?

Whib. I am commonly his journeyman, sir.

Treed. How?

Whib. I look to his horses, sir.

Treed. Wilt serve me when I'm married?

Whib. Alas! I have no good parts to commend me.

Treed. No good parts! an thou hast but skill in horses and dogs, thou art fit for any gentleman in England.

Vio. Just at that place assault him.

Tutor. By your fair hand I will.   [*Exit.*

Vio. [*Coming forward.*] My delight, how fare you?

Treed. I am studying some witty poesy for thy wedding-ring ; let me see—

Vio. Trouble not your head.—Whibble, entreat my father hither.

Treed. No matter; I will send to the university.

Vio. Were you ever of any college?

Treed. College! I have had a head in most of the butteries of Cambridge, and it has been sconced to purpose. I know what belongs to sizing, and have answered to my cue in my days; I am free of the whole university, I commenced with no worse than his majesty's footmen.

Vio. And ever since you have had a running wit. You were better consult our wits at home; we have excellent poets in the town, they say.

Treed. In the town? What makes so many scholars

then come from Oxford and Cambridge, like market-women, with dossers [1] full of lamentable tragedies, and ridiculous comedies, which they might here vent to the players, but they will take no money for them.

Vio. Oh, my dearest! How happy shall I be when I'm married.   [*Kisses him.*

     Enter Sir GEORGE RICHLEY *and* WORTHY.

Wor. Look! they are ingendering at the lip.

Rich. I like it well.

Vio. Why are our joys deferred?

Rich. But till to-morrow.

Vio. 'Tis an age, methinks.

Treed. Kind worm!

Wor. This cannot be deceit.

Vio. I want some trifles, the Exchange will furnish me; Let it be your motion to my father.

Treed. Father and uncle, you will excuse our familiar conversation; I vow I will be honest till I be married; not a touch of my flesh within the walls, only the suburbs of her lips or hands, or so, and when, and when?—is to morrow the day, the day of coupling and so forth? have you got a license?

Rich. It shall be my next work.

Treed. Pray do, we will be married here, but keep our wedding at my own house at Croydon, we will have the city waites down with us, and a noise [2] of trumpets; we can have drums in the country, and the train-band, and then let the Spaniards come an they dare!—Dost hear? here is twenty pieces, you shall fribble them away at the Exchange presently.

Rich. How, sir?

Treed. By this gold she shall, father.—Lay it out in tooth-picks, I will wear them in my hat.—Come, I will with you for the license.

Rich. Who shall with her?

----

       [1] Baskets.   [2] Band.

Wor. I must attend a project of my daughter's.

Rich. Brains! 　　　　　　　　　　　　　　*[Exit.*

Enter BRAINS.

Bra. Sir.

Rich. Wait on my daughter to the Exchange; observe her carefully.

Bra. 'Point me a minute to return with her; if I fail, put my brains into the pot, and let them be served up with a calf's head, to-morrow for dinner.

Vio. It succeeds to my wish. 　　　　　　*[Aside.*

Treed. Violetta, look you lay out my gold at the Exchange in Bartholomew-fairings; farewell, Violetta.

　　　　　　　　　　[Exeunt RICH. *and* TREED.

Bra. Come, mistress, will you walk? I would fain see any mortal wit cozen me of my charge now. I will live to be the shame of politicians, and when I am dead, be clapt up into the Chronicles. 　　　　*[Exeunt.*

SCENE III.—*A Room in* WORTHY'S *House.*

Enter FOWLER.

Fow. Ah, the desire of unlawful flesh! what a conjuring dost thou keep within us to lay this little spirit of concupiscence! The world and the devil are tame and sprightless temptations, poor traffic, to this staple commodity of whoring: this is the place where I must take shipping for the summer islands; if she keep touch, I will call them Fortunate, and once a week make a love voyage to them. *[Music within]*—Ha! are we entertained with music? 　　　　　　　*[One sings within.*

SONG.

Back, back again! fond man forbear,
Buy not a minute's play too dear;
Come with holy flame, and be
Welcome to virtue and to me.

Fow. " Come with holy flame, and be
      Welcome to virtue and to me."
Flame ! I bring none with me, and I should be sorry to
meet any fireworks here; for those hereafter I look on
them afar off, and apprehend them with less fear.—
Again !   [*Music.*

SONG.

Love a thousand sweets distilling,
And with nectar bosoms filling,
Charm all eyes that none may find us;
Be above, before, behind us ;
And while we thy pleasures taste,
    Enforce time itself to stay,
And by the fore-lock hold him fast,
    Lest occasion slip away.

Fow. Ay, marry this is another manner of invitement ;
I will to her ; but—

Enter WINNIFRED.

Here comes the squire of her mistress's body,—How
does my little taper of virgin wax ? thou hast been in
some damp, thou burn'st blue, methinks.

Win. [*In a hoarse voice.*] Noble sir.

Fow. What ! a cold ?

Win. A great cold ; I have lost my voice.

Fow. An thou hast not lost thy maidenhead, it is no
matter ; have a little care of thy frank tenement, and
thy tongue will come time enough to itself, I'll warrant
thee : what place has she chosen for the encounter ?

Win. Her chamber.

Fow. Her chamber !

Win. It is all dark.

Fow. Is it all dark ? I commend her policy the
better ; then the room, and the deed that must be done
in it, will be of one complexion ; so she be light I care
not : prythee convey me to her.

Win. Follow me.

Fow. As thy shadow.—Woe be to some of the dear sex when a chambermaid is usher to a gentleman.

[*Exeunt.*

SCENE IV.—*Another Room in the same, darkened.*

Enter PENELOPE *and* WORTHY.

Pen. It shall be a harmless trial, sir.

Wor. Go too; I know thou art virtuous; put in execution thy purpose, I will be within the reach of thy voice.

[*Retires.*

Pen. It shall be my security.—
What ill star ruled at my nativity,
That I should be so miserable to love
A man, whose glory is his vice, whose study
Is but to ruin virtue!

Enter WINNIFRED.

Win. Mistress!

Pen. Here, Winnifred.

Win. The gamester waits his entrance, jocund as a bridegroom; he has forgot his fever.

Pen. Away; you know your charge; be ready.—[*Exit* WIN. PEN. *goes to the door, and speaks hoarsely.*]—Where are you, sir? Master Fowler.

Enter FOWLER.

Fow. In hell, if darkness will carry it; yet hell cannot be so black, there are too many flames in it. Thy hand; what monk's hole hast thou brought me to? where is thy mistress?

Pen. This is the way.

Fow. Is this the way? it is a very blind one; the devil can hardly know me if he meet here, that is my comfort: yet if he did, he loves the sin too well to interrupt so precious a meeting. Prithee, child of darkness, conduct me to the handsome fairy I must dance withal.

Pen. It seems your fever hath left you.

Fow. My fever! I forget myself, I should have coun-
terfeited sick all this while, but no matter, an thy mistress
know it not; thou art skilful in secrets, and I will
deserve it: two or three fits when I am in her presence,
will make her keep her promise with me about the cure,
for that she thinks I was so: Prithee do thy office, and
bring me to her; I hope she is not within hearing.

Pen. Fear not.

Fow. So, about it then.

Pen. There is a fee belongs to my place first.

Fow. A fee belonging to your place? as I hope for a
limb of thy mistress I had forgot it; there is gold, I can feel
it: by this darkness, for thou seest I have no light to swear
by, it is weight; quick, periwinkle! to thy mistress now.

Pen. This is not enough.

Fow. There is more; take silver and all.

Pen. This is nothing.

Fow. Is it nothing? by this hand, would I could see
it; it is all I have; wilt search me?

Pen. There is another fee belongs to us.

Fow. Another fee belongs to us! what is that? I
must kiss her:—[*Kisses her.*]—thou hast a down lip, and
dost twang it handsomely; now to the business.

Pen. This is not all I look for.

Fow. She will not tempt me to come aloft, will she?
[*Aside.*]

Pen. If you could see me, I do blush.

Wor. What does my daughter mean? [*Aside.*]

Fow. If I could see her she does blush, she says; it is
so: oh the insatiable desires of chambermaids! they were
wont to look no higher than the groom or servingman,
and be thankful; or if the master would be pleased to
let them show him this lobby, t'other withdrawing chamber, or the turret, in summer, and take occasion to commend the situation and so forth, it was after the lady had
been served, out of his own mere motion and favour,

and it was taken as an indearment for ever of their
service and secrecy ; now they must be tasters to them
in the sweet sin ; fees of the court must be paid, or no
suit commenced with iniquity.—O Venus, what will this
world come to !

Pen. Hear me.

Fow. Yes, I cannot see thee.

Pen. This chamber, by my policy, was made dark.

Fow. "This chamber, by your policy, was made
dark," so.

Pen. My mistress expected you without this ceremony.

Fow. "Your mistress expects me without this ceremony."—Cunning gipsy !   [*Aside.*

Pen. But if you condescend not first—

Fow. "But if I condescend not first ;" will she
threaten me ?   [*Aside.*

Pen. To impart to me the sweet pleasure of your
body—

Fow. "To impart to you the sweet pleasure of my
body ! "

Pen. Indeed, you shall not embrace my mistress, and
so forth.

Fow. "Indeed I shall not embrace your mistress, and
so forth ! " You will justify this to her face ? 'tis not
that I stand upon a carriere,[1] but I will not be compelled
to lie with any whore in Christendom. Was ever such a
goat in nature ! Why, hark ye, virgin above ground,
for a dark room or a cellar are all one for you, you that
are a degree above the kitchen, and make your master's
man run mad to hear you play on the virginals : whose
breath, though strengthened with garlic, you would suck
like a domestic cat at midnight, will not diet down with
you, but what is reserved for your mistress's palate ?
You are in hope to filch a point from my breeches, which,
executed at both ends, you will wear about your smutchy
wrist for a bracelet. I will seek out thy mistress, rifle
her lady-ware, in spite of thee, and give my footman

[1] Meaning, not caring what he does.

charge not to kiss thee, an it would keep thee from starv-
ing.—Would I could see the way out again!

Pen. I can betray, and will.

Fow. She'll betray us, she has voice enough for such
a mischief. [*Aside.*]—Dost hear? do but consider she is
thy mistress, there's some reason she should be preferred.

Pen. I'll hear none.

Fow. She'll hear no reason! If the devil hath fed
her blood with the hope of me, would he would furnish
her with an incubus in my shape, to serve her, or let a
satyr leap her! Oh, unmerciful chambermaids! the grave
is sooner satisfied than their wantonness. [*Aside.*]—Dost
hear? wilt have the truth on't? 'twas a condition between
us, and I swore no woman should enjoy me before her;
there's conscience I should be honest to her; prithee be
kind to a young sinner; I will deserve thee hereafter in
the height of dalliance.

Pen. I am in the same humour still.

Fow. "She is in the same humour still!" I must go
through her to her mistress. [*Aside.*]—Art thou a Christian? Well, thou art a brave girl, and I do love thy
resolution, and so soon as I have presented my first fruits
to thy mistress only for oath's sake, I'll return and ply
thee with embraces, as I am a gentleman. Prithee show
me the way.

Pen. I will not trust you, sir.

Fow. Will not you trust me? why, come on then, an
there be no remedy.

Pen. Will you satisfy my desire?

Fow. I'll do my endeavour; I am untrussing as fast as
I can; nay, an I be provoked, I'm a tyrant; have at your
bacon.

Pen. [*Aloud.*] Winnifred!

Re-enter WINNIFRED *with a light.*

Fow. Have you found your voice? what mean you by
this light?

Pen. That you should see your shame.

Fow. Cheated; ha?

Pen. Is this your love to me, your noble love? I did
suspect before how I should find you.

Fow. Penelope!

Pen. Degenerated man! what mad disease
Dwells in thy veins, that does corrupt the flowings
Of generous blood within thee?

Fow. Shall I not vault, gentlewoman?

Pen. What behaviour
Of mine gave thee suspicion I could be
So lost to virtue, to give up mine honour?
Poor man!
How thou didst fool thyself to thy devouring
Lust, for 'twas it made thee so late a counterfeit.—
Go home, and pray
Thy sin may be forgiven, and with tears
Wash thy polluted soul.

Wor. I like this well,
And find her noble aim.   [*Aside.*

Pen. Be man again;
For yet thou art a monster, and this act
Published, will make thee appear so black
And horrid, that even beasts will be ashamed
Of thy society.   My goodness,
In hope of your conversion, makes me chide you so—
Ha! Win, dost thou observe him?   Oh, my heart
Is full of fear; I tremble to look on him:
See, of a sudden, what a paleness has
Possessed his face; do not his eyes retire
Into their hollow chambers?   Sir, how do you?

Fow. Well.

Wor. What new project's this?   [*Aside.*

Win. A sudden change.
Sure, Heaven is just unto thy late imposture,
And thou art punished now indeed with sickness,
For mocking Heaven, I fear.   Oh, dost thou see?

Fow. What?

Pen. Death sits upon his forehead; I ne'er saw
The horror of a dying countenance,
But in this gentleman.—Winnifred, to my closet,
Fetch me the cordial.

Fow. What do you mean, gentlewoman?
I do not feel any such dangerous sickness.

Pen. What a hollow voice he has! oh, my misfortune,
If he should die here! Fetch me some strong waters.

Fow. No, no, I can walk for them myself, if need be.

Pen. He talks wildly;
I may suspect him; if you have so much strength
To walk, go home, call your physician,
And friends; dispose of your estate, and settle
Your peace for Heaven, I do beseech you, sir;
My prayers shall beg a mercy on your soul,
For I have no encouragement to hope
Your glass hath many sands. Farewell, sir; cherish
Pure holy thoughts, that if your life soon end,
Your better part may to yon court ascend.—
Come, to my father. [*Exeunt all but* FOWLER.

Fow. What's the meaning of this? sick and dying! I
feel no pains. I have heard of some died with conceit;
if it should kill me, I were a precious coxcomb. Was
ever poor gentleman brought into such a foolish paradise? prepared for a race, and mounted into the saddle,—
I must go home and die! well, if I live I'll quit your
cunning, and for the more certainty my revenge may
prosper, I will not say my prayers till it take effect.

[*Exit.*

SCENE V.—*The Street, near* Sir GEORGE RICHLEY'S
House.

Enter Tutor.

Tutor. This is the place where I must exercise my
valour upon Brains; I was ne'er given to fight, but I'm

Shir. F

engaged for such a prize as I would challenge all the noble sciences in my own defence.

[*Walks about practising with his sword.*

Enter AIMWELL, CLARE, *and* MANLY.

Aim. I cannot spy them yet; pray Heaven no disaster cross our project.

Clare. What thing's that walks about the door?

Aim. One practising, I think,
The postures of a fencer.

Tutor. Things occur worthy consideration. Were I best to speak before I strike him, or give him blows, and tell him the reason afterwards? I do not like expostulations, they proclaim our anger, and give the enemy warning to defend himself; I'll strike him valiantly, and in silence.

Clare. What does he mutter?

Aim. What business stays him here? some treachery.

Tutor. Being resolved to strike before I speak,
'Tis worth my judgment, whether fist or sword
Shall first salute him : I'll be generous,
And give him first two or three wholesome buffets,
Which, well laid on, may haply so amaze him,
My weapon may be useless ; for I fear,
Should I begin with steel, her very face
Would force me make too deep incision,
And so there may be work for sessions:
I like not that, as valiant as I am :
Killing is common.

Aim. They are in sight! down, down! oh, my ravished soul ! what bliss is in this object !   [*Retires.*

Tutor. Ha ! they are coming ; 'tis she and the old ruffian ; he has but a scurvy countenance ; I have the advantage in the first blow, and I should be very sorry he should beat me in the conclusion.

Clare. Why does this fellow stay?

Tutor. I must on; she has spied me through her mask ;

I see her smile already ; and command
A present battery.

Enter BRAINS *before* VIOLETTA.

Clare. Will this fellow prevent my office ? he goes
towards him with a quarrelling face. — Ha ! I'll not
engage myself then ; 'tis so.

[CLARE *and* MANLY *withdraw.* Tutor *strikes* BRAINS.

Vio. Help ! help !

[*She runs in, and presently* SENSIBLE *slips out, dressed like her* Mistress.

Bra. Mistress, stay. Fear nothing ; alas, good gentlewoman.—[*Beats the* Tutor]—You black maggot; death !
I'll tread him into the kennel amongst his kindred.

[*Beats him again.*

Tutor. Hold ! help ! murder !

Bra. We shall have the whole street about us presently. Let's on our journey. Who is this mole-catcher?
—An ye had not been with me, I would have cut him
into more pieces than a tailor's cushion.—Sir Nicholas,
you shall know on't too. [*Exeunt* BRAINS *and* SENSIBLE.

Tutor. They are gone together ; pox on this tough-
ness ! He has made an ass of me ; next him do I hate
the law most abominably, for if I might kill and not be
hanged for him, 'twould never trouble me. Shall I lose
my reputation so? I'll venture another pounding, but
I'll be revenged on him. [*Exit.*

SCENE VI.—*Another part of the same.*

Enter BRAINS *before* SENSIBLE.

Bra. My mistress has grown very thrifty of her voice
o' the sudden ; I have asked her two or three questions,
and she answers me with holding out her hand, as the
post at St. Alban's, that points the way to London ;
either she is grown sullen, or the fright she was in of late,
like a wolf that sees a man first, hath taken away her

voice.—I'll make her speak to me.—[*He stops, she puts him forward with her hand.*]—Said you, forsooth?— 'twill not do—what a blessed comfort shall he enjoy if she continue speechless! the Persians did worship a god under the name of Silence, and, sure, Christians may have an excuse for their idolatry, if they can find a woman whom nature hath posted into the world with a tongue, but no ability to make use of that miserable organ.—What do you think 'tis o'clock? two not struck, ha?—[SENSIBLE *slips away.*]—How now, mistress, treading on t'other side? this is your way to the Exchange.

Sens. My way, you saucy clown!—take that.

[*Strikes him.*

Bra. You are bountiful; 'tis more than I looked for.

Sens. [*Unmasking.*]—What have you to say to me, sirrah? Cannot a gentlewoman—

Bra. Ha, ah! my brains melt; I am undone, I am undone; you succuba, where is my mistress? Proserpine, speak!

Enter Tutor, *with* Serjeants.

Tutor. That's he; your office.

Serj. We arrest you, sir.

Bra. Me, you toads?

Sens. How's this?

Tutor. Away with him to prison; 'tis no slight action: at your perils, serjeants.—My fairest mistress.

Sens. Mistress!—I'll humour this plot for the mirth' sake.

[*Aside, and putting on her mask again, exit with* Tutor.

Bra. Sirrah, tadpole; what do you mean?—I owe him not a penny, by this flesh; he has a conspiracy upon me; I charge you, in the king's name, unbind me.

Serj. We charge you, in the king's name, obey us.

Bra. May you live to be arrested of the pox, and die in a dungeon! may inns o' court gentlemen, at next trimming, shave your ears and noses off, and then duck you in their own boggards! [*Exeunt.*

ACT THE FIFTH.

SCENE I.—*The Street before* Sir GEORGE RICHLEY'S *House.*

Enter Sir GEORGE RICHLEY, Sir NICHOLAS TREEDLE, *and* WORTHY.

REED. So, now we have got a license, I would see who dares marry your daughter besides myself. Is she come from the Exchange yet?

Wor. Not yet, sir.

Enter a Messenger.

Mes. Your servant Brains remembers his duty in this paper.

Rich. Letters.

Treed. Letters! let me read them.

Rich. Your patience, sir.

Wor. I doubt all is not well; what if some misfortune should now befall your mistress? I hope you have armour of patience?

Treed. Ay, and of proof too, at home, as much as my hall can hold; the story of the Prodigal can hardly be seen for't;[1] I have pikes and guns, enow for me and my predecessors, a whole wardrobe of swords and bucklers; when you come home you shall see them.

Rich. A conspiracy!

Treed. Oh, treason!

---

[1] The story worked in the tapestry against which the arms hung.

Rich. My man Brains is arrested by your Tutor; a plot to take away my daughter; she is gone.

Wor. I did prophesy too soon.

Treed. My Tutor read travel to me, and run away with my wench! a very peripatetic—what shall I do, then? an some one had arrested and clapped her up, too, we should have known where to find her. Do you hear? I did not mean to n.arry with a licence.

Wor. How, sir?

Treed. No, sir, I did mean to marry with your daughter. Am I a gull?

Wor. Have patience.

Treed. I will have no patience; I will have Violetta: why does not Brains appear?

Wor. His heels are not at liberty; he's in prison.

Treed. In prison! why, an he had been hanged, he might have brought us word.

Rich. I am rent with vexation.—Sirrah, you go with me to the prison.   [*Exeunt* RICH. *and* MES.

Wor. What will you do, sir?

Treed. I'll geld my Tutor.

Wor. You were best find him first.

Treed. Nay, I will find him, and find him again, an I can light on him; let me alone, I'll take half-a-dozen with me, and about it instantly.   *Exit.*

Wor. I wish thee well, niece, but a better husband.

Enter FOWLER.

Who's yonder? 'tis Master Fowler, at an excellent opportunity.   [*Exit.*

Fow. I do walk still; by all circumstance I am alive, not sick in part but my head, which has only the pangs of invention, and in travail of some precious revenge for my worse than masculine affront: what if I report abroad she's dishonest? I cannot do them a worse turn than to say so: some of our gallants take a pride to belie poor gentlewomen in that fashion, and think the discourse an honour to them; confidently boast the fruition of this or that lady, whose hand they never kissed with the glove off: and why may not I make it my revenge, to blur their fames a little for abusing me?

Enter two Gentlemen *at several doors.*

1st Gent. Well met, friend; what! thou lookest sad.

2nd Gent. You will excuse me, and bear a part, when I tell the cause.

1st Gent. What's the news?

2nd Gent. Our friend, Master Fowler's dead.

Fow. Fowler! ha!

1st Gent. Master John Fowler?

Fow. That's I, that's I, ha!

2nd Gent. The same.

Fow. Dead! am I dead?

1st Gent. It cannot be; I saw him but this morning Lusty and pleasant; how died he?

2nd Gent. Suddenly.

1st Gent. Where?

2nd Gent. At Master Worthy's house.

1st Gent. Dead?

2nd Gent. Too true, sir.

Fow. I would not believe myself sick; belike I am dead; 'tis more than I know yet.

1st Gent. He was a suitor to Master Worthy's daughter.

2nd Gent. Mistress Penelope; right.

Fow. By all circumstance they mean me: these gentlemen know me, too; how long is it since I departed? Some mistake——

1st Gent. How poor a thing is life, that we cannot Promise a minute's certainty; i' the height And strength of youth, falling to dust again!

Fow. Ha, ha, gentlemen! what do you think of the dead man?

2nd Gent. 'Tis the last office I can do him, now, To wait on him to the earth.

Fow. Coxcombs, do ye not know me? I'm alive, do
you not see me?

1st Gent. He was a noble fellow, and deserves
A memory; if my brain have not lost
All his poetic juice, it shall go hard
But I'll squeeze out an elegy.

Fow. For whom, my furious poet? Ha! not know
me! do I walk invisible, or am I my own ghost?—An
you will not see me, you shall feel me, you have a nimble
pate, I may chance strike out some flash of wit—[*Strikes
him.*]—No—

Re-enter WORTHY.

Here comes another.—Save you, Master Worthy.

1st Gent. Sir, I heard ill news, Master Fowler's dead.

Wor. He is indeed, sir.

Fow. Indeed you lie, sir.

Wor. I saw his eyes sealed up by death, and him
Wrapt in his last sheet.

1st Gent. Where's his body?

Wor. At my sad house, sir.

Fow. Is my body at your house?

Wor. I did hope, gentlemen, we should have found
My house his bridal chamber, not his coffin.
But Heaven must be obeyed, my daughter loved him,
And much laments his loss.

Fow. Very good; then I am dead, am I not?

Wor. You both were in the number of his friends,
I hope you'll add your presence to the rest
At the funeral.

Fow. Whose funeral, you man of Bedlam?

2nd Gent. Cry you mercy, sir; pray keep your way.

1st Gent. It is a duty which, without invitement, we
are both prompt to discharge.

Fow. Master Worthy! Gentlemen! do ye hear?
[*Exeunt all but* FOWLER.]—Is't possible? not know me,
not see me! I am so thin, and airy, I have slipped out
o' the world, it seems, and did not know on't.—If I be

dead, what place am I in? where am I? This is not
hell, sure? I feel no torment, and there is too little
company; no, 'tis not hell—and I have not lived after
the rate of going to Heaven yet; beside, I met just now
a usurer, that only deals upon ounces, and carries his
scales at his girdle, with which he uses to weight, not
men's necessities, but the plate he is to lend money upon:
can this fellow come to heaven? Here a poor fellow is
put in the stocks for being drunk, and the constable
himself reeling home, charges others in the king's name
to aid him. There's a spruce captain, newly crept out
of a gentleman-usher, and shuffled into a buff jerkin with
gold lace, that never saw service beyond Finsbury or the
Artillery-garden,[1] marches waving a desperate feather in
his lady's beaver, while a poor soldier, bred up in the
school of war all his life, yet never commenced any
degree of commander, wants a piece of brass, to discharge a wheaten bullet to his belly;—no, this is not
Heaven, I know by the people that traffic in't: where
am I, then? Umph! I'll to Worthy's before they bury
me, and inform myself better what's become of me; If I
find not myself there in a coffin, there's hope I may
revive again; if I be dead, I am in a world very like the
other; I will get me a female spirit to converse withal,
and kiss, and be merry, and imagine myself alive again.

[*Exit.*

SCENE II.—*A Street.*

Enter Sir NICHOLAS TREEDLE, WHIBBLE, *and*
Footman.

Treed. Come, follow me, and be valiant, my masters.

Whib. Remember yourself, sir; this is your worship's
footman, and, for mine own part, though I be not cut

---

[1] The usual places of exercise for the city train-bands.

according to your cloth, I am a true servant of yours;
where do you think we shall find them?

Treed. Where! where dost thou think?

Foot. I think where his worship thinks.

Treed. No matter, whether we find them or no; but,
when we have taken them,—as if they be not, it is their
own fault, for we are ready,—for Violetta, upon submission, I will commit marriage with her; but for the
rogue, my Tutor——

Whib. What will you do with him?

Treed. I'll do nothing to him; thou shalt kill him for
me.

Whib. It will show better in your footman.

Treed. Thou sayest right, he can run him through
quickly; but it is no matter who; an the worst come to
the worst, it is but a hanging matter, and I'll get a
pardon first or last. I would kill him myself, but that I
should be taxed to kill a poor worm more than ever I
did in my life; besides, it is not with my credit to be
hanged.

Whib. An't please your worship, I'll make a fair
motion; take your choice, Sir Nicholas, whether we shall
kill him and you'll be hanged for him, or you shall be
hanged for him, and we'll kill him.

Foot. Under correction, I think it were better to take
him prisoner.

Treed. I like my footman's reason; we will take him
first prisoner, and whosoever hath a mind to be hanged,
may kill him afterwards.—Oh that I had him here now,
I could cut him in pieces on my rapier's point!

Whib. Has not your worship been at fence-school?

Treed. At fence-school? I think I have, I'll play so
many for so many, I name no weapons, with any high
German English fencer of them all.—Canst not thou
fence, Whibble?

Whib. I, sir? alas.——

Treed. It is but thus and thus, and there is a man at

your mercy; I would cleave a button, an it were as broad as the brim of your hat now. Oh that I had but any friend but to kill a little! prithee try me, Whibble.

Whib. I am none of your friends.

Treed. Why, then, an thou lovest me, be my foe a little, for a bout or so.

Whib. I care not much to exercise your worship; stand aside.

Treed. Stay, let me see first—there is it—I cannot with my honour wound thee, I do not stand upon the odds of my weapon, which is longer than thine, but thou seest thine is shorter than mine by an handful;— too much is too much.

Enter Tutor, *and* SENSIBLE *masked as before.*

Foot. Your Tutor, sir, and Mistress Violetta!

Treed. How! down with him, somebody!—[*Exit* Tutor.]—he is gone, follow him close!—Oh, run away, cowardly rascal, will ye not fight against three? Mistress, it is my fortune, you see, or my destiny, to recover your lost virginity; I am sorry for nothing, but that I have shed no blood in your rescue: but where there is no valour to be expected, it is best to put up with valour and reputation. Would the rascal my Tutor have popped in before me? I am glad I have prevented him,—do you hear!—your father is mad, and I am little better myself: but let us be wise, lose no time; I know a parson shall divide us into man and wife ere any body think on it; I will make all sure now, I will not be put into any more of these frights, I will marry you; if any man dare run away with you afterwards, let it light upon mine own head, and that is the worse I am sure they can do me.

[*Exeunt.*

SCENE III.—WORTHY'S *House.* PENELOPE'S *Bed-chamber.*

Enter WORTHY *and two* Gentlemen.

Wor. Gentlemen, I thank you; you carried it to my desire, most cunningly.

1st Gent. Do you think it has taken?

2nd Gent. I am covetous to see the event.

Wor. Pray sit.—Penelope!

Enter PENELOPE *in mourning.*

2nd Gent. In mourning!

Wor. All parties in the engagement.

Pen. You oblige a woman's service.

2nd Gent. Gentle lady,
And if it prove fortunate, the design
Will be your honour, and the deed itself
Reward us in his benefit: he was ever wild.

1st Gent. Assured your ends are noble, we are happy in't.

Enter WINNIFRED.

Win. Master Fowler.

Wor. Is he come already?

Pen. Remove the hearse into this chamber.
                    [*A hearse is brought in with tapers.*
In your nobleness I desire you will
Interpret fairly what I am to personate,
And by the story you will find I have
Some cause of passion.   [*They sit round the hearse.*

Enter FOWLER.

Fow. This is the room I sickened in, and by report died in; umph! I have heard of spirits walking with aerial bodies, and have been wondered at by others, but I must only wonder at myself, for if they be not mad, I am come to my own burial; certain these clothes are substantial, I owe my tailor for them to this hour, if the devil be not my tailor, and hath furnished me with another suit very like it.—[*Rings his money.*]—This is no magical noise, essential gold and silver. What do I with it if I be dead? Here are no reckonings to be paid with it, no tavern bills, no midnight revels, with the costly tribe of amorous she-sinners; now I cannot spend it, would the poor had it; by their prayers I might hope to get out of this new pitiful purgatory, or at least know which way I came into it.—Here they are in mourning, what a devil do they mean to do with me?—Not too many tears, lady, you will but spoil your eyes, and draw upon them the misery of spectacles: do not you know me neither?

Pen. Oh, Master Fowler!

Fow. Ha! out with it; nay, an the woman but acknowledged me alive, there is some hope of me.

Pen. I loved thee living with a holy flame,
To purge the errors of thy wanton youth.

Fow. I'm dead again.

Pen. This made
Thy soul sue out so hasty a divorce,
And flee to airy dwellings: this hath left us
Thy cold pale figure,
Which we have commission but to chamber up
In melancholy dust, where thy own worms,
Like the false servants of some great man, shall
Devour thee first.

Fow. I am worms' meat!

Pen. We must all die.

Fow. Would some of you would do it quickly, that I might have company!

Pen. But, wert
Thou now to live again with us, and that,
By miracle, thy soul should with thy body
Have second marriage, I believe thou'd'st study
To keep it a chaste temple, holy thoughts,
Like fumes of sacred incense, hovering

About this heart, then thou would'st learn to be
Above thy frailties, and resist the flatteries
Of smooth-faced lust.

Fow. This is my funeral sermon.

Pen. The burden of which sin, my fears persuade me,
Both hastened and accompanied thy death.

Wor. This sorrow is unfruitful.

Pen. I have done ;
May this prayer profit him ! would his soul were
As sure to gain Heaven as his body is here !

2nd Gent. We must hope the best, he was an inconstant
young man ; frequenting of some companies had corrupted his nature, and a little debauched him.

Fow. In all this sermon I have heard little commendations of our dear brother departed ; rich men do not go
to the pit-hole without complement of christian burial.
It seems, if I had lived to have made a will, and bequeathed so much legacy as would purchase some
preacher a neat cassock, I should have died in as good
estate and assurance for my soul as the best gentleman
in the parish, had my monument in a conspicuous place
of the church, where I should have been cut in a form of
prayer, as if I had been called away at my devotion, and
so for haste to be in Heaven, went thither with my book
and spectacles.—Do you hear, lady, and gentlemen, is it
your pleasure to see me, though not know me ? and to
inform a walking puisne when this so much lamented
brother of yours departed out of this world ? In his life
I had some relation to him : what disease died he of,
pray ? who is his heir yet at common law? for he was
warm in the possession of lands, thank his kind father,
who having been in a consumption sixteen years, one
day, above all the rest, having nothing else to do, died,
that the young man might be a landlord, according to
the custom of his ancestors.

1st Gent. I doubt the project.   [*Aside.*

Fow. You should be his heir or executor at least, by

your dry eyes, sir; I commend thee; what a miserable
folly it is to weep for one that is dead, and has no sense
of our lamentation.   Wherefore were blacks invented?
to save our eyes their tedious distillations; it is enough
to be sad in our habits, they have cause to weep that
have no mourning cloth, it is a sign they get little by the
dead, and that is the greatest sorrow now-a-days.   You
loved him, lady; to say truth, you had little cause, a
wild young man, yet an he were alive again, as that is in
vain to wish, you know, he may perchance be more
sensible, and reward you with better service, so you
would not proclaim his weakness.—Faith, speak well of
the dead hereafter, and bury all his faults with him, will
ye? what, are these all the guests? ha! what papers?[1]
some elegy or epitaph? who subscribes? oh, this is your
poetry.   [*Reads.*

> " How he died some do suppose,
>   How he lived the parish knows;
>   Whether he's gone to Heaven or hell,
>   Ask not me, I cannot tell."

Very well, would the gentleman your friend were alive to
give you thanks for them. What, have we more? [*Reads.*

> " Underneath, the fair not wise,
>   Too self-loved Narcissus lies,
>   Yet his sad destruction came
>   From no fountain but a flame.
>   Then, youth, quench your hot desires,
>   Purge your thoughts with chaster fires,
>   Lest with him it be too late,
>   And death triumph in your fate.
>   Hither all your virgins come,
>   Strew your tears upon this tomb,
>   Perhaps a timely weeping may
>   So dispose his scorched clay,
>   That a chaste and snowy flower
>   May reward your gentle shower.

---

[1] These were the elegies or epitaphs fixed to the hearse.

Very well done upon so dead a subject; by the virgin
that is in it, you should owe this parcel of poetry, lady.

Pen. A woman's muse, sir.

Fow. Oh, now you can answer me; am I dead still?

Pen. Yes.

Fow. Then you talk to a dead man?

Pen. I do.

Fow. Where am I dead?

Pen. Here, everywhere.

You're dead to virtue, to all noble thoughts,
And, till the proof of your conversion
To piety win my faith, you are to me
Without all life; and charity to myself
Bids me endeavour with this ceremony
To give you burial.   If hereafter I
Let in your memory to my thoughts, or see you,
You shall but represent his ghost or shadow
Which never shall have power to fright my innocence,
Or make my cheek look pale.   My ends are compassed,
And here, in sight of Heaven——

Fow. Stay,
Thou art a noble girl, and dost deserve
To marry with an emperor.   Remove
This sad thing from us.——

                    [*The hearse and lights are taken out.*
                 You do know me, gentlemen;
Witness my death to vanity, quitting all
Unchaste desires:——revive me in thy thoughts,
And I will love as thou hast taught me, nobly,
And like a husband, by this kiss, the seal
That I do shake my wanton slumber off,
And wake to virtue.

Wor. Meet it daughter.

Pen. Now you begin to live.

Fow. I will grow old in the study of my honour! this
last conflict hath quite o'ercome me, make me happy in
the style of your son,

Wor. My blessings multiply.

Gent. We congratulate this event.

Wor. See, my brother.

Enter SIR GEORGE RICHLEY *and* BRAINS.

Bra. Let not your rage be so high, sir, I have more cause to be mad.

Rich. Thou?

Bra. I.

Rich. I have lost my daughter.

Bra. But I have lost my credit, that had nothing else to live by. I was more proud of that than you could be of twenty daughters.

Wor. Have you found them?

Rich. No, not I; and yet this old ruffian will not let me vex for it; he says the greatest loss is his.

Bra. And I will maintain it, it was my boast that I was never cozened in my life; have I betrayed so many plots, discovered letters, deciphered characters, stript knavery to the skin, and laid open the very soul of conspiracy, deserved for my cunning to be called Brains both town and country over, and now to forfeit them, to see them drenched in a muddy stratagem, cheated by a woman, and a pedantical lousy wordmonger! it is abominable; patience, I abhor thee. I desire him that bids me go hang myself, which is the way to Surgeon's Hall? I will beg to have my skull cut, I have a suspicion my brains are filched, and my head has been late stuffed with woodcocks' feathers.

Fow. Be not mad.

Bra. I will, in spite of any man here; who shall hinder me, if I have a mind to it?

Rich. Your happiness removes my affliction.—Ha!

Enter WHIBBLE *and* Tutor.

Whib. Where is Sir Nicholas? we have brought the gentleman.

Shir.

Bra. Are you there!—this was the champion that jostled me; shall I fetch a dog-whip? or let me cut him up, he will make excellent meat for the devil's trencher; I will carve him.—Sirrah!

Rich. Forbear;—where is my daughter? villain, confess.

Tutor. Alas, sir, I was waiting upon her home, Sir Nicholas met me, and took her from me.

Rich. Wor. Sir Nicholas!

Whib. Yes, Sir Nicholas hath Mistress Violetta, I am a witness.

Bra. Why did he jostle me? there began the treachery, ask him that.

Tutor. I pray you, sir, let it be forgotten, I have been kicked for it.

Enter at one door AIMWELL, VIOLETTA, MANLY, *and* CLARE, *at the other* Sir NICHOLAS TREEDLE, *and* SENSIBLE *disguised as before.*

Whib. Here she is; no, there she is.

Rich. Sir Nicholas.

Wor. I am amazed.

Treed. Stay, which is my wife?

Rich. Here is my daughter.

Bra. Mistress!

Fow. Fine juggling! Frank, whence comest thou?

Aim. From the priest, if you have any joy for me. We are married.

Treed. Are there not two Sir Nicholases? pray what do you call this gentlewoman?

Aim. Her name is Violetta.

Vio. Father, your pardon.

Treed. This is fine, i' faith; well may a woman mistake her husband, when a man, that is the wiser vessel, cannot know his own wife.

Rich. Married to Aimwell!

Man. Clare. We are witnesses.

Treed. A good jest, faith; hark you, were you ever catechised? What is your name, forsooth?

Sens. Faith, sir, guess.   [*Unmasks.*

Aim. All passion will be fruitless but of joy.

Treed. Sensible! Came I from Croydon for a chambermaid? do you hear, every body? I have married Sensible.

Man. Clare. We are witnesses of that, too.

Treed. No, no, this is my wife.

Aim. Touch her not with a rude hand.

Treed. Why, I know she meant to be my wife, and only I have married her, as folks go to law, by attorney; she is but her deputy; for the more state I married her proxy.

Bra. [*Aside to* TREED.]—Do not deceive yourself, sir: though princes depute men to marry their wives, women do not use to be ciphers; she is your wife in law, let me counsel you, sir, to prevent laughter;—somebody hath been cozened, I name nobody; sure it was your fortune to marry this wench, which cannot now be undone; seem not to be sorry for it, they do purpose to jeer you out of your skin else.

Treed. Sayest thou so?

Bra. Be confident, and laugh at them first that they are so simple to think that you are gulled: commend your choice, and say it was a trick of yours to deceive their expectation.

Treed. Come hither, Madam Treedle.—Gentlemen, you think now I have but an ill match on't, and that, as they say, I am cheated; do not believe it—a lady is a lady, a bargain is a bargain, and a knight is no gentleman—so much for that.—I grant I married her, in her mistress's name, and though (as great men, that use to choose wifes for their favourites or servants, when they have done with them) I could put her off to my footman or my Tutor here, I will not; I will maintain her my wife, and publish her, do you see, publish her to any man that shall laugh at it, my own lady-bird.

Fow. You are happy, sir, in being deceived; he is a noble gentleman.

Wor. Sir Nicholas has released her,
Let your consent be free, then.

Rich. You have won it.
Be my loved children, and I wish a joy
Flow in all bosoms.—Brains, we are reconciled.

Treed. Tutor, we pardon.

Vio. You may, sir; he was my engine. Now, what says my factious servant? nay, we are friends; the greatest politician may be deceived sometimes; wit without brains, you see.

Bra. And Brains without wit too.

Fow. Frank, thou art married, and Sir Nicholas has made a lady, I have lived loose a great while, and do purpose to be made fast to this gentlewoman, to whose act I owe my true conversion.
When all things have their trial, you shall find
Nothing is constant but a virtuous mind.   [*Exeunt.*

THE TRAITOR.

 HE TRAITOR was licensed in 1631,
acted by Her Majesty's Servants, and
published in 1635. "The plot," Ward
remarks, "is based on history; but
the author has treated both the character and the fate of the principal
personage of his drama with considerable freedom. The real Lorenzino
de' Medici seems to have been singularly heedless in his
talk, if cautious in his designs; and instead of (as in the
play) falling an immediate victim to his own evil ambition,
he had survived his assassination of Duke Alessandro for
eleven years, when vengeance (real or pretended) at last
overtook him."

Towards the end of the seventeenth century an attempt
was made to show that this play was written by Rivers, a
Jesuit, in Newgate, where he died, and that Shirley "only
ushered it to the stage."

The Traitor was revived several times after the Restoration, and a successful play, written at the beginning of the
present century, Sheil's *Evadne*, is an adaptation or recon-
struction of it.

To the Right Honourable

WILLIAM CAVENDISH,

EARL OF NEWCASTLE, VISCOUNT MANSFIELD,
LORD BOLSOVER AND OGLE.

My Lord,

THE honour of your name, and clearness of soul, which want no living monuments in the heart of princes, have already made the title of this poem innocent, though not the author; who confesseth his guilt of a long ambition, by some service to be known to you, and his boldness at last, by this rude attempt to kiss your Lordship's hands.

Fame with one breath hath possessed the world with your Lordship's general knowledge and excellent nature, both an ornament to your blood, and in both you stand the rare and justified example to our age. To the last, these cold papers address themselves, which if (with truce to your richer contemplations) you vouchsafe to read and smile upon, not only they shall receive a life, beyond what the scene exactly gave them, in the presentment, rewarded with frequent applause, but your Lordship shall infinitely honour him, whose glory is to be mentioned

the humblest of your Lordship's servants,

JAMES SHIRLEY.

DRAMATIS PERSONÆ.

ALEXANDER, Duke of Florence.

LORENZO, his Kinsman and Favourite.

SCIARRHA, Brother to AMIDEA.

PISANO, Lover to ORIANA.

COSMO, his Friend.

FLORIO, SCIARRHA's Brother.

DEPAZZI, a Creature of LORENZO's.

FREDERICO, } Noblemen.
ALONZO,

PETRUCHIO, PISANO's Servant.

ROGERO, Page to DEPAZZI.

Gentlemen.

Servants.

AMIDEA, SCIARRHA's Sister.

ORIANA, beloved of PISANO.

MOROSA, her Mother.

Youth.

Lust.

Pleasure.

Death.

Furies.

SCENE—FLORENCE.

THE TRAITOR.

ACT THE FIRST.

SCENE I.—*A Room in* PISANO'S *House.*

Enter PISANO *and* PETRUCHIO.

IS. Didst bid him come?

    Pet. I did.

    Pis. Go back again,

And tell him I am gone abroad.

    Pet. He's here

Already, sir.

Enter COSMO.

    Pis. Oh, Cosmo!

    Cos. Dear Pisano,

That I could let thee nearer into me!

My heart counts this embrace a distance yet;

Let us incorporate.

    Pis. I was wooing, Cosmo,

My man, to tell thee I was gone abroad,

Before thou cam'st.

    Cos. How's this? your words and looks

Are strange, and teach me to infer I am

Not welcome; that, on riper counsel, you

Do wish my absence.

Pis. What, for telling truth?
He thus should have but made thee fit to see
Thy friend ; thou com'st with expectation
To hear me talk sense, dost not?

Cos. Yes.

Pis. La, now!
And to discourse as I was wont, of state,
Our friendship, or of women? no such matter.

Cos. This is more wild than usual ; your language
Is not so clear as it was wont ; it carries
Not the same even thread ; although some words
May knit, the sense is scattered.

Pis. Right, right, Cosmo,
The reason is, I have straggled,
And lost myself, I know not where, in what
Part of the world :—and would not this have shown
As well in him [*Points to* PET.] to have prepared thee now?

Cos. What humour's this, Pisano? I am yet
To understand.

Pis. To understand? why, Cosmo,
Had I not changed my dialect and method,
What need this tedious apology?
That's it, I would have had thee know before.
Thou canst not understand me, yet thou hast
A name in Florence, for a ripe young man,
Of nimble apprehension, of a wise
And spreading observation ; of whom
Already our old men do prophesy
Good, and great things, worthy thy fair dimensions!

Cos. This is an argument above the rest.
Pisano is not well ; for being temperate,
He was not wont to flatter and abuse
His friend.

Pis. Beside, there is another reason,
Thou shouldst discover me at heart, through all
These mists ; thou art in love, too, and who cannot,
That feels himself the heat, but shrewdly guess

At every symptom of that wanton fever ?—
Oh, Cosmo !

   Cos. What misfortune can approach
Your happy love in fairest Amidea ?
You have been long contracted, and have passed
The tedious hope ; Hymen doth only wait
An opportunity to light his torch,
Which will burn glorious at your nuptials :
Let jealous lovers fear, and feel what 'tis
To languish, talk away their blood, and strength,
Question their unkind stars ; you have your game
Before you, sir.

   Pis. Before me ? Where ? why dost
Thou mock me, Cosmo ? she's not here.

   Cos. It is
No pilgrimage to travel to her lip.

   Pis. 'Tis not for you.

   Cos. How, sir ; for me ? you've no
Suspicion I can be guilty of
A treason to our friendship. Be so just,
If malice have been busy with my fame,
To let me know—

   Pis. You hastily interpret.
Thy pardon, I have only erred, but not
With the least scruple of thy faith and honour
To me. Thou hast a noble soul, and lov'st me
Rather too well ; I would thou wert my enemy,
That we had been born in distant climes, and never
Took cement from our sympathies in nature.
Would we had never seen, or known each other !
This may seem strange from him that loves thee, Cosmo,
More precious than his life.

   Cos. Love me, and wish
This separation ?

   Pis. I will give the proof ;
So well I love thee, nothing in the world
Thy soul doth heartily affect, but I

Do love it too : does it not trouble thy
Belief? I wear not my own heart about me,
But thine exchanged ; thy eyes let in my objects ;
Thou hear'st for me, talk'st, kissest, and enjoy'st
All my felicities.

   Cos. What means this language?

   Pis. But what's all this to thee? Go to Oriana,
And bathe thy lips in rosy dew of kisses ;
Renew thy eye, that looks as Saturn hung
Upon the lid ; take in some golden beam,
She'll dart a thousand at one glance ; and if,
At thy return, thou find'st I have a being
In this vain world, I'll tell thee more.   [*Exit.*

   Cos. But, sir, you must not part so.

   Pet. Not with my good will ;
I have no great ambition to be mad.

   Cos. Petruchio, let me conjure thee, tell
What weight hangs on thy master's heart? why does he
Appear so full of trouble?

   Pet. Do you not guess?

   Cos. Point at the cause ; I cannot.

   Pet. Why he loves—

   Cos. The beauteous Amidea, I know that.

   Pet. Some such thing was ; but you are his friend, my
       lord :
His soul is now devoted to Oriana,
And he will die for her, if this ague hold him.

   Cos. Ha !

   Pet. Your doublet pinch you, sir? I cannot tell,[1]
But ne'er a woman in the world should make
Me hang myself. It may be, for his honour,
He'll choose another death, he is about one ;
For 'tis not possible, without some cure,
He should live long ; he has forgot to sleep,
And for his diet, he has not eaten this se'nnight
As much as would choke a sparrow ; a fly is

---

   [1] *i.e.* I know not what to think of it.

An epicure to him.—Good sir, do you counsel him.—
                                    [*Exit* COSMO.
So, so, it works ;
This was my Lord Lorenzo's plot, and I
Have been his engine in the work, to batter
His love to Amidea, by praising
Oriana to him.—He is here.—My lord—

Enter LORENZO *attended.*

  Lor. Petruchio, where's your lord ? how moves the
    work ?
  Pet. To your own wish, my lord ; he has thrown off
The thought of Amidea, and is mad
For Cosmo's mistress, whom, by your instructions,
I have commended so.
  Lor. My witty villain !
  Pet. Cosmo is with him, to whom cunningly
I have discovered his disease, and I
Beseech you interrupt them not.
  Lor. This may
Have tragical effects, Petruchio :
For Cosmo, we shall prune his fortune thus.
Oriana's wealth would swell him in the state ;
He grows too fast already.—Be still ours.
  Pet. My lord, you bought my life, when you procured
My pardon from the duke.   [*Exit* LORENZO.

Re-enter PISANO *and* COSMO.

  Pis. O, friend, thou canst not be so merciful,
To give away such happiness : my love
Is, for some sin I have committed, thus
Transplanted.   I looked rather thou shouldst kill me,
Than give away this comfort ; 'tis a charity
Will make thee poor, and 'twere a great deal better
That I should languish still, and die.
  Cos. While I have art to help thee ? Oriana
And I were but in treaty ; howsoever,

I were not worthy to be called his friend,
Whom I preferred not to a mistress.   If
You can find dispensation to quit
With Amidea, your first love, be confident
Oriana may be won ; and it were necessary
You did prepare the mother ; be not modest.

    Pis. Each syllable is a blessing.—Hark, Petruchio.
                                [*Whispers him.*

    Cos. There is an engine levelled at my fate,
And I must arm.   [*Aside.*

    Pis. Away !   [*Exit* PETRUCHIO.

    Cos. This for thy comfort :
Although some compliments have passed between
Me and Oriana, I am not warm
Yet in the mother's fancy, whose power may
Assist you much ; but lose no time : let's follow.

    Pis. Thou miracle of friendship !   [*Exeunt.*

SCENE II.—*A Room in the* Duke's *Palace.*

Enter DUKE, FREDERICO, FLORIO, *and* ALONZO.

    Duke. Letters to us ? from whom ?
    Alon. Castruchio.
    Duke. The exile ? whence ?
    Alon. Sienna, my good lord ;
It came enclosed within my letter, which
Imposed my care and duty, in the swift
Delivery.   [*He delivers letters, which the* Duke *reads.*
    Fred. The duke is pale o' the sudden.
    Duke. A palsey does possess me ; ha ! Lorenzo ?
Our cousin the enemy of our life and state !
My bosom kinsman ?—Not too loud ; the traitor
May hear, and by escape prevent our justice.   [*Aside.*
    Flo. What traitor ?

Duke. Signior Alonzo, come you hither;
What correspondence maintain you with this
Castruchio?

Alon. None, my lord; but I am happy
In his election, to bring the first
Voice to your safety.

Duke. Most ingrateful man!
Turn rebel! I have worn him in my blood.

Alon. 'Tis time to purge the humour.

Duke. I will do it.——
Our guard!—Were he more precious, had he shared
Our soul, as he but borrows of our flesh,
This action makes him nothing; had I been
In heaven, I could have leant him my eternity.
He turn conspirator? oh, the fate of princes!
But stay, this paper speaks of no particular;
He does not mention what design, what plot.

Alon. More providence is necessary.

Duke. Right,
Right, good Alonzo; thou'rt an honest man,
And lov'st us well.—What's to be done?

Alon. 'Tis best
To make his person sure; by this you may
Discover soonest who are of his faction.

Duke. And at our leisure study of his punishment,
Which must exceed death; every common trespass
Is so rewarded: first, apply all tortures
To enforce confession, who are his confederates,
And how they meant to murder us; then some rare
Invention to execute the traitor,
So as he may be half a year in dying,
Will make us famed for justice.

Enter LORENZO *and* DEPAZZI.

Alon. He is here,
Shall we apprehend him?

Lor. Happy morning to
My gracious sovereign !

Duke. Good morrow, coz.—
Can treason couch itself within that frame ?—　　[*Aside.*
We have letters for you.　　[*Gives* LORENZO *the letters.*

Lor. Letters ! these, dread sir,
Have no direction to me, your highness
Is only named.

Duke. They will concern your reading.—
Alonzo, now observe and watch him.—Florio,
Depazzi, come you hither; does Lorenzo
Look like a traitor ?

Dep. How, sir ? a traitor ?

Duke. Ay, sir.

Dep. I, sir ? by my honour, not I, sir ; I defy him that
speaks it.—I am in a fine pickle.　　　　[*Aside.*

Lor. I have read.

Duke. Not blush ? not tremble ? read again.

Lor. The substance is, that you maintain
A vigilant eye over Lorenzo, who
Hath threatened, with your death, his country's liberty ;
And other things, touching reducing [1] of
A commonwealth.

Duke. I like not that.　　　　　　　　[*Aside.*
Dep. All's out !
A pox upon him for a traitor, he
Has hedged me in ; but I'll confess.　　　[*Aside.*

Duke. What answer
Make you to this, Lorenzo ?

Lor. This, o' the sudden,
Sir : I must owe the title of a traitor
To your high favours ; envy first conspired,
And malice now accuses : but what story
Mentioned his name, that had his prince's bosom
Without the people's hate ? 'tis sin enough,
In some men, to be great ; the throng of stars,

---

[1] *i.e.* Bringing back.

The rout and common people of the sky,
Move still another way than the sun does,
That gilds the creature : take your honours back,
And if you can, that purple of my veins,
Which flows in your's, and you shall leave me in
A state I shall not fear the great ones' envy,
Nor common people's rage ; and yet, perhaps,
You may be credulous against me.

 Duke. Ha !

 Alon. The duke is cool.

 Duke. Alonzo, look you prove
Lorenzo what you say.

 Alon. I say, my lord ?
I have discovered all my knowledge, sir.

 Dep. Stand to 't.

 Lor. With license of your highness, what
Can you imagine I should gain by treason ?
Admit I should be impious, as to kill you—
I am your nearest kinsman, and should forfeit
Both name and future title to the state,
By such a hasty, bloody disposition ;
The rabble hate me now, how shall I then
Expect a safety ?   Is it reformation
Of Florence they accuse me of ? suggesting
I disaffect a monarchy, which how
Vain and ridiculous would appear in me,
Your wisdom judge ; in you I live and flourish ;
What, in your death, can I expect, to equal
The riches I enjoy under your warmth ?
Should I, for the air and talk of a new government,
A commonwealth, lose all my certainties ?
And you above them all, whose favours have
Fallen like the dew upon me ? have I a soul
To think the guilt of such a murder easy,
Were there no other torments ? or can I
Expect the people will reward your murderer
With anything but death ? a parricide !

 Shir.   H

Alon. So, so, the duke's already in his circle.   [*Aside.*

Lor. But I am tame, as if I had no sense,
Nor other argument to vindicate
My loyalty, thus poisoned by a paper,
In my eternal fame, and by a slave?
Call to my brow some one that dare accuse me,
Let him have honour, great as mine, to forfeit,
Or, since your grace hath taken me so near
Your own height, that my scale may not expect
Such a proportioned adversary, yet let him
Have name within his country, and allow him
A soul, 'gainst which I may engage my more
Than equal honour, then I'll praise your justice;
But let him not be one condemned already,
A desperate exile.—Is it possible
A treason hatched in Florence, 'gainst the duke,
Should have no eyes at home to penetrate
The growing danger, but at Siena one
Must with a perspective discover all?
Ask this good counsellor, or these gentlemen,
Whose faiths are tried, whose cares are always waking
About your person, how have I appeared
To them, that thus I should be rendered hateful
To you and my good country? they are virtuous,
And dare not blemish a white faith, accuse
My sound heart of dishonour.   Sir, you must
Pardon my bold defence; my virtue bleeds
By your much easiness, and I am compelled
To break all modest limits, and to waken
Your memory (if it be not too late
To say you have one) with the story of
My fair deservings.   Who, sir, overthrew
With his designs, your late ambitious brother,
Hippolito, who, like a meteor, threatened
A black and fatal omen?

Duke. 'Twas Lorenzo.

Lor. Be yet as just, and say whose art directed

A countermine to check the pregnant hopes
Of Salviati, who for his cardinal's cap,
In Rome was potent, and here popular?

    Duke. None but Lorenzo.

    Dep. Admirable traitor!   [*Aside.*

    Lor. Whose service was commended when the exiles,
One of whose tribe accuseth me, had raised
Commotions in our Florence? When the hinge
Of state did faint under the burthen, and
The people sweat with their own fears, to think
The soldier should inhabit their calm dwellings,
Who then rose up your safety, and crushed all
Their plots to air?

    Duke. Our cousin, dear Lorenzo.

    Lor. When he that should reward, forgets the men
That purchased his security, 'tis virtue
To boast a merit. With my services
I have not starved your treasury; the grand
Captain Gonzales accounted to King Ferdinand
Three hundred thousand crowns, for spies; what bills
Have I brought in for such intelligence?

    Dep. I do grow hearty.   [*Aside.*

    Duke. All thy actions
Stand fresh before us, and confirm thou art
Our best and dearest friend; thus we assure
Our confidence; they love us not that feed
One jealous thought of our dear coz, Lorenzo.
New welcome to us all; for you, Alonzo,
Give o'er your paper kites, learn wit, 'tis time.—

                  [*Walks aside with* LORENZO.
Where shall we meet to-night?

    Lor. Pardon me, sir;
I am a dangerous man.

    Duke. No more of that;
I'll credit my soul with thee.—Shall we revel
This night with Amidea?

    Dep. The duke courts him.

Well, go thy ways, for one of the most excellent,
Impudent traitors—   [*Aside.*

    Duke. Yet a murmuring
Of traitor? we shall soon suspect him
That thinks Lorenzo guilty.

    Dep. I, my lord,
Dare boldly swear, his honour is as free
From any treason, as myself;—
I did prophesy this issue.   [*Aside.*

    Duke. 'Tis an age
Till night; I long to fold her in my arms.
Prepare Sciarrha, but be very wise
In the discovery; he is all touchwood.

    Lor. I know he is her brother; leave the managing
Of things to me.

    Duke. Still when we expect
Our bliss, time creeps; but when the happier things
Call to enjoy, each saucy hour hath wings.   [*Exeunt.*

ACT THE SECOND.

SCENE I.—*A Room in* SCIARRHA'S *House.*

Enter SCIARRHA *and* LORENZO.

SCI. My sister ! Though he be the duke,
   he dares not.—
   Patience, patience ! if there be such a
    virtue,
   I want it, Heaven ; yet keep it a little
    longer,
It were a sin to have it ; such an injury
Deserves a wrath next to your own.—My sister !
It has thrown wild-fire in my brain, Lorenzo,
A thousand Furies revel in my skull.
Has he not sins enough in's court to damn him,
But my roof must be guilty of new lusts,
And none but Amidea ? these the honours
His presence brings our house !

 Lor. Temper your rage.

 Sci. Are all the brothels rifled ? no quaint piece
Left him in Florence, that will meet his hot
And valiant luxury, that we are come to
Supply his blood out of our families ?
Diseases gnaw his title off !

 Lor. My lord—

 Sci. He is no prince of mine ; he forfeited
His greatness that black minute he first gave
Consent to my dishonour.

 Lor. Then I'm sorry—

Sci. Why should you be sorry, sir?
You say it is my sister he would strumpet,
Mine! Amidea! 'tis a wound you feel not;
But it strikes through and through the poor Sciarrha.
I do not think but all the ashes of
My ancestors do swell in their dark urns,
At this report of Amidea's shame:
It is their cause, as well as mine; and should
Heaven suffer the duke's sin to pass unpunished,
Their dust must of necessity conspire
To make an earthquake in the temple.

   Lor. Sir,
You said you would hear me out.

   Sci. Why, is there more
Behind?

   Lor. And greater: master your high blood
Till I conclude, Sciarrha. I accuse not
Your noble anger, which, I have observed,
Is not on every cheap and giddy motion
Inflamed; but, sir, be thrifty in your passion,
This is a petty trespass.

   Sci. Has mischief any name
Beyond this? will it kill me with the sound?

   Lor. My lord, though the dishonouring your sister
Be such a fact, the blood of any other
But Alexander could no less than expiate,
Yet this sin stretches farther, and involves,
With her's, your greater stain. Did you e'er promise
Yet, why do I make any question?   [him?—
It were another crime to think Sciarrha
Could entertain a thought so far beneath
His birth.—You stoop to such a horrid baseness!
Then all the virtue of mankind would sicken,
And soon take leave of earth.

   Sci. You torture me.

   Lor. What then could the duke find, to give him any
Encouragement, you would be guilty of

An act so fatal unto honour?   What,
When you were least yourself (as we are all
Frail compositions), did appear so wicked
In you, he should conceive a hope, and flatter
Himself with possibility to corrupt
Your soul to a deed so monstrous?

Sci. To what?

Lor. Though all the teeming glories of his dukedom,
Nay, Florence' state, offered itself a bribe,
And tempted the betraying of your name
To infamy, yet to imagine you
Would turn officious pander to his lust,
And interpose the mercenary bawd
To court your sister to his sinful coupling!
'Tis horrid, affrights nature; I grow stiff
With the imagination.

Sci. Ha!

Lor. Yet this
Was his command I should impose.

Sci. Lorenzo,
I do want breath; my voice is ravished from me;
I am not what I was; or—if I be
Sciarrha thou hast talked to all this while,
Look heedfully about me, and thou may'st
Discover, through some cranny of my flesh,
A fire within; my soul is but one flame,
Extended to all parts of this frail building.
I shall turn ashes, I begin to shrink;—
Is not already my complexion altered?
Does not my face look parched, and my skin gather
Into a heap? my breath is hot enough
To thaw the Alps.

Lor. Your fancy would transport you.

Sci. It is my rage; but let it cool, Lorenzo;
And then we'll talk of something, something, sir,
Shall be to purpose.

Lor. Now the flame is mounted,

My lord, I have given proof, although he be
My duke, and kinsman, I abhor his vices,
Howe'er the world, without examination,
Shoot their malicious noise, and stain my actions:
'Tis policy in princes to create
A favourite, who must bear all the guilt
Of things ill managed in the state; if any
Design be happy, 'tis the prince's own.
Heaven knows, how I have counselled this young man,
By virtue to prevent his fate; and govern
With modesty : O the religious days
Of commonwealths ! we have outlived that blessing.

   Sci. But I have thought a cure for this great state
Imposthume.

   Lor. What?

   Sci. To lance it; is't not ripe?
Let us draw cuts, whether your hand or mine
Shall do an act for Florence' liberty,
And send this tyrant to another world.

   Lor. How! I draw cuts?

   Sci. Coy it not thus, Lorenzo,
But answer: by your name and birth, you are
His kinsman, we all know it ; that you dwell
In's bosom, great in favour as in blood,
We know that too; and let me tell you more,
We know you but disguise your heart, and wish
Florence would change her title.

   Lor. How is this?

   Sci. We know you have firm correspondence with
The banished men, whose desperate fortunes wait
Your call to tumult in our streets ; all this,
Not to feed your ambition with a dukedom,
By the remove of Alexander, but
To serve your country, and create their peace
Who groan under the tyranny of a proud,
Lascivious monarch.—Is't not true, Lorenzo?
My phrase is blunt, my lord.

Lor. My genius
And thine are friends; I see they have conversed,
And I applaud the wisdom of my stars,
That made me for his friendship who preserves
The same religious fire.   I will confess,
When Alexander left his piety
To Florence, I placed him beneath my country,
As we should all; but we have lost our souls,
Or changed our active spirits, for a dull
And lazy sufferance; let this secret be
An argument, how much I dare repose
Upon Sciarrha's honour; virtue witness,
I choose no other destiny: command
Lorenzo's fate, dissolve me with your breath;
I'll either live, in your exchange of faith,
A patriot, or die my country's martyr.

Sci. Thou hast a fire beyond Prometheus',
To quicken earth; thy flame is but a prophecy
Of that high pyramid the world shall build
To thy immortal name: it was the glory
Of Romans to prefer their empire's safety
To their own lives; they were but men like us,
And of the same ingredients, our souls
Create of no inferior substance; ha?—

Lor. Heaven knows, I've no particular design
To leap into a throne; I will disclaim
The privilege of blood; let me advance
Our liberty, restore the ancient laws
Of the republic, rescue from the jaws
Of lust your mothers, wives, your daughters, sisters—

Sci. Sisters!

Lor. From horrid rape—'las, Amidea!

Sci. I am resolved; by all that's blest, he dies.
Return my willingness to be his pander,
My sister's readiness to meet his dalliance;
His promises have bought our shame:—he dies;
The roof he would dishonour with his lust

Shall be his tomb;—bid him be confident;
Conduct him, good Lorenzo, I'll dispose
My house for this great scene of death.

    Lor. Be constant.   [*Exit.*

Enter FLORIO *and* AMIDEA.

    Flo. Now, brother, what news brings the great Lorenzo?

    Sci. Let me have truce, vexation, for some minutes.—
                                [*Aside.*

What news? preferments, honours, offices.—
Sister, you must to court.

    Ami. Who, I to court?

    Sci. Or else the court will come to you. The duke
Hath sent already for us, Amidea:
O that I knew what happy stars did govern
At thy nativity! It were no sin
To adore their influence.

    Ami. What means my brother?

    Flo. He is transported.

    Ami. I shall suspect your health.

    Sci. I easily could forget I am Sciarrha,
And fall in love myself.—Is she not fair,
Exceeding beautiful, and tempting, Florio?
Look on her well, methinks I could turn poet,
And make her a more excellent piece than Heaven.
Let not fond men hereafter commend what
They most admire, by fetching from the stars,
Or flowers, their glory of similitude,
But from thyself the rule to know all beauty;
And he that shall arrive at so much boldness,
To say his mistress' eyes, or voice, or breath,
Are half so bright, so clear, so sweet as thine,
Hath told the world enough of miracle.
These are the duke's own raptures, Amidea;
His own poetic flames; an argument
He loves my sister.

    Ami. Love me?

Sci. Infinitely.
I am in earnest; he employed Lorenzo,
No meaner person, in this embassy;
You must to court.   Oh happiness!
   Ami. For what?
   Sci. What do great ladies do at court, I pray?
Enjoy the pleasures of the world, dance, kiss
The amorous lords, and change court breath; sing;
     lose
Belief of other Heaven; tell wanton dreams,
Rehearse their sprightly bed-scenes, and boast, which
Hath most idolaters; accuse all faces
That trust to the simplicity of nature,
Talk witty blasphemy,
Discourse their gaudy wardrobes, plot new pride,
Jest upon courtiers' legs, laugh at the wagging
Of their own feathers, and a thousand more
Delights, which private ladies never think of.
But above all, and wherein thou shalt make
All other beauties envy thee, the duke,
The duke himself shall call thee his, and single
From the fair troop thy person forth, to exchange
Embraces with, lay siege to these soft lips,
And not remove, till he hath sucked thy heart,
Which soon dissolved with thy sweet breath, shall be
Made part of his, at the same instant he
Conveying a new soul into thy breast
With a creating kiss.
   Ami. You make me wonder;
Pray speak, that I may understand.
   Sci. Why will you
Appear so ignorant?   I speak the dialect
Of Florence to you.   Come, I find you're cunning;[1]
The news does please, the rolling of your eye
Betrays you, and I see a guilty blush
Through this white veil, upon your cheek; you would

---

[1] Knowing.

Have it confirmed ; you shall ; the duke himself
Shall swear he loves you.

   Ami. Love me ! why ?

   Sci. To court,
And ask him ; be not you too peevish now,
And hinder all our fortune : I have promised him,
To move you for his armful, as I am
Sciarrha, and your brother ; more, I have sent
Word to him by Lorenzo, that you should
Meet his high flame ; in plain Italian,
Love him, and—

   Ami. What, for Heaven ! be the duke's whore ?

   Sci. No, no, his mistress ; command him, make us.

   Ami. Give up my virgin honour to his lust ?

   Sci. You may give it a better name ; but do it.

   Ami. I do mistake you, brother, do I not ?

   Sci. No, no, my meaning is so broad, you cannot.

   Ami. I would I did then.   Is't not possible
That this should be a dream ? where did you drop
Your virtue, sir ?—Florio, why move you not ?
Why are you slow to tell this man,—for sure
'Tis not Sciarrha,—he hath talked so ill,
And so much, that we may have cause to fear,
The air about's infected ?

   Flo. Are not you
My brother ?

   Sci. Be not you a fool, to move
These empty questions, but join to make her
Supple and pliant for the duke.   I hope
We are not the first have been advanced by a wagtail : [1]
No matter for the talk of musty people,
Look up to the reward ; thou art young, and skilled
In these court temptings, naturally soft,
And moving, I am rough-hewn ; assist, wilt,
With some quaint charm, to win her to this game ?

   Flo. My sister ?

   Sci. Ay, ay.

               [1] Wanton.

Ami. Come not near him, Florio,
'Tis not Sciarrha; sure, my brother's nurse
Played the imposter, and with some base issue
Cheated our house.

   Sci. Gipsy, use better language,
Or I'll forget your sex.

   Flo. Offer to touch her
With any rudeness, and by all that's virtuous—

   Sci. Why, how now, boy?

   Flo. I do not fear your sword,   [*Draws.*
This, with my youth and innocence, is more
Defence than all thy armoury; what devil
Has crept into thy soul?

   Sci. You will not help?

   Flo. I'll never[1] kill thee.

   Sci. 'Tis very well.
Have you considered better o' the motion?

   Ami. Yes.

   Sci. And what is your resolve?

   Ami. To have my name
Stand in the ivory register of virgins
When I am dead. Before one factious thought
Should lurk within me to betray my fame
To such a blot, my hands shall mutiny,
And boldly with a poniard teach my heart
To weep out a repentance.

   Sci. Let me kiss thee,
My excellent, chaste sister.—Florio,
Thou hast my soul; I did but try your virtues.—
'Tis truth, the duke does love thee, viciously,
Let him, let him! he comes to be our guest;
This night he means to revel at our house,—
The Tarquin shall be entertained; he shall.

Enter a Servant.

   Ser. My lord, Pisano is come.   [*Exit.*

         [1] Query, rather.

Sci. I had forgot his promise.—Look up, sister,
And shine with thy own smiles; Pisano's come,
Pisano, thy contracted, honoured friend;
A gentleman so rich in hopes, we shall
Be happy in's alliance.—

    Enter PISANO, COSMO, *and* FREDERICO.

                           Welcome all,
But you above the rest, my brother shortly.—
Sister, and Florio, entertain your noble
Friends; some few minutes I am absent. We
Must not forget t' prepare for the duke's coming;
I'll soon return.   [*Exit.*
    Ami. You are not cheerful, sir;
How is't, my lord? you were not wont to look
So sad when you came hither.
    Pis. I am not well, Amidea.
    Ami. Oh my heart!
    Pis. Be you
Comforted, lady; let all griefs repair
To this, their proper centre.   [*Lays his hand on his breast.*
    Flo. Sir, how fare you?
    Pis. Altered of late a little.
    Fred. Virtuous lady,
I cannot choose but pity her, and accuse
Pisano's levity.   [*Aside.*
    Pis. Would he were come back!
I might have finished ere he went, and not
Delayed his business much; two or three words,
And I had dispatched.
    Ami. How, sir? your language is
Another than you used to speak; you look not
With the same brow upon me.
    Cos. 'Las! sweet lady.—
But who shall accuse me?   [*Aside.*
    Pis. We shall expect too long.—Lady, I am come
To render all my interest in your love,

And to demand myself again; live happier
In other choice, fair Amidea, 'tis
Some shame to say my heart's revolted.

Ami. Ha!

Pis. Here's witness, all is cancelled betwixt us;
Nay, an you weep—Farewell!

Ami. He's gone!

Flo. I am amazed.

Pis. Now lead me to my blessing.

[*Exeunt* PISANO, COSMO, *and* FREDERICO.

Flo. Shall a long suit and speeding in his love,
With the world's notice, and a general fame
Of contract too, just in the instant, when
A marriage is expected, be broke off
With infamy to our house?

Ami. Brother, if ever
You loved poor Amidea, let not this
Arrive Sciarrha's ear, there's danger in
His knowledge of it; this may be a trial
Of my affection.

Flo. A trial! no, it showed
Too like a truth.

Ami. My tears entreat your silence.

Flo. You have power to command it; dry your eyes
then,
He is returned.

Re-enter SCIARRHA.

Sci. How now!
Weeping? Where is Pisano, and his friends?

Flo. They're gone, sir.

Sci. Ha!

Ami. Guess by my eyes you may,
Something of sorrow hath befallen; no sooner
You were departed, but some strange distemper
Invaded him; we might discern a change
In's countenance, and though we prayed him to
Repose with us, he would straight back again;

So, with Frederico,
And Signior Cosmo, he returned.

Flo. The alteration was strange and sudden.

Sci. 'Las! noble gentleman—but come, clear up
Your face again, we hope it will not last:
Look bright again, I say, I have given order—

Enter a Gentleman.

Gent. My lord, the duke's already come.   [*Exit.*

Sci. Remove,
Good Amidea, and reserve thy person
To crown his entertainment; be not seen yet.
                                        [*Exit* AMIDEA.

Enter DUKE, LORENZO, ALONZO, *and* Attendants.

Duke. Sciarrha, we are come to be your guest.

Sci. Your highness doth an honour to our house.

Duke. But where's thy sister? she must bid us wel-
        come.

Sci. She is your grace's handmaid.

Duke. For this night,
Let the whole world conspire to our delight.—
Lorenzo—   [*Whispers him.*

Lor. Sir, be confident——and perish.   [*Aside.*

SCENE II.—*The Garden of* MOROSA'S *House.*

Enter MOROSA, ORIANA, *and* Servant.

Mor. You should not rashly give away your heart,
Nor must you, without me, dispose yourself.—
Pray give access to none—yet, if Pisano
Enquire, direct him to the garden. —[*Exit* Servant.
        Cosmo
Is young, and promising, but, while Lorenzo
Lives, must expect no sunshine.

Re-enter Servant *with* PISANO *and* COSMO.

Pis. There's for thy pains.—   [*Exit* Servant.
They are now at opportunity.

Cos. My lord,
Do you prepare the mother, and let me close
With Oriana.

Pis. What service can reward thee?

Cos. Take occasion
To leave us private; this hour be propitious!
Win but the matron to you.

Pis. She is prepared already.

Cos. Lose no time,
Take the other walk.   [*Exeunt* PISANO *and* MOROSA.

Ori. My dear Cosmo.

Cos. My best Oriana.   [you.

Ori. You have been too much absent, I must chide

Cos. You cannot, sweet; I would I knew which way
To make thee angry; yes, that I might see
How well it would become thee. I do fear
Thou art some angel, and that sin would be
An argument to me, that thou wert mortal;
I must suspect thy too much goodness else,
And leave thee for the fellowship of saints,
I am too wicked.

Ori. You will make me angry.

Cos. But you will love me still, I fear.

Ori. Do you fear it?
Is't a misfortune?

Cos. What?

Ori. My love.

Cos. Your anger;
And yet the t'other oftentimes may carry
An evil with it; we may love too well,
And that's a fault.

Ori. Not where the object's good.

Cos. O yes: always beware of the extremes.

Shir.   I

Ori. What mean you ? I affect none but my Cosmo,
Nor him with too much flame.

Cos. If you should, lady,
'Twere nobly done.

Ori. To love another?

Cos. Yes,
If there be cause, that may be called a virtue :
For what have I to engross the affection
Of any lady, if she can discern
A greater merit in some other man ?
Wisdom forbid, but she command her smiles,
To warm and cherish him.

Ori. So we should be
Inconstant.

Cos. Why not? if our reason be
Convinced that's no such fault, as the world goes.
Let us examine all the creatures, read
The book of nature through, and we shall find
Nothing doth still the same ; the stars do wander,
And have their divers influence, the elements
Shuffle into innumerable changes:
Our constitutions vary ; herbs and trees
Admit their frost and summer; and why then
Should our desires, that are so nimble, and
More subtle than the spirits in our blood,
Be such stayed things within us, and not share
Their natural liberty ?   Shall we admit a change
In smaller things, and not allow it in
What most of all concerns us?

Ori. What ?

Cos. Our loves.

Ori. Have you suspicion I am changed, and thus
Would school me for it ? or shall I imagine
That you are altered ?

Cos. Yes, I am, and therefore
Proclaim thy freedom ; I do love thee less,
To show I love thee more.

Ori. What riddle's this?

Cos. I will explain.   Upon maturity
Of counsel, Oriana, I have found
I am not worthy of thee, therefore come
To make thee satisfaction for my sin
Of loving thee, by pointing out a way,
And person, will become thy affection better.

Ori. You have a pretty humour.

Cos. What dost think
Of brave Pisano? shall his merit plead
Succession in thy chaste thoughts?

Ori. I do know him.

Cos. Thou canst not choose, and I could study
　　　none
Worthy thy love but him.

Ori. 'Tis very likely
You would resign then?

Cos. Ay, to honour thee;
His service will deserve thee at the best
And richest value.

Ori. Why, it shall be so.

Cos. Nay, but be serious, and declare me happy,
That I may say, I have made thee just amends,
And I will thank thee.

Ori. Why, sir, I do love him.

Cos. Oh, when did Cupid aim that golden shaft?
But dost thou love him perfectly, with a
Desire, when sacred rites of marriage
Are past, to meet him in thy bed, and call him
Thy husband?

Ori. Why, sir, did you ever think
I was so taken with your worth and person,
I could not love another lord as well?
By your favour, there be many as proper men,
And as deserving; you may save your plea,
And be assured I need no lesson to
Direct my fancy.   I did love Pisano

Before, but for your sake, I mean to place him
A great deal nearer.—Sure he does but jest.   [*Aside.*
You did love me.

 Cos. Now, by my heart, I love thee.
This act shall crown our story, Oriana,
Thou dost not know how much thou honourest me,
For he's not in the common list of friends,
And he does love thee past imagination.
Next his religion he has placed the thought
Of Oriana, he sleeps nothing else,
And I shall wake him into Heaven, to say
Thou hast consented to be his.

 Ori. Pray tell me,
But truly, I beseech you ; do you wish
Pisano mine indeed ? or are you jealous,
And name him to accuse me ?

 Cos. Not, by goodness ;
But if there be a charm beyond thy innocence,
By that I would conjure thee, Oriana,
Love him, and make three happy; it shall be
My bliss to call you his, let me but own
A servant in your memory.

 Ori. Unkind
And cruel Cosmo ! dost thou think it possible
I can love any but thyself ? thou wilt
Undo my heart for ever.

Re-enter PISANO *and* MOROSA.

 Mor. You shall be
Ever most welcome ; If I be her mother,
She must declare obedience.—Oriana—

 Cos. Go cheerfully, thy mother calls, to him
Whose orator I have been.—'Las, poor lady !
I half repent me, since she is so constant:
But a friend's life weighs down all other love ;
Beside I thus secure my fate ; Lorenzo
Threatens my spring, he is my enemy.   [*Aside.*

Ori. You'll not compel affection?

Pis. No, but court it;
With honour, and religion, thus invite it.

Mor. I shall forget the nature of a parent,
Unless you show more softness, and regard
To what is urged. What promise could you make
To Cosmo without me? or, if you had—

Cos. Here Cosmo doth give up all title to it;
I have no part in Oriana now.

Ori. I've heard too much; do with me what you
    please,
I am all passive, nothing of myself,
But an obedience to unhappiness.   [*Exit.*

Cos. Follow her, Pisano.

Pis. Thou art all friendship.

Cos. Trace their warm steps, virgins' resolves are
    weak.
Leave not her eyes until you see day break.   [*Exeunt.*

ACT THE THIRD.

SCENE I.—*A Room in* DEPAZZI'S *House.*

Enter DEPAZZI *and* ROGERO.

EP. Rogero!

Rog. My lord.

Dep. Make fast the chamber door, stifle the keyhole and the crannies, I must discourse of secret matters; dost thou smell nothing, Rogero? ha?

Rog. Smell? not any thing, my lord, to offend my nostril.

Dep. Come hither; what do the people talk abroad of me? Answer me justly, and to the point; what do they say?

Rog. Faith, my lord, they say that you are—

Dep. They lie, I am not; they are a lousy, impudent multitude, a many-headed, and many-horned generation, to say that I am—

Rog. A noble gentleman, a just and discreet lord, and one that deserved to have his honours without money.

Dep. Oh, is that it? I thought the rabble would have said, I had been a traitor.—I am half mad, certainly, ever since I consented to Lorenzo; 'tis a very hard condition, that a man must lose his head to recompense the procuring of his honours: what if I discover him to the duke?—ten to one, if Lorenzo come but to speak, his grace will not have the grace to believe me, and then I run the hazard to be thrown out of all on t'other side:

'tis safest to be a traitor. [*Aside.*]—Hum, who is that you whispered to?

Rog. I whisper?

Dep. Marry did you, sirrah.

Rog. Not I, good faith, my lord.

Dep. Sirrah, sirrah, sirrah, I smell a rat behind the hangings. [*Takes up the hangings.*]—Here's nobody; ha? are there no trunks[1] to convey secret voices?

Rog. Your lordship has a pair[2] on.

Dep. I do not like that face in the arras; on my conscience he points at me. 'Pox upon this treason, I have no stomach to't; I do see myself upon a scaffold, making a pitiful speech already; I shall have my head cut off. Seven years ago I laid my head upon a wager, I remember, and lost it; let me see,—it shall be so, 'tis good policy to be armed. [*Aside.*]—Rogero, imagine I were a traitor.

Rog. How, sir?

Dep. I but say "imagine;" we may put the case; and that I were apprehended for a traitor.

Rog. Heaven defend!

Dep. Heaven has something else to do, than to defend traitors. I say, imagine I were brought to the bar.

Rog. Good, my lord! you brought to the bar?

Dep. I will beat you, if you will not imagine, at my bidding: I say, suppose I now were at the bar, to answer for my life.

Rog. Well, sir.

Dep. Well, sir? that's as it happens; you must imagine I will answer the best I can for myself. Conceive, I prithee, that these chairs were judges, most grave and venerable beards and faces, at my arraignment, and that thyself wert, in the name of the duke and state, to accuse me, what couldst thou say to me?

Rog. I accuse your good honour? for what, I beseech

Dep. For high treason, you blockhead.   [you?

Rog. I must be acquainted with some particulars first.

---

[1] Tubes.   [2] *i.e.* Trunk-hose, large breeches.

Dep. Mass, thou sayest right: why imagine,—do you hear? you must but imagine,—that some great man had a conspiracy against the duke's person, and that I, being an honest lord, and one of this great man's friends, had been drawn in, for that's the plain truth on't; 'twas against my will, but that's all one. Well, thou understand'st me; show thy wit, Rogero, scratch thy nimble pericranium, and thunder out my accusation *ex tempore.* Here I stand, Signior Depazzi, ready to answer the indictment.

Rog. Good, my lord, it will not become me, being your humble servant.

Dep. Humble coxcomb! is it not for my good? I say, accuse me, bring it home, jerk me soundly to the quick, Rogero, tickle me, as thou lov'st thy lord; I do defy thee, spare me not, and the devil take thee if thou be'st not malicious.

Rog. Why then have at you. First, Signior Depazzi, thou art indicted of high treason, hold up thy hand; guilty, or not guilty?

Dep. Very good.

Rog. Nay, very bad, sir:—answer, I say; guilty or not guilty?

Dep. Not guilty.

Rog. 'Tis your best course to say so:—well, imagine I rise up the duke's most learned in the laws, and his nimble-tongued orator; have at you signior.

Dep. Come, come on, sir, here I stand.

Rog. I will prove thou liest in thy throat, if thou deniest thy treason, and so I address myself to the most understanding seats of justice.—"Most wise, most honourable, and most incorrupt judges, sleep not, I beseech you; my place hath called me to plead, in the behalf of my prince and country, against this notable, this pernicious, and impudent traitor, who hath plotted and contrived such high, heinous, and horrible treasons, as no age nor history hath ever mentioned the like. Here he stands, whose birth I will not touch, because it is altogether unknown who begot him. He was brought up among the small wares in the city, became rich by sinister and indirect practices, married a merchant's wife at adventures, and was soon after advanced to be a head-officer."

Dep. Why, you rascal!

Rog. Peace, sirrah, peace!—" Nay, your lordships shall find him very audacious: this fellow, not content to have his branches spread within the city, I speak it to his face, let him deny it, was afterward, by the corruption of his confederate, and the mere grace of his highness, raised to honour, received infinite favours from his prince of blessed memory, yet, like a wretch, a villain, a viper, a rat of Nilus, he hath practised treasons against the sacred person of the duke, for which he deserveth not only to die, but also to suffer tortures, whips, racks, strapadoes, wheels, and all the fiery brazen bulls that can be invented, as I shall make it appear to this honourable and illustrious court."

Dep. This rogue's transported.

Rog. With all my heart; " I obey your lordships:— thus then I pass from these circumstances, and proceed to the principal villainies that we have to lay to his charge. *Imprimis*, thou, Signior Depazzi, didst offer to a groom one hundred crowns to poison his highness' hunting-saddle."

Dep. Did I?

Rog. Do not interrupt me, varlet; I will prove it;— "his hunting saddle, and woe shall be unto thy breech therefore; and finding this serpentine treason broken in the shell,—do but lend your reverend ears to his next designs—I will cut them off presently,—this irreligious, nay, atheistical traitor, did with his own hands poison the duke's prayer-book; oh, impiety! and had his highness, as in former times he accustomed, but prayed once in a month, which, by special grace, he omitted, how fatal had it been to Florence! but as by justice his excellence did then, and by his own want of devotion, prevent this assassinate's purpose, so we hope, in his own discretion, and the counsel of his state, he will take heed how he prays hereafter while he lives, to which every true subject will say, Amen."

Dep. " May it please your honours——"

Rog. Thou impudent, brazen-faced traitor, wilt thou deny it? " Moreover, an't like your good lordships, he hath for this fortnight or three weeks before his apprehension, walked up and down the court with a case[1] of pistols charged, wherewith, as he partly confessed, he intended to send the duke to Heaven with a powder!"

Dep. This rogue will undo the devil at invention.— " May it please this honourable——"

Rog. " These are but sprinklings of his treason."

Dep. Will you justify this? did I any of these things, you tadpole?

Rog. Hold yourself contented, my lord; he that is brought to the bar in case of treason, must look to have more objected than he can answer, or any man is able to justify.

Dep. " I confess, an't please your good lordships——"

Rog. " Mark, he will confess——"

Dep. That's the way to be sent of a headless errand:— " Indeed I confess that I never intended any treason to his highness, nor ever sought the prince's life; true it is, that I heard of a conspiracy."

Rog. " That, that, my lords, hath overthrown him; he saith he never sought the prince's life, *ergo*, he sought his death; besides, he hath heard of treason; now, he that heareth and discovereth not, is equally guilty in fact: for in offences of this nature there are no accessories, *ergo*, he is a principal, and being a principal traitor, he deserveth condemnation."

Dep. Shall I not speak?

Rog. No, traitors must not be suffered to speak, for

---

[1] Couple.

when they have leave, they have liberty, and he that is a traitor deserveth to be close prisoner.

Dep. "All that this fellow hath uttered is false and forged, abominable lies."

Rog. I will speak truth, and I will be heard, and no man else, in this place.

Dep. "I never dreamt of a hunting-saddle, nor never had so much as a thought of any prayer-book."

Rog. "You sit here to do justice; I speak for the duke, and the safety of the commonwealth."

Dep. "As for pistols, 'tis well known I could never endure the report of them. I defy powder and shot as I do him that accuseth me."

Rog. "I defy all the world that will hear a traitor speak for himself; 'tis against the law, which provides that no man shall defend treason, and he that speaks for himself, being a traitor, doth defend his treason: thou art a capital obstreperous malefactor."

Dep. Thou art a madman.

Rog. Go to, you have played the fool too much.

Dep. Thou continual motion cease; a pox upon thee, hold thy tongue.

Rog. The pox will not serve your turn.

Dep. Why then this shall. [*Beats him.*

Rog. Hold, hold, good my lord, I am sensible; I have done, imagine I have done; I but obeyed your lordship, whose batoon[1] I find stronger than my imagination.— My lord, you will answer this, to strike in the court thus?

Dep. I am as weary—hark, Rogero, [*Knocking within.*] —one knocks; see, see; there's to make thee amends; [*Gives him money.*]—see, good Rogero, and say nothing. [*Exit* ROGERO.]—Pray Heaven it be no pursuivant.

Re-enter ROGERO *with* PETRUCHIO *bearing a letter.*

Rog. Petruchio, my Lord Pisano's secretary.

Dep. But Lorenzo's engine a very knave. [*Aside.*

---

[1] Stick. Fr. *Bâton.*

Pet. My very good lord.   [*Gives him the letter.*

Dep. What's here? it can be no goodness. [*Reads aside.*]—" My lord, I would not have you go to bed to-night,"—he will not let me sleep now, I dreamt as much; —" something will be done to give Florence liberty. In the depth of night you may cunningly disperse some rumours in the city, that the duke is dead; the people must be distracted; in the common fright be not you wanting in your person to assist their fears, and speak well of—Lorenzo.—" Speak well of the devil.—My humble service to your lord, and say he has power to command me in all things.

Pet. My very good lord.

Dep. No matter, an you were both hanged. [*Aside.*]— Rogero, show him the wine cellar. [*Exeunt* ROGERO *and* PETRUCHIO.]—Let me see, I must report the duke's death; I cannot abide this word "death;" yet he desires me but to report it: hum, if it be false, why so much the better; there will be the less harm in it; if it should prove true, they will believe me another time: well, I will drink myself half drunk, and be fortified.   [*Exit.*

SCENE II.—*A Room in* SCIARRHA'S *House.*

Preparations for a Masque.

Enter DUKE, AMIDEA, LORENZO, SCIARRHA, FLORIO, *and* Attendants.

Duke. Sciarrha, you exceed in entertainment;
Banquet our eyes too?

Lor. He will feast all senses.

Sci. Only a toy, my lord; I cannot call't
A masque, nor worthy of this presence, yet
It speaks the freedom of my heart, and gratitude
For this great honour.

Duke. Amidea must
Sit near us.

Sci. Lords, your places; 'twill not be
Worth half this ceremony.—Let them begin.

Enter Lust, richly apparelled, the Pleasures attending.

Duke. Who's the presenter?

Sci. Lust, sir; pray observe.

Lust.   Now let Lust possess the throne
      Of Love, and rule in hearts alone:
      You sweet tempters to my sin,
      Beauty, smiles, and kisses win
      Upon frail mortals, let them know
      There is no happiness, but you.
      Shoot no arrows tipped with lead,
      Each shaft have his golden head.
      Call no love, delude men still,
      Through the flesh their spirits kill,
      Nor spend all your heart to take
      Common persons; greatness make,
      By your potent charms, to be
      Subjects unto hell and me:
      Inflame but kings with loose desire,
      You soon set all the world on fire.

Enter a Young Man richly habited, and crowned.

Duke. What's he?

Sci. A wild young man, that follows Lust;
He has too much blood it seems.

Duke. Why looks he back?

Sci. There is a thing called Death, that follows
    him;
With a large train of Furies; but the Syrens
Of Lust make him secure, and now the hag
Embraces him, and circles him with pleasures;
The harpies mean to dance too.—[*Here* Lust, *the* Plea-
    sures, *and the* Young Man *join in a Dance.*]—
        Hang his conscience!
It whines too much.

Lor. This is too plain. [*Aside.*

Sci. He does not tremble yet.—
By-and-by, sir, you shall see all his tormentors
Join with them; there's the sport on't.

Lor. Methinks they
Should have been first, for th' antimasque.[1]

Sci. Oh no!
In hell they do not stand upon the method,
As we at court; the grand masque and the glory
Begin the revels.—

Enter Death.

Sister, you do ill
To keep the duke in talk; he cannot see
The devil for you, and the whips: does not
That death's head look most temptingly? the worms
Have kissed the lips off.—

Enter Furies, *who join in the dance, and in the end carry
the* Young Man *away. The rest flee in confusion.*

How does your highness like this dance?

Duke. My eyes so feasted here, I did not mark it,
But I presume 'twas handsome.

Sci. O the lethargy
Of princes!—We have kept you, sir, from bed.—
More lights.

Duke. Good night to all; to you the best:—
Sciarrha, bind us ever by performance.

Sci. We are all your's.

Duke. And Florence thine.—Once more—
Brightest of ladies.

Lor. You are firm? [*Aside to* SCIARRHA.

Sci. Suspect not. [*Exeunt all but* AMIDEA *and* FLORIO.

Flo. I do not like my brother's moral masque;
The duke himself was personated: I
Wonder it did not startle him.

---

[1] A burlesque interlude in the masque.

Ami. I hope
Sciarrha does not mean so ill as that
Did promise. He's returned; his looks are full

Re-enter SCIARRHA.

Of threat'ning.

Sci. Amidea, go not to bed;
And yet no matter; I can do 't alone.
Take both your rest, and in your prayers commend
The duke to Heaven, 'tis charity; he has made
His will already, and bequeathed his body
To you, sister; pity his soul, for 'tis now
Within few minutes of departing.

Ami. How?

Sci. Why, this way; [*Showing a poniard.*]—I must
　　help him in his groans,
To bring his flesh a-bed.

Ami. You will not kill him?

Sci. I am not of your mind.

Ami. I know you cannot.

Sci. You are not studied so perfect in
His destiny, I hope; I will endeavour—

Ami. To kill your prince?

Flo. What, here?

Sci. No, in his chamber.

Ami. Shall it be read in stories of our Florence,
Sciarrha first did stain his family
With such a treason?

Flo. Was he not invited?

Sci. Yes, by his lust.

Flo. And in your crownèd tables,
And hospitality, will you murder him?

Sci. Yes, and the reason wherefore he was mur-
　　dered,
Shall justify the deed to all posterity;
He came to wrong my sister.

Flo. Wanton heat;
Let youthful blood excuse him.

Sci. So it must.

Flo. Mistake me not; oh, think but who he is,
The duke, that word must needs awake your piety.

Ami. How will good men in this remembrance
Abhor your cruelty, that send to hell
One with the weight of all his sins upon him?

Sci. It is too late to cool with argument
My incensed blood. Will you go dally with him,
And let him board your pinnace? I have gone
So far in promise, if you clasp not with him,
It will be dangerous if he outlive
This night.

Ami. I have thought on't; send him to my bed.

Sci. Ha!

Ami. Do not question what I purpose; Heaven
Witness to my chaste thoughts.

Sci. Wilt thou trust him?

Ami. I will do much, sir, to preserve his life,
And your innocence: be not you suspectful;
At the worst you can but respite your revenge.

Sci. Dost thou not fear unhappy Lucrece' chance,
Or wretched Philomel's dishonour?

Ami. No:
Give me his life, and send your wanton to me:
I'll to my chamber; fear me not, Sciarrha,
Have not one thought so bad, I shall not prosper;
Virgins in Heaven will suffer with me.

Flo. Trust her.   [*Exeunt* AMIDEA *and* FLORIO.

Sci. 'Tis but deferring of my justice;
She will not kill him, sure; draw on her soul
The guilt she hates in mine; if she do yield
To the hot encounter, ha! 'twill then be just,
That both their hearts weep blood, to purge their lust.

[*Exit.*

SCENE III.—*Another Room in the same.*

Enter FLORIO *and* AMIDEA.

Flo. My poniard?

Ami. I've no black intent
To stain't with any blood.

Flo. Take it, I know
Thou art my virtuous sister, it were wickedness
To doubt thy purpose, or the event.

Ami. Now leave me.

Flo. Thou hast a guard of angels.

Ami. They are coming.

[FLORIO *conceals himself behind the hangings.*

Enter SCIARRHA *and the* DUKE.

Sci. Look, there she is, sir: you know how to undress
Duke. Dearest Sciarrha.   [her.
Sci. To your recreation.—
Here I'll obscure myself. [*Aside: sees* FLORIO *as he retires
behind the hangings.*]—Florio? 'tis well.

Duke. Lady, you know me?

Ami. Yes; my prince.

Duke. I was so
Till I saw thee, but I gave up that title
A conquest to thy beauty, which, among
Her other wonders, hath created me
A subject and a servant, and I shall
Be happier to be received your's by
One of those names, than Duke of Tuscany.

Ami. Oh, take yourself again, sir; use your greatness
To make the hearts of Florence bow to you,
And pay their duties thus.   [*Kneels.*

Duke. Rise, Amidea,
And since you have given my power back, it will
Become me to command.

Ami. And me to obey.   [*Rises.*

Duke. I see thy noble brother hath been faithful

Shir.   K

To my desires ; he has prepared thee with
A story of my love, which thou reward'st
With too much humbleness : thou hast a quarrel,
And a just one, with thy stars, that did not make thee
A princess, Amidea ; yet thou'rt greater,
And born to justify unto these times,
Venus, the queen of Love, was but thy figure,
And all her graces prophecies of thine,
To make our last age best.   I could dwell ever
Here, and imagine I am in a temple,
To offer on this altar of thy lip,   [*Kisses her often.*
Myriads of flaming kisses, with a cloud
Of . . . . .[1] sighs breathed from my heart,
Which, by the oblation, would increase his stock,
To make my pay eternal.

    Ami. What mean you?

    Duke. That question is propounded timely : hadst thou
Not interrupted me, I should have lost
Myself upon thy lips, and quite forgot
There is a bliss beyond it, which I came for.
Let others satisfy themselves to read
The wonders in thy face, make proud their eye,
By seeing thine, turn statues at thy voice,
And think they never fix enough to hear thee.
A man half dead with famine would wish here
To feed on smiles, of which the least hath power
To call an anchorite from his prayers, tempt saints
To wish their bodies on.   Thou dost with ease
Captivate kings with every beam, and mayst
Lead them like prisoners round about the world,
Proud of such golden chains; this were enough,
Had not my fate provided more, to make me
Believe myself immortal in thy touches.
Come to thy bed, transform me there to happiness ;
I'll laugh at all the fables of the gods,

    [1] Something appears to have dropped out here.

And teach our poets after I know thee,
To write the true Elysium.

   Ami. Good, my lord,
I understand you not, and yet I fear
You do not mean well; if you have brought with you
A sinful purpose, which I may suspect—

   Duke. Why, lady, what do you imagine I
Came hither for?

   Ami. I know not.

   Duke. How!
Is't come to that? your brother gave you more
Desirous of the sport, and brought me hither,
Ripe for your dalliance.   Did you not expect me?

   Ami. Yes.

   Duke. And to what other purpose?

   Ami. To tell you, that you are not virtuous.

   Duke. I'm of your mind.

   Ami. But I am not so wicked
To be of your's: oh, think but who you are,
Your title speaks you nearest Heaven, and points
You out a glorious reign among the angels;
Do not depose yourself of one, and be
Of the other disinherited.

   Duke. I would
Your brother heard you; prithee, do not waste
This tedious divinity, I am
Resolved to grapple with you.

   Ami. Keep off.   [*Shows the poniard.*

   Duke. Ha!
Turned Amazon?

   Ami. Prince, come not too near me,
For, by my honour, since you have lost your own,
Although I bow in duty to your person,
I hate your black thoughts; tempt not my just hand
With violent approach, I dare, and will
Do that will grieve you, if you have a soul.

   Duke. Thou dar'st not kill me.

Ami. True, but I dare die.

Duke. Be thy own murderer?

Ami. Rather than you should be my ravisher.

Duke. Thou canst not be so merciless, 'tis less sin
To be unchaste; I am thy prince, I prithee
Throw by that cruel weapon, let our war
Be soft embraces, shooting amorous smiles,
Kill and restore each other with a kiss,
I know thou canst not be unkind so long:
Then, I command thee.

Ami. I must not obey
To be your strumpet: though my hand be unskilful,
I shall soon find my heart.

Duke. I'll not believe—

Ami. Let this deserve your faith I dare be just,
[*She wounds her arm.*
This crimson river issuing from my arm.

Duke. Hold!

Ami. Never; it shall flow, and if this channel
Yield not enough, I'll strike another vein,
And after that, another, and not pity
The murmuring stream, till through a prodigal wound
I have drained the fountain: this doth weep for you,
And shall extol my death, if it may teach
You to correct your blood.

Duke. There's so much gone
From me, I cool apace; this action
Hath shot an ague through me; Amidea,
Pity thyself.

Ami. Not, till you swear repentance;
I do not faint yet, 'tis somewhat about,
But I can find a nearer way; this does it.
[*Offering to strike herself again.*

Duke. Contain [1]; I am sorry, sorry from my soul,
Trust me, I do bleed inward, Amidea,
Can answer all thy drops: oh, pardon me,

[1] *i.e.* Abstain.

Thou faint'st already, dost not? I am fearful.
The phœnix, with her wings, when she is dying,
Can fan her ashes into another life;
But when thy breath, more sweet than all the spice
That helps the other's funeral, returns
To Heaven, the world must be eternal loser.
Look to thy wound.

   Ami. May I believe you, sir?

   Duke. I dare not think awry; again I ask
Forgiveness; in thy innocence I see
My own deformity.

   [SCIARRHA, *followed by* FLORIO, *comes hastily from
      behind the hangings and embraces* AMIDEA.

   Sci. Now a thousand blessings
Reward thy goodness; thou deserv'st a statue,
A tall one, which should reach above the clouds,
Jostle the moon, that people afar off
Beholding it, may be invited hither,
In hope to climb to Heaven by't; but apply
Betimes unto thy wound.—Florio, assist her.—

               [FLORIO *leads off* AMIDEA.

And now, my lord—

   Duke. Sciarrha, I'll begin to be thy lord;
I brought intentions of dishonour to thee,
And thy fair sister, but I am reconciled
To virtue, and will study how to satisfy
For you and Florence.

   Sci. You will be more precious,
Than had you never fallen; I am all joy
In your conversion.

   Duke.   .   `    `   .   .   .[1]

   Sci. Lorenzo! I think, he has not said his prayers yet,
But—

   Duke. What?

   Sci. I cannot tell, may be he does not use it.

---

[1] Some words have probably dropped out here, as Sciarrha
appears to reply to a question from the duke relating to Lorenzo.

Duke. How?

Sci. My lord, you now are lovely;
'Twere better you'd forget him; he's not right
At heart, I fear.

Duke. Fear nothing.

Sci. To be plain,
You cherish your disease in him, and are
Not safe while he is near you.

Duke. Do not envy him.[1]

Sci. Then I must tell you, sir, he is a traitor,
Within my knowledge, hath conspired your death.

Duke. With whom?

Sci. With me; I should have killed you, sir,
This night, and every minute he expects
To hear you numbered with the dead.   I can
Demonstrate this: your pardon, but in truth,
The injuries you meant us were severe,
And he with as much violence did urge them
To your destruction; but your piety
Hath charmed my purpose, and I look upon you
With new obedience.

Re-enter FLORIO.

Duke. Impossible!

Sci. We will not shift the scene till you believe it.—
Florio, entreat my Lord Lorenzo hither.—[*Exit* FLO.
Step but behind the arras, and your ear
Shall tell you who's the greatest traitor living.
Observe but when I tell him you are slain,
How he'll rejoice, and call me Florence' great
Preserver, bless my arm, that in your blood
Hath given our groaning state a liberty;
Then trust Sciarrha: but obscure, I hear him.

[*The* DUKE *retires behind the hangings.*

Enter LORENZO.

Lor. Whom talked he to?   [*Aside.*

———
[1] *i.e.* Do not bear him any ill-will; do not injure him.

Sci. 'Tis done—

Lor. What, good Sciarrha !

Sci. The duke is dead.

Lor. We are not left so miserable !
Heav'n is more kind to Florence.

Sci. With this hand
I made a passage for his soul.

Lor. Defend,
Omnipotence ! what ! murdered ? and by noble
Sciarrha ? how my ear abuses me !

Sci. Did not we plot it too ?

Lor. How ! we ? collect,
I fear you are not well : pray tell me why
You talk thus ? where's the duke ? he hath a guard,
An army of Heaven about him ; who in Florence
Dares be so black a devil to attempt
His death ?

Sci. This is fine cunning ; why, that devil is
Lorenzo, if he dare deny it ; we are in private,
You need appear no stranger to that's done
By your direction.

Lor. I in the practice ?
Then let me creep into the earth, and rise
A monster to affright mankind.   Sciarrha,
I must abhor thee for it.—Oh my prince !
My dearest kinsman !—may thy hand rot off !—
Treason, treason !

Sci. Then my sword shall fetch
Another witness in thy heart.

[*As they draw the* DUKE *comes hastily forth, and
    interposes.*

Duke. Hold !

Lor. Tush, let him come,
My royal lord ; nay, let him kill me now :
I've so much joy and peace about me, 'twere
A sin to wish my life beyond this minute.

Duke. Put up, I say.

Sci. My lord, we are both cozened :
That very smile's a traitor.

Duke. Come, be calm :
You are too passionate, Sciarrha, and
Mistook Lorenzo.

Lor. But I hold him noble :
I see he made this trial of my faith,
And I forgive him.

Duke. You shall be friends ; you shall, I say.

Enter hastily COSMO *and* ALONZO.

Cos. The duke—

Alon. Where's the duke ?

Cos. My lord, we are blest to see you safe ; report
Hath frighted all the city with your death :
People forsake their beds, and seeking how
To be informed, increase the wretched tumult.

Alon. There's nothing but confusion ; all men tremble,
As if some general fire invaded Florence.

Sci. Have comfort, sir.

Duke. What's to be done ?

Lor. Depazzi has remembered.—   [*Aside.*
My, lord, there is no safety for the state,
Unless you personally appease them.

Duke. How ?

Lor. I hope they'll tear him ; would he were dead any
            way !   [*Aside.*

Alon. He hath counselled well.

Cos. Your presence only hath the power to charm them.

Duke. I fear their rage : where is our guard ?
Alonzo, haste afore, proclaim our pardon,
And that we live to give the offenders mercy.
Why are we born to greatness, mocked with state,
When every tumult staggers our proud fate ?

Sci. [*Aside to* LOR.]—Our quarrel is deferred, sir.
            [*Exeunt.*

ACT THE FOURTH.

SCENE I.—*A Room in* LORENZO'S *House.*

Enter LORENZO.

LOR. My plots thrive not; my engines
    all deceive me,
    And in the very point of their dis-
    charge
    Recoil with danger to myself: are
    there
    No faithful villains left in nature? all
Turned honest? man nor spirit aid Lorenzo,
Who hath not patience to expect his fate,
But must compel it. How Sciarrha played
The dog-bolt with me! and had not I provided
In wisdom for him, that distress had ruined me.
His frozen sister, Amidea, too,
Hath half converted him; but I must set
New wheels in motion, to make him yet
More hateful, and then cut him from his stalk,
Ripe for my vengeance. I'll not trust the rabble;
Confusion on 'em!—the giddy multitude,
That, but two minutes ere the duke came at them,
Bellowed out "Liberty," shook the city with
Their throats, no sooner saw him, but they melted
With the hot apprehension of a gallows:
And when a pardon was proclaimed (a fine
State-snaffle for such mules), they turned their cry
To acclamations, and deafed Heaven to beg

His long and prosperous reign.   A sudden rot
Consume this base herd ! an the devil want
Any cattle for his own teeth, these are for him.

Enter a Servant.

Serv. Sciarrha, my lord, desires to speak with you.

Lor.   Sciarrha !   come near—[*Whispers him.*]—you
   understand ? admit him.   [*Exit* Serv.

Enter SCIARRHA.

Welcome, my noble lord ;
You were not wont to visit me.

Sci.   Nor mean
Ever to do't again.

Lor.   You bring frowns ;
I can be sullen too : what is your pleasure ?

Sci.   You have abused me.

Lor.   You have injured me.

Sci.   In what ?

Lor.   Betrayed me basely to the duke.

Sci.   You denied then you were a traitor ?

Lor.   Yes,
I was no fool to run my neck upon
The axe, and give you such a cause of triumph.
Were it again in question—

Sci.   You are a villain, sir.
And I
Must have it certified under your own hand,
To show the duke.

Lor.   You shall be humbled to
Confess the contrary, nay, subscribe
That I am honest, and desire my pardon.
Look, I have a sword, and arm, and vigour ;
Dare fight with thee, didst ride upon a whirlwind,
Provoke thee on a rock, in waves, in fire,
And kill thee without scruple ; such a strength
Is innocence.

Sci.   Innocence ! dost not fear a thunderbolt ?

I shall be charitable to the world, an I
Cut thee in pieces; and yet then I fear
Thou wilt come together again: the devil does
Acknowledge thee on earth the greater mischief,
And has a fear, when thou art dead, he shall not
Be safe in hell; thou wilt conspire with some
Of his black fiends, and get his kingdom from him.
Didst not thou rail upon the duke?

Lor. I grant it.

Sci. Call him a tyrant?

Lor. More, I do confess
I did exasperate you to kill or murder him;
Give it what name you please; with joy I brought him,
Under the colour of your guest, to be
The common sacrifice: all this I remember;
But is Heaven's stock of mercy spent already,
That sins, though great and horrid, may not be
Forgiven, to the heart that groans with penitence?
Are the eternal fountains quite sealed up?
I was a villain, traitor, murderer,
In my consenting to his death, but hope
Those stains are now washed off.

Sci. Hast thou repented?

Lor. Trust me, I have.

Sci. The devil is turned religious!
Augment not thy damnation.

Lor. As he was
A lustful duke, a tyrant, I had lost him.
In his return to piety, he commanded
My prayers, and fresh obedience to wait on him;
He's now my prince again.

Sci. This is but cunning
To save your life.

Lor. My life!—Within there! Ha! Welcome.

Enter divers Gentlemen *armed.*

1*st Gent.* My gracious lord.

2nd Gent. Wilt please your honour
Command my service?

3rd Gent. Or me?

4th Gent. Or any?

5th Gent. Our swords and lives are yours.

Sci. Perhaps your lordship hath some business with
These gentlemen, I'll take some other time.

Lor. By no means, good Sciarrha:
You visit seldom; those are daily with me,
Men that expect employment, that wear swords,
And carry spirits, both to be engaged,
If I but name a cause.—Gentlemen draw.

Sci. My providence has betrayed me.   [*Aside.*

Lor. Now, Sciarrha,
You that with single valour dare come home
To affront me thus; know, but too late, thy heart
Is at the mercy of my breath: these swords
Can fetch it when I please; and, to prevent
Your boast of this great daring—I beseech,
As you do love and honour your Lorenzo,
No hand advance a weapon, sheath again,
And leave us; I owe service to your loves,
But must not so dishonour you.

All Gent. We obey.   [*Exeunt.*

Sci. They're gone: this is some nobleness.   [*Aside.*

Lor. You see
I do not fear your sword; alone, I have,
Too much advantage; yet you may imagine
How easily I could correct this rashness:
But in my fear to offend gracious Heaven
With a new crime, having so late obtained
My peace, I give you freedom.

Sci. Do I dream?

Lor. Pray chide me still, I will be patient
To hear my shame.

Sci. Is this to be believed?

Doth not Lorenzo counterfeit this virtue?
He does: it is impossible he should repent.

Lor. Why? tell me, Sciarrha, and let us argue awhile
In cooler blood; did not you once resolve
To kill the duke too?

Sci. I confess—

Lor. To give him death with your own hand?
Methinks it should be the same parricide
In you, if not a greater; yet you changed
Your purposes; why did you not go through,
And murder him?

Sci. He was converted.

Lor. Good!
That taught you mercy, and perhaps repentance
For your intent.

Sci. It did.

Lor. Why should not, sir,
The same conversion of the duke possess
My heart, with as much piety to him,
And sorrow for myself? If I should say
You are but cunning in this shape of honesty,
And still suspect your soul to be a traitor,
Might you not blame my want of charity?

Sci. He says but right, we are both men, frail things.
                                                    [*Aside.*

'Tis not impossible.

Lor. I am reconciled
To Heaven already, and the duke: if you
Be still unsatisfied, I am ready, sir—

Sci. The circumstance considered, I incline
To think this may be honest.

Lor. Come, Sciarrha,
We are both hasty: pardon my rash language
In the beginning, I will study service
Shall make you love me; I have been too wicked,
Too full of passion, inexorable:
My nature is corrected; at this minute

I'm friends with all the world, but in your love
Shall number many blessings.

Sci. I am converted.

Enter PETRUCHIO.

Lor. [*Takes* PET. *aside.*]—What's the news?

Pet. My lord, Depazzi prays some conference
In the next chamber; we arrived by chance
Together at your gate: I do not like
His talk, sir.

Lor. Hang him, property! let him
Expect; thou art come in the opportunity
I could have wished; be wise, and second me.

[*Whispers him.*

Sci. He waits upon Pisano,
Whose health I may enquire; I have not seen him
Since he departed sick; a fit occasion.

Lor. [*Aloud.*] Married to Oriana? thou mistak'st,
'Tis Amidea, Lord Sciarrha's sister.

Pet. That contract's broken, and the old lady Morosa
is violent to have the marriage finished with her daughter.

Lor. [*Coming forward.*]—Sciarrha,
Is't true Pisano marries Oriana,
The rich Morosa's daughter?

Sci. Ha!

Lor. We did expect to hear your sister should
Have been his bride; has he forsaken Amidea?

Sci. Do not you serve Pisano?

Pet. Yes, my lord.

Sci. And dare you talk he's to be married
To Oriana?

Pet. If they live till to-morrow:
There's great provision, to my knowledge, and—

Sci. Take that, and learn to speak a truth hereafter.

[*Strikes him.*

Lor. That blow shall cost his life.—   [*Aside.*
It is not possible he dare affront

You thus; the world takes notice of a contract;
He's much to blame if he should wrong so sweet
A lady as Amidea. Now, by Hymen,
'Tis not so honourable; he need not scorn
Such an alliance.

   Pet. I am not to give
Account for my lord's actions, let him answer
And justify his honour: but, my lord,
Since I am provoked, I must declare he has
Called back his vows to Amidea, given
Her freedom, and does mean to use his own,
And this he dares publish.

   Lor. What! disclaimed
A lady of her birth and glorious merit?

   Sci. Thou art a villain.

   Lor. My lord, he is not worth your anger; he
Declares but what his master hath committed,
'Tis none of his fault.

   Pet. It becomes my duty
To take correction, my lord, from you;
I am a servant, a poor gentleman.

   Sci. Shall I
Suspect the circumstance at his departure?   [*Aside.*

   Lor. It is strange you knew not this before.

   Sci. I must examine if he dares—

   Lor. Be patient.

   Sci. Teach fools and children patience.
May dogs eat up Sciarrha: let me live
The prodigy of sorrow; die a death
That may draw tears from Scythians, if Pisano
Lead o'er his threshold any soon-won dame,
To be my sister's shame! I am calm now.
One thus false, Heaven, why should thy altars save?
'Tis just that Hymen light him to his grave.   [*Exit.*

   Lor. A thousand Furies swell his rage! although
Pisano bleed, this is the safest killing;
Wise men secure their fates, and execute

Invisibly, like that most subtle flame
That burns the heart, yet leaves no part or touch
Upon the skin to follow or suspect it.—
Farewell, dull, passionate fool! how this doth feed me;
Kill, and be lost thyself; or, if his sword
Conclude thy life, both ways I am revenged.
Petruchio, thou didst hit my instructions rarely,
And I applaud thee: now send in Depazzi,
And visit me anon.

 Pet. I shall, my lord.   [*Exit.*

 Lor. Some politician,
That is not wise but by a precedent,
Would think me weak for using such an instrument
As this Depazzi; but I know by proof,
Such men whom fear and honour make our creatures,
Do prove safe engines; fools will still obey,
When cunning knaves our confidence betray.

Enter DEPAZZI.

 Dep. My lord, I would speak a word or two in private.

 Lor. You may.

 Dep. Is no body within hearing? all clear behind the arras?

 Lor. Make do doubt, sir.

 Dep. My lord, the truth is—I am very fearful—is your lordship sure there are no eaves-droppers?

 Lor. What needs this circumstance? I pray come to the point.

 Dep. 'Tis not unknown to your lordship, that you have been my very good lord,[1] neither am I ignorant, that I am your humble servant; you advanced me, brought me into the number of the nobles, and I brought you a reasonable number of crowns: I am not the first wise citizen that hath been converted into a foolish courtier; but, my lord, I beseech you pardon me:—it will out.

---

[1] *i.e.* My patron.

Lor. What's the matter?

Dep. I am ready to burst.

Lor. With what?

Dep. Treason, treason;—now 'tis out, and I feel my body the lighter for it already. The last plot did not take, you see; and I would humbly entreat your lordship to excuse me, and get somebody else hereafter to be your traitor, in my stead.

Lor. How, sir?

Dep. If you did but know the tenderness of my constitution, or feel the pangs and convulsions that I suffer, you would pity me: I fall away, you see, I cannot sleep for dreaming of an axe; I have caused my hangings of Holofernes to be taken down in my drawing-room, because I dare not look upon a head that is cut off in it, something of my complection: my wisdom tells me I am a fool to be so fearful; but my conscience tells me I am a greater fool if I have not wit enough in my pate to keep my head on my shoulders. I beseech your lordship take me into your consideration; I am but a mortal, though I be a lord; every man hath not the like gift of impudence; I have a weak stomach, and treason is physic to me, and although I do not vomit up your secrets, they may out some other way.

Lor. You will not betray me?

Dep. But alas! in such a case I may soon bewray myself, and then your lordship may be smelt out: to prevent, therefore, some mischief that may happen, I desire to leave off while I am well, and that your lordship may know I mean plainly, I have brought you all your letters; I durst not trust any other place with them, for fear of state rats; I have unript my bosom to you, and there they are to a title—now, I may safely swear I have no hand with your lordship.

Lor. This is very strange.

Dep. Mistake not, my good lord, I am still your creature, but I have a great mind to be honest a little,

Shir.   L while among the weaker sort of nobility: yet thus much persuade yourself, I will never wrong your lordship in a syllable; should you tell me of a thousand treasons and stratagems, I will never reveal any; I scorn that: but your lordship must pardon me, I will be a traitor no longer, that's certain, I will be honest, and the rather because no body shall hit me in the teeth after I am dead, and say, "Look where Depazzi carries his head very high!"—And, my lord, the more to induce your lordship to dismiss me—Rogero!

Enter ROGERO.

Rog. My lord.

Dep. Give me the gold.—I have brought fifteen hundred crowns more.

Lor. Wherefore?

Dep. That I may have your lordship's good will, to leave my office before it be taken from me, and preferred to a worse; 'tis half the price I paid for't. I love peace, and a little honesty; I know your honour will find an abler man for it, and it is fit I should pay for my *quietus*.

Lor. And what do you resolve?

Dep. To return to the dunghill, from whence I came; for though I was born in the city, I have some land in the country, dirty acres, and mansion-house, where I will be the miracle of a courtier, and keep good hospitality, love my neighbours, and their wives, and consequently get their children; be admired amongst the justices, sleep upon every bench, keep a chaplain in my own house to be my idolater, and furnish me with jests; and when I have nothing else to do, I will think of the court, and how much I have been obliged to your lordship. My lord, I may do you service with a leading voice in the country; the kennel will cry on my side if it come to election: you or your friend shall carry it against the commonwealth.

Lor. Well, sir, since you have expressed yourself so freely, I will not counsel you against your disposition to stay at court ; you may go when and whither you please ; and though at parting I have nothing worth your acceptation, I will bestow these crowns upon your servant.

[*Gives* ROGERO *the money.*

Dep. Thou shalt give them me again.

Rog. Indeed, my lord, I love a little honesty, 'tis his lordship's bounty, it will be a stock to set me up for myself at court, when your lordship is retired into the country.—I humbly thank your lordship, and take my leave of yours. [*Exit with the money.*

Enter a Servant.

Serv. The duke, my lord. [*Exit* Servant.
Dep. How ! the duke ?

Enter the DUKE.

Duke. Signior Depazzi.

Lor. He has been earnest with me, an't please your highness,
To be his humble suitor, he may have
Freedom to leave the court.

Duke. He shall be banished.

Dep. How ?

Lor. What time will your grace allow him to provide ?

Duke. Two hours.

Dep. I had rather lose my head at home, and save charges of travel, I beseech your grace.

Duke. Well, 'tis granted ; let him not trouble us.

Lor. Enjoy the country, and return when the duke sends for you.

Dep. I humbly thank his highness, and will pray for your increase of grace. [*Exit.*

Duke. Lorenzo, are we private ?

Lor. Yes, my lord.

Duke. I am very melancholy.

Lor. I know the cause, 'tis Amidea.

Duke. Right.

Lor. I do wish her dead.

Duke. It were a sin.

Lor. Not in Heaven, sir; yet there be ladies, that
would think it a promotion.

Duke. It were a pity she should leave the world,
Till she hath taught the rest by her example
The nearest way.

Lor. I am very confident she's yet honest.[1]

Duke, Yet, Lorenzo?

Lor. Ay, sir, but I'm not of opinion
It is impossible to know a change.

Duke. Take heed.

Lor. I must confess she has been very valiant,
In making you remove your siege, and showed a
Pretty dexterity at the poniard;
Let herself blood;—but this a mortal virgin
Might do, and not be adored for't : other women
Have gone as far, or else false legends have
Been thrust upon the easy world; some say
There have been creatures that have killed themselves,
To save their sullen chastities; but I
Have no strong faith that way; yet you were startled
To see her strike her arm, and grew compassionate.

Duke. I was not marble; we break adamant
With blood,[2] and could I be a man, and not
Be moved to see that hasty ebb of life
For my sake?

Lor. I have read some aged stories :
What think you of Lucrece? she is remembered.

Duke. Chastity's great example.

Lor. How the world
Was cozened in her? she knew of Tarquin first,
And then suspecting she should never meet
Again the active gentleman, and having
Determined of his death, with well dissembled

---

[1] Chaste.
[2] This is a very ancient notion; it is mentioned by Greene and
Lyly, and many more of our old writers, who had it from Pliny,
Solinus, &c.—*Gifford.*

Sorrow did stab herself, in hope to meet
The gamester in Elysium.   Amidea
You will allow beneath this Roman dame?

   Duke. Lorenzo, had the burning ravisher
Made this attempt on Amidea, she
Would have compelled his penitence, to quench
His fire with holy tears.   I had a body
Refined to air, or I was borne up by
A thousand wings: methought I could have flown
And kissed the cheek of Cynthia, thence with ease
Have leaped to Venus' star, but I was wounded,
And the gay feathers, in whose pride I had
My confidence, served now but with their weight
To hasten me to earth.

   Lor. Ascend again,
And fix in your loved orb; he brings this comfort
That can assure it, if you have not lost
A heart to entertain with love and pleasure
The beauteous Amidea.

   Duke. Ha!

   Lor. You shall enjoy her.

   Duke. Enjoy fair Amidea? do not tempt
Or rather mock my frailty with such promise.

   Lor. Shake off your melancholy slumber, I
Have here decreed you shall possess her: she
Be sent submissive to your arms, and you
Be gracious to accept what she made coy of.

   Duke. Is this in nature?

   Lor. Thus: Sciarrha's life
And fortunes are already growing forfeit,
These brains have plotted so: your mercy shall
Purchase what you can wish for, in his sister;
And he acknowledge rifling of her honour
A fair and cheap redemption.

   Duke. Do this;
And I'll repent the folly of my penitence,
And take thee to my soul, a nearer pledge,

Than blood or nature gave me : I'm renewed,
I feel my natural warmth return. When, where
Is this to be expected? I grow old,
While our embraces are deferred.

Lor. I go
To hasten your delight; prepare your blood
For amorous game : Sciarrha's fate is cast
Firmer than destiny.

Duke. Thou art my prophet,
I'll raise thee up an altar.

Lor. Trust these brains.

Duke. Thou makest my spirit caper in my veins.

[*Exeunt.*

SCENE II.—*A Street.*

COSMO *and* TWO GENTLEMEN *appear at an Upper
Window.*

1st Gent. This way they pass.

Cos. I would not see them.

2nd Gent. Why?

1st Gent. What! melancholy o' the sudden? it is now
Past cure.

Cos. I know it is, and therefore do not
Desire to witness their solemnity.
Should Oriana see me to-day—

2nd Gent. What then?

Cos. The object,
I fear, would be too prodigious.

2nd Gent. We dispute not
Those nice formalities.

Enter ALONZO, PISANO, ORIANA, *and* MOROSA

1st Gent. She has spied you already.

Cos. I am sorry for't.

[ORIANA *faints.* COSMO *and* Gentlemen *retire.*

Mor. How is't, my child?

Pis. My dearest Oriana;—

She faints! what grief is so unmannerly
To interrupt thee now? Oriana!

Mor. Daughter!

Pis. Will Heaven divorce us ere the priest have made
Our marriage perfect? we in vain hereafter
Shall hear him teach, that our religion binds
To have the church's ceremony. She returns.

Ori. Why were you so unkind to call me from
A pleasing slumber? Death has a fine dwelling.

Alon. This shows her heart's not yet consenting; 'tis
Her mother's fierce command.

Ori. Something spake to me from that window.

Pis. There is nothing.

Ori. Nothing now.

Pis. Set forward.

Alon. I do not like this interruption; it
Is ominous.

Enter AMIDEA *hastily.*

Ami. Not for my sake, but for your own, go back,
Or take some other way, this leads to death;
My brother—

Pis. What of him;

Ami. Transported with
The fury of revenge for my dishonour,
As he conceives, for 'tis against my will,
Hath vowed to kill you in your nuptial glory.
Alas! I fear his haste; now, good my lord,
Have mercy on yourself; I do not beg
Your pity upon me, I know too well
You cannot love me now, nor would I rob
This virgin of your faith, since you have pleased
To throw me from your love: I do not ask
One smile, nor one poor kiss; enrich this maid,
Created for those blessings; but again

I would beseech you, cherish your own life,
Though I be lost for ever.

Alon. It is worth
Your care, my lord, if there be any danger.

Pis. Alas! her grief hath made her wild, poor lady
I should not love Oriana to go back;
Set forward.—Amidea, you may live
To be a happier bride: Sciarrha is not
So irreligious to profane these rites.

Ami. Will you not then believe me?—Pray persuade
     him,
You are his friends.—Lady, it will concern
You most of all, indeed; I fear you'll weep
To see him dead, as well as I.

Pis. No more;
Go forward.

Ami. I have done; pray be not angry,
That still I wish you well: may Heaven divert
All harms that threaten you; full blessings crown
Your marriage! I hope there is no sin in this;
Indeed, I cannot choose but pray for you.
This might have been my wedding-day—

Ori. Good Heaven,
I would it were! my heart can tell, I take
No joy in being his bride, none in your prayers;
You shall have my consent to have him still ·
I will resign my place, and wait on you,
If you will marry him.

Ami. Pray do not mock me,
But if you do, I can forgive you too.

Ori. Dear Amidea, do not think I mock
Your sorrow; by these tears, that are not worn
By every virgin on her wedding-day,
I am compelled to give away myself:
Your hearts were promised, but he ne'er had mine.
Am not I wretched too.

Ami. Alas, poor maid!

We two keep sorrow alive then; but I prithee,
When thou art married, love him, prithee love him,
For he esteems thee well; and once a day
Give him a kiss for me; but do not tell him,
'Twas my desire: perhaps 'twill fetch a sigh
From him, and I had rather break my heart.
But one word more, and Heaven be with you all.—
Since you have led the way, I hope, my lord,
That I am free to marry too?

   Pis. Thou art.

   Ami. Let me beseech you then, to be so kind,
After your own solemnities are done,
To grace my wedding; I shall be married shortly.

   Pis. To whom?

   Ami. To one whom you have all heard talk of,
Your fathers knew him well: one, who will never
Give cause I should suspect him to forsake me;
A constant lover, one whose lips, though cold,
Distil chaste kisses: though our bridal bed
Be not adorned with roses, 'twill be green;
We shall have virgin laurel, cypress, yew,
To make us garlands; though no pine do burn,
Our nuptial shall have torches, and our chamber
Shall be cut out of marble, where we'll sleep,
Free from all care for ever: Death, my lord,
I hope, shall be my husband.   Now, farewell;
Although no kiss, accept my parting tear,
And give me leave to wear my willow here.   [*Exit.*

   Enter SCIARRHA; *followed at a distance by* LORENZO,
              with a Guard.

   Alon. Sciarrha! then I prophesy—

   Sci. Pisano! where's Pisano?

   Pis. Here, Sciarrha.
I should have answered with less clamou..

   Sci. But
I would not lose my voice; I must be heard,

And it does concern you.   I profess no augury,
I have not quartered out the heavens, to take
The flight of birds, nor by inspection
Of entrails made a divination;
But I must tell you, 'tis not safe to marry.

 Pis. Why?

 Sci. 'Twill be fatal; Hymen is gone abroad,
And Venus, lady of your nativity,
Is found, by wise astrologers, this day,
I' the House of Death.

 Pis. This must not fright me, sir.—Set forward.

 Sci. One cold word,—you are a villain!
I do not flatter.

 Pis. I am patient:
This day I consecrate to love, not anger;
We'll meet some other time.

 Sci. Deride my fury?
Then to thy heart I send my own revenge, [*Stabs him.*
And Amidea's.

 Pis. I am murdered.

 Mor. Help! murder! gentlemen! oh, my unhappiness!
      [LORENZO *and* Guard *come forward.*

 Pis. Bloody Sciarrha!
    [*Dies.   They offer to seize* SCIARRHA.

 Lor. Hold!

 Sci. Come all at once;
Yet let me tell you, my revenge is perfect,
And I would spare your blood, if you despise not
My charity—

 Lor. No man attempt his death;
I'll give you reasons: this fell deed deserves
An exemplary justice.

 Sci. I am above
Your politic reach, and glory in the wound
That punished our dishonour.   Is he dead?
I would not be so miserable, not to have sped him,
For the empire.

Enter COSMO.

Cos. Oh, my friend! poor Oriana!

Lor. [*To the* Guard.]—Disarm him:
Return and comfort one another; some
Remove Pisano's body, while I make it
My care Sciarrha 'scape not.

         [*Exeunt, bearing the body of* PISANO, *all but*
              LORENZO, SCIARRHA, *and* Guard.

Sci. None of all
Give me a scratch?

Lor. [*To the* Guard.]—You have forced him with dis-
Sci. Now what must I expect?   [cretion.

Lor. You are my prisoner.

Sci. I am so.

Lor. And be confident to find
That favour.—

Sci. Favour!

Lor. Be at distance more.—   [*The* Guard *retire.*
My lord, I am sorry for your great misfortune,
And if you can but study how I may
Assist you, you shall soon discern my love,
My readiness to serve you.

Sci. Ha! this honest?

Lor. I would deserve your faith,
A friend but in affliction justifies
His heart and honour, I durst run some hazard,
Might I secure your fate; name something to me
That may declare my friendship.

Sci. Be still safe,
And teach the world repentance for mistaking thee;
I pity not myself, but envy thy
Heroic honours.

Lor. I will impose no more
Restraint, than your own house; you're honourable:
You have many severe enemies; the duke
Looked graciously upon Pisano, but—

Sci. You shall not lose the smallest beam of favour,
To buy a man so desperate.   I never
Thought death the monster that weak men have fancied,
As foil to make us more in love with life.
The devil's picture may affright poor souls
Into their bodies' paleness, but the substance
To resolute man's a shadow ; and cold sweat
Dare not approach his forehead.   I am armed
To die, and give example of that fortitude
Shall shame the law's severity : my sister
May now give back Pisano his false vows,
To line his coffin : one tear shed on me is
Enough, the justice I have done shall make
My memory beloved.

 Lor. I have thought a way
To recover you, if you incline to it ;
Dare you consent ?

 Sci. To any thing that's noble ;
Although I never feared to suffer, I
Am not so foolish to despise a life.

 Lor. There is no difficulty attends it ; listen,
The time will not permit much circumstance :
The duke, you know, did love your sister.

 Sci. Viciously.

 Lor. Her virtue did but cool him for the present,
As sprinklings on a flame ; he's now more passionate
To enjoy her.

 Sci. Ha !

 Lor. If she consent to meet
His soft embrace, with his first kiss he seals
Your pardon ; then the act upon Pisano
Appears a true revenge, when none dares question it.
Beside addition of state and fortune,
To you and Amidea, weigh your danger,
And what a trifle she gives up, to save
Your life, that never can be valued,
Less recompensed ; the duke may be so taken

With her return to his delight, who knows
But he may marry her, and discharge his duchess
With a quaint salad—[1] You do apprehend me?

　Sci. And repent more I had one good thought of thee,
Than I had killed a thousand :—save my life,
And prostitute my sister !　Though I have
No weapon, I will look thee dead, or breathe
A damp shall stifle thee : that I could vomit
Consuming flames, or stones, like Etna ! make
The earth with motion of my feet shrink lower,
And take thee in alive ! oh that my voice
Could call a serpent from corrupted Nile,
To make thee part of her accursed bowels !
Is this your noble friendship? readiness
To save my life? let malice read all stories
Famous for cruelty, awake dead tyrants,
Or be instructed by their ghosts with tortures,
Such as will make a damned Fury weep
Only to see inflicted, I would bear them,
And weary my tormenters, ere consent
In thought to thy temptation.

　Lor. I have done,
And praise your heathen resolution
Of death ; go practise immortality,
And tell us, when you can get leave to visit
This world again, what fine things you enjoy
In hell, for thither these rash passions drive thee :
And ere thy body hath three days inhabited
A melancholy chamber in the earth,
Hung round about with skulls and dead men's bones,
Ere Amidea have told all her tears
Upon thy marble, or the epitaph
Bely thy soul, by saying it is fled
To Heaven, this sister shall be ravished,
Maugre thy dust and heraldry.

　Sci. Ha ! ravished

---

[1] A salad dressed with poisonous oils.

When I am dead ? Was't not so ? oh my soul!
I feel it weep within me, and the tears
Soften my flesh : Lorenzo, I repent
My fury.

Lor. I advised you the best way
My wisdom could direct.

Sci. I thank you for't,
You have awaked my reason, I am ashamed
I was no sooner sensible ; does the duke
Affect my sister still, say you ?

Lor. Most passionately.

Sci. She shall obey him then, upon my life ;
That's it, my life. I know she loves me dearly.
I shall have much ado to win her to't,
But she shall come ; I'll send her.

Lor. Perform this.

Sci. I will not only send her, but prepared
Not to be disobedient to his highness ;
He shall command her any thing.

Lor. Do this,
And be for ever happy. When these have
Only for form waited on you home,
This disengages them.

Sci. My humblest service
To the duke I pray, and tell him, Amidea
This night shall be at his dispose, by this.[1]

Lor. I'm confident ; farewell!—Attend Sciarrha.

[*Exit.*

Sci. Pity the seaman, that to avoid a shelf,
Must strike upon a rock to save himself.

[*Exit, with* Guard.

[1] That is, as I conceive, by some token, probably a ring, or
signet, which he puts into Lorenzo's hand.—*Gifford.*

ACT THE FIFTH.

SCENE I.—*A Room in* SCIARRHA'S *House.*

Enter SCIARRHA *and* AMIDEA.

CI. The doors are fast;
Enough is wept already for Pisano:
There's something else that must be
thought on, and
Of greater consequence: I am yet
unsafe,
That, for thy sake, am guilty of his blood.

Ami. Though all my stock of tears were spent already
Upon Pisano's loss, and that my brain
Were banquèrupt of moisture, and denied
To lend my grief one drop more for his funeral
Yet the remembrance that you have made
A forfeit for my sake of your dear life
Is able to create a weeping spring
Within my barren head : oh, my lost broth
Thou hast a cruel destiny! my eyes,
In pity of thy fate, desire to drown thee.
The law will only seek thee upon land;
Hid in my tears, thou shalt prevent the stroke
Kills both our name and thee.

Sci. I know thou lov'st me,
Poor girl. I shall desire to cherish life,
If thou lament me thus: so rich a comfort

Will tempt me wish I might delay my journey
To Heaven.

Ami. Good Heaven, that we might go together!

Sci. That must not be.

Ami. Then let me go before.

Sci. How?

Ami. Make my suit unto the prince, my blood
May be your ransom; let me die, Sciarrha,
My life is fruitless unto all the world;
The duke in justice will not deny this:
And though I weep in telling thee, I shall
Smile on the scaffold.

Sci. How my honour blushes
To hear thee, Amidea! in this love
Thou wound'st me more, than thou desir'st to save.
Suffer for me? why, thou art innocent:
I have provoked the punishment, and dare
Obey it manly; if thou could'st redeem me
With anything but death, I think I should
Consent to live, but I'd not have thee venture
All at one chance.

Ami. Nothing can be too precious
To save a brother, such a loving brother
As you have been.

Sci. Death's a devouring gamester,
And sweeps up all: what think'st thou of an eye?
Couldst thou spare one, and think the blemish recom-
pensed,
To see me safe with t'other? Or a hand?
This white hand, Amidea, that hath so often,
With admiration, trembled on the lute,
Till we have prayed thee leave the strings awhile,
And laid our ears close to thy ivory fingers,
Suspecting all the harmony proceeded
From their own motion, without the need
Of any dull or passive instrument.
No, Amidea, thou shalt not bear one scar

To buy my life; the sickle shall not touch
A flower that grows so fair upon his stalk;
Thy t'other hand will miss a white companion,
And wither on thy arm: what then can I
Expect from thee to save me? I would live,
And owe my life to thee, so 'twere not bought
Too dear.

    Ami. Do you believe I should not find
The way to Heaven? were both mine eyes thy ransom,
I shall climb up those high and rugged cliffs
Without a hand.

    Sci. One way there is, if thou
Dost love me with that tenderness.

    Ami. Pronounce it,
And let no danger that attends, incline you
To make a pause.

    Sci. The duke, thou know'st, did love thee.

    Ami. Ha!

    Sci. Nay, do not start already, nor mistake me;
I do not, as before, make trial of thee,
Whether thou canst, laying aside thy honour,
Meet his lascivious arms; but, by this virtue,
I must beseech thee to forego it all,
And turn a sinful woman.

    Ami. Bless me!

    Sci. I know the kingdoms of the world contain not
Riches enough to tempt thee to a fall
That will so much undo thee; but I am
Thy brother, dying brother; if thou lov'st
Him, therefore, that for thee hath done so much;
Dyed his pale hands in blood, to revenge thee,
And in that murder wounded his own soul
Almost to death, consent to lose thy innocence;
I know it makes thee grieve, but I shall live
To love thee better for it: we'll repent
Together for our sins, and pray and weep
Till Heaven hath pardoned all.

    Shir.

Ami. Oh, never, never.

Sci. Do but repeat thy words, to " save my life,"
And that will teach compassion, my life ;
Our shame, the stain of all our family,
Which will succeed in my ignoble death,
Thou washest off.

Ami. But stain myself for ever.

Sci. Where ? In thy face, who shall behold one
   blemish,
Or one spot more in thy whole frame ? thy beauty
Will be the very same, thy speech, thy person
Wear no deformity.

Ami. Oh, do not speak
So like a rebel to all modesty,
To all religion ; if these arguments
Spring from your jealousy that I am fallen,
After a proof you did so late applaud—

Sci. I had not killed Pisano then ; I am now
More spotted than the marble : then my head
Did own no forfeiture to law,
It does ache now ; then I but tried thy virtue,
Now my condition calls for mercy to thee,
Though to thyself thou appear cruel for't :
Come, we may live both, if you please.

Ami. I must never
Buy my poor breath at such a rate. Who has
Made you afraid to die ? I pity you,
And wish myself in any noble cause
Your leader. When our souls shall leave this dwelling,
The glory of one fair and virtuous action
Is above all the 'scutcheons on our tomb,
Or silken banners over us.

Sci. So valiant !
I will not interpose another syllable
To entreat your pity ; say your prayers, and then
Thou'rt ripe to be translated from the earth,
To make a cherubin.

Ami. What means my brother?

Sci. To kill you.

Ami. Do not fright me, good Sciarrha.

Sci. And I allow three minutes for devotion.

Ami. Will you murder me?

Sci. Do you tremble?

Ami. Not at the terror of your sword,
But at the horror will affright thy soul,
For this black deed. I see Pisano's blood
Is texted in thy forehead, and thy hands
Retain too many crimson spots already;
Make not thyself, by murthering of thy sister,
All a red letter.

Sci. You shall be the martyr.[1]

Ami. Yet stay; is there no remedy but death,
And from your hand? then keep your word, and let me
Use one short prayer.   [*Kneels.*

Sci. I shall relent.   [*Aside.*

Ami. Forgive me, Heaven, and witness I have still
My virgin thoughts; 'tis not to save my life,
But his eternal one.——
Sciarrha, give me leave to veil my face,   [*Rises.*
I dare not look upon you, and pronounce
I am too much a sister; live; hereafter,
I know, you will condemn my frailty for it.
I will obey the duke.

Sci. Darest thou consent?   [*Stabs her.*

Ami. [*Unveiling.*]—Oh, let me see the wound;
'Tis well, if any other hand had done it:
Some angel tell my brother now, I did
But seem consenting.

Sci. Ha! "but seem"?

Ami. You may believe my last breath.

Sci. Why didst say so?

---

[1] The allusions here are to the custom, still observed, of printing the names of the martyrs in the Roman Calendar in red letters.— *Gifford.*

Ami. To gain some time, in hope you might call in
Your bloody purpose, and prevent the guilt
Of being my murderer ; but Heaven forgive thee.

Sci. Again, again forgive me, Amidea,
And pray for me ; live but a little longer,
To hear me speak ; my passion hath betrayed
Thee to this wound, for which I know not whether
I should rejoice, or weep, since thou art virtuous.
The duke, whose soul is black again, expects thee
To be his whore :—Good Death, be not so hasty.—
The agent for his lust, Lorenzo, has
My oath to send thee to his bed : for otherwise,
In my denial, hell and they decree,
When I am dead, to ravish thee—mark that,
To ravish thee !—and I confess, in tears
As full of sorrow, as thy soul of innocence,
In my religious care to have thee spotless,
I did resolve, when I had found thee ripe,
And nearest Heaven, with all thy best desires,
To send thee to thy peace : thy feigned consent
Hath brought thy happiness more early to thee,
And saved some guilt ; forgive me altogether.

Ami. With the same heart I beg Heaven for myself ;
Farewell.   [*Swoons.*

Sci. Thou shalt not die yet. Amidea ! sister !—
                                [*Knocking within.*
I cannot come :—
But one word more : Oh, which way went thy soul ?
Or is it gone so far it cannot hear me ?—

FLORIO *breaks open the door and enters.*

Look, here's our sister ! so, so ; chafe her :
She may return ; there is some motion.

Flo. Sister !

Sci. Speak aloud, Florio ; if her spirit be not
Departed, I will seal this passage up ;

I feel her breath again.—Here's Florio, would
Fain take his leave.—So, so, she comes!

Flo. Amidea,
How came this wound?

Ami. I drew the weapon to it:
Heaven knows, my brother loved me: now, I hope,
The duke will not pursue me with new flames.
Sciarrha, tell the rest: love one another
The time you live together; I'll pray for you
In Heaven: farewell! kiss me when I am dead,
You else will stay my journey. [*Dies.*

Sci. Didst not hear
An angel call her? Florio, I have much
To tell thee: take her up; stay, I will talk
A little more with her; she is not dead,
Let her alone;—nay then, she's gone indeed.
But hereabouts her soul must hover stil'
Let's speak to that: fair spirit—

Flo. You talk idly.

Sci. Do you talk wisely then? An excellent pattern,
As she now stands, for her own alabaster;
Or may she not be kept from putrefaction,
And be the very figure on her tomb?
Cannot thy tears and mine preserve her, Florio?
If we want brine, a thousand virgins shall
Weep every day upon her, and themselves,
In winter, leaning round about her monument,
Being moist creatures, stiffen with the cold,
And freeze into so many white supporters.
But we lose time.—I charge thee, by thy love
To this pale relic, be instructed by me,
Not to thy danger; some revenge must be,
And I am lost already; if thou fall,
Who shall survive, to give us funeral? [*Exeunt.*

SCENE II.—*A Room in* Lorenzo's *House.*

Enter Lorenzo *and* Petruchio.

Lor. Petruchio.

Pet. My lord.

Lor. Thou art now my servant.

Pet. I ever was in heart your humblest vassal.

Lor. Thou art faithful ; I must cherish thy desert ;
I shortly shall reward it, very shortly :
Next morning must salute me duke · the sun
And I must rise together.

Pet.   I shall pray
Your glory may outshine him in your Florence,
And when he sets, we may enjoy your sunbeam.

Lor. 'Tis handsome flattery, and becomes a courtier,

Pet. I flatter not, my lord.

Lor. Then, thou'rt a fool :
No music to a great man chimes so sweetly,
And men must thrive ; come hither,
How many hast thou killed ?

Pet. But one, my lord.

Lor. But one !

Pet.   And I must owe
My life to your lordship, I had been hanged else.

Lor. But one ? wait at the door ;   [*Exit* Petruchio.
    He is
Not fit to kill a duke, whose hand is guilty
But of a single murder ; or at least
Not fit alone to act it : I have been
Practised already, and though no man see it,
Nor scarce the eye of Heaven, yet every day
I kill a prince.—Appear, thou tragic witness,
    [*Brings forth the duke's picture, a poniard sticking in it.*
Which, though it bleed not, I may boast a murder.
Here first the duke was painted to the life,
But with this pencil, to the death : I love
My brain for the invention, and thus

Confirmed, dare trust my resolution.
I did suspect his youth and beauty might
Win some compassion when I came to kill him;
Or the remembrance that he is my kinsman,
Might thrill my blood; or something in his title
Might give my hand repulse, and startle nature:
But thus I have armed myself against all pity,
That when I come to strike, my poniard may
Through all his charms as confidently wound him,
As thus I stab his picture, and stare on it.

　　　　　　　　　　　　　[Stabs the picture.

Methinks the duke should feel me now: is not
His soul acquainted? can he less than tremble,
When I lift up my arm to wound his counterfeit?
Witches can persecute the lives of whom
They hate, when they torment their senseless figures,
And stick the waxen model full of pins.
Can any stroke of mine carry less spell
To wound his heart, sent with as great a malice?
He smiles, he smiles upon me! I will dig
Thy wanton eyes out, and supply the dark
And hollow cells with two pitch-burning tapers;
Then place thee porter in some charnel-house,
To light the coffins in.——

Re-enter PETRUCHIO.

Pet. My lord.

Lor. The duke's not come already?

Pet. Signior Florio
Desires to speak with you.

Lor. This must retire
Again into my closet.　　　　*[Puts back the picture.*
　　Admit him.

Enter FLORIO.

Welcome! how does Sciarrha?

Flo. He commends
His service to your lordship, and hath sent——

Lor. His sister?

Flo. Much ado he had to affect it:
He hopes his grace will quickly sign his pardon.

Lor. It shall be done.

Flo. I have a suit, my lord.

Lor. To me?

Flo. My sister would intreat your honour,
She may be admitted privately, and that
I may have privilege to prepare her chamber:
She does retain some modesty, and would not
Trust every servant with her shame; their eyes
Are apt to instruct their tongues.

Lor. I will not see her myself.
Command what you desire.

Flo. You are gracious.

Lor. I'll give directions instantly: poor lady,
This is the duke's hot blood; but Heaven convert him!
Follow me, good Florio.

Flo. I attend, my lord.

Lor. Things shall be carried honourably.

Flo. We are all bound to you.   [*Exeunt.*

SCENE III.—*Another Room in the same.*

Recorders[1] sound. The body of AMIDEA *discovered on a
bed, prepared by two* Gentlewomen.

1st Gent. This is a sad employment.

2nd Gent. The last we c'er shall do my lady.

Enter FLORIO.

Flo. So; now you may return: it will become
Your modest duties not to enquire the reason
Of this strange service, nor to publish what
You have been commanded.—[*Exeunt* Gentlewomen.]—

---

[1] Flageolets.

Let me look upon
My sister now ; still she retains her beauty,
Death has been kind to leave her all this sweetness.
Thus in a morning have I oft saluted
My sister in her chamber, sat upon
Her bed, and talked of many harmless passages;
But now 'tis night, and a long night with her,
I ne'er shall see these curtains drawn again,
Until we meet in Heaven.—The duke already !

Enter DUKE *and* LORENZO.

Duke. May I believe ?
Lor. Trust me, my lord, hereafter.
Duke. Call me no more thy lord, but thy companion ;
I will not wear that honour in my title,
Shall not be thine.—Who's that ?
Lor. Her brother Florio.
Duke. She is abed.
Lor. The readier for your pastime.
She means to make a night on't.
Flo. This shall declare thee to posterity
The best of sisters.—What of that ? and is not
A brother's life more precious than a trifle ?
I prithee do not sigh : how many ladies
Would be ambitious of thy place to-night,
And thank his highness ? yes, and virgins too.
Duke. He pleads for me.
Lor. He will deserve some office 'bout your person.
Duke. With what words
Shall I express my joy ?
Lor. I leave you, sir, to action ; Florio
Is soon dismissed.　　　　　　　　　　　　[*Exit.*
Flo. He's come : good night—
Duke. Florio !
Flo. [*Coming forward.*]—Your slave.
Duke. My friend !
Thou shalt be near our bosom.

Flo. Pleasures crown

Your expectation!   [*Exit.*

Duke. All perfect; till this minute, I could never

Boast I was happy: all this world has not

A blessing to exchange: this world! 'tis Heaven;

And thus I take possession of my saint:

                                [*Goes up to the bed.*

Asleep already? 'twere great pity to

Disturb her dream, yet if her soul be not

Tired with the body's weight, it must convey

Into her slumbers I wait here, and thus

Seal my devotion. [*Kisses the corpse.*]—What winter dwells

Upon this lip! 'twas no warm kiss; I'll try

Again—[*Kisses it again.*]—the snow is not so cold; I have

Drunk ice, and feel a numbness spread through all

My blood at once.—Ha! let me examine

A little better; Amidea! she is dead, she is dead!

What horror doth invade me?—Help, Lorenzo!

Murder! where is Lorenzo?

Re-enter LORENZO *with* PETRUCHIO.

Lor. Here, my lord.

Duke. Some traitor's hid within the chamber; see,

My Amidea's dead!

Lor. Dead! 'tis impossible,   [*Goes up to the bed.*

Yet, she has a wound upon her breast.

Duke. I prithee kill me:—   [*They stab him.*

Ha! wilt thou murder me, Lorenzo?—Villain!—

                                [*To* PETRUCHIO.

Oh, spare me to consider; I would live

A little longer: treason!

Lor. A little longer, say you?

It was my duty to obey you, sir.

Pet. Let's make him sure, my lord.

Lor. What would you say?—No ears but ours

Can reach his voice;—but be not tedious.

Duke. Oh, spare me; I may live, and pardon thee:

Thy prince begs mercy from thee, that did never
Deny thee any thing ; pity my poor soul ;
I have not prayed.

    Lor. I could have wished you better
Prepared, but let your soul e'en take his chance.

                                         [*Stabs him again.*

    Duke. No tears prevail ! oh, whither must I wander ?
Thus Cæsar fell by Brutus.   I shall tell
News to the world I go to, will not be
Believed, Lorenzo killed me.

    Lor. Will it not ?
I'll presently put in security.   [*Stabs him again.*

    Duke. I am coming, Amidea, I am coming.—
For thee, inhuman murderer, expect
My blood shall fly to Heaven, and there inflamed,
Hang a prodigious meteor all thy life,
And when by some as bloody hand as thine
Thy soul is ebbing forth, it shall descend
In flaming drops upon thee : oh, I faint !—
Thou flattering world, farewell ! let princes gather
My dust into a glass, and learn to spend
Their hour of state, that's all they have ; for when
That's out, Time never turns the glass agen.   [*Dies.*

    Lor. So !
Lay him beside his mistress; hide their faces.
The duke dismissed the train came with him ?

    Pet. He did, my lord.

    Lor. Run to Sciarrha, pray him come and speak with me;
Secure his passage to this chamber : haste !—

                                   [*Exit* PETRUCHIO.

He's dead; I'll trust him now, and his ghost too ;
Fools start at shadows, I'm in love with night
And her complexion.

Re-enter PETRUCHIO.

    Pet. My lord, he's come without your summons.

    Lor. Already ? leave us.   [*Exit* PETRUCHIO.

Enter SCIARRHA *and* FLORIO.

Welcome, let embraces
Chain us together.—Noble Florio, welcome :—
But I must honour thy great soul.

Sci. Where's the duke?

Lor. They are abed together.

Sci. Ha!

Lor. He's not stirring yet:
Thou kill'dst thy sister, didst not?

Sci. I preserved her.

Lor. So! it was bravely done.

Sci. But where's the wanton duke?

Lor. Asleep, I tell you.

Sci. And he shall sleep eternally.

Lor. You cannot wake him; look you.

[*Leads* SCIARRHA *up to the bed.*

Sci. Is he dead?

Lor. And in his death we two begin our life
Of greatness, and of empire; nay, he's dead.

Sci. That labour's saved.

Lor. Now I pronounce, Sciarrha,
Thy pardon, and to recompense thy loss,
The share of Florence; I'll but wear the title,
The power we'll divide.

Sci. I like this well:
You told a tale once of a commonwealth,
And liberty.

Lor. It was to gain a faction
With discontented persons, a fine trick
To make a buz of reformation.
My ends are compassed; hang the ribble rabble!

Sci. Shall we sweat for the people? lose our breath
To get their fame?

Lor. I'll have it given out
The duke did kill thy sister.

Sci. Excellent!

Lor. Having first ravished her : he cannot be
Too hateful ; it will dull the examination
Of his own death ; or, if that come to question—

Sci. What if I say, I killed him in revenge
Of Amidea ? they will pity me ;
Beside, it will be in your power to pardon
Me altogether.

Lor. Most discreetly thought on.

Sci. The devil will not leave us o' the sudden.

Lor. Rare wit !—
How hastily he climbs the precipice,
From whence one fillip topples him to ruin.   [*Aside.*
We two shall live like brothers.

Sci. Stay ; we two ?—
Now I consider better, I have no mind
To live at all—and you shall not—
I'll give you proof ; if you but make a noise,
You gallop to the devil.

Lor. I'm betrayed.

Sci. To death inevitable.—Brother, be you
Spectator only.

Lor. This is somewhat noble.

Sci. Thank me not, Lorenzo ; I will not engage
His innocence to blood.—Thy hands are white,
Preserve them, Florio, and unless my arm
Grow feeble, do not interpose thy sword,
I charge thee.

Lor. None to assist me ? help, Petruchio ! help !
[*They fight.*

Enter PETRUCHIO, *and offers to run at* SCIARRHA, *but is
intercepted by* FLORIO. *He runs out, crying* Help !
FLORIO *makes fast the door.*

Stretch thy jaws wider, villain ! cry out Murder !
Treason ! anything ; hold—oh !

Sci. Will you not fall, colossus ?
[LORENZO *falls, and dies.*

Flo. Are not you hurt?

Sci. I know not. Ha? yes, he has pricked me some-where,

But I'll make sure of him; [*Stabs him again.*]—Now must
   I follow:

I'll fight with him in the t'other world—thy hand,

Florio; farewell.   [*Dies.*

Flo. He's dead too? 'tis in vain for me to fly.

[*Within.*] Break ope the doors!

Flo. You shall not need.   [*Opens the door.*

Re-enter PETRUCHIO, *with* COSMO, ALONZO, FREDERICO,
          and Guard.

Alon. Disarm him.

Cos. Lorenzo and Sciarrha slain?

Alon. Where is the duke?

Pet. Look here, my lords.

Alon. What traitor?

Fred. See, Amidea murdered too.

Cos. I tremble; here is a heap of tragedies.

Alon. We must have an account from Florio.

Flo. He can inform you best that brought you hither.

Alon. Lay hands upon Petruchio! disarm him!

Cos. What blood is that upon his sword? 'tis fresh.

Pet. I'm caught.

Cos. To tortures with him.

Pet. Spare your fury; know

'Twas the best blood in Florence: I must quit[1]

Young Florio; Lorenzo, and myself,

Are only guilty of the prince's death.

Alon. Inhuman traitors!

Cos. But who killed Amidea?

Flo. The duke's lust:

There was no other way to save her honour;

My brother has revenged it here, but fate

Denied him triumph.

            [1] *i.e.* Acquit.

Alon. I never heard
Such killing stories ; but 'tis meet we first
Settle the state.—Cosmo, you are the next
Of blood to challenge Florence.

    Cos. Pray defer
That till the morning.   Drag that murderer
To prison.—Florio, you must not expect
Your liberty, till all things be examined.—
Lorenzo, now I am above thy malice,
And will make satisfaction to Oriana.—
'Tis a sad night, my lords ; by these you see
There is no stay in proud mortality.   [*Exeunt.*

HYDE PARK.

YDE PARK was licensed in 1632, acted at Drury Lane by her Majesty's servants, and published in 1637. It appears to have been a favourite with the public. After the Restoration it was revived (in 1668), and Pepys tells us that horses were brought upon the stage.

To the Right Honourable

HENRY EARL OF HOLLAND,[1]

*Knight of the most noble Order of the Garter, one of his Majesty's
most Honourable Privy Council, Chancellor of the
University of Cambridge, &c.*

MY LORD,

HE comedy, in the title, is a part of your
lordship's command, which heretofore
graced and made happy by your smile,
when it was presented, after a long
silence, upon first opening of the Park,
is come abroad to kiss your lordship's
hand. The applause it once received in
the action, is not considerable with that
honour your lordship may give it in your acceptance;
that was too large, and might with some narrow and
stoical judgment render it suspected: but this, depending
upon your censure (to me above many theatres) is able to
impart a merit to the poem, and prescribe opinion. If your
lordship retired from business into a calm, and at truce with
those high affairs wherein your counsel and spirit is fortu-
nately active, vouchsafe to peruse these unworthy papers,
you not only give a life to the otherwise languishing numbers,
but quicken and exalt the genius of the author, whose
heart pointeth at no greater ambition, than to be known,

MY LORD,

to your name and honour,

the most humbly devoted,

JAMES SHIRLEY.

[1] This was Henry Rich, the first Earl of Holland, created in the
23rd of James the First, and beheaded with the Duke of Hamilton
and Lord Capel, in 1648-9, "dying a martyr," as Langbaine says,
"to retrieve his former forfeited loyalty to his prince."—*Gifford*.

DRAMATIS PERSONÆ.

LORD BONVILE.

FAIRFIELD, ⎫
RIDER,   ⎬ amorous Servants to MISTRESS CAROL.
VENTURE, ⎭

LACY, suitor to MISTRESS BONAVENT.

TRIER, suitor to JULIETTA.

BONAVENT, a Merchant, supposed to have been lost at sea.

JARVIS, Servant to MISTRESS BONAVENT.

Page to BONVILE.

Gentlemen.

Jockey.

Officers.

Runners.

Bagpipers.

Park-keepers, Servants, &c.

MISTRESS CAROL.

MISTRESS BONAVENT, supposed to be a Widow.

JULIETTA, Sister to FAIRFIELD.

Waiting-woman.

Milkmaid, &c.

SCENE—LONDON and HYDE PARK.

ACT THE FIRST.

SCENE I.—*A Street.*

Enter TRIER *and* LACY.

RI. And how, and how?

    Lacy. The cause depends—

    Tri. No mistress?

    Lacy. Yes, but no wife.

    Tri. For now she is a widow.

    Lacy. But I resolve—

    Tri. What does she say to thee?

  Lacy. She says—I know not what she says—but I
Must take another course; and yet she is—

  Tri. A creature of much sweetness, if all tongues
Be just in her report; and yet 'tis strange,
Having seven years expected, and so much
Remonstrance of her husband's loss at sea,
She should continue thus.

  Lacy. What if she should
Renew the bond of her devotion
For seven years more?

  Tri. You will have time enough
To pay in your affection.

  Lacy. I would make
A voyage to Cassandra's temple first,
And marry a deformed maid; yet I must
Confess, she gives me a fair respect.

Tri. Has she
A hope her husband may be living yet?

Lacy. I cannot tell; she may have a conceit
Some dolphin has preserved him in the storm,
Or that he may be tenant to some whale,
Within whose belly he may practise lent,
And feed on fish till he be vomited
Upon some coast: or, having 'scaped the seas,
And bills of exchange failing, he might purpose
To foot it o'er the Alps in his return,
And by mischance is fallen among the mice
With whom, perhaps, he battens upon sleep,
Beneath the snow.

Tri. This were a vagary.

Lacy. I know not what to think; or, is she not
The worse for the coy lady that lives with her?

Tri. Her kinswoman?

Lacy. Such a malicious piece,
(I mean to love,) 'tis pity any place
But a cold nunnery should be troubled with her.
If all maids were but her disciples, we
Should have no generation, and the world,
For want of children, in few years undone by't:
Here's one can tell you more.   Is not that Jarvis,
The widow's servant?

Enter VENTURE *and* JARVIS *meeting.*

Vent. Whither in such haste, man?

Jar. I am commanded, sir, to fetch a gentleman.

Vent. To thy mistress? to give her a heat this morning?

Jar. I have spied him.—With your pardon—
                              [*Goes to* LACY.

Tri. Good morrow, Master Venture.

Vent. Frank Trier?

Tri. You
Look high and jocund, Venus has been propitious;
I dreamt last night thou wert a bridegroom.

Vent. Such a thing may be ; the wind blows now
From a more happy coast.

Lacy. I must leave you ; I am sent for.

Tri. To thy mistress?

Lacy. Without more ceremony, gentlemen, my service.
Farewell.   [*Exit.*

Vent. I'll tell thee, I have a mistress.

Tri. I believe it.

Vent. And yet I have her not.

Tri. But you have hope.

Vent. Or rather certainty.

Tri. Why, I hear she is
A very tyrant over men.

Vent. Worse, worse,
The needle of a dial never had
So many waverings ; but she is touched,
And she points only this way now, true north ;
I am her pole.

Tri. And she your *Ursa minor.*

Vent. I laugh to think how other of her rivals
Will look, when I enjoy her.

Tri. You are not yet contracted ?

Vent. No, she changed
Some amorous tokens ; do you see this diamond?
A toy she gave me.

Tri. 'Cause she saw you a spark.

Vent. Her flame of love is here ; and in exchange
She took a chain of pearl.

Tri. You'll see it hanged.

Vent. These to the wise are arguments of love,
And mutual promises.

Enter Lord BONVILE *and* Page.

Tri. Your lordship's welcome to town :
I am blest to see your honour in good health.

Lord B. Prithee visit my lodgings.

Tri. I shall presume to tender my humble service.

               [*Exeunt* Lord B. *and* Page.

Vent. What's he?

Tri. A sprig of the nobility,
That has a spirit equal to his fortunes ;
A gentleman that loves clean napery.

Vent. I guess your meaning.

Tri. A lady of pleasure ; 'tis no shame for men
Of his high birth to love a wench ; his honour
May privilege more sins : next to a woman,
He loves a running horse.—
Setting aside these recreations,
He has a noble nature, valiant, bountiful.

Vent. I was of his humour till I fell in love,
I mean for wenching ; you may guess a little,
By my legs ; but I will now be very honest,
And when I am married—

Tri. Then you are confident
To carry away your mistress from them all ?

Vent. From Jove himself, though he should prac-
     tise all
His shapes to court her ; 'tis impossible
She should put any trick upon me, I
Have won her very soul.

Tri. Her body must
Needs be your own then.

Vent. I have a brace of rivals,
Would they were here, that I might jeer them !
And see how opportuncly one is come !

Enter RIDER.

I'll make you a little sport.

Tri. I have been melancholy,
You will express a favour in't.

Rid. Master Venture ! the first man in my wish ;
What gentleman is that ?

Vent. A friend of mine.

Rid. I am his servant; look you, we are friends,
And't shall appear, however things succeed,
That I have loved you; and you cannot take
My counsel in ill part.

Vent. What is the business.

Rid. For my part, I have
Used no enchantment, philter, no devices
That are unlawful, to direct the stream
Of her affection; it flows naturally.

Vent. How's this?—Prithee observe.   [*Aside to* TRIER.

Tri. I do, and shall laugh presently.

Rid. For your anger,
I wear a sword, though I have no desire
It should be guilty of defacing any
Part of your body; yet upon a just
And noble provocation, wherein
My mistress' love and honour is engaged,
I dare draw blood.

Tri. Ha, ha, ha!

Vent. A "mistress' love and honour!" this is pretty.

Rid. I know you cannot
But understand me; yet, I say I love you,
And with a generous breast, and in the confidence
You will take it kindly, I return to that
I promised you, good counsel; come, leave off
The prosecution.

Vent. Of what, I prithee?

Rid. There will be less affront than to expect
Till the last minute, and behold the victory
Another's; you may guess why I declare this.
I am studious to preserve an honest friendship;
For though it be my glory, to be adorned
With trophies of her vanquished love—

Vent. Whose love?

Tri. This sounds as if he jeered you.

[*Aside to* VENTURE.

Vent. Mushroom!   [*Draws.*

Tri. What do you mean, gentlemen? friends and fall
About good counsel!   [out

Vent. I'll put up again,
Now I think better on't.

Tri. 'Tis done discreetly.
Cover the nakedness of your tool, I pray.

Vent. Why, look you, sir; if you bestow this counsel
Out of your love, I thank you; yet there is
No great necessity, why you should be at
The cost of so much breath; things well considered:
A lady's love is mortal, I know that,
And if a thousand men should love a woman,
The dice must carry her; but one of all
Can wear the garland.

Tri. Now you come to him.

Vent. For my own part, I loved the lady well,
But you must pardon me, if I demonstrate
There's no such thing as you pretend, and therefor
In quittance of your loving, honest counsel,
I would not have you build an airy castle;
Her stars have pointed her another way,
This instrument will take her height.

                              [*Shows the diamond ring.*

Rid. Ha!

Vent. And you may guess what cause you have to
            triumph;
I would not tell you this, but that I love you
And hope you will not run yourself into
The cure of Bedlam. He that wears this favour,
Hath sense to apprehend.

Rid. That diamond?

Vent. Observe it perfectly, there are no trophies
Of vanquished love, I take it, coming toward you;
" It will be less affront, than to expect
Till the last minute, and behold the victory
Another's."

Rid. That ring I gave her.

Tri. Ha, ha, ha!

Vent. This was his gift to her; ha, ha, ha!
Have patience, spleen; ha, ha!

Tri. The scene is changed!

Rid. She will not use me thus; she did receive it
With all the circumstance of love.

Vent. I pity him; my eyes run o'er.   Dost hear?—
I cannot choose but laugh, and yet I pity thee.
She has a jeering wit, and I shall love her
More heartily for this.   What dost thou think?
Poor gentleman, how he has fooled himself!

Rid. I'll to her again.

Vent. Nay, be not passionate!
I' faith, thou wert too confident, I knew
It could not hold; dost think I'd say so much else?
I can tell thee more; but lose her memory.

Rid. Were it more rich   [*He shows a chain of pearl.*
Than that which Cleopatra gave to Antony,
With scorn I would return it.

Tri. She give you this chain?

Rid. She shall be hanged in chains ere I will keep it.

Vent. Stay, stay; let my eye
Examine that——this chain?—

Rid. Who would trust woman after this?

Vent. The very same
She took of me, when I received this diamond!

Rid. Ha, ha! you do but jest; she will not fool
You o' this fashion; look a little better,
One may be like another.

Vent. 'Tis the same.

Rid. Ha, ha! I would it were, that we might laugh
At one another; by this hand I will
Forgive her: prithee tell me—ha, ha, ha!

Tri. You will " carry her
From Jove himself, though he should practise all
His shapes to court her."

Rid. By this pearl,—O rogue,

How I do love her for't!—be not dejected;
"A lady's love is mortal, one of all
Must wear the garland; do not fool yourself
Beyond the cure of Bedlam."

Tri. She has fitted you
With a pair of fools' coats, and as handsomely
As any tailor, that had taken measure.

Vent. Give me thy hand.

Tri. Nay, lay your heads together
How to revenge it; and so, gentlemen,
I take my leave.   [*Exit.*

Vent. She has abused us.

Rid. Let us take his counsel;
We can be but what we are.

Vent. A pair of credulous fools.

Rid. This other fellow, Fairfield, has prevailed.

Vent. Which if he have—

Rid. What shall we do?

Vent. I think we were best let him alone.

Rid. Do you hear? We'll to her again; (you will
Be ruled by me); and tell her what we think of her.

Vent. She may come to herself, and be ashamed on't.

Rid. If she would affect one of us, for my part
I am indifferent.

Vent. So say I too, but to give us both the canvas![1]
Let's walk, and think how to behave ourselves.
                                        [*Exeunt.*

SCENE II.—*A Room in* BONAVENT'S *House.*

Enter Mistress BONAVENT *and* Mistress CAROL.

Mis. Car. What do you mean to do with him?

---

[1] *i.e.* Dismiss us both. From the practice of journeymen mechanics carrying their tools with them, when dismissed they were said to get the canvas or the bag, or, as we should say, the sack

Mis. Bon. Thou art
Too much a tyrant ; the seven years are past,
That did oblige me to expect my husband,
Engaged to sea ; and though within those limits
Frequent intelligence hath reported him
Lost, both to me, and his own life, I have
Been careful of my vow ; and were there hope
Yet to embrace him, I would think another
Seven years no penance : but I should thus
Be held a cruel woman, in his certain
Loss, to despise the love of all mankind.
And therefore I resolve, upon so large
A trial of his constancy, at last
To give him the reward of his respects
To me, and—

Mis. Car. Marry him.

Mis. Bon. You have apprehended.

Mis. Car. No marvel if men rail upon you then,
And doubt whether a widow may be saved.
We maids are thought the worse on, for your easiness.
How are poor women overseen ! We must
Cast away ourselves upon a whining lover,
In charity : I hope my cousin's ghost
Will meet you as you go to church, or if
You 'scape it then, upon the wedding night—

Mis. Bon. Fie ! fie !

Mis. Car. When you are both abed, and candles out.

Mis. Bon. Nay, put not out the candles.

Mis. Car. May they burn blue then, at his second kiss,
And fright him from—well, I could say something ;
But take your course—He's come already.

Enter LACY.

Put him off but another twelvemonth. [Mis. BONAVENT
      walks aside with LACY.]—So, so.
Oh love, into what foolish labyrinths
Dost thou lead us ! I would all women were

But of my mind, we would have a new world
Quickly.   I will go study poetry
On purpose to write verses in the praise
Of th' Amazonian ladies, in whom only
Appears true valour (for the instruction
Of all posterity), to beat their husbands.

    Lacy. How you endear your servant !

    Mis. Car. I will not
Be guilty of more stay.

Enter FAIRFIELD.

    Fair. Sweet lady !

    Mis. Car. You're come in time, sir, to redeem me.

    Fair. Why, lady ?

    Mis. Car. You will be as comfortable as strong
      waters ;
There's a gentleman—

    Fair. So uncivil to affront you ?

    Mis. Car. I had no patience to hear him longer ;
Take his offence, before you question him.

    Fair. And be most happy if, by any service,
You teach me to deserve your fair opinion.

    Mis. Car. It is not civil to eavesdrop him, but
I'm sure he talks on't now.

    Fair. Of what?

    Mis. Car. Of love ; is any thing more ridiculous ?
You know I never cherish that condition : [1]
In you 'tis the most harsh, unpleasing discord ;
But I hope you will be instructed better,
Knowing how much my fancy goes against it.
Talk not of that, and welcome.

    Fair. You retain,
I see, your unkind temper ; will no thought
Soften your heart ? disdain agrees but ill
With so much beauty ; if you would persuade
Me not to love you, strive to be less fair ;

<hr>

[1] Humour, disposition.

Undo that face, and so become a rebel
To heaven and nature.

   Mis. Car. You do love my face then?

   Fair. As heavenly prologue to your mind; I do not
Doat, like Pygmalion, on the colours.

   Mis. Car. No, you cannot; his was a painted mistress.
Or, if it be the mind you so pretend
To affect, you increase my wonder of your folly,
For I have told you that so often.

   Fair. What?

   Mis. Car. My mind, so opposite to all your courtship,
That I had rather hear the tedious tales
Of Hollinshed, than any thing that trenches
On love. If you come fraught with any o'
Cupid's devices, keep them for his whirligigs;
Or load the next edition of his messenger,
Or post, with a mad packet, I shall but laugh
At them, and pity you.

   Fair. That pity—

   Mis. Car. Do not mistake me, it shall be a very
Miserable pity, without love?
Were I a man, and had but half that handsomeness,
(For though I have not love, I hate detraction),
Ere I would put my invention to the sweat
Of compliment, to court my mistress' hand,
And call her smile, blessing beyond a sun-beam,
Entreat to wait upon her, give her rings
With wanton, or most lamentable poesies,
I would turn thrasher.

   Fair. This is a new doctrine,
From women.

   Mis. Car. 'Twill concern your peace, to have
Some faith in it.

   Fair. You would not be neglected?

   Mis. Car. You neglect
Yourselves, the nobleness of your birth and nature,
By servile flattery of this jigging,

And that coy mistress; keep your privilege,
Your masculine property.

    Fair. Is there so great
A happiness in nature?

    Mis. Car. There is one   [*Points to* LACY.
Just of your mind; can there be such happiness
In nature? Fie upon't, if it were possible,
That ever I should be so mad to love,
To which, I thank my stars, I am not inclined,
I should not hold such servants worth my garters,
Though they would put me in security
To hang themselves, and ease me of their visits.

    Fair. You are a strange gentlewoman; why, look you,
        lady:
I am not so enchanted with your virtues,
But I do know myself, and at what distance
To look upon such mistresses; I can
Be scurvily conditioned; you are—

    Mis. Car. As thou dost hope for any good, rail now
But a little.

    Fair. I could provoke you.

    Mis. Car. To laugh, but not to lie down. Why,
        prithee do.

    Fair. Go, you are a foolish creature, and not worth
My services.

    Mis. Car. Aloud, that they may hear;
The more the merrier, I'll take't as kindly
As if thou hadst given me the Exchange. What, all this
        cloud
Without a shower?

    Fair. You are most ingrateful.

    Mis. Car. Good!
Abominable peevish, and a wench
That would be beaten, beaten black and blue,
And then, perhaps, she may have colour for't.
Come, come, you cannot scold
With confidence, nor with grace; you should look big,

And swear you are no gamester ; practise dice
And cards a little better, you will get
Many confusions and fine curses by't.

Fair. Is not she mad ?

Mis. Car. To show I have my reason,
I'll give you some good counsel, and be plain with you ;
None that have eyes will follow the direction
Of a blind guide, and what do you think of Cupid ?
Women are either fools, or very wise,
Take that from me ; the foolish women are
Not worth your love, and if a woman know
How to be wise, she will not care for you.

Fair. Do you give all this counsel without a fee ?
Come, be less wild. I know you cannot be
So hard of soul.   [*Offers to take her hand.*

Mis. Car. Prithee let my body alone !

Fair. Why are you thus peremptory ? Had
Your mother been so cruel to mankind,
This heresy to love, with you had been
Unborn.

Mis. Car. My mother was no maid.

Fair. How, lady ?

Mis. Car. She was married long ere I was born, I
     take it,
Which I shall never be, that rule's infallible ;
I would not have you fooled in the expectation,
A favour all my suitors cannot boast of.
Go home, and say your prayers, I will not look
For thanks till seven year hence.

Fair. I know not what
To say ; yes, I will home, and think a satire.—
Was ever man jeered thus for his good will !   [*Exit.*

Mis. Bon. The license will be soon dispatched.

Lacy. Leave that
To my care, lady, and let him presume,
Whom you intend to bless with such a gift,
Seal on your lips the assurance of his heart. [*Kisses her.*

Shir.   o

I have more wings than Mercury : expect
Your servant in three minutes.
    Mis. Car. Take more time.
You'll overheat yourself, and catch a surfeit.
    Lacy. My nimble lady, I have business ; we
Will have a dialogue another time.   [*Exit.*
    Mis. Car. You do intend to marry him, then ?
    Mis. Bon. I have promised
To be his wife ; and, for his more security,
This morning—
    Mis. Car. How ! this morning?
    Mis. Bon. What should one,
That has resolved, lose time ?   I do not love
Much ceremony ; suits in love should not,
Like suits in law, be racked from term to term.
    Mis. Car. You will join issue presently, without your
        council,
You may be o'erthrown ; take heed, I have known wives
That have been o'erthrown in their own case, and after
Nonsuited too, that's twice to be undone.
But take your course ; some widows have been mortified.
    Mis. Bon. And maids do now and then meet with their
        match.
    Mis. Car. What is in your condition makes you weary ?
You are sick of plenty and command ; you have
Too, too much liberty, too many servants ;
Your jewels are your own, and you would see
How they will show upon your husband's wagtail.[1]
You have a coach now, and a Christian livery
To wait on you to church, and are not catechised
When you come home ; you have a waiting-woman,
A monkey, squirrel, and a brace of islands,[2]
Which may be thought superfluous in your family,
When husbands come to rule. A pretty wardrobe,

---

    [1] Mistress.
    [2] *i.e.* Shock-dogs. They seem to have been favourites of ladies.
Island is the old way of writing Iceland.

A tailor of your own, a doctor too,
That knows your body, and can make you sick
I' the spring, or fall, or when you have a mind to't,
Without control; you have the benefit
Of talking loud and idle at your table,
May sing a wanton ditty, and not be chid,
Dance, and go late to bed, say your own prayers,
Or go to Heaven by your chaplain.

   Mis. Bon. Very fine.

   Mis. Car. And will you lose all this, for
"I, Cicely, take thee, John, to be my husband"?
Keep him still to be your servant;
Imitate me; a hundred suitors cannot
Be half the trouble of one husband.   I
Dispose my frowns and favours like a princess;
Deject, advance, undo, create again;
It keeps the subjects in obedience,
And teaches 'em to look at me with distance.

Enter VENTURE and RIDER.

   Mis. Bon. But you encourage some.

   Mis. Car. 'Tis when I have nothing else to do, for
     sport,
As, for example—

   Mis. Bon. But I am not now in tune to hear 'em;
     prithee
Let's withdraw.   [*Exeunt.*

   Vent. Nay, nay, lady, we must follow you.
                  [*Exeunt* VENTURE *and* RIDER.

ACT THE SECOND.

SCENE I.—*An outer Room in* BONAVENT'S *House.*

Enter BONAVENT *in disguise, listening.*

Bona. Music and revels! they are very merry.

Enter a Servant.

By your favour, sir.

Ser. You are welcome.

Bona. Pray, is this a dancing school?

Ser. No dancing school.

Bona. And yet some voices sound like women.

Ser. Wilt please you
To taste a cup of wine? 'tis this day free
As at a coronation; you seem
A gentleman.

Bona. Prithee, who dwells here?

Ser. The house this morning was a widow's, sir,
But now her husband's; without circumstance,
She is married.

Bona. Prithee, her name?

Ser. Her name was Mistress Bonavent.

Bona. How long is't since her husband died?

Ser. 'Tis two years since she had intelligence
He was cast away; at his departure, he
Engaged her to a seven years expectation,

Which full expired, this morning she became
A bride.

Bona. What's the gentleman she has married?

Ser. A man of pretty fortune, that has been
Her servant many years.

Bona. How do you mean?
Wantonly? or does he serve for wages?

Ser. Neither, I mean a suitor.

Bona. Cry mercy; may I be acquainted with his name?

Ser. And his person too, if you have a mind to't;
Master Lacy; I'll bring you to him.

Bona. Master Lacy, may be 'tis he; would thou couldst
help me to
A sight of this gentleman! I have business with
One of his name, and cannot meet with him.

Ser. Please you walk in.

Bona. I would not be an intruder
In such a day; if I might only see him.—

Ser. Follow me, and I'll do you that favour. [*Exeunt.*

SCENE II.—*Another Room in the same.*

Enter LACY, Mistress BONAVENT, RIDER, Mistress
CAROL, *and* VENTURE, *dancing; followed at a distance by* BONAVENT.

Vent. Who is that peeps?

Lacy. Peeps!—Who is that? [*Bringing forward* BONA-
VENT]—Faith, you shall dance.

Bona. Good sir, you must excuse me, I am a stranger.

Lacy. Your tongue does walk our language, and your
Shall do as we do: take away his cloak   [feet
And sword.—By this hand, you shall dance, Monsieur,
No *pardonnez moi.*

Mis. Car. Well said, master bridegroom,
The gentleman may perhaps want exercise.

Mis. Bon. He will not take it well.

Vent. The bridegroom's merry.

Lacy. Take me no takes;
Come, choose your firk,[1] for dance you shall.

Bona. I cannot;
You'll not compel me?

Lacy. I have sworn.

Bona. 'Tis an affront; as I am a gentleman,
I know not how to foot your chamber jigs.

Lacy. No remedy; here's a lady longs for one
       vagary.—
Fill a bowl of sack, and then to the Canaries.

Bona. You are circled with your friends, and do not well
To use this privilege to a gentleman's
Dishonour.

Lacy. You shall shake your heels.

Bona. I shall?
Ladies, it is this gentleman's desire
That I should make you mirth; I cannot dance,
I tell you that afore.

Mis. Bon. He seems to be a gentleman and a soldier.

Mis. Car. Good Mars, be not so sullen; you'll do
       more
With Venus privately.

Bona. Because this gentleman is engaged, I'll try.
                                         [*A Dance.*
Will you excuse me yet?

Lacy. Play excuse me; yes, any thing you'll call for.

Mis. Car. This motion every morning will be wholesome
And beneficial to your body, sir.

Bona. So, so.

Mis. Car. Your pretty lump requires it.

Bona. Where's my sword, sir? I have been your
       hobby-horse.

Mis. Car. You danced something like one.

---

[1] *i.e.* Your dance, or your partner.

Bona. Jeer on, my whimsy lady.

Mis. Bon. Pray impute it
No trespass studied to affront you, sir,
But to the merry passion of a bridegroom.

Lacy. Prithee stay: we'll to Hyde Park together.

Bona. There you may meet with morris-dancers: for
You, lady, I wish you more joy, so farewell.   [*Exit.*

Lacy. Come, let's have t'other whirl, lustily, boys!
                                        [*They dance off.*

SCENE III.—*A Room in* FAIRFIELD'S *House.*

Enter FAIRFIELD, JULIETTA, *and* Waiting-woman.

Jul. You are resolved then?

Fair. I have no other cure left,
And if I do it not quickly, my affection
May be too far spent, and all physic will
Be cast away.

Jul. You will show a manly fortitude.

Fair. When saw you Master Trier?

Jul. Not since yesterday.

Fair. Are not his visits frequent?

Jul. He does see me sometimes.

Fair. Come, I know thou lov'st him, and he will
Deserve it; he's a pretty gentleman.

Jul. It was your character, that first commended
Him to my thoughts.

Fair. If he be slow to answer it,
He loses me again; his mind, more than
His fortune, gain'd me to his praise: but I
Trifle my precious time.
Farewell! all my good wishes stay with thee.   [*Exit.*

Enter TRIER.

Jul. And mine attend you!—Master Trier!

Tri. I come to kiss your hand.

Jul. And take your leave?

Tri. Only to kiss't again!

Jul. You begin to be a stranger; in two mornings
Not one visit, where you profess affection!

Tri. I should be surfeited with happiness
If I should dwell here.

Jul. Surfeits in the spring
Are dangerous, and yet I never heard,
A lover would absent him from his mistress
Through fear to be more happy; but I allow
That for a compliment, and dispute not with you
A reason of your actions. You are now welcome,
And though you should be guilty of neglect,
My love would overcome any suspicion.

Tri. You are all goodness.—

Enter a Servant, *and whispers* TRIER.

With me? prithee admit him.   [*Exit* Servant.

Enter Page.

Page. Sir, my lord saw you enter, and desires
To speak with you.

Tri. His lordship shall command; where is he?

Page. Below, sir.

Tri. Say, I instantly wait on him.—   [*Exit* Page.
Shall I presume upon your favour, lady?

Jul. In what?

Tri. That I may entreat him hither? you will honour
    me
To bid him welcome; he is a gentleman
To whom I owe all services, and in
Himself is worthy of your entertainment.

Jul. If he be your's command me.

Enter Lord BONVILE *and* Page.

Tri. My lord, excuse—

Lord B. Nay, I prevent your trouble.—Lady, I am

Your humble servant.—Pardon my intrusion.
I have no business, only I saw you enter.

Tri. Your lordship honours me.

Lord B. What gentlewoman's this?

Tri. Why—   [*Whispers him.*

Lord B. A lady of pleasure! I like her eye, it has
A pretty twirl with't; will she bid one welcome?

Tri. Be confident, my lord.—Sweet lady, pray
Assure his lordship he is welcome.

Jul. I want words.

Lord B. Oh, sweet lady, your lip in silence
Speaks the best language.

Jul. Your lordship's welcome to this humble roof.

Lord B. I am confirmed.   [*Aside.*

Tri. If you knew, lady, what
Perfection of honour dwells in him,
You would be studious, with all ceremony
To entertain him! besides, to me
His lordship's goodness hath so flowed, you cannot
Study, what will oblige me more than in
His welcome.

Lord B. Come, you compliment.

Jul. Though I want both ability and language,
My wishes shall be zealous to express me
Your humble servant.

Lord B. Come, that humble was
But compliment in you, too.

Jul. I would not
Be guilty of dissembling with your lordship;
I know words that have more proportion
With my distance to your noble birth and fortune,
Than humble servant.

Lord B. I do not love these distances.

Tri. You would have her be more humble.—
This will try her,
If she resist his siege, she is a brave one,
I know he'll put her to't. He that doth love

Wisely, will see the trial of his mistress,
And what I want in impudence myself,
Another may supply for my advantage;
I'll frame excuse.   [*Aside.*

   Lord B. Frank, thou art melancholy.

   Tri. My lord, I now reflected on a business
Concerns me equal with my fortune, and
It is the more unhappy that I must
So rudely take my leave.

   Lord B. What! not so soon?

   Tri. Your honour's pardon.

   Jul. Are you, sir, in earnest?

   Tri. Love will instruct you to interpret fairly;
They are affairs that cannot be dispensed with.—
I leave this noble gentleman.

   Jul. He's a stranger;
You will not use me well, and show no care
Of me, nor of my honour; I pray stay.

   Tri. Thou hast virtue to secure all; I am confident,
Temptations will shake thy innocence
No more than waves that climb a rock, which soon
Betray their weakness,—and discover thee
More clear and more impregnable.

   Jul. How is this?

   Tri. Farewell.
I will not sin against your honour's clemency,
To doubt your pardon.

   Lord B. Well, an there be no remedy, I shall see
     you
Anon in the Park; the match holds.—[*Exit* TRIER.] I
     am not willing
To leave you alone, lady.

   Jul. I have a servant.

   Lord B. You have many; in their number pray write
     me,
I shall be very dutiful.

   Jul. Oh, my lord.

Lord B. And when I have done a fault, I shall be
    instructed,
But with a smile, to mend it.

Jul. Done what fault?

Lord B. Faith, none at all, if you but think so.

Jul. I think your lordship would not willingly
Offend a woman.

Lord B. I would never hurt 'em,
It has been my study still to please those women
That fell within my conversation.
I am very tender-hearted to a lady,
I can deny them nothing.

Jul. The whole sex
Is bound to you.

Lord B. If they well considered things,
And what a stickler I am in their cause,
The common cause, but most especially
How zealous I am in a virgin's honour,
As all true knights should be, no woman could
Deny me hospitality, and let down,
When I desire access, the rude portcullice :
I have a natural sympathy with fair ones,
As they do, I do ; there's no handsome woman
Complains, that she has lost her maidenhead,
But I wish mine had been lost with it.

Jul. Your lordship's merry.

Lord B. 'Tis because you look pleasant.—
A very handsome lodging ; is there any
Accommodations that way.

Jul. There's a garden,
Will't please your lordship taste the air on't.

Lord B. I meant other conveniency ; but if
You please, I'll wait upon you thither.

          [*Exeunt* Lord BONVILE *and* JULIETTA.

Page. You and I had better stay, and in their absence
Exercise one another.

Wait. How mean you, page?

Page. I'll teach you a way that we may follow 'em,
And not remove from hence.

Wait. How, prithee?

Page. Shall I beg your lip?

Wait. I cannot spare it.

Page. I'll give you both mine.

Wait. What means the child?

Page. Because I have no upper lip, do you scorn me?
I have kissed ladies before now, and have
Been sent for to their chambers.

Wait. You sent for!

Page. Yes, and been trusted with their closets too!
We are such pretty things, we can play at
" All hid under a fardingale ; " how long
Have you been a waiting creature?

Wait. Not a month yet.

Page. Nay then, I cannot blame your ignorance ;
You have perhaps your maidenhead.

Wait. I hope so.

Page. Oh, lamentable ! away with it, for shame.
Chaffer it with the coachman, for the credit
Of your profession ; do not keep it long,
'Tis fineable in court.

Wait. Good master page,
How long have you been skilled in those affairs?

Page. E'er since I was in breeches ; and you'll find
Your honesty so troublesome.

Wait. How so?

Page. When you have trucked[1] away your maidenhead,
You have excuse lawful to put off gamesters,
For you may swear, and give 'em satisfaction,
You have not what they looked for ; beside the benefit
Of being impudent as occasion serves,
A thing much in request with waiting creatures :
We pages can instruct you in that quality,
So you be tractable.

[1] Trafficked.

Wait. The boy is wild.

Page. An you will lead me a chase, I'll follow you.

[*Exeunt.*

SCENE IV.—*A Room in* BONAVENT'S *House.*

Enter Mistress CAROL, RIDER, *and* VENTURE.

Mis. Car. Why, did you ever think I could affect,
Of all men living, such a thing as you are?
What hope, or what encouragement did I give you?
Because I took your diamond, must you presently
Bound like a stoned horse?

Rid. She's a very colt.   [dancer,

Mis. Car. 'Cause you can put your hat off like a
And make a better leg[1] than you were born to,
For, to say truth, your calf is well amended,
Must this so overtake me, that I must
Straight fall in love with you? one step to church.
Another into the streets? more to a bargain;
You are wide a bow, and something overshot.

Vent. Then this is all that I must trust to, you
Will never have me?

Mis. Car. In my right mind, I think so.
Why, prithee tell me, what I should do with thee?

Vent. Can you find nothing to do with me?

Mis. Car. To find my monkey spiders, were an office,
Perhaps, you would not execute?

Vent. You are a gipsy,
And none of the twelve Sybils in a tavern,
Have such a tanned complexion; there be dogs
And horses in the world.

Mis. Car. They'll keep you company.

Vent. Tell me of spiders!
I'll wring your monkey's neck off.

---

[1] Bow.

Mis. Car. And then puzzle
Your brain to make an elegy, which shall be sung
To the tune of " The Devil and the Baker ; " good !
You have a pretty ambling wit in summer ;
Do you let it out, or keep't for your own riding ?
Who holds your stirrup, while you jump
Into a jest, to the endangering
Of your ingenious quodlibets ?

Rid. Come, thou hast said enough.

Mis. Car. To him ; you would have some ?

Rid. Some testimony of your love, if it please you.

Mis. Car. Indeed, I have heard you are a precious gentleman,
And in your younger days could play at trap well.

Rid. Fare you well, gentlewoman ! by this light a devil ;
I'll follow my old game of horse-racing.

Vent. I could tear her ruff ! I would thou wert
A whore, then I'd be revenged, and bring the 'prentices
To arraign thee on Shrove Tuesday ; [1] a pox upon you !

Enter FAIRFIELD.

Mis. Car. A third man, a third man ! two fair gamesters ;

Rid. For shame ! let's go.

Mis. Car. Will you stay, gentlemen ? you have no more wit   [*Exeunt* VENTURE *and* RIDER.
To vent ! keep your heads warm in any case,
There may be dregs in the bottom o' the brain pan,
Which may turn to somewhat in seven years ; and set
You up again.—Now, sir.

Fair. Lady, I am come to you.

Mis. Car. It does appear so.

Fair. To take my leave.

Mis. Car. 'Tis granted, sir ; good bye.

---

[1] Shrove Tuesday was noted for the riotous conduct of the London apprentices, who used to attack the brothels, etc.

Fair. But you must stay and hear a little more.
I promise not to trouble you with courtship,
I am as weary as you can be displeased with't,

  Mis. Car. On these conditions, I would have the patience
To hear the brazen head speak.[1]

  Fair. Whether, or how I purpose to dispose
Myself hereafter, as I know you have
No purpose to enquire, I have no great
Ambition to discourse ; but how I have
Studied your fair opinion, I remit
To time, and come now only to request
That you would grant, in lieu of my true service,
One boon at parting.

  Mis. Car. *Fort bon!* proceed.

  Fair. But you must swear to perform truly what
I shall desire ; and that you may not think
I come with any cunning to deceive you,
You shall accept whate'er you would deny me ;
And after all, I'll make request.

  Mis. Car. How's this?

  Fair. But it concerns my life, or what can else
Be nearer to me, that you swear.

  Mis. Car. To what?

  Fair. When you have made exceptions, and thought
What things in all the world you will exempt
From my petition, I'll be confident
To tell you my desire.

  Mis. Car. This is fair play.

  Fair. I would not for an empire, by a trick
Oblige you to perform what should displease you.

  Mis. Car. 'Tis a very strange request ; are you in earnest?
Ere you begin, shall I except? 'tis odds

---

[1] In the prose-tract of the *Famous Historie of Fryer Bacon* it is related how "Friar Bacon made a brazen head to speak, by which he would have walled England about with brass."

But I may include, what you have a mind to, then
Where's your petition?

    Fair. I will run that hazard.

    Mis. Car. You will? why, look you; for a little mirth's
        sake,
And since you come so honestly, because
You shall not say, I am composed of marble,
I do consent.

    Fair. Swear.

    Mis. Car. I am not come to that;
I'll first set bounds to your request, and when
I have left nothing for you worth my grant,
I'll take a zealous oath to grant you any thing.

    Fair. You have me at your mercy.

    Mis. Car. First, you shall not
Desire that I should love you.

    Fair. That's first; proceed.

    Mis. Car. No more but "proceed"? Do you know
        what I say?

    Fair. Your first exception forbids to ask
That you should love me.

    Mis. Car. And you are contented?

    Fair. I must be so.

    Mis. Car. What, in the name of wonder, will he ask
        me?   [*Aside.*
You shall not desire me to marry you.

    Fair. That's the second.

    Mis. Car. You shall neither directly nor indirectly,
        wish me to lie with you.
Have I not clipt the wings of your conceit?

    Fair. That's the third.

    Mis. Car. "That's the third!" is there any thing a
        young man would
Desire of his mistress, when he must neither love, marry,
        nor lie with her?

    Fair. My suit is still untouched.

    Mis. Car. Suit! if you have another 'tis out of fashion,

You cannot beg my state, yet I would willingly
Give part of that, to be rid of thee.

Fair. Not one jewel.   [poison,

Mis. Car. You would not have me spoil my face, drink
Or kill any body?

Fair. Goodness forbid, that I should wish you danger!

Mis. Car. Then you would not have me ride through
   the city naked,
As once a princess of England did through Coventry?

Fair. All my desires are modest.

Mis. Car. You shall not beg my parrot, nor entreat me
To fast, or wear a hairy smock.

Fair. None of these.

Mis. Car. I will not be confined to make me ready
At ten, and pray till dinner; I will play
At gleek [1] as often as I please, and see
Plays when I have a mind to't, and the races,
Though men should run Adamites [2] before me.

Fair. None of these trench on what I have to ask.

Mis. Car. Why, then I swear—stay,
You shall not ask me before company
How old I am, a question most untoothsome.
I know not what to say more; I'll not be
Bound from Spring-garden, [3] and the 'Sparagus. [4]
I will not have my tongue tied up, when I've
A mind to jeer my suitors, among which
Your worship shall not doubt to be remembered,
For I must have my humour, I am sick else;
I will not be compelled to hear your sonnets,
A thing before I thought to advise you of;
Your words of hard concoction, your rude poetry,

---

[1] A game at cards.

[2] Religious enthusiasts who are said to have dispensed with
clothing at their meetings.

[3] Situated near Charing Cross and noted for its bowling alley
and ordinary, and for its "continual bibbing and drinking wine all
day under the trees, and two or three quarrels every week."

[4] A place of amusement frequented by Pepys, in Lambeth
Marsh.

Have much impaired my health, try sense another while
And calculate some prose according to
The elevation of our pole at London,
As says the learned almanack—but, come on,
And speak your mind, I have done; I know not what
More to except; if it be none of these,
And, as you say, feasible on my part,
I swear.

 Fair. By what?

 Mis. Car. For once, a kiss, it may be a parting blow.
By that I will perform what you desire. [*Kisses him.*

 Fair. In few words thus receive it: by that oath
I bind you never to desire my company
Hereafter; for no reason to affect me;
This, I am sure, was none of your exceptions.

 Mis. Car. What has the man said?

 Fair. 'Tis clear, I am confident,
To your understanding.

 Mis. Car. You have made me swear
That I must never love you, nor desire
Your company.

 Fair. I know you will not violate
What you have sworn, so all good thoughts possess you.
            [*Exit.*

 Mis. Car. Was all this circumstance for this? I never
Found any inclination to trouble him
With too much love; why should he bind me from it,
And make me swear? an oath that, for the present,
I had no affection to him, had been reasonable;
But for the time to come, never to love,
For any cause or reason, that may move me
Hereafter, very strange! I know not what to think on't,
Although I never meant, to think well of him,
Yet to be limited, and be prescribed,
I must not do it,—'twas a poor trick in him;
But I'll go practise something to forget it. [*Exit.*

ACT THE THIRD.

SCENE I.—*A part of Hyde Park.*

Enter Lord BONVILE *and* JULIETTA.

ORD B. Lady, you are welcome to
the spring; the Park
Looks fresher to salute you: how the birds
On every tree sing, with more cheerfulness
At your access, as if they prophesied
Nature would die, and resign her providence
To you, fit only to succeed her!

Jul. You express
A master of all compliment; I have
Nothing but plain humility, my lord,
To answer you.

Lord B. But I'll speak our own English,
Hang these affected strains, which we sometimes
Practise, to please the curiosity
Of talking ladies; by this lip thou'rt welcome, [*Kisses her.*
I'll swear a hundred oaths upon that book,
An't please you.

Enter TRIER, *behind.*

Tri. They are at it.

Jul. You shall not need, my lord, I'm not incredulous,
I do believe your honour, and dare trust
For more than this.

Lord B. I will not break my credit
With any lady that dares trust me.

Jul. She had a cruel heart, that would not venture
Upon the engagement of your honour.

Lord B. What?
What durst thou venture now, and be plain with me?

Jul. There's nothing in the verge of my command,
That should not serve your lordship.

Lord B. Speak, speak truth,
And flatter not, on what security?

Jul. On that which you propounded, sir, your honour:
It is above all other obligation,
And he that's truly noble, will not stain it.

Lord B. Upon my honour will you lend me then
But a night's lodging?

Jul. How, sir?

Lord B. She is angry;
I shall obtain, I know the trick on't; had
She yielded at the first, it had been fatal.   [*Aside.*

Jul. It seems your lordship speaks to one you know not.

Lord B. But I desire to know you better, lady.

Jul. Better I should desire, my lord.

Lord B. Better or worse, if you dare venture one,
I'll hazard t'other.

Jul. 'Tis your lordship's mirth.

Lord B. You're in the right, 'tis the best mirth of all.

Jul. I'll not believe, my lord, you mean so wantonly
As you profess.

Lord B. Refuse me,[1] if I do not.
Not mean? I hope you have more charity
Than to suspect, I'll not perform as much,
And more than I have said; I knew my fault,
I am too modest when I undertake,
But when I am to act, let me alone.

Tri. You shall be alone no longer.— [*Comes forward.*
My good lord.

─────────────
[1] A fashionable oath.

Lord B. Frank Trier.

Tri. Which side holds your honour

Lord B. I am o' thy side, Frank.

Tri. I think so,

For all the Park's against me; but six to four

Is odds enough.

Jul. Is it so much against you?

Tri. Lady, I think 'tis two to one.

Lord B. We were on even terms till you came hither.—

I find her yielding.—And when do they run?

Tri. They say presently.

Lord B. Will you venture anything, lady?

Tri. Perhaps she reserves herself for the horse-race.

Jul. There I may venture somewhat with his lord-
    ship.

Lord B. That was a witty one.   [*Aside.*

Tri. You will be doing.

Lord B. You are for the footmen.

Tri. I run with the company.

Enter RIDER *and* VENTURE.

Vent. I'll go your half.

Rid. No, thank you, Jack; would I had ten pieces
    more on't!

Lord B. Which side?

Rid. On the Irishman.

Lord B. Done; I'll maintain the English.

As many more with you;

I love to cherish our own countrymen.

Vent. 'Tis done, my lord.

Tri. I'll rook for once; my lord,

I'll hold you twenty more.

Lord B. Done with you, too.

Jul. Your lordship is very confident.

Lord B. I'll lay with you, too.

Tri. Lie with her, he means.   [*Aside.*

Lord B. Come; you shall venture something.

What gold against a kiss? but if you lose,
You shall pay it formally down upon my lip.

Tri. Though she should win, it would be held extortion
To take your money.

Jul. Rather want of modesty,
A greater sin, if you observe the circumstance.
I see his lordship has a disposition
To be merry, but proclaim not this free lay
To every one; some women in the world
Would hold you all day.

Lord B. But not all night, sweet lady.

Vent. Will you not see them, my lord?

Lord B. Frank Trier, you'll wait upon this gentle-
woman;
I must among the gamesters, I shall quickly
Return to kiss your hand.   [*Exit.*

Tri. How do you like this gallant?

Jul. He's one it becomes not me to censure.

Tri. Do you not find him coming? a wild gentleman;
You may in time convert him.

Jul. You made me acquainted with him to that purpose,
It was your confidence; I'll do what I can,
Because he is your noble friend, and one
In whom was hid so much perfection
Of honour, for at first 'twas most invisible,
But it begins to appear, and I do perceive
A glimmering, it may break out a flame,
I shall know all his thoughts at our next conference;
He has a secret to impart, he says,
Only to me.

Tri. And will you hear it?

Jul. Yes, sir;
If it be honourable, there is no harm in't,
If otherwise, you do not doubt my innocence.

Tri. But do not tempt a danger.

Jul. From his lordship?

Tri. I do not say from him.

Jul. From mine own frailty?

Tri. I dare not conclude that, but from the matter
Of his discourse, on which there may depend
A circumstance, that may not prove so happy.

Jul. Now I must tell you, sir, I see your heart
Is not so just as I deserve; you have
Engaged me to this conversation,
Provoked by jealous thoughts, and now your fear
Betrays your want of goodness, for he never
Was right at home, that dare suspect his mistress.
Can love degenerate in noble breasts?
Collect the arguments, that could invite you
To this unworthy trial, bring them to
My forehead, where you shall inscribe their names
For virgins to blush at me, if I do not
Fairly acquit myself.

Tri. Nay, be not passionate.

Jul. I am not, sir, so guilty to be angry;
But you shall give me leave, unless you will
Declare, you dare not trust me any further,
Not to break off so rudely with his lordship.
I will hear what he means to say to me,
And if my counsel may prevail with you,
You shall not interrupt us; have but patience,
I'll keep the story for you, and assure
My ends have no base mixture, nor my love
To you could bribe me to the least dishonour,
Much less a stranger; since I have gone so far
By your commission, I will proceed
A little further, at my peril, sir.

Tri. I know thou art proof against a thousand engines.
Pursue what ways you please.   [*They walk aside.*

Enter LACY, Mistress BONAVENT, Mistress CAROL, *and*
Servant.

Jul. This morning married?—

Tri. That's your brother's mistress.

Jul. She that jeers
All within gun-shot?

Tri. In the way of suitors,
She is reported such a tyrant.

Jul. My brother.

Enter FAIRFIELD.

Fair. Frank Trier.

Jul. Brother, do you know that gentlewoman?

Fair. 'Tis she; then you and I must seem more familiar,
And you—[*To* LACY.]—shall not be angry,

Lacy. What gentlewoman's that?

Tri. She does not know thee.

Mis. Car. [*Seeing* FAIRFIELD *and* JULIETTA.]—Was this his reason?   [*Aside.*]—Pray, if you love me, let's
Walk by that gentleman.

Lacy. Master Fairfield.

Mis. Car. Is that well-trussed gentleman one of them that run?

Mis. Bon. Your sweetheart.

Mis. Car. Ha, ha! I'd laugh at that.
If you allow a bushel of salt to acquaintance,
Pray vouchsafe two words to a bargain, while you live,
I scarce remember him.—Keep in, great heart.   [*Aside.*]

Enter BONAVENT.

Lacy. Oh sir, you are very well met here.

Bona. We are met indeed, sir; thank you for your music.

Lacy. It is not so much worth.

Bona. I made you merry, Master Bridegroom.

Lacy. I could not choose but laugh.

Bona. Be there any races here?

Lacy. Yes, sir, horse and foot.

Bona. You'll give me leave to take my course, then.

Mis. Car. This is the captain that did dance.

Bona. Not so nimbly as your wit; pray let me ask you
    a question,   [*Takes* Mistress CAROL *aside.*
I hear that gentlewoman's married.

Mis. Car. Married! without question, sir.

Bona. Do you think he has been aforehand?

Mis. Car. How do you mean?

Bona. In English, has he played the forward gamester,
And turned up trump?

Mis. Car. Before the cards be shuffled?—
I lay my life you mean a coat card.
Deal again, you gave one too many
In the last trick, yet I'll tell you what I think.

Bona. What?

Mis. Car. I think she and you might have shown
    more wit.

Bona. Why she and I?

Mis. Car. She to have kept herself a widow, and you
Not to have asked me such a foolish question;
But if she had been half so wise, as in
My conscience she is honest, you have missed
That excellent occasion, to show
Your notable skill in dancing; but it pleased
The learned Destinies to put things together,
And so we separate.   [*They come forward.*

Bona. Fare you well, mistress.

Mis. Car. [*To* RIDER.]—Come hither; go to that
    gentleman, Master Fairfield—   [*Whispers him.*

Mis. Bon. Prithee, sweetheart, who runs?

Lacy. An Irish and an English footman.

Mis. Bon. Will they run this way?

Lacy. Just before you; I must have a bet.   [*Exit.*

Mis. Bon. Nay, nay, you shall not leave me.

Mis. Car. Do it discreetly; [*Exit* RIDER.] I must
    speak to him,
To ease my heart, I shall burst else,   [*Aside.*
We'll expect 'em here.—Cousin, do they run naked?

Mis. Bon. That were a most immodest sight.

Mis. Car. Here have been such fellows, cousin.

Mis. Bon. It would fright the women.

Mis. Car. Some are of opinion it brings us hither.

[*Noise within.*

Hark, what a confusion of tongues there is !
Let you and I venture a pair of gloves
Upon their feet; I'll take the Irish.

Mis. Bon. 'Tis done; but you shall pay if you lose.

Mis. Car. Here's my hand, you shall have the gloves,
if you win.

[*A cry within.*] A Teague ! a Teague ! Make way, for
shame !

Mis. Bon. I think they are started.

The two Runners *cross the stage, followed by* Lord Bon-
ville, Venture, *and others.*

Lord B. I hold any man forty pieces, yet.

Vent. A hundred pounds to ten ! a hundred pieces to
ten ! will no man take me ?

Bona. I hold you, sir.

Vent. Well, you shall see.—

[*Within.*]—A Teague ! a Teague ! hey !

Tri. Ha ! well run Irish !

[*Exeunt all but* Mis. Carol *and* Mis. Bonavent.

Mis. Bon. He may be in a bog anon.

Mis. Car. Can they tell what they do in this noise ?
Pray Heaven it do not break into the tombs
At Westminster, and wake the dead.

Re-enter Fairfield *and* Julietta.

Fair. She's yonder still, she thinks thee a new mistress.

Jul. I observe her.

Re-enter Trier.

Fair. How go things, Frank ?
Prithee, observe that creature.

Tri. She leers this way.

Fair. I have done such a strange cure upon her !
She has sent for me, and I entreat thee, Frank,
To be a witness of my triumph ; 'tis
Now in my power to punish all her jeers ;
But I'll go to her : thou shalt keep at distance,
Only to hear how miraculously
I have brought things about.

    Tri. The cry returns. [*Exeunt* FAIRFIELD *and* TRIER.

    [*Within.*]—Make way there ! a Teague ! a Teague ! a
        Teague !

The two Runners *re-cross the stage, followed by* Lord BON-
    VILE, VENTURE, BONAVENT, &c.

    Vent. Forty, fifty, a hundred pieces to ten !

    Bona. I hold you.

    Vent. Well, you shall see, you shall see.

    Bona. This gentleman does nothing but talk ; he makes
good no bet.

    Vent. Talk ? you prate ; I'll make good what I please,
        sir.

    Bona. Make the best you can of that.

                    [*They switch, and then draw.*

    Mis. Bon. For Heaven's sake, let's remove.

    Mis. Car. What ! for a naked weapon ?

            [*Exeunt* Mis. BONAVENT *and* CAROL.

    Lord B. Fight, gentlemen,
You are fine fellows, 'tis a noble cause.—

            [*Exeunt* VENTURE *and* BONAVENT.

Come, lady, I'll discharge your fears.
A cup of sack, and Anthony at the Rose.[1]
Will reconcile their furies.

           [*Exeunt* BONVILE *and* JULIETTA.

---

[1] A famous tavern in Russell Street, Covent Garden.

SCENE II.—*Another part of the Park.*

Enter FAIRFIELD *and* TRIER.

Fair. I make a doubt whether I should go to her,
Upon a single summons.

Tri. By any means.

Fair. What women are forbidden
They're mad to execute; she's here, be you
In the reach of her voice, and see how I will humble her.

Enter Mistress CAROL *and* RIDER.

Mis. Car. But keep at some fit distance.

Rid. You honour me, and shall
Command me any service.   [*Exit.*

Mis. Car. He has gone a strange way to work with me.
                                                 [*Aside.*

Fair. Well advised; observe and laugh, without a
     noise.   [TRIER *drops behind.*

Mis. Car. I am ashamed to think what I must say
     now.   [*Aside.*

Fair. By your leave, lady! I take it you sent for me?

Mis. Car. You will not be so impudent? I send for
By whom, or when?   [you!

Fair. Your servant[1]—

Mis. Car. Was a villain, if he mentioned
I had any such desire; he told me, indeed,
You courted him to entreat me, that I would
Be pleased to give you another audience,
And that you swore, I know not what, confound you,
You would not trouble me above six words.

Fair. You are prettily disposed.

Mis. Car. With much ado, you see, I have consented.
What is it you would say?

Fair. Nay, what is't you would say?

Mis. Car. Have you no prompter, to insinuate

---

[2]. *i.e.* Your lover; Fairfield means Rider.

The first word of your studied oration ?—
He's out on's part.—Come, come, I will imagine it,
Was it not something to this purpose—" Lady,"
Or " Mistress," or what you will, " although
I must confess, you may with justice laugh at
My most ridiculous suit, and you will say
I am a fool—"

   Fair. You may say any thing.

   Mis. Car. " To come again, whom you have so tor-
      mented ;
For ne'er was simple camomile so trod on,
Yet still I grow in love ;[1] but since there is
No hope to thaw your heart, I now am desperate ;
Oh give me, lend me but the silken tie
About your leg, which some do call a garter,
To hang myself, and I am satisfied."
Am not I a witch ?

   Fair. I think thou art past it.
Which of the Furies art thou made already ?
I shall depart the world, ne'er fear it, lady,
Without a necklace.   Did not you send for me ?

   Tri. I shall laugh aloud sure.

   Mis. Car. What madness has possessed you ? have I
      not sworn,
You know by what, never to think well of you,
Of all men living, not to desire your company ?
And will you still intrude ?   Shall I be haunted
For ever ? no place give me privilege ?
Oh man, what art thou come to ?

   Fair. Oh woman !
How far thy tongue and heart do live asunder !
Come, I have found you out ; off with this veil,
It hides not your complexion ; I do tell thee,
I see thy heart, and every thought within it ;

---

[1] Falstaff in *Henry IV.* says, " Though the camomile the more
it is trodden on the faster it grows, yet youth the more it is wasted
the sooner it wears."

A little peevishness, to save your credit,
Had not been much amiss, but this over-
Over-doing the business,—it appears
Ridiculous, like my suit, as you inferred ;
But I forgive thee, and forget thy tricks
And trillabubs, and will swear to love thee heartily ;
Wenches must have their ways.

Mis. Car. Pardon me, sir, if I have seemed too light ;
It was not rudeness from my heart, but a
Disguise to save my honour, if I found
You still incredulous.

Fair. I love thee better
For thy vagaries.

Mis. Car. In vain, I see, I should dissemble with you,
I must confess you have caught me ; had you still
Pursued the common path, I had fled from you ;
You found the constitution of women
In me, whose will, not reason, is their law ;
Most apt to do, what most they are forbidden,
Impatient of curbs, in their desires.

Fair. Thou say'st right,

Mis. Car. Oh love, I am thy captive ;—
But I am forsworn, am I not, sir ?

Fair. Ne'er think of that.

Mis. Car. Ne'er think on't !

Fair. 'Twas a vain oath, and well may be dispensed
    with.

Mis. Car. Oh, sir, be more religious ; I never
Did violate an oath in all my life ;
Though I have been wild, I had a care of that.
An oath's a holy obligation,
And never dreaming of this chance, I took it
With true intention to perform your wishes.

Fair. 'Twas but a kiss, I'll give it thee again.

Mis. Car. But 'tis enrolled in that high court already.
I must confess, I could look on you now
With other eyes, for my rebellious heart

Is soft and capable of love's impression ;
Which may prove dangerous, if I cherish it,
Having forsworn your love.

    Fair. Now I am fitted !
I have made twigs to jerk myself. [*Aside.*]—Well
        thought on !
You shall absolve yourself; your oath does not
Oblige you to perform what you excepted,
And among them, if you remember, you
Said you must have your humour, you'd be sick else ;
Now, if your humour be to break your oath,
Your obligation's void.

    Mis. Car. You have relieved me !
But do not triumph in your conquest, sir,
Be modest in your victory.

    Fair. Will not you
Fly off again, now you're at large ?

    Mis. Car. If you
Suspect it, call some witness of my vows,
I will contract myself.

    Fair. And I am provided.—
Frank Trier, appear, and shew thy physnomy.—
He is a friend of mine, and you may trust him.

                   [TRIER *comes forward.*

    Mis. Car. What sum of money is it you would
        borrow ?

    Tri. I borrow ?

    Mis. Car. This gentleman, your friend, has fully
Possessed me with your wants ; nay, do not blush,
Debt is no sin : though my own monies, sir,
Are all abroad, yet, upon good security,
Which he answers you can put in, I will speak
To a friend of mine.

    Fair. What security?

    Mis. Car. Yourselves, and two sufficient aldermen,
For men are mortal, and may break.

    Fair. What mean you ?

Mis. Car. You shall have fifty pounds for forty weeks,
To do you a pleasure.

Fair. You'll not use me thus?

Tri. Fare you well;
You have miraculously brought things about.   [*Exit.*

Mis. Car. You work by stratagem and ambuscado.
Do you not think yourself a proper gentleman,
Whom by your want of hair some hold a wit too?
You know my heart, and every thought within it!
How I am caught! do I not melt like honey
I' the dog-days? Why do you look so staring?

Fair. Do not you love me for all this?

Mis. Car. Would I had art enough to draw your
picture,
It would show rarely at the Exchange;[1] you have
A medley in your face of many nations:
Your nose is Roman, which your next debauchment
At tavern, with the help of pot or candlestick,
May turn to Indian, flat; your lip is Austrian,
And you do well to bite it; for your chin,
It does incline to the Bavarian poke,
But seven years may disguise it with a beard,
And make it—more ill favoured; you have eyes,
Especially when you goggle thus, not much
Unlike a Jew's, and yet some men might take 'em
For Turk's by the two half moons that rise about 'em.—
I am an infidel to use him thus.   [*Aside.*

Fair. Till now, I never was myself; farewell
For ever, woman, not worth love or anger.

Mis. Car. Do you hear? one word.—I'd fain speak
kindly to him.   [*Aside.*
Why dost not rail at me?

Fair. No, I will laugh at thee, and at myself,

---

[1] *i.e.* The new Exchange in the Strand, occupying part of the site
of the present Adelphi, and at the time a place of great resort with
people of fashion. It is frequently referred to in the plays of the
period.

To have been so much a fool; you are a fine may game.

   Mis. Car. I shall fool too much. [*Aside.*]—But one
      word more;

By all the faith and love of womankind,

Believe me now—it will not out.   [*Aside.*

   Fair. Farewell;

When next I doat upon thee, be a monster.

   Mis. Car. Hark, sir, the nightingale; there is better
      luck

Coming towards us.

   Fair. When you are out of breath,

You will give over; and for better luck,

I do believe the bird, for I can leave thee,

And not be in love with my own torment.

   Mis. Car. How, sir?

   Fair. I have said; stay you and practise with the
      bird,

'Twas Philomel, they say; an thou wert one,

I should new ravish thee.   [*Exit.*

   Mis. Car. I must to the coach and weep, my heart
      will break else;

I'm glad he does not see me.   [*Exit.*

ACT THE FOURTH.

SCENE I.—*Another part of the Park.*

Enter Lord BONVILE *and* JULIETTA.

UL. Whither will you walk, my lord?
you may engage
Yourself too far, and lose your sport.

Lord B. I would
Go farther for a little sport; you
mean

The horse-race; they're not come
into the Park yet,
I might do something else, and return time
Enough to win five hundred pieces.

Jul. Your lordship had no fortune in the last match ;
I wished your confidence a happier success.

Lord B. We must lose sometimes. — Hark the
nightingale !

Jul. You win, my lord, I dare engage myself.

Lord B. You make the omen fortunate ; this bird
Doth prophesy good luck.

Jul. 'Tis the first time I heard it.

Lord B. And I, this spring ; let's walk a little
further.

Jul. I am not weary, but—

Lord B. You may trust your person, lady.

Jul. I were too much wicked to suspect your honour,
And in this place.

Lord B. This place! the place were good enough.
If you were bad enough, and as prepared
As I.   There have been stories, that some have
Struck many deer within the Park.

   Jul. Foul play.
If I did think your honour had a thought
To venture at unlawful game, I should
Have brought less confidence.

Enter TRIER, *at a distance.*

   Lord B. Ha! Trier?
What, does he follow us?

   Jul. To show I dare
Be bold upon your virtue, take no notice,
I'll waft him back again; my lord, walk forward.
       [*Waves her hand, and exit with* Lord BONVILE.

   Tri. Thus far alone? yet why do I suspect?
Hang jealousy, 'tis naught, it breeds too many   [me—
Worms in our brains; and yet she might have suffered

Enter LACY *and* Mistress BONAVENT.

Master Lacy, and his bride!

   Mis. Bon. I was wont to have one always in my
      chamber.

   Lacy. Thou shalt have a whole quire of nightingales.

   Mis. Bon. I heard it yesterday warble so prettily!

   Lacy. They say 'tis lucky, when it is the first
Bird that salutes our ear.

   Mis. Bon. Do you believe it?

   Tri. I am of his mind, and love a happy augury.

   Lacy. Observe the first note always—
[*Within.*] Cuckoo!

   Lacy. Is this the nightingale?

   Mis. Bon. Why do you look so?

   Lacy. Are not we married?
I would not have been a bachelor to have heard it.

   Mis. Bon. To them they say 'tis fatal.

Tri. And to married men
Cuckoo is no delightful note; I shall
Be superstitious.

Mis. Bon. Let's walk a little further.

Lacy. I wait upon thee.   [" Cuckoo!" *again within.*]
         Hark, still, ha, ha, ha!

                    [*Exeunt* Mistress BONAVENT *and* LACY.

Tri. I am not much in love with the broad ditty.

Enter FAIRFIELD.

Fair. Frank Trier, I have been seeking thee
About the Park.

Tri. What to do?

Fair. To be merry for half an hour; I find
A scurvy melancholy creep upon me,
I'll try what sack will do; I have sent my footman
To the Maurice[1] for a bottle, we shall meet him.
I'll tell thee t'other story of my lady.

Tri. I'll wait on you.

Fair. But that she is my sister,
I'd have thee forswear women; but let's walk.   [*Exeunt.*

SCENE II.—*The same.*

Enter BONAVENT.

Bona. This way they marched; I hope they will not
    leap
The pale; I do not know the disposition
Of my capering gentleman, and therefore 'twill not
Be indiscretion to observe him; things
Must be a little better reconciled.—
The nightingale!—this can presage no hurt,
But I shall lose my pigeons;—they are in view,
Fair and far off.   [*Exit.*

---

[1] The lodge, with the sign of Grave Maurice's head.

SCENE III.—*Another part of the same.*

Enter VENTURE *and* RIDER.

Vent. He must be a Pegasus that beats me.

Rid. Yet your confidence may deceive you; you will ride

Against a jockey, that has horsemanship.

Vent. A jockey! a jackanapes on horseback rather;

A monkey or a masty [1] dog would show

A giant to him; an I were Alexander,

I would lay the world upon my mare; she shall

Run with the devil for a hundred pieces,

Make the match who will.

Rid. Not I, you shall excuse me,

Nor would I win his money.

Vent. Whose?

Rid. The devil's;

My gold has burnt this twelve months in my pocket;

A little of his amongst, would scorch my thighs,

And make such tinder of my linings, that

My breeches never after would hold money;

But let this pass; where's Lacy and his bride?

Vent. They are walked to hear the nightingale.

Rid. The nightingale! I have not heard one this year

Vent. Listen, and we shall hear one presently.

[*Within.*]—Cuckoo!

Vent. The bird speaks to you.

Rid. No, 'tis to you.

Vent. Now do I suspect

I shall lose the race.

Rid. Despair for a cuckoo!

Vent. A cuckoo will not flatter,

His word will go before a gentleman's,

In the city; 'tis an understanding bird,

And seldom fails; a cuckoo! I'll hedge in

My money presently.

[1] Mastiff.

Rid. For shame, be confident.

Vent. Will you go half?

Rid. I'll go it all, or any thing.

Vent. Hang cuckoos then.

Enter Lord BONVILE, JULIETTA, LACY, *and* Mistress
BONAVENT.

Lord B. How now, gentlemen?

Vent. Your honour's servants.

Rid. Ladies, I kiss your hands.

Lord B. You are the man will run away with all
The gold anon.

Vent. Your jockey must fly else.

Rid. I'll hold your honour thirty pieces more.

Lord B. 'Tis done.

Jul. Do you ride yourself?

Vent. I shall have the reins in my own hand, lady.

Mis. B. Master Rider, saw you not my cousin?

Enter Mistress CAROL.

Cry mercy, she is here.—I thought you'd followed us.

Lord B. Your kinswoman?—
I shall be honoured to be your servant, lady.

Mis. Car. Alas, my lord, you'll lose by't!

Lord B. What?

Mis. Car. Honour, by being my servant; here's a
brace
Of gentlemen will tell you as much.

Vent. But will
Say nothing, for our credits.

Mis. Bon. You look as you had wept.

Mis. Car. I weep! For what?
Come towards the lodge, and drink a syllabub.

Mis. Bon. A match!

Lacy. And as we walk, Jack Venture, thou shalt sing
The song thou mad'st o' the horses.

Vent. You shall pardon me.

Rid. What, among friends? my lord, if you'd speak
  to him.

Lord B. A song by all means,
Prithee let me entreat it; what's the subject?

Lacy. Of all the running horses.

Vent. Horses and mares, put them together.

Lord B. Let's have it; come, I hear you can sing rarely,

Rid. An excellent voice.

Lacy. A ravishing tone.

Vent. 'Tis a very ballad, my lord, and a coarse tune.

Lord B. The better; why, does any tune become
A gentleman so well as a ballad? hang
Curiosity[1] in music; leave those crotchets
To men that get their living with a song.—
Come, come, begin.   [VENTURE *sings.*

SONG.

Come, Muses all, that dwell nigh the fountain.
Made by the wingèd horse's heel,
Which firked[2] with his rider over each mountain,
Let me your galloping raptures feel.
  I do not sing of fleas, or frogs,
  Nor of the well-mouthed hunting dogs.
Let me be just, all praises must
Be given to well-breathed Jilian Thrust.

Young Constable and Kill Deer's famous,
The Cat, the Mouse, and Neddy Gray;
With nimble Peggybrig, you cannot shame us
With Spaniard nor with Spinola.
  Hill-climbing White Rose praise doth not lack,
  Handsome Dunbar, and Yellow Jack;
But if I be just, all praises must
Be given to well-breathed Jilian Thrust.

Sure-spurred Sloven, true-running Robin,
Of Young Shaver I do not say less,

---

[1] Nicety.   [2] Hastened.

Strawberry Soam, and let Spider pop in,
Fine Brackly, and brave Lurching Bess.
 Victorious too was Herring Shotten,
 And Spit-in's-arse is not forgotten ;
But if I be just, all honour must
Be given to well-breathed Jilian Thrust.

Lusty George, and, gentlemen, hark yet,
To winning Mackarel, fine-mouthed Freak,
Bay Tarrall, that won the cup at Newmarket,
Thundering Tempest, Black Dragon eke.
 Precious Sweet Lips, I do not lose,
 Nor Toby with his golden shoes ;
But if I be just, all honour must
Be given to well-breathed Jilian Thrust.

Lord B. Excellent! how think you, lady?
Jul. I like it very well.
Mis. Car. I never thought you were a poet, sir.
Vent. No, no, I do but dabble.
Mis. Car. You can sing rarely too ; how were these parts
Unobserved, invisible?
Vent. You may see, lady.
Jul. Good sir, your pardon.
Vent. Do you love singing? hum ; la, la. [*Sings.*
Mis. Car. Who would have thought these qualities were in you?
Vent. Now or never.
Mis. Car. Why, I was cozened.
Vent. You are not the first I have cozened; shall I wash
Your faces with the drops of Helicon?
I have fancies in my head.
Mis. Car. Like Jupiter, you want a Vulcan but
To cleave your skull, and out peeps bright Minerva.
Jul. When you return I'll tell you more, my lord.
Vent. Give me a subject.

Mis. Bon. Prithee coz, do.

Mis. Car. Let it be — How much you dare suffer
   for me.

Vent. Enough — hum, fa, la, la.

Enter Page.

Page. Master Venture, you are expected.

Lord B. Are they come?

Page. This half hour, my lord.

Lord B. I must see the mare: you will excuse this
   rudeness.—

Sirrah, stay you, and wait upon these ladies.

                           [Exit Lord BONVILE.

Vent. 'Tis time to make me ready.—

Ladies, I take this leave in prose,

You shall see me next in other feet.   *[Exit.*

Rid. I wish your syllabub were nectar, lady.

Mis. Bon. We thank you, sir, and here it comes
   already.

Enter Milkmaid *with a bowl.*

Jul. So, so; is it good milk?

Mis. Bon. Of a red cow?

Mis. Car. You talk as you inclined to a consumption;
Is the wine good?

Milk. It comes from his Excellence' head.[1]

Mis. Car. My service to you, lady, and to him
Your thoughts prefer.

Mis. Bon. A health!

Mis. Car. No deep one; 'tis lawful for gentlewomen
To wish well to their friends.

Jul. You have obliged me — the wishes of all happiness
To him your heart hath chosen!

Mis. Bon. Duty now
Requires I should be willing to receive it:
As many joys to you both, when you are married!

---

[1] Grave Maurice's.

Mis. Car. Married?

Jul. You have not vowed to die a virgin,
I know an humble servant of your's, lady.

Mis. Car. Mine!

Jul. Would be sorry you should be a nun.

Mis. Car. Do you think he loves me, then?

Jul. I do not think
He can dissemble where he does profess
Affection; I know his heart by mine:
Fairfield is my brother!

Mis. Car. Your brother? then the danger's not so
    great;
But let us change our argument. With your pardon,
Come hither, pretty one; how old are you?

Page. I am young, lady;
I hope you do not take me for a dwarf.

Mis. Bon. How young, I pray then?

Page. Four summers since my life was questioned,
And then a jury of years did pass upon me.

Mis. Car. He is upon the matter, then, fifteen.

Page. A game at noddy.[1]

Mis. Car. You can play your cards already, it seems:
Come, drink of this syllabub.

Page. I shall spoil your game, ladies;
For if there be sack in it, it may make
You flush a three.

Jul. The boy would seem witty.

Page. I hope, ladies, you will pardon me; my lord
commanded me to wait upon you, and I can do you no
better service than to make you laugh.

Enter FAIRFIELD *and* TRIER.

Fair. They're here, bless you!

Mis. Bon. Master Fairfield, you are welcome.

Fair. I presume so, but howsoever it skills[2] not.

---

[1] An old game at cards.   [2] Matters.

Tri. I do not come to borrow money.

Mis. Car. And yet all they that do so are no fools ;
Money or lands make not a man the wiser,
I know handsome gentlemen have pawned their clothes.

Tri. I'll pawn my skin too, with a woman.

Mis. Car. Wipe your mouth; here's to you, sir !

Tri. I'll pledge you, quicksilver. Where is your lord ?

Page. He has left Virgo, sir, to go to Libra,
To see the horsemen weighed.

Tri. Lady, my service !

Jul. Brother, you interpose too far ; my lord
Has used me honourably, and I must tell you,
Somebody has made a fault.

Mis. Bon. Master Fairfield !

Fair. I kiss your hand.

Tri. My lord and you have walked.

Jul. Yes, sir.

Fair. My sister shall excuse ; here's to thee and thy
    cream bowl.

Milk. I thank your worship.

Fair. There is more honesty in thy petticoat,
Than twenty satin ones.

Mis. Bon. Do you know that?

Fair. I know by her pail ; an she were otherwise,
T'would turn her milk.—Come hither, let me kiss thee.

　　　　　　　　　　　　　　　　[*Kisses the* Milkmaid.

Now I am confirmed, he that shall marry thee
Shall take thee a virgin at my peril.

Mis. Bon. Have you such skill in maidenheads ?

Fair. I'll know't by a kiss,
Better than any doctor by her urine.—
Be merry with thy cow, farewell !—Come, Frank :
That wit and good clothes should infect a woman !

Jul. I'll tell you more hereafter ; pray let's hear
Who wins.

Tri. Your servant, ladies.

　　　　　　　　　　　　　　[*Exeunt* FAIRFIELD *and* TRIER.

Enter Jockey *and* Gentlemen.

1st Gent. What dost think, Jockey?

2nd Gent. The crack o' the field's against you.

Jock. Let 'em crack nuts.

1st Gent. What weight?

2nd Gent. I think he has the heels.

3rd Gent. Get but the start.

Jock. However, if I get within his quarters
Let me alone.

3rd Gent. Montez à cheval.   [*Exeunt.*

    [*Confused noise of betting within, after that a shout.*
Mis. Car. They are started.

Re-enter Lord BONVILE, RIDER, TRIER, *and* FAIRFIELD.

Rid. Twenty pounds to fifteen!

Lord B. 'Tis done wi' ye!

Fair. Forty pounds to thirty!

Lord B. Done! done! I'll take all odds.

Tri. My lord, I hold as much.

Lord B. Not so.

Tri. Forty pounds to twenty.

Lord B. Done, done!

Re-enter LACY.

Lacy. You have lost all, my lord, an it were a million.

Lord B. In your imagination; who can help it?

Lacy. Venture had the start, and keeps it.

Lord B. Gentlemen, you have a fine time to triumph,
'Tis not your odds that makes you win.

    [*Within.*] Venture! Venture!

                    [*Exeunt all but the ladies.*
Jul. Shall we venture nothing o' the horses?
What odds against my lord!

Mis. Car. Silk stockings.

Jul. To a pair of perfumed gloves? I take it.

Mis. Car. Done!

Mis. Bon. And I as much.

Jul. Done, with you both!

Mis. Car. I'll have 'em Spanish scent.

Jul. The stockings shall be scarlet; if you choose
Your scent, I'll choose my colour.

Mis. Car. 'Tis done; if Venture
Knew but my lay, it would half break his neck now.

> [*A shout within, and cry of* A jockey!

Jul. Ha! is the wind in that coast? hark! the noise
Is jockey now.

Mis. Car. 'Tis but a pair of gloves.

[*Within.*] A jockey!

Jul. Still it holds.—

Re-enter Lord BONVILE.

How have you sped, my lord?

Lord B. Won, won! I knew by instinct
The mare would put some trick upon him.

Mis. Bon. Then we have lost; but, good my lord, the
circumstance.

Lord B. Great John-at-all-adventure, and grave Joc-
key.
Mounted their several mares.—I shall not tell
The story out for laughing, ha, ha, ha!—
But this in brief—Jockey was left behind,
The pity and the scorn of all; the odds
Played 'bout my ears like cannon, but less dangerous.
I took all still, the acclamations were
For Venture, whose disdainful mare threw dirt
In my old Jockey's face, all hopes forsaking us,
Two hundred pieces desperate, and two thousand
Oaths sent after them, upon the sudden,
When we expected no such trick, we saw
My rider, that was domineering ripe,
Vault o'er his mare into a tender slough,
Where he was much beholding to one shoulder,
For saving of his neck; his beast recovered,

And he by this time somewhat mortified,
Besides mortarified,[1] hath left the triumph
To his Olympic adversary, who shall
Ride hither in full pomp on his Bucephalus,
With his victorious bagpipe.

   Mis. Car. I would fain see
How Venture looks.

   Lord B. He's here; ha, ha!

      Enter VENTURE, *covered with mud, and* RIDER.

   Vent. I told you as much before;
You would not believe the cuckoo.

   Mis. Car. Why, how now, sir?

   Vent. An I had broke my neck in a clean way,
'Twould ne'er have grieved me.—Lady, I am your's;
Thus Cæsar fell.

   Lord B. Not in a slough, dear Jack.

   Vent. You shall hear further from me.

   Rid. Come to Knightsbridge.

   Vent. That cuckoo was a witch, I'll take my death
      on't.   [*Exit.*

   Lord B. Here comes the conqueror.

Enter a Bagpiper, *and* Jockey *in triumph, followed by*
    BONAVENT, TRIER, *and* FAIRFIELD.

" Lo, from the conquest of Jerusalem
Returns Vespasian !"—Ha, ha! mer—mercy, Jockey.

   Jock. I told you, if I came within his quarters.

   All. A jockey, a jockey!

   [*Exeunt all but* LACY, *his* Bride, *and* Mistress CAROL.

      Re-enter BONAVENT *and* Bagpiper.

   Bona. This shall be but your earnest; [*Gives him
     money.*]—follow me
At pretty distance, and when I say " draw,"

---

[1] Suggested by Gifford in place of the " mortified   of the old
copy.

Play me a galliard.[1]—By your favour, sir,
Shall I speak a cool word with you?

   Lacy. With all my heart.

   Bona. You do owe me a dance, if you remember,
And I will have it now; no dispute.—Draw!

            [Bagpiper *plays.* LACY *draws his sword.*
That will not serve your turn; come, shake your
     heels,
You hear a tune; I will not change my tool
For a case[2] of rapiers; keep off, at your perils,
I have sworn.

   Mis. Bon. For Heaven's sake some to part 'em.

   Lacy. Dost hear?

   Bona. And you may hear the bagpipe is not dumb:
Will you to this gear? or do you mean to try
                [*Draws his sword.*
How this will scower you? Come, come, I will have it.

   Lacy. Hold! I will.

   [*He dances, meantime enter* Lord BONVILE *and* TRIER.

   Bona. So; now we are on equal terms, and if
You like it not, I'll use my t'other instrument.

   Lacy. Thou art a brave fellow; come your ways.

   Lord B. Hold!
You shall not fight, I'll understand your quarrel.

   Lacy. Good my lord.
Let's have one pass.

   Mis. Bon. Your weapons shall run through me;
And I must tell you, sir, you have been injurious—

   Bona. Good lady, why? in doing myself right?

   Mis. Bon. In wronging me.

   Bona. I am not sensible of that.

   Mis. Bon. Could any shame be fastened upon him,
Wherein I have no share?

   Bona. I was provoked
By him, if you remember, and was not

---

      [1] A lively dance tune.   [2] Couple.

Born so unequal to him, I should suffer
His poor affront.

 Mis. Bon. This was a day of peace,
The day wherein the holy priest hath tied
Our hearts together ; Hymen's tapers yet
Are burning, and it cannot be a sin
Less than a sacrilege, to extinguish them
With blood, and in contempt of Heaven's proceeding,
Thus to conspire our separation.
No Christian would profane the marriage day :
And when all other wish us joys, could you
Intrude yourself to poison all our mirth,
Blast, in the very budding, all our happiness
Our hopes had laid up for us ?

 Bona. I was a stranger.

 Mis. Bon. That makes you more uncivil; we were merry,
Which could not offend you.

 Bona. I had no thought
To violate your mirth.

 Mis. Bon. What came you for ?
With whom had you acquaintance ? or what favour
Gave you access, at so unfit a time,
To interrupt our calm and free delights ?
You cannot plead any abuse, where you
Were never known, that should incite you to
Revenge it there : I take it you were never
His rival.

 Bona. 'Tis confessed.

 Mis. Bon. What malice then
Prevailed above your reason to pursue us
With this injustice ?

 Bona. Lady, give me leave.
I were a villain to be guilty of
The baseness you accuse me : your servant
Shall quit me from intrusion, and my soul
Is my best witness, that I brought no malice
But unstained thoughts into your roof ; but when

I was made the common laughter, I had been
Less than a man, to think of no return,
And had he been the only of my blood,
I would not be so much the shame of soldier,
To have been tamed, and suffered ; and you are
Too hasty in your judgment; I could say more,
But 'tis dishonour to expostulate
These causes with a woman : I had reason
To call him to account, you know not all
My provocation ; things are not with me
As with another man.

    Mis. Bon. How is that ? the matter
May spread too far ; some former quarrel,—'tis
My best to reconcile 'em. [*Aside.*]—Sir, I may
Be ignorant; if anything have passed
Before this morning, I pray pardon me ;
But as you are a gentleman, let me
Prevail, your differences may here conclude ;
'Las, I am part of him now, and between
A widow and his wife, if I be thus
Divorced—

    Bona. I'll be his servant.

    Mis. Bon. Sir, you show
A noble disposition.—Good my lord,
Compose their differences. — Prithee meet his friend-
    ship.

    Bona. I have satisfaction, and desire his love.

    Lacy. Thou hast done but like a gentleman ; thy
    hand,
I'll love thee while I live.

    Lord B. Why so ; all friends.

    Bona. I meet it with a heart; and for disturbing
Your mirth to-day—

    Lacy. No, no disturbance.

    Bona. Then give me but the favour
To show I wish no sorrow to the bride :
I have a small oblation, which she must

    Shir.   R

Accept, or I shall doubt we are not friends;
'Tis all I have to offer at your wedding.

                        [*Gives* Mistress BONAVENT *a paper.*

  Mis. Bon. Ha!

  Bona. There's my hand
To justify it at fit time.—Peruse it,
My lord, I shall be studious
How to deserve your favour.

  Lord B. I am yours.

  Lacy. My lord, let me obtain you'll honour me
To-night.

[Mistress BONAVENT *walks aside with the paper, and reads.*
"I was taken by a Turkish pirate, and detained many
years a prisoner in an island, where I had died his captive, had not a worthy merchant thence redeemed and
furnished me."—

  Mis. Bon. Blessed delivery!

Enter a Servant *and delivers a letter to* Mistress CAROL.

  Mis. Car. To me! from Venture? he is very mindful;
                                   [*Reads.*
Good, I shall make use of this.

  Mis. Bon. [*Reading.*]—"Till then conceal me."

  Mis. Car. Excellent stuff,
But I must have another name subscribed.

  Lord B. Will you walk, ladies?
                   [*Gives money to the* Park-keepers.

  Mis. Car. Your servants wait upon you.

  Keepers. We humbly thank your honour.

  2nd Keep. A brave spark.

  1st Keep. Spark! he's the very Bonfire of nobility.
                             [*Exeunt.*

ACT THE FIFTH.

SCENE I.—*A Room in* BONAVENT'S *House.*

Enter LACY, Mistress BONAVENT, Lord BONVILE,
JULIETTA, Mistress CAROL, *and* TRIER.

L ACY. My lord, you honour us.

  Mis. Bon. And what we want
  In honourable entertainment, we beseech
  Our duties may supply in your construction.

   Lord B. What needs this cere-

Lacy. Thou art welcome, too, Frank Trier. [mony?

Tri. I give you thanks, and wish you still more joy,
  sir.

Mis. Bon. We'll show your lordship a poor gallery.

Lacy. But, where's my new acquaintance?

Mis. Bon. His nag outstripped the coaches,
He'll be your guest anon, fear not!

   [*Exeunt all but* Mistress CAROL *and* JULIETTA.

Mis. Car. While they
Compliment with my lord, let you and I
Change a few words.

  Jul. As many as you please.

Mis. Car. Then to the purpose. Touching your
  brother, lady,
'Twere tedious to repeat he has been pleased
To think well of me; and to trouble you

With the discourse how I have answered it,
'Twere vain ; but thus—howe'er he seem to carry it
While you were present, I do find him desperate.

   Jul. How !

   Mis. Car. Nay, I speak no conjecture ;
I have more intelligence than you imagine.
You are his sister,
And nature binds you to affect his safety.
By some convenient messenger send for him ;
But, as you love his life, do not delay it :
Alas, I shall be sorry any gentleman
Should, for my sake, take any desperate course.

   Jul. But are you serious?

   Mis. Car. Perhaps good counsel
Applied while his despair is green, may cure him,
If not—

   Jul. You make me wonder.

   Mis. Car. I know the inconsiderate will blame
Me for his death ; I shall be railed upon,
And have a thousand cruelties thrown on me ;
But would you have me promise love, and flatter him ?
I would do much to save his life : I could
Show you a paper that would make you bleed
To see his resolution, and what
Strange and unimitable ways he has
Vowed to pursue ; I tremble to think on 'em.
There's not a punishment in fiction,
(And poets write enough of hell, if you
Have read their story,) but he'll try the worst.
Were it not that I fear him every minute,
And that all haste were requisite to save him,
You should peruse his letter.

   Jul. Letter !   Since
We saw him?

   Mis Car. Since ; I must confess I wondered,
But you in this shall see I have no malice.
I pray send for him ; as I am a gentlewoman,

I have pure intention to preserve his life;
And 'cause I see the truth of his affliction,
Which may be your's, or mine, or anybody's,
Whose passions are neglected, I will try
My best skill to reduce[1] him. Here's Master Trier.

Re-enter TRIER.

He now depends upon your charity;
Send for him, by the love you bear a brother.

Tri. Will you not chide my want of manners, gentle-
    women,
To interrupt your dialogue?

Jul. We have done, sir.

Mis. Car. I shall be still your servant.

Jul. Here's a riddle;
But I will do't.—
Shall I presume upon you for a favour?

Re-enter Lord BONVILE.

Tri. You shall impose on me a greater trouble.
My lord!

Jul. Your ear.   [*Whispers* TRIER.

Lord B. We miss you above, lady.

Jul. My lord, I wait upon you; I beseech
Your pardon but a minute.—Will you do this?
It is an office he may thank you for,
Beside my acknowledgment.

Tri. Yes, I'll go,—
And yet I do not like to be sent off,
This is the second time.   [*Aside, and exit.*

Jul. Now I am for your lordship. What's your plea-
    sure?

Lord B. I would be your echo, lady, and return
Your last word—pleasure.

Jul. May you never want it!

Lord B. This will not serve my turn.

---

[1] Recover.

Jul. What, my lord?

Lord B. This is the charity of some rich men,
That, passing by some monument that stoops
With age, whose ruins plead for a repair,
Pity the fall of such a goodly pile,
But will not spare from their superfluous wealth,
To be the benefactor.

Jul. I acknowledge
That empty wishes are their shame, that have
Ability to do a noble work,
And fly the action.

Lord B. Come, you may apply it.
I would not have you a gentlewoman of your word
Alone, they're deeds that crown all; what you wish me,
Is in your own ability to give;
You understand me: will you at length consent
To multiply? we'll 'point a place and time,
And all the world shall envy us.

Jul. My lord!

Lord B. Lord me no lords; shall we join lips upon't?
Why do you look as you still wondered at me?
Do I not make a reasonable motion?
Is't only in myself? shall not you share
I' the delight? or do I appear a monster
'Bove all mankind, you shun my embraces thus?
There be some ladies in the world have drawn
Cuts for me; I have been talked on and commended,
Howe'er you please to value me.

Jul. Did they
See you thus perfectly?

Lord B. Not always; 'twas
Sometimes a little darker, when they praised me.
I have the same activity.

Jul. You are
Something—I would not name, my lord.

Lord B. And yet you do; you call me lord, that's
        something,
And you consider all men are not born to't.

Jul. 'Twere better not to have been born to honours,
Than forfeit them so poorly; he is truly
Noble, and then best justifies his blood,
When he can number the descents of virtue.

　　Lord B. You'll not degrade me?

　　Jul. 'Tis not in my power,
Or will, my lord, and yet you press me strangely.
As you are a person, separate and distinct,
By your high blood, above me and my fortunes,
Thus low I bend; you have no noble title
Which I not bow to, they are characters
Which we should read at distance, and there is
Not one that shall with more devotion
And honour of your birth, express her service:
It is my duty, where the king has sealed
His favours, I should show humility,
My best obedience, to his act.

　　Lord B. So should
All handsome women, that will be good subjects.

　　Jul. But if to all those honourable names,
That marked you for the people's reverence,
In such a vicious age, you dare rise up
Example too of goodness, they which teach
Their knees a compliment, will give their heart;
And I among the number of the humblest,
Most proud to serve your lordship, and would refuse
No office or command, that should engage me
To any noble trial; this addition
Of virtue is above all shine of state,
And will draw more admirers: but I must
Be bold to tell you, sir, unless you prove
A friend to virtue, were your honour centupled,
Could you pile titles till you reach the clouds,
Were every petty manor you possess
A kingdom, and the blood of many princes
United in your veins, with these had you
A person that had more attraction
Than poesy can furnish, love withal,

Yet I, I in such infinite distance, am
As much above you in my innocence.

    Lord B. This becomes not.

    Jul. 'Tis the first liberty
I ever took to speak myself; I have
Been bold in the comparison, but find not
Wherein I have wronged virtue, pleading for it.

    Lord B. How long will you continue thus?

    Jul. I wish
To have my last hour witness of these thoughts;
And I will hope, before that time, to hear
Your lordship of another mind.

    Lord B. I know not,
'Tis time enough to think o' that hereafter:
I'll be a convertite within these two days,
Upon condition you and I may have
One bout to-night; nobody hears.

    Jul. Alas!
You plunge too far, and are within this minute,
Further from Heaven than ever.

    Lord B. I may live to
Requite the courtesy.

    Jul. Live, my lord, to be
Your country's honour and support, and think not
Of these poor dreams.

    Lord B. I find not
Desire to sleep;—an I were abed with you—

    Jul. 'Tis not improbable, my lord, but you
May live to be an old man, and fill up
A seat among the grave nobility;
When your cold blood shall starve your wanton thoughts,
And your slow pulse beat like your body's knell,
When time hath snowed upon your hair, oh then
Will it be any comfort to remember
The sins of your wild youth? how many wives
Or virgins you have dishonoured? in their number,
Would any memory of me (should I

Be sinful to consent), not fetch a tear
From you, perhaps a sigh, to break your heart?
Will you not wish then you had never mixed
With atheists, and those men whose wits are vented
In oaths and blasphemy, (now the pride of gentle-
        men,)
That strike at Heaven, and make a game of thunder?
    Lord B. If this be true, what a wretched thing
        should I
Appear now, if I were any thing but a lord?
I do not like myself.—   [*Aside.*
Give me thy hand; since there's no remedy,
Be honest!—there's no harm in this, I hope.
I will not tell thee all my mind at once;
If I do turn Carthusian, and renounce
Flesh upon this, the devil is like to have
The worst on't.   But I am expected.   [*Exit.*
    Jul. My lord, I'll follow you.—

Enter FAIRFIELD *and* TRIER.

Brother, welcome!—
Sir, we are both obliged to you.
A friend of your's desires some private conference.
    Fair. With me?
    Jul. He does not look so desperate.—   [*Aside.*
How do you, brother?
    Fair. Well:—dost not see me?—
    Jul. I'll come to you presently.   [*Exit.*
    Fair. What's the meaning?
    Tri. Nay, I know not;
She is full of mysteries of late.

Re-enter JULIETTA *with* Mistress CAROL.

She's here again; there is some trick in it.
    Jul. Brother, I sent for you, and I think 'twas time;
Pray hearken to this gentlewoman, she will
Give you good counsel.—You and I withdraw, sir.

Tri. Whither you please.

                  [*Exeunt* JULIETTA *and* TRIER.

    Mis. Car. You are a strange gentleman;
Alas! what do you mean? is it because
I have dealt justly with you, without flattery
Told you my heart, you'll take these wicked courses?
But I am loath to chide, yet I must tell you,
You are to blame; alas! you know affection
Is not to be compelled; I have been as kind
To you as other men, nay, I still thought
A little better of you, and will you
Give such example to the rest?
Because, forsooth, I do not love you, will you
Be desperate?

    Fair. Will I be desperate?

    Mis. Car. 'Twere a fine credit for you, but perhaps
You'll go to hell to be revenged on me,
And teach the other gentlemen to follow you,
That men may say, 'twas long of me, and rail at
My unkindness; is this all your Christianity?
Or could you not prosecute your impious purpose,
But you must send me word on't, and perplex
My conscience with your devilish devices?
Is this a letter to be sent a mistress?

    Fair. I send a letter?   [*Gives him the letter.*

    Mis. Car. You were best deny your hand.

    Fair. My name subscribed! who has done this?—

                            [*Reads.*

"Rivers of hell, I come; Charon, thy oar
Is needless, I will swim unto the shore,
And beg of Pluto, and of Proserpine,
That all the damnèd torments may be mine;
With Tantalus I'll stand up to the chin
In waves; upon Ixion's wheel I'll spin
The sister's thread; quail Cerberus with my groan,
And take no physic for the rolling stone:
I'll drown myself a hundred times a day—"

Mis. Car. There be short days in hell.

Fair. " And burn myself as often, if you say
The word.—"

Mis. Car. Alas! not I.

Fair. " And if I ever chance to come
Within the confines of Elysium,
The amazèd ghosts shall be aghast to see,
How I will hang myself on every tree,
    Your's, till his neck be broke, Fairfield."
Here's a strange resolution!

Mis. Car. Is it not?
Whither is fled your piety? but, sir,
I have no meaning to exasperate
Thoughts that oppose your safety, and to show
I have compassion, and delight in no
Man's ruin, I will frame myself to love you.

Fair. Will you? why, thank you.

Mis. Car. Here's my hand, I will;
Be comforted; I have a stronger faith.

Fair. I see then you have charity for a need.

Mis. Car. I'll lose my humour to preserve a life.
You might have met with some hard-hearted mistress,
That would have suffered you to hang or drown
Yourself.

Fair. I might indeed.

Mis. Car. And carried news
To the distressed ghosts; but I am merciful:
But do not you mistake me, for I do not
This out of any extraordinary
Former good will, only to save your life.
There be so many beams convenient,
And you may slip out of the world before
We are aware; beside, you dwell too near
The river; if you should be melancholy,
After some tides, you would come in, and be
More talked off than the pilchards; but I have done.
You shall go to hell for me: I now

Am very serious, and if you please
To think well of me, instantly we'll marry;
I'll see how I can love you afterward.
Shall we to the priest?

   Fair. By your good favour, no;
I am in no such tune.

   Mis. Car. You do suspect
I jeer still: by my troth, I am in earnest.

   Fair. To save my life, you are content to marry me?

   Mis. Car. Yes.

   Fair. To save thy life, I'll not be troubled with thee.

   Mis. Car. How?

   Fair. No, madam jeer-all, I am now resolved:
Talk, and talk out thy heart, I will not lose
Myself a scruple; have you no more letters?
They're pretty mirth; would I knew who subscribed
My name! I am so far from hanging of myself,
That I will live yet to be thy tormentor.
Virtue, I thank thee for't! and for the more
Security, I'll never doat again;
Nor marry, nor endure the imagination
Of your frail sex: this very night I will
Be fitted for you all; I'll geld myself,
'Tis something less than hanging; and when I
Have carved away all my concupiscence,
Observe but how I'll triumph; nay, I'll do it,
An there were no more men in the world.   [*Going.*

   Mis. Car, Sir, sir! as you love goodness,—
I'll tell you all; first hear me, and then execute;
You will not be so foolish; I do love you.

   Fair. I hope so, that I may revenge thy peevishness.

   Mis. Car. My heart is full, and modesty forbids
I should use many words; I see my folly,
You may be just, and use me with like cruelty,
But if you do, I can instruct myself,
And be as miserable in deed as I
Made you in supposition: my thoughts

Point on no sensuality; remit
What's past, and I will meet your best affection.
I know you love me still; do not refuse me.
If I go once more back, you ne'er recover me.

    Fair. I am as ticklish.

    Mis. Car. Then, let's clap it up wisely,
While we are both i' the humour; I do find
A grudging, and your last words stick in my stomach.
Say, is't a match? speak quickly, or for ever
Hereafter hold your peace.

    Fair. Done!

    Mis. Car. Why, done!

    Fair. Seal and deliver.

    Mis. Car. My hand and heart; this shall suffice till
        morning.

    Fair. Each other's now by conquest, come let's to
If you should fail now!—   ['em.

    Mis. Car. Hold me not worth the hanging. [*Exeunt.*

SCENE II.—*Another Room in the same.*

Enter JULIETTA, *Lord* BONVILE, *and* TRIER.

    Lord B. I knew not
She was thy mistress, which encouraged
All my discourses.

    Tri. My lord, you have richly satisfied me, and
Now I dare write myself the happiest lover
In all the world.   Know lady, I have tried you.

    Jul. You have, it seems!

    Tri. And I have found thee right
And perfect gold, nor will I change thee for
A crown imperial.

    Jul. And I have tried you,
And found you dross; nor do I love my heart
So ill, to change it with you.

Tri. How's this?

Jul. Unworthily you have suspected me,
And cherished that bad humour, for which know
You never must have hope to gain my love.
He that shall doubt my virtue, out of fancy,
Merits my just suspicion and disdain.

Lord B. Oh fie, Frank, practise jealousy so soon!
Distrust the truth of her thou lov'st! suspect
Thy own heart sooner.—What I have said I have
Thy pardon for; thou wert a wife for him
Whose thoughts were ne'er corrupted.

Tri. 'Twas but a trial, and may plead for pardon.

Jul. I pray deny me not that liberty:
I will have proof, too, of the man I choose
My husband; and believe me, if men be
At such a loss of goodness, I will value
Myself, and think no honour equal to
Remain a virgin.

Tri. I have made a trespass,
Which if I cannot expiate, yet let me
Dwell in your charity.

Jul. You shall not doubt that.—

Enter FAIRFIELD, Mistress CAROL, LACY, and Mistress
BONAVENT.

Pray, my lord, know him for your servant.

Fair. I am much honoured.

Lord B. You cannot but deserve more
By the title of her brother.

Lacy. Another couple!

Mis. Bon. Master Fairfield and my cousin are contracted.

Mis. Car. 'Tis time, I think; sister I'll shortly call you.

Jul. I ever wished it.

Fair. Frank Trier is melancholy.—How hast thou
sped?

Tri. No, no, I am very merry.

Jul. Our banns, sir, are forbidden.

Fair. On what terms?

Lacy. My lord, you meet but a coarse entertainment.
How chance the music speaks not? Shall we dance?

Enter VENTURE *and* RIDER.

Vent. " Rivers of hell, I come !"

Rid. " Charon, thy oar
Is needless."—Save you, gallants !

Vent. " I will swim unto thy shore." Art not thou
    Hero ?

Mis. Car. But you are not Leander, if you be
Not drowned in the Hellespont.

Vent. I told thee "I would drown myself a hundred
    times a day."

Mis Car. Your letter did.

Vent. Ah ha !

Mis. Car. It was a devilish good one.

Vent. Then I am come
To tickle the "confines of Elysium."—
My lord,—I invite you to my wedding, and all this good
    company.

Lord B. I am glad your shoulder is recovered ;
When is the day ?

Vent. Do thou set the time.

Mis. Car. After to-morrow, name it.
This gentleman and I
Shall be married in the morning, and you know
We must have a time to dine, and dance to bed.

Vent. Married ?

Fair. Yes, you may be a guest, sir, and be welcome.

Vent. I am bobbed[1] again !
I'll bob for no more eels ; let her take her course.

Lacy. Oh for some willow garlands !
                 [*Recorders*[2] *sound within.*

---

[1] Tricked.   [2] Flageolets.

Enter Page, *followed by* Bonavent *in another disguise,
with willow garlands in his hand.*

Lord B. This is my boy; how now, sirrah?
Page. My lord, I am employed in a device.
    Room for the melancholy wight,
    Some do call him willow knight,
    Who this pains hath undertaken,
    To find out lovers are forsaken,
    Whose heads, because but little witted,
    Shall with garlands straight be fitted.
    Speak, who are tost on Cupid's billows,
    And receive the crown of willows,
    This way, that way, round about,

        [Bonavent *goes round the company with the
        garlands.*

    Keep your heads from breaking out.
Lacy. This is excellent! Nay, nay, gentlemen,
You must obey the ceremony.
Vent. He took measure of my head.
Rid. And mine.
Tri. It must be my fate too.

        [Bonavent *puts a garland on* Trier's *head.*
Vent. Now we be three.
Bona. And if you please to try, I do not think
But this would fit you excellently.
Lacy. Mine!
What does he mean?
Mis. Bon. I prithee, Master Lacy, try for once;
Nay, he has some conceit.
Lacy. For thy sake, I'll do any thing; what now?

        [Bonavent *puts a garland on* Lacy's *head.*
Bona. You are now a mess of willow—gentlemen—
And now, my lord, [*Throws off his disguise.*]—I'll pre-
sume to bid you welcome.

        [Mistress Bonavent *takes* Lord Bonvile *aside.*
Fair. Is not this the gentleman you made dance?
Lacy. My new acquaintance! where's thy beard?

Bona. I left it at the barber's; it grew rank,
And he has reaped it.

Lacy. Here, take thy toy again.

[*Takes off the garland.*

Bona. It shall not need.

Lord B. You tell me wonders, lady; is this gentleman
Your husband?

Lacy and Mis. Car. How! her husband, my lord?

Bona. Yes, indeed, lady; if you please you may
Call me your kinsman: seven year and misfortune,
I confess, had much disguised me, but I was,
And by degrees may prove again, her husband.

Mis. Bon. After a tedious absence, supposed death,
Arrived to make me happy.

Vent. This is rare!

Bona. My lord, and gentlemen,
You are no less welcome than before.—Master Lacy,
Droop not.

Lord B. This turn was above all expectation,
And full of wonder; I congratulate
Your mutual happiness.

Vent. All of a brotherhood!

Lacy. Master Bonavent! on my conscience it is he!
Did fortune owe me this?

Mis. Car. A thousand welcomes.

Mis. Bon. Equal joys to thee and Master Fairfield.

Lord B. Nay, then, you but obey the ceremony.

Lacy. I was not ripe for such a blessing; take her
And with an honest heart I wish you joys.
Welcome to life again! I see a providence
In this, and I obey it.

Vent. In such good company 'twould never grieve
A man to wear the willow.

Bona. You have but changed
Your host, whose heart proclaims a general welcome.

Mis. Bon. He was discovered to me in the Park,
Though I concealed it.

Shir.   s

Bona. Every circumstance
Of my absence, after supper we'll discourse of.
I will not doubt your lordship means to honour us.

Lord B. I'll be your guest, and drink a jovial health
To your new marriage, and the joys of your
Expected bride ; hereafter you may do
As much for me.—Fair lady, will you write
Me in your thoughts? if I desire to be
A servant to your virtue, will you not
Frown on me then?

Jul. Never in noble ways ;
No virgin shall more honour you.

Lord B. By thy cure
I am now myself, yet dare call nothing mine,
Till I be perfect blest in being thine.   [*Exeunt.*

THE
LADY OF PLEASURE.

T was in October, 1635, that the comedy of *The Lady of Pleasure* was licensed by the Master of the Revels and acted by her Majesty's Servants at the Private House in Drury Lane. The play seems to have been much liked. The first and only edition of it issued during Shirley's lifetime was published in 1637.

To the Right Honourable

RICHARD LORD LOVELACE, OF HURLEY.[1]

MY LORD,

 CANNOT want encouragement to present a poem to your lordship, while you possess so noble a breast, in which so many seeds of honour, to the example and glory of your name, obtained, before your years, a happy maturity. This comedy, fortunate in the scene, and one that may challenge a place in the first form of the author's compositions, most humbly addresseth itself to your honour; if it meet your gracious acceptance, and that you repent not to be a patron, your lordship will only crown the imagination, and for ever, by this favour, oblige,

My Lord,
The most humble services of your honourer,

JAMES SHIRLEY.

[1] Sir Richard Lovelace was created Lord Lovelace of Hurley in Berkshire in 1627.

DRAMATIS PERSONÆ.

Sir Thomas Bornwell.
Lord A.
Sir William Scentlove, ⎫
Master Alexander Kickshaw, ⎬ Gallants.
Master John Littleworth, ⎭
Haircut, a Barber.
Master Frederick, nephew to Lady Bornwell.
Steward to Sir Thomas Bornwell.
Steward to Celestina.
Secretary to Lord A.
Servants, &c.

Lady Bornwell, Wife of Sir Thomas.
Celestina, a young Widow.
Isabella, ⎫
Mariana, ⎬ Friends of Celestina.
Decoy, a Procuress.
Gentlewoman.

SCENE—The Strand.

THE LADY OF PLEASURE.

ACT THE FIRST.

SCENE I.—*A Room in* Sir THOMAS BORNWELL'S *House.*

Enter Lady BORNWELL, *and* Steward.

STEW. Be patient, madam; you may have
    your pleasure.
    Lady B. 'Tis that I came to town for.
    I would not
Endure again the country conversation,
To be the lady of six shires! The men,
So near the primitive making, they retain
A sense of nothing but the earth; their brains,
And barren heads standing as much in want
Of ploughing as their ground. To hear a fellow
Make himself merry and his horse, with whistling
Sellinger's Round![1] To observe with what solemnity
They keep their wakes, and throw for pewter candle-
    sticks !
How they become the morris, with whose bells
They ring all in to Whitsun-ales; and sweat,
Through twenty scarfs and napkins, till the hobby-horse
Tire, and the Maid Marian, dissolved to a jelly,
Be kept for spoon meat !

[1] A tune adapted to country dances.

Stew. These, with your pardon, are no argument
To make the country life appear so hateful;
At least to your particular, who enjoyed
A blessing in that calm, would you be pleased
To think so, and the pleasure of a kingdom;
While your own will commanded what should move
Delights, your husband's love and power joined
To give your life more harmony.   You lived there
Secure, and innocent, beloved of all;
Praised for your hospitality, and prayed for:
You might be envièd; but malice knew
Not where you dwelt.   I would not prophesy,
But leave to your own apprehension,
What may succeed your change.
    Lady B. You do imagine,
No doubt, you have talked wisely, and confuted
London past all defence.   Your master should
Do well to send you back into the country,
With title of superintendent-bailiff.
    Stew. How, madam!
    Lady B. Even so, sir.
    Stew. I am a gentleman,
Though now your servant.
    Lady B. A country gentleman,
By your affection to converse with stubble.
His tenants will advance your wit, and plump it so
With beef and bag-pudding!
    Stew. You may say your pleasure,
It becomes not me dispute.
    Lady B. Complain to
The lord of the soil, your master.
    Stew. You're a woman
Of an ungoverned passion, and I pity you.

Enter Sir THOMAS BORNWELL.

Born. How now?   What's the matter?
Stew. Nothing, sir.   [*Exit.*

Born. Angry, sweetheart?

Lady B. I am angry with myself,
To be so miserably restrained in things,
Wherein it doth concern your love and honour
To see me satisfied.

Born. In what, Aretina,
Dost thou accuse me? Have I not obeyed
All thy desires? against mine own opinion
Quitted the country, and removed the hope
Of our return, by sale of that fair lordship
We lived in? changed a calm and retired life
For this wild town, composed of noise and charge?

Lady B. What charge, more than is necessary for
A lady of my birth and education?

Born. I am not ignorant how much nobility
Flows in your blood; your kinsmen great and powerful
I' the state; but with this, lose not you memory
Of being my wife. I shall be studious,
Madam, to give the dignity of your birth
All the best ornaments which become my fortune;
But would not flatter it, to ruin both,
And be the fable of the town, to teach
Other men loss of wit by mine, employed
To serve your vast expenses.

Lady B. Am I then
Brought in the balance? So, sir!

Born. Though you weigh
Me in a partial scale, my heart is honest,
And must take liberty to think you have
Obeyed no modest counsel, to affect,
Nay, study ways of pride and costly ceremony:
Your change of gaudy furniture, and pictures
Of this Italian master, and that Dutchman;
Your mighty looking-glasses, like artillery,
Brought home on engines; the superfluous plate,
Antique and novel; vanities of tires;
Fourscore-pound suppers for my lord, your kinsman,

Banquets for t' other lady aunt, and cousins,
And perfumes that exceed all: train of servants,
To stifle us at home, and show abroad
More motley than the French or the Venetian,
About your coach, whose rude postillion
Must pester every narrow lane, till passengers
And tradesmen curse your choking up their stalls;
And common cries pursue your ladyship,
For hindering of their market.

 Lady B. Have you done, sir?

 Born. I could accuse the gaiety of your wardrobe,
And prodigal embroideries, under which
Rich satins, plushes, cloth of silver, dare
Not show their own complexions; your jewels,
Able to burn out the spectators' eyes,
And show like bonfires on you by the tapers:
Something might here be spared, with safety of
Your birth and honour, since the truest wealth
Shines from the soul, and draws up just admirers.—
I could urge something more.

 Lady B. Pray do, I like
Your homily of thrift.

 Born. I could wish, madam,
You would not game so much.

 Lady B. A gamester too!

 Born. But are not come to that acquaintance yet,
Should teach you skill enough to raise your profit.
You look not through the subtilty of cards,
And mysteries of dice; nor can you save
Charge with the box, buy petticoats and pearls,
And keep your family by the precious income;
Nor do I wish you should: my poorest servant
Shall not upbraid my tables, nor his hire,
Purchased beneath my honour. You make play
Not a pastime but a tyranny, and vex
Yourself and my estate by it.

 Lady B. Good! proceed.

Born. Another game you have, which consumes more
Your fame than purse ; your revels in the night,
Your meetings called the Ball, to which repair,
As to the court of pleasure, all your gallants,
And ladies, thither bound by a subpœna
Of Venus, and small Cupid's high displeasure ;
'Tis but the Family of Love[1] translated
Into more costly sin !   There was a play on't,
And had the poet not been bribed to a modest
Expression of your antic gambols in't,
Some darks had been discovered, and the deeds too
In time he may repent, and make some blush,
To see the second part danced on the stage.
My thoughts acquit you for dishonouring me
By any foul act ; but the virtuous know,
'Tis not enough to clear ourselves, but the
Suspicions of our shame.

    Lady B. Have you concluded
Your lecture ?

    Born. I have done ; and howsoever
My language may appear to you, it carries
No other than my fair and just intent
To your delights, without curb to their modest,
And noble freedom.

    Lady B. I'll not be so tedious
In my reply ; but, without art or elegance,
Assure you, I keep still my first opinion :
And though you veil your avaricious meaning
With handsome names of modesty and thrift,
I find you would intrench and wound the liberty
I was born with.   Were my desires unprivileged
By example, while my judgment thought 'em fit,
You ought not to oppose ; but when the practice
And track of every honourable lady

---

[1] The supposed licentiousness of this religious sect is often
noticed by the writers of our poet's age. Middleton has a drama
with this title.

Authorise me, I take it great injustice
To have my pleasures circumscribed, and taught me.
A narrow-minded husband is a thief
To his own fame, and his preferment too ;
He shuts his parts and fortunes from the world,
While, from the popular vote and knowledge, men
Rise to employment in the state.

Born. I have
No great ambition to buy preferment at
So dear a rate.

Lady B. Nor I to sell my honour,
By living poor and sparingly ; I was not
Bred in that ebb of fortune, and my fate
Shall not compel me to it.

Born. I know not,
Madam ; but you pursue these ways—

Lady B. What ways ?

Born. In the strict sense of honesty, I dare
Make oath they are innocent.

Lady B. Do not divert,
By busy troubling of your brain, those thoughts
That should preserve 'em.

Born. How was that?

Lady B. 'Tis English.

Born. But carries some unkind sense.

Enter DECOY.

Dec. Good morrow, my sweet madam.

Lady B. Decoy ! welcome ;
This visit is a favour.

Dec. Alas, sweet madam,
I cannot stay ; I came but to present
My service to your ladyship ; I could not
Pass by your door, but I must take the boldness
To tender my respects.

Lady B. You oblige me, madam ;
But I must not dispense so with your absence.

Dec. Alas, the coach, madam, stays for me at the
    door.

Lady B. Thou shalt command mine; prithee, sweet
    Decoy—

Dec. I would wait on you, madam, but I have many
Visits to make this morning; I beseech—

Lady B. So you will promise to dine with me.

Dec. I shall
Present a guest.

Lady B. Why, then good morrow, madam.

Dec. A happy day shine on your ladyship!   [*Exit.*

Re-enter Steward.

Lady B. What's your news, sir?

Stew. Madam, two gentlemen.

Lady B. What gentlemen?   Have they no names?

Stew. They are,
The gentleman with his own head of hair,
Whom you commended for his horsemanship
In Hyde Park, and becoming so the saddle,
The t'other day.

Lady B. What circumstance is this
To know him by?

Stew. His name's at my tongue's end:—
He liked the fashion of your pearl chain, madam;
And borrowed it for his jeweller to take
A copy by it.

Born. What cheating gallant's this?   [*Aside.*

Stew. That never walks without a lady's busk,
And plays with fans—Master Alexander Kickshaw,—
I thought I should remember him.

Lady B. What's the other?

Stew. What an unlucky memory I have!
The gallant that still danceth in the street,
And wears a gross of ribbon in his hat;
That carries oringado in his pocket,
And sugar-plums, to sweeten his discourse;

That studies compliment, defies all wit
In black, and censures plays that are not bawdy—
Master John Littleworth.

   Lady B. They are welcome; but
Pray entertain them a small time, lest I
Be unprovided.

   Born. Did they ask for me?

   Stew. No, sir.

   Born. It matters not, they must be welcome.

   Lady B. Fie! how's this hair disordered? Here's a
     curl
Straddles most impiously. I must to my closet. [*Exit.*

   Born. Wait on 'em; my lady will return again.
                                [*Exit* Steward.
I have to such a height fulfilled her humour,
All application's dangerous: these gallants
Must be received, or she will fall into
A tempest, and the house be shook with names
Of all her kindred. 'Tis a servitude
I may in time shake off.

       Enter KICKSHAW *and* LITTLEWORTH.

   Kick and Little. Save you, Sir Thomas!

   Born. Save you, gentlemen!

   Kick. I kiss your hand.

   Born. What day is it abroad?

   Little. The morning rises from your lady's eye:
If she look clear, we take the happy omen
Of a fair day.

   Born. She'll instantly appear,
To the discredit of your compliment;
But you express your wit thus.

   Kick. And you modesty,
Not to affect the praises of your own.

   Born. Leaving this subject, what game's now on
     foot?
What exercise carries the general vote

O' the town, now? nothing moves without your know-
          ledge.

Kick. The cocking now has all the noise; I'll have
A hundred pieces on one battle.—Oh,
These birds of Mars!

Little. Venus is Mars' bird too.

Kick. Why, and the pretty doves are Venus's,
To show that kisses draw the chariot.

Little. I am for that skirmish.

Born. When shall we have
More booths and bagpipes upon Banstead downs?
No mighty race is expected?—But my lady
Returns!

Re-enter Lady BORNWELL.

Lady B. Fair morning to you, gentlemen!
You went not late to bed by your early visit.
You do me honour.

Kick. It becomes our service.

Lady B. What news abroad? you hold precious intelli-
          gence.

Little. All tongues are so much busy with your praise,
They have not time to frame other discourse.
Will't please you, madam, taste a sugar-plum?

Born. What does the goldsmith think the pearl is
          worth
You borrowed of my lady?

Kick. 'Tis a rich one.

Born. She has many other toys, whose fashion you
Will like extremely : you have no intention
To buy any of her jewels?

Kick. Understand me—

Born. You had rather sell, perhaps. But leaving this.
I hope you'll dine with us.

Kick. I came o' purpose.

Lady B. And where were you last night

Kick. I, madam? where

I slept not ; it had been sin, where so much
Delight and beauty was to keep me waking.
There is a lady, madam, will be worth
Your free society ; my conversation
Ne'er knew so elegant and brave a soul,
With most incomparable flesh and blood ;
So spirited ! so courtly ! speaks the languages,
Sings, dances, plays o' the lute to admiration !
Is fair, and paints not ; games too, keeps a table,
And talks most witty satire ; has a wit
Of a clean Mercury—

 Little. Is she married ?

 Kick. No.

 Lady B. A virgin ?

 Kick. Neither.

 Little. What ! a widow ! something
Of this wide commendation might have been
Excused.   This such a prodigy !

 Kick. Repent,
Before I name her : she did never see
Yet full sixteen, an age, in the opinion
Of wise men, not contemptible. She has
Mourned out her year too for the honest knight
That had compassion of her youth, and died
So timely.   Such a widow is not common ;
And now she shines more fresh and tempting
Than any natural virgin.

 Lady B. What's her name ?

 Kick. She was christened Celestina ; by her husband,
The Lady Bellamour : this ring was hers.

 Born. You borrowed it to copy out the posy.

 Kick. Are they not pretty rubies ? 'twas a grace
She was pleased to show me, that I might have one
Made of the self-same fashion ; for I love
All pretty forms.

 Lady B. And is she glorious ?

 Kick. She is full of jewels, madam ; but I am

Most taken with the bravery of her mind,
Although her garments have all grace and ornament.

Lady B. You have been high in praises.

Kick. I come short;
No flattery can reach her.

Born. Now my lady
Is troubled, as she feared to be eclipsed :
This news will cost me somewhat.   [*Aside.*

Lady B. You deserve
Her favour, for this noble character.

Kick. And I possess it, by my stars benevolence.

Lady B. You must bring us acquainted.

Born. I pray do, sir ;
I long to see her too.—Madam, I have
Thought upon't, and corrected my opinion.
Pursue what ways of pleasure your desires
Incline you to, not only with my state,
But with my person ; I will follow you
I see the folly of my thrift, and will
Repent in sack and prodigality,
To your own heart's content.

Lady B. But do not mock.

Born. Take me to your embraces, gentlemen,
And tutor me.

Little. And will you kiss the ladies ?

Born. And sing and dance. I long to see this beauty;
I would fain lose a hundred pounds at dice now.—
Thou shalt have another gown and petticoat
To-morrow ;—will you sell me running-horses ?
We have no Greek wine in the house, I think ;
Pray send one of our footmen to the merchant,
And throw the hogsheads of March-beer into
The kennel, to make room for sack and claret.
What think you to be drunk yet before dinner?
We will have constant music, and maintain
Them and their fiddles in fantastic liveries :
I'll tune my voice to catches.—I must have

Shir.

T

My dining-room enlarged, to invite ambassadors
We'll feast the parish in the fields, and teach
The military men new discipline,
Who shall charge all their great artillery
With oranges and lemons, boy, to play
All dinner upon our capons.

 Kick. He's exalted!

 Born. I will do anything to please my lady,
Let that suffice; and kiss o' the same condition.
I am converted; do not you dispute,
But patiently allow the miracle.

 Lady B. I am glad to hear you, sir, in so good tune

Enter Servant.

 Serv. Madam, the painter.

 Lady B. I am to sit this morning.

 Born. Do.
While I give new directions to my steward.

 Kick. With your favour, we'll wait on you.
Sitting's but a melancholy exercise without
Some company to discourse.

 Lady B. It does conclude
A lady's morning work. We rise, make fine,
Sit for our picture, and 'tis time to dine.

 Little. Praying's forgot.

 Kick. 'Tis out of fashion.   [*Exeunt.*

SCENE II.—*A Room in* CELESTINA'S *House.*

Enter CELESTINA *and her* Steward.

 Cel. Fie! what an air this room has!

 Stew. 'Tis perfumed.

 Cel. With some cheap stuff. Is it your wisdom's thrift
To infect my nostrils thus? or is't to favour
The gout in your worship's hand, you are afraid

To exercise your pen in your account book ?
Or do you doubt my credit to discharge
Your bills?

Stew. Madam, I hope you have not found
My duty, with the guilt of sloth or jealousy,
Unapt to your command.

Cel. You can extenuate
Your faults with language, sir ; but I expect
To be obeyed.   What hangings have we here !

Stew. They are arras, madam.

Cel. Impudence ! I know't.
I will have fresher, and more rich; not wrought
With faces that may scandalize a Christian,
With Jewish stories stuffed with corn and camels.[1]
You had best wrap all my chambers in wild Irish,
And make a nursery of monsters here,
To fright the ladies come to visit me.

Stew. Madam, I hope—

Cel. I say I will have other,
Good Master Steward, of a finer loom ;
Some silk and silver, if your worship please
To let me be at so much cost.   I'll have
Stories to fit the seasons of the year,
And change as often as I please.

Stew. You shall, madam.

Cel. I am bound to your consent, forsooth ! And is
My coach brought home ?

Stew. This morning I expect it.

Cel. The inside, as I gave directions,
Of crimson plush ?

Stew. Of crimson camel plush.

Cel. Ten thousand moths consume't !   Shall I ride through
The streets in penance, wrapt up round in hair cloth ?
Sell't to an alderman, 'twill serve his wife
To go a feasting to their country-house;

[1] The story of Joseph and his brethren.

Or fetch a merchant's nurse-child, and come home
Laden with fruit and cheese-cakes. I despise it!

Stew. The nails adorn it, madam, set in method,
And pretty forms.

Cel. But single gilt, I warrant.

Stew. No, madam.

Cel. Another solecism! Oh fie!
This fellow will bring me to a consumption
With fretting at his ignorance. Some lady
Had rather never pray, than go to church in't.
The nails not double gilt! To market with't;
'Twill hackney out to Mile-end, or convey
Your city tumblers, to be drunk with cream
And prunes at Islington.

Stew. Good madam, hear me.

Cel. I'll rather be beholding to my aunt
The countess, for her mourning coach, than be
Disparaged so. Shall any juggling tradesman
Be at charge to shoe his running-horse with gold,[1]
And shall my coach nails be but single gilt!
How dare these knaves abuse me so?

Stew. Vouchsafe
To hear me speak.

Cel. Is my sedan yet finished,
And liveries for my men-mules, according
As I gave charge?

Stew. Yes, madam, it is finished,
But without tilting-plumes at the four corners;
The scarlet's pure, but not embroidered.

Cel. What mischief were it to your conscience
Were my coach lined with tissue, and my harness
Covered with needle-work? if my sedan
Had all the story of the prodigal
Embroidered with pearl?

---

[1] See *ante* p. 232, where "Toby with his golden shoes" is
enumerated among the running-horses; the above allusion is probably to the same animal, whose successes perhaps had led his
owner to distinguish him in so peculiar a way.—*Gifford.*

Stew. Alas, good madam,
I know 'tis your own cost; I am but your steward,
And would discharge my duty the best way.
You have been pleased to hear me; 'tis not for
My profit that I manage your estate,
And save expense, but for your honour, madam.

Cel. How, sir! my honour?

Stew. Though you hear it not,
Men's tongues are liberal in your character,
Since you began to live thus high. I know
Your fame is precious to you.

Cel. I were best
Make you my governor: audacious varlet!
How dare you interpose your doating counsel!
Mind your affairs with more obedience,
Or I shall ease you of an offence, sir.
Must I be limited to please your honour,
Or, for the vulgar breath, confine my pleasures?
I will pursue 'em in what shapes I fancy,
Here, and abroad; my entertainments shall
Be oftener, and more rich. Who shall control me?
I live i' the Strand, whither few ladies come
To live, and purchase, more than fame. I will
Be hospitable then, and spare no cost
That may engage all generous report
To trumpet forth my bounty and my bravery,
Till the court envy, and remove. I'll have
My house the academy of wits, who shall
Exalt their genius with rich sack and sturgeon,
Write panegyrics of my feasts, and praise
The method of my witty superfluities.
The horses shall be taught, with frequent waiting
Upon my gates, to stop in their career
Toward Charing-cross, spite of the coachman's fury;
And not a tilter but shall strike his plume,
When he sails by my window: my balcony
Shall be the courtier's idol, and more gazed at

Than all the pageantry at Temple Bar,
By country clients.

Stew. Sure my lady's mad.

Cel. Take that for your ill manners.   [*Strikes him.*

Stew. Thank you, madam.—
I would there were less quicksilver in your fingers.
[*Exit.*

Cel. There's more than simple honesty in a servant
Required to his full duty ; none should dare
But with a look, much less a saucy language,
Check at their mistress' pleasure.   I'm resolved
To pay for some delight, my estate will bear it;
I'll rein it shorter when I please.

Re-enter Steward.

Stew. A gentleman
Desires to speak with your ladyship.

Cel. His name?

Stew. He says you know him not · he seems to be
Of quality.

Cel. Admit him.   [*Exit* Steward.

Enter HAIRCUT.

Sir, with me?

Hair. Madam, I know not how you may receive
This boldness from me ; but my fair intents
Known, will incline you to be charitable.

Cel. No doubt, sir.

Hair. He must live obscurely, madam,
That hath not heard what virtues you possess;
And I, a poor admirer of your fame,
Am come to kiss your hand.

Cel. That all your business?

Hair. Though it were worth much travel, I have more
In my ambition.

Cel. Speak it freely, sir.

Hair. You are a widow.

Cel. So !

Hair. And I a bachelor.

Cel. You come a wooing, sir, and would perhaps
Show me a way to reconcile the two?

Hair. And bless my stars for such a happiness.

Cel. I like you, sir, the better, that you do not
Wander about, but shoot home to the meaning;
It is a confidence will make a man
Know sooner what to trust to: but I never
Saw you before, and I believe you come not
With hope to find me desperate upon marriage.
If maids, out of their ignorance of what
Men are, refuse these offers, widows may,
Out of their knowledge, be allowed some coyness
And yet I know not how much happiness
A peremptory answer may deprive me of;—
You may be some young lord, and though I see not
Your footmen and your groom, they may not be
Far off, in conference with your horse. Please you
To instruct me with your title, against which
I would not willingly offend.

Hair. I am
A gentleman; my name is Haircut, madam.

Cel. Sweet Master Haircut! are you a courtier?

Hair. Yes.

Cel. I did think so, by your confidence.
Not to detain you, sir, with circumstance,
I was not so unhappy in my husband,
But that 'tis possible I may be a wife
Again; but I must tell you, he that wins
My affection, shall deserve me.

Hair. I will hope,
If you can love, I shall not present, madam,
An object to displease you in my person:
And when time, and your patience, shall possess you
With further knowledge of me, and the truth
Of my devotion, you will not repent
The offer of my service.

Cel. You say well.
How long do you imagine you can love, sir?
Is it a quotidian, or will it hold
But every other day?

Hair. You are pleasant, madam.

Cel. Does it take you with a burning at the first,
Or with a cold fit? for you gentlemen
Have both your summer and your winter service.

Hair. I am ignorant what you mean; but I shall never
Be cold in my affection to such beauty.

Cel. And 'twill be somewhat long ere I be warm in't.

Hair. If you vouchsafe me so much honour, madam,
That I may wait on you sometimes, I shall not
Despair to see a change.

Cel. But, now I know
Your mind, you shall not need to tell it when
You come again; I shall remember it.

Hair. You make me fortunate.

Re-enter Steward.

Stew. Madam, your kinswomen,
The lady Novice, and her sister, are
New lighted from their coach.

Cel. I did expect 'em,
They partly are my pupils.   I'll attend them.

[*Exit* Steward.

Hair. Madam, I have been too great a trespasser
Upon your patience; I will take my leave:
You have affairs, and I have some employment
Calls me to court; I shall present again
A servant to you.   [*Exit.*

Cel. Sir, you may present,
But not give fire, I hope.   Now to the ladies.
This recreation's past, the next must be
To read to them some court philosophy.   [*Exit.*

ACT THE SECOND.

SCENE I.—*A Room in* Sir Thomas Bornwell's *House.*

Enter Sir Thomas Bornwell.

Born. 'Tis a strange humour I have undertaken,
To dance, and play, and spend as fast as she does;
But I am resolved: it may do good upon her,
And fright her into thrift.   Nay, I'll endeavour
To make her jealous too; if this do not
Allay her gamboling, she's past a woman,
And only a miracle must tame her.

Enter Steward.

Stew. 'Tis master Frederick, my lady's nephew
Born. What of him?
Stew. Is come from the university.
Born. By whose directions?
Stew. It seems, my lady's.
Born. Let me speak with him
Before he sees his aunt. [*Exit* Stew.]—I do not like it.—

Re-enter Steward, *with* Frederick, *in his college dress.*

Master Frederick, welcome!   I expected not
So soon your presence; what's the hasty cause?
Fred. These letters, from my tutor, will acquaint you.
[*Gives* Bornwell *letters.*

Stew. Welcome home, sweet Master Frederick!

Fred. Where's my aunt?

Stew. She's busy about her painting, in her closet;
The outlandish man of art is copying out
Her countenance.

Fred. She is sitting for her picture?

Stew. Yes, sir; and when 'tis drawn she will be hanged
Next the French cardinal, in the dining-room.
But when she hears you are come, she will dismiss
The Belgic gentleman, to entertain
Your worship.

Fred. Change of air has made you witty.

Born. Your tutor gives you a handsome character,
Frederick, and is sorry your aunt's pleasure
Commands you from your studies; but I hope
You have no quarrel to the liberal arts:
Learning is an addition beyond
Nobility of birth.   Honour of blood,
Without the ornament of knowledge, is
A glorious ignorance.

Fred. I never knew
More sweet and happy hours than I employed
Upon my books.   I heard
A part of my philosophy, and was so
Delighted with the harmony of nature,
I could have wasted my whole life upon it.

Born. 'Tis pity a rash indulgence should corrupt
So fair a genius!   She's here; I'll observe.   [*Aside.*

Enter Lady BORNWELL, KICKSHAW, *and* LITTLEWORTH.

Fred. My most loved aunt!

Lady B. Support me, I shall faint.

Little. What ails your ladyship?

Lady B. Is that Frederick,
In black?

Kick. Yes, madam; but the doublet's satin

Lady B. The boy's undone!

Fred. Madam, you appear troubled.

Lady B. Have I not cause? Was not I trusted with
Thy education, boy, and have they sent thee
Home like a very scholar!

Kick. 'Twas ill done,
Howe'er they used him in the university,
To send him to his friends thus.

Fred. Why, sir? black,
(For 'tis the colour that offends your eye-sight,)
Is not, within my reading, any blemish;
Sables are no disgrace in heraldry.

Kick. 'Tis coming from the college thus, that makes it
Dishonourable. While you wore it for
Your father, it was commendable; or were
Your aunt dead, you might mourn, and justify.

Lady B. What luck I did not send him into France
They would have given him generous education,
Taught him another garb, to wear his lock,[1]
And shape, as gaudy as the summer; how
To dance, and wag his feather *à-la-mode*,
To compliment, and cringe; to talk not modestly,
Like, " ay forsooth," and " no forsooth;" to blush,
And look so like a chaplain!—There he might
Have learned a brazen confidence, and observed
So well the custom of the country, that
He might, by this time, have invented fashions
For us, and been a benefit to the kingdom;
Preserved our tailors in their wits, and saved
The charge of sending into foreign courts
For pride and antic fashions.—Observe
In what a posture he does hold his hat now!

Fred. Madam, with your pardon you have practised
Another dialect than was taught me when
I was commended to your care and breeding.
I understand not this; Latin or Greek
Are more familiar to my apprehension:

---

[1] Hair.

Logic was not so hard in my first lectures
As your strange language.

 Lady B. Some strong waters; oh!

 Little. Comfits will be as comfortable to your stomach,
  madam.   [*Offers his box.*

 Lady B. I fear he's spoiled for ever! he did name
Logic, and may, for aught I know, be gone
So far to understand it. I did always
Suspect they would corrupt him in the college.—
Will your Greek saws and sentences discharge
The mercer? or is Latin a fit language
To court a mistress in?—Master Alexander,
If you have any charity, let me
Commend him to your breeding.—I suspect
I must employ my doctor first, to purge
The university that lies in's head;
It alters his complexion.

 Kick. If you dare
Trust me to serve him—

 Lady B. Master Littleworth,
Be you joined in commission.

 Little. I will teach him
Postures and rudiments.

 Lady B. I have no patience
To see him in this shape; it turns my stomach.
When he has cast his academic skin
He shall be your's. I am bound in conscience
To see him bred; his own state shall maintain
The charge, while he's my ward.—Come hither, sir.

 Fred. What does my aunt mean to do with me?

 Stew. To make you a fine gentleman, and translate
  you
Out of your learned language, sir, into
The present Goth and Vandal, which is French.

 Born. Into what mischief will this humour ebb?
She will undo the boy; I see him ruined.
My patience is not manly: but I must

Use stratagem to reduce her : open ways
Give me no hope.   [*Aside.*

 Stew. You shall be obeyed, madam.
    [*Exeunt all but* FREDERICK *and* Steward.
 Fred. Master Steward, are you sure we do not dream?
Was't not my aunt you talked to ?
 Stew. One that loves you
Dear as her life.   These clothes do not become you,
You must have better, sir——
 Fred. These are not old.
 Stew. More suitable to the town and time; we keep
No Lent here, nor is't my lady's pleasure you
Should fast from anything you have a mind to ;
Unless it be your learning, which she would have you
Forget with all convenient speed that may be,
For the credit of your noble family.
The case is altered since we lived i' the country ;
We do not now invite the poor o' the parish
To dinner, keep a table for the tenants ;
Our kitchen does not smell of beef ; the cellar
Defies the price of malt and hops ; the footmen
And coach-drivers may be drunk like gentlemen,
With wine; nor will three fiddlers upon holidays,
With aid of bag-pipes, that called in the country
To dance, and plough the hall up with their hob-nails,
Now make my lady merry.   We do feed
Like princes, and feast nothing else but princes ;
And are these robes fit to be seen amongst 'em ?
 Fred. My lady keeps a court then ! Is Sir Thomas
Affected with this state and cost ?
 Stew. He was not;
But is converted: and I hope you will not
Persist in heresy, but take a course
Of riot, to content your friends ; you shall
Want nothing, if you can be proud, and spend it
For my lady's honour.   Here are a hundred
Pieces, will serve you till you have new clothes ;

I will present you with a nag of mine,
Poor tender of my service, please you accept;
My lady's smile more than rewards me for it.
I must provide fit servants to attend you,
Monsieurs, for horse and foot.

 Fred. I shall submit,
If this be my aunt's pleasure, and be ruled;
My eyes are opened with this purse already,
And sack will help to inspire me.   I must spend it?

 Stew. What else, sir?

 Fred. I'll begin with you: to encourage
You to have still a special care of me,
There is five pieces,—not for your nag.

 Stew. No, sir; I hope it is not.

 Fred. Buy a beaver
For thy own block;[1] I shall be ruled.   Who does
Command the wine cellar?

 Stew. Who commands but you, sir?

 Fred. I'll try to drink a health or two, my aunt's,
Or anybody's; and if that foundation
Stagger me not too much, I will commence
In all the arts of London.

 Stew. If you find, sir,
The operation of the wine exalt
Your blood to the desire of any female
Delight, I know your aunt will not deny
Any of her chambermaids to practise on;
She loves you but too well.

 Fred. I know not how
I may be for that exercise—Farewell, Aristotle
Prithee commend me to the library
At Westminster; my bones I bequeath thither,
And to the learned worms that mean to visit 'em.
I will compose myself; I begin to think
I have lost time indeed.—Come to the wine cellar.

          [*Exeunt.*

---

[1] The block was the mould on which the hat was shaped, but here
the head is evidently intended.

SCENE II.—*A Room in* CELESTINA'S *House.*

Enter CELESTINA, MARIANA, *and* ISABELLA.

Mar. But shall we not, madam, expose ourselves
To censure for this freedom?

Cel. Let them answer,
That dare mistake us. Shall we be so much
Cowards, to be frighted from our pleasure,
Because men have malicious tongues, and show
What miserable souls they have? No, cousin,
We hold our life and fortunes upon no
Man's charity; if they dare show so little
Discretion to traduce our fames, we will
Be guilty of so much wit to laugh at them

Isab. 'Tis a becoming fortitude.

Cel. My stars
Are yet kind to me; for, in a happy minute
Be it spoke, I'm not in love, and men shall never
Make my heart lean with sighing, nor with tears
Draw on my eyes the infamy of spectacles.
'Tis the chief principle to keep your heart
Under your own obedience; jest, but love not.
I say my prayers, yet can wear good clothes,
And only satisfy my tailor for them.
I will not lose my privilege.

Mar. And yet they say your entertainments are,
Give me your pardon, madam, to proclaim
Yourself a widow, and to get a husband.

Cel. As if a lady of my years, some beauty,
Left by her husband rich, that had mourned for him
A twelvemonth too, could live so obscure i' the town,
That gallants would not know her, and invite
Themselves, without her chargeable proclamations!
Then we are worse than citizens: no widow
Left wealthy can be thoroughly warm in mourning,
But some one noble blood, or lusty kindred,
Claps in, with his gilt coach, and Flandrian trotters.

And hurries her away to be a countess.
Courtiers have spies, and great ones with large titles,
Cold in their own estates, would warm themselves
At a rich city bonfire.

 Isab. Most true, madam.

 Cel. No matter for corruption of the blood:
Some undone courtier made her husband rich,
And this new lord receives it back again.
Admit it were my policy, and that
My entertainments pointed to acquaint me
With many suitors, that I might be safe,
And make the best election, could you blame me?

 Mar. Madam, 'tis wisdom.

 Cel. But I should be
In my thoughts miserable, to be fond
Of leaving the sweet freedom I possess,
And court myself into new marriage fetters.
I now observe men's several wits, and windings,
And can laugh at their follies.

 Mar. You have given
A most ingenious satisfaction.

 Cel. One thing I'll tell you more, and this I give you
Worthy your imitation, from my practice :
You see me merry, full of song and dancing,
Pleasant in language, apt to all delights
That crown a public meeting ; but you cannot
Accuse me of being prodigal of my favours
To any of my guests.   I do not summon,
By any wink, a gentleman to follow me,
To my withdrawing chamber ; I hear all
Their pleas in court, nor can they boast abroad,
And do me justice, after a salute,
They have much conversation with my lip.
I hold the kissing of my hand a courtesy,
And he that loves me, must, upon the strength
Of that, expect till I renew his favour.
Some ladies are so expensive in their graces,

To those that honour them, and so prodigal,
That in a little time they have nothing but
The naked sin left to reward their servants
Whereas, a thrift in our rewards will keep
Men long in their devotion, and preserve
Ourselves in stock, to encourage those that honour us.

   Isab. This is an art worthy a lady's practice.

   Cel. It takes not from the freedom of our mirth,
But seems to advance it, when we can possess
Our pleasures with security of our honour;
And, that preserved, I welcome all the joys
My fancy can let in. In this I have given
The copy of my mind, nor do I blush
You understand it.

   Isab. You have honoured us.

     Enter CELESTINA'S Gentlewoman.

   Gentlew. Madam, Sir William Scentlove's come, to
wait on you.

   Cel. There's one would be a client.—Make excuse
For a few minutes.   [*Exit* Gentlewoman.

   Mar. One that comes a wooing?

   Cel. Such a thing he would seem, but in his guiltiness
Of little land, his expectation is not
So valiant as it might be. He wears rich clothes
And feeds with noblemen; to some, I hear,
No better than a wanton emissary,
Or scout for Venus' wild fowl; which made tame,
He thinks no shame to stand court sentinel,
In hope of the reversion.

   Mar. I have heard
That some of them are often my lord's tasters,
The first fruits they condition for, and will
Exact as fees, for the promotion.

   Cel. Let them agree, there's no account shall lie
For me among their traffic.

    Shir.   U

Re-enter Gentlewoman.

Gentlew. Master Haircut, madam,
Is new come in, to tender you his service.

Cel. Let him discourse a little with Sir William.

Mar. What is this gentleman, Master Haircut, madam?
I note him very gallant, and much courted
By gentlemen of quality.

Cel. I know not,
More than a trim gay man; he has some great office,
Sure, by his confident behaviour:
He would be entertained under the title
Of servant to me, and I must confess,
He is the sweetest of all men that visit me.

Isab. How mean you, madam?

Cel. He is full of powder;
He will save much in perfume for my chamber,
Were he but constant here.   Give them access.
                                    [*Exit* Gentlewoman.

Enter Sir WILLIAM SCENTLOVE *and* HAIRCUT.

Scent. Madam, the humblest of your servants is
Exalted to a happiness, if you smile
Upon my visit.

Hair. I must beg your charity
Upon my rudeness, madam; I shall give
That day up lost to any happiness,
When I forget to tender you my service.

Cel. You practise courtship, gentlemen.

Scent. But cannot
Find wherewith more desert to exercise it.
What lady's this, I pray?

Cel. A kinswoman
Of mine, Sir William.

Scent. I am more her servant.

Cel. You came from court, now, I presume?

Hair. 'Tis, madam,

The sphere I move in, and my destiny
Was kind to place me there, where I enjoy
All blessings that a mortal can possess,
That lives not in your presence ; and I should
Fix my ambition, when you would vouchsafe
Me so much honour, to accept from me
An humble entertainment there.

Cel. But by
What name shall I be known ? in what degree
Shall I be of kindred to you ?

Hair. How mean you, madam ?

Cel. Perhaps you'll call me sister, I shall take it
A special preferment ; or it may be
I may pass under title of your mistress,
If I seem rich, and fair enough, to engage
Your confidence to own me.

Hair. I would hope—

Cel. But 'tis not come to that yet : you will, sir.
Excuse my mirth.

Hair. Sweet madam !

Cel. Shall I take
Boldness to ask what place you hold in court?
'Tis an uncivil curiosity ;
But you'll have mercy to a woman's question.

Hair. My present condition, madam, carries
Honour and profit, though not to be named
With that employment I expect i' the state,
Which shall discharge the first maturity
Upon your knowledge ; until then, I beg
You allow a modest silence.

Cel. I am charmed, sir ;
And if you 'scape ambassador, you cannot
Reach a preferment wherein I'm against you.
But where is Sir William Scentlove?

Hair. Give him leave
To follow his nose, madam, while he hunts
In view,—he'll soon be at a fault.

Cel. You know him?

Hair. Know Scentlove? not a page but can decipher
     him;

The waiting-women know him to a scruple;

He's called the blister-maker of the town.

Cel. What's that?

Hair. The laundry ladies can resolve you,

And you may guess: an arrant epicure,

As this day lives, born to a pretty wit,

A knight, too; but no gentleman. I must

Be plain to you;—your ladyship may have

Use of this knowledge, but conceal the author.

Scent. I kiss your fairest hand.

Mar. You make a difference;

Pray reconcile them to an equal whiteness.

Scent. You wound my meaning, lady.

Cel. Nay, Sir William

Has the art of compliment.

Scent. Madam, you honour me

'Bove my desert of language.

Cel. Will you please

To enrich me with your knowledge of that gentleman?

Scent. Do you not know him, madam?

Cel. What is he?

Scent. A camphire ball; you shall know more here-
     after;

He shall tell you himself, and save my character;

Till then,—you see he's proud.

Cel. One thing, gentlemen,

I observe in your behaviour, which is rare

In two that court one mistress: you preserve

A noble friendship; there's no gum within

Your hearts; you cannot fret,[1] or show an envy

Of one another's hope; some would not govern

Their passions with that temper!

---

[1] An allusion to Shakespeare's *Henry IV*. "I have hid Falstaff's
horse, and he frets like gummed velvet."– *Gifford*.

Scent. The whole world
Shall nor divorce our friendship.—Master Haircut!
Would I had lives to serve him! he is lost
To goodness does not honour him.

Hair. My knight!

Cel. This is right playing at court shuttlecock. [*Aside.*

Re-enter Gentlewoman.

Gentlew. Madam, there is a gentleman desires
To speak with you, one Sir Thomas Bornwell.

Cel. Bornwell?

Gentlew. He says he is a stranger to your ladyship.

Scent. I know him.

Hair. Your neighbour, madam.

Scent. Husband to
The lady that so revels in the Strand.

Hair. He has good parts, they say, but cannot help
His lady's bias.

Cel. They have both much fame
I' the town, for several merits. Pray admit him.
[*Exit* Gentlewoman.

Hair. What comes he for? [*Aside.*

Enter Sir THOMAS BORNWELL.

Born. Your pardon, noble lady, that I have
Presumed, a stranger to your knowledge,—
[*Salutes* CELESTINA.

Cel. Sir,
Your worth was here before you, and your person
Cannot be here ungrateful.

Born. 'Tis the bounty
Of your sweet disposition, madam.—Make me
Your servant, lady, by her fair example,
To favour me. [*Offers to salute* ISABELLA, *who turns
from him.*]—I never knew one turn
Her cheek to a gentleman that came to kiss her,

But she'd a stinking breath [*Aside.*]—Your servant, gen-
     tlemen.
Will Scentlove, how is't?

   Cel. I am sorry, coz,
To accuse you; we in nothing more betray
Ourselves to censure of ridiculous pride,
Than answering a fair salute too rudely.
Oh, it shows ill upon a gentlewoman
Not to return the modest lip, if she
Would have the world believe her breath is not
Offensive.

   Born. Madam, I have business
With you.

   Scent. His looks are pleasant.

   Cel. With me, sir?

   Born. I hear you have an excellent wit, madam;
I see you are fair.

   Cel. The first is but report;
And do not trust your eye-sight for the last,
'Cause I presume you're mortal, and may err.

   Hair. He is very gamesome.

   Born. You have an excellent voice,
(They say you catched it from a dying swan,)
With which, joined to the harmony of your lute,
You ravish all mankind.

   Cel. Ravish mankind?

   Born. With their consent.

   Cel. It were the stranger rape;
But there's the less indictment lies against it:
And there is hope your little honesties
Cannot be much the worse, for men do rather
Believe they had a maidenhead, than put
Themselves to the rack of memory how long
'Tis since they left the burden of their innocence.

   Born. Why, you are bitter, madam!

   Cel. So is physic;
I do not know your constitution.

Born. You shall, if 't please you, madam.

Cel. You're too hasty,
I must examine what certificate
You have first, to prefer you.

Born. Fine! certificate?

Cel. Under your lady's hand and seal.

Born. Go to;
I see you are a wag.

Cel. But take heed how
You trust to 't.

Born. I can love you in my wedlock,
As well as that young gallant o' the first hair,
Or the knight-bachelor; and can return
As amorous delight to your soft bosom.

Cel. Your person and your language are both
strangers.

Born. But may be more familiar; I have those
That dare make affidavit for my body.

Cel. Do you mean your surgeon?

Born. My surgeon, madam?
i know not how you value my abilities,
But I dare undertake as much, to express
My service to your ladyship, and with
As fierce ambition fly to your commands,
As the most valiant of these lay siege to you.

Cel. You dare not, sir.

Born. How, madam?

Cel. I will justify it.
You dare not marry me; and I imagine
Some here, should I consent, would fetch a priest
Out of the fire.

Born. I have a wife indeed.

Cel. And there's a statute not repealed, I take it.

Born. You're in the right; I must confess you'v
hit
And bled me in a master vein.

Cel. You think

I took you on the advantage ; use your best
Skill at defence, I'll come up to your valour,
And show another work you dare not do :
You dare not, sir, be virtuous.

   Born. I dare,
By this fair hand I dare ; and ask a pardon,
If my rude words offend your innocence,
Which, in a form so beautiful, would shine
To force a blush in them suspected it,
And from the rest draw wonder.

   Hair. I like not
Their secret parley ; shall I interrupt them?

   Isab. By no means, sir.

   Scent. Sir Thomas was not wont
To show so much a courtier.

   Mar. He cannot
Be prejudicial to you ; suspect not
Your own deserts so much ; he's married.

   Born. I have other business, madam: you keep
     music :
I came to try how you can dance.

   Cel. You did?—I'll try his humour out of breath.
                                    [Aside.
Although I boast no cunning, sir, in revels,
If you desire to show your art that way,
I can wait on you.

   Born. You much honour me ;
Nay, all must join to make a harmony.   *[They dance.*

   Born. I have nothing now, madam, but to be-
     seech,
After a pardon for my boldness, you
Would give occasion to pay my gratitude :
I have a house will be much honoured,
If you vouchsafe your presence ; and a wife
Desires to present herself your servant.
I came with the ambition to invite you,

Deny me not ; your person you shall trust
On fair security.

   Cel. Sir, although I use not
This freedom with a stranger, you shall have
No cause to hold me obstinate.

   Born. You grace me.
Sir William Scentlove—

   Hair. I must take my leave.
You will excuse me, madam ; court attendance

   Cel. By any means.

   Born. Ladies, you will vouchsafe
Your company?

   Isab. We wait upon you, sir.   *[Exeunt.*

ACT THE THIRD.

SCENE I.—Lord A.'s *House.*—*A dressing Room, with table and looking-glass;* HAIRCUT *preparing a peruke.*

ORD. [*Within.*]—What hour is't?

    Hair. 'Bout three o'clock, my lord.

    Lord. 'Tis time to rise.

    Enter Lord A., *in his dressing-gown.*

    Hair. Your lordship went but late
To bed last night.

Lord. 'Twas early in the morning.

Sec. [*Within.*]—Expect awhile, my lord is busy.

    Enter Secretary.

Lord. What's the matter?

Sec. Here is a lady
Desires access to you upon some affairs,
She says, may specially concern your lordship.

Lord. A lady? what's her name?

Sec. Madam Decoy.

Lord. Decoy? Prithee admit her.— [*Exit* Secretary.

    Re-enter Secretary, *with* DECOY.

Have you business, madam,
With me?

Dec. And such, I hope, as will not be
Offensive to your lordship.

Lord. I pray speak it.

Dec. I would desire your lordship's ear more private.

Lord. Wait i' the next chamber till I call. [*Exeunt*
    HAIRCUT *and* Secretary.]—Now, madam.
Dec. Although I am a stranger to your lordship,
I would not lose a fair occasion offered,
To show how much I honour, and would serve you.
Lord. Please you to give me the particular,
That I may know the extent of my engagement.
I am ignorant by what desert you should
Be encouraged to have care of me.
Dec. My lord,
I will take boldness to be plain ; beside
Your other excellent parts, you have much fame
For your sweet inclination to our sex.
Lord. How do you mean, madam?
Dec. I' that way your lordship
Hath honourably practised upon some
Not to be named.   Your noble constancy
To a mistress, hath deserved our general vote;
And I, a part of womankind, have thought
How to express my duty.
Lord. In what, madam?
Dec. Be not so strange, my lord; I knew the beauty
And pleasures of your eyes; that handsome creature
With whose fair life all your delight took leave,
And to whose memory you have paid too much
Sad tribute.
Lord. What's all this?
Dec. This : if your lordship
Accept my service, in pure zeal to cure
Your melancholy, I could point where you might
Repair your loss.
Lord. Your ladyship, I conceive,
Doth traffic in flesh merchandize.
Dec. To men
Of honour, like yourself.   I am well known
To some in court, and come not with ambition
Now to supplant your officer.

Lord. What is
The Lady of Pleasure you prefer?

Dec. A lady
Of birth and fortune, one upon whose virtue
I may presume, the Lady Aretina.

Lord. Wife to Sir Thomas Bornwell?

Dec. The same, sir.

Lord. Have you prepared her?

Dec. Not for your lordship, till I have found your pulse.
I am acquainted with her disposition,
She has a very appliable nature.

Lord. And, madam, when expect you to be whipped
For doing these fine favours?

Dec. How, my lord?
Your lordship does but jest, I hope; you make
A difference between a lady that
Does honourable offices, and one
They call a bawd. Your lordship was not wont
To have such coarse opinion of our practice.

Lord. The Lady Aretina is my kinswoman.

Dec. What if she be, my lord? the nearer blood,
The dearer sympathy.

Lord. I'll have thee carted.

Dec. Your lordship will not so much stain your honour
And education, to use a woman
Of my quality—

Lord. 'Tis possible you may
Be sent off with an honourable convoy
Of halberdiers.

Dec. Oh, my good lord!

Lord. Your ladyship shall be no protection,
If you but stay three minutes.

Dec. I am gone.—
When next you find rebellion in your blood,
May all within ten mile o' the court turn honest! [*Exit.*

Lord. I do not find that proneness, since the fair
Bella Maria died; my blood is cold,

Nor is there beauty enough surviving
To heighten me to wantonness.—Who waits?

Re-enter HAIRCUT *and* Secretary.

And what said my lady?

Hair. The silent language of her face, my lord,
Was not so pleasant, as it showed upon
Her entrance.

Lord. Would any man that meets
This lady take her for a bawd?

Hair. She does
The trade an honour, credit to the profession.
We may, in time, see baldness, quarter noses,
And rotten legs to take the wall of footcloths.

Lord. I have thought better; call the lady back.—
I will not lose this opportunity.—
Bid her not fear. [*Exit* Secretary.]—The favour is not
    common,
And I'll reward it.   I do wonder much
Will Scentlove was not here to-day.

Hair. I heard him say this morning he would wait
Upon your lordship.—
She is returned, sir.

Re-enter Secretary *and* DECOY.

Sec. Madam, be confident, my lord's not angry.

Lord. You return welcome, madam; you are better
Read in your art, I hope, than to be frighted
With any shape of anger, when you bring
Such news to gentlemen.   Madam, you shall
Soon understand how I accept the office.

Dec. You are the first lord, since I studied carriage,
That showed such infidelity and fury
Upon so kind a message.   Every gentleman
Will show some breeding; but if one right honourable
Should not have noble blood—

Lord. You shall return
My compliment, in a letter, to my lady
Aretina.   Favour me with a little patience.—
Show her that chamber.

Dec. I'll attend your lordship.

    [*Exeunt* DECOY *and* HAIRCUT.—*Secretary seats
       himself at a table.*

Lord. Write,—" Madam, where your honour is in
danger, my love must not be silent."

    Enter Sir WILLIAM SCENTLOVE *and* KICKSHAW.

Scentlove and Kickshaw !

Kick. Your lordship's busy,

Lord. Writing a letter ;—nay, it shall not bar
Any discourse.

    [*Walks alternately to ·the* Secretary *and to* SCENTLOVE
       and KICKSHAW.

Sec. "Silent."

Lord. " Though I be no physician, I may prevent a
fever in your blood."—
And where have you spent the morning's conversation ?

Scent. Where you would have given the best barbary
In your stable, to have met on honourable terms.

Lord. What new beauty?   You acquaint yourselves
With none but wonders.

Scent. 'Tis too low,—a miracle.

Lord. It will require a strong faith.

Sec. "Your blood."

Lord. " If you be innocent, preserve your fame, lest
this Decoy-madam betray it, to your repentance."—
By what name is she known?

Scent. Ask Alexander.
He knows her.

Kick. Whom?

Scent. The lady Celestına.

Lord. He has a vast knowledge of ladies. 'Las, poor
    Alexander !
When dost thou mean thy body shall lie fallow?

Kick. When there is mercy in a petticoat:
I must turn pilgrim for some breath.

Lord. I think
'Twere cooler travel, if you examine it,
Upon the hoof through Spain.

Scent. Through Ethiopia.

Lord. Nay, less laborious to serve a prenticeship
In Peru, and dig gold out of the mine,
Though all the year were dog-days.

Sec. " To repentance."

Lord. " In brief, this lady, could you fall from virtue,
within my knowledge, will not blush to be a bawd."

Scent. But hang 't, 'tis honourable journey-work;
Thou art famous by it, and thy name's up.

Kick. So, sir!
Let me ask you a question, my dear knight:
Which is less servile, to bring up the pheasant,
And wait, or sit at table uncontrolled,
And carve to my own appetite?

Scent. No more;
Thou'rt witty, as I am.

Sec. " A bawd."

Scent. How's that?

Kick. Oh,
You are famous by't, and your name's up, sir.

Lord. " Be wise, and reward my caution with timely
care of yourself, so I shall not repent to be known your
loving kinsman and servant"—
Gentlemen, the lady Celestina,
Is she so rare a thing?

Kick. If you'll have my
Opinion, my lord, I never saw
So sweet, so fair, so rich a piece of nature.

Lord. I'll show thee a fairer presently, to shame
Thy eyes and judgment; look on that. [*Gives him a
     miniature.*]—So; I'll subscribe. [*Signs his name
     to the letter.*
Seal it; I'll excuse your pen for the direction.

Kick. Bella Maria's picture ! she was handsome.

Scent. But not to be compared—

Lord. Your patience, gentlemen ; I'll return instantly.

[*Exit.*

Kick. Whither is my lord gone ?

Sec. To a lady i' the next chamber.

Scent. What is she ?

Sec. You shall pardon me, I am his secretary.

Scent. I was wont to be of his counsel. A new officer,
And I not know't ? I am resolved to batter
All other with the praise of Celestina:
I must retain him.

Re-enter Lord A.

Lord. Has not that object
Convinced your erring judgments ?

Kick. What ! this picture ?

Lord. Were but your thoughts as capable as mine
Of her idea, you would wish no thought
That were not active in her praise, above
All worth and memory of her sex.

Scent. She was fair,
I must confess ; but had your lordship looked
With eyes more narrow, and some less affection,
Upon her face,—

Kick. I do not love the copies
Of any dead, they make me dream of goblins ;
Give me a living mistress, with but half
The beauty of Celestina. [*Returns the miniature.—*
    Come, my lord,
'Tis pity that a lord of so much flesh
Should waste upon a ghost, when they are living
Can give you a more honourable consumption.

Scent. Why, do you mean, my lord, to live an infidel?
Do, and see what will come on't ; observe still,
And dote upon your vigils ; build a chamber
Within a rock, a tomb among the worms,
Not far off, where you may, in proof apocryphal,

Court 'em not to devour the pretty pile
Of flesh your mistress carried to the grave.
There are no women in the world ; all eyes,
And tongues, and lips, are buried in her coffin!

Lord. Why, do you think yourselves competent judges
Of beauty, gentlemen ?

Both. What should hinder us ?

Kick. I have seen and tried as many as another,
With a mortal back.

Lord. Your eyes are bribed,
And your hearts chained to some desires ; you cannot
Enjoy the freedom of a sense.

Kick. Your lordship
Has a clear eyesight, and can judge and penetrate.

Lord. I can, and give a perfect censure of
Each line and point ; distinguish beauty from
A thousand forms, which your corrupted optics
Would pass for natural.

Scent. I desire no other
Judge should determine us, and if your lordship
Dare venture but your eyes upon this lady,
I'll stand their justice, and be confident
You shall give Celestina victory,
And triumph, o'er all beauties past and living.

Kick. I dare, my lord, venture a suit of clothes,
You'll be o'ercome.

Lord. You do not know my fortitude.

Scent. Nor frailty ; you dare not trust yourself to see
her.   [ture

Lord. Think you so, gentlemen ? I dare see this crea-
To make you know your errors, and the difference
Of her, whose memory is my saint. Not trust
My senses ! I dare see, and speak with her.
Which holds the best acquaintance to prepare
My visit to her ?

Scent. I will do't, my lord.

Kick. She is a lady free in entertainments.

  Shir.

X

Lord. I would give this advantage to your cause,
Bid her appear in all the ornaments
Did ever wait on beauty, all the riches
Pride can put on, and teach her face more charms
Than ever poet drest up Venus in ;
Bid her be all the Graces, and the queen
Of love in one, I'll see her, Scentlove, and
Bring off my heart, armed but with a single thought
Of one that's dead, without a wound ; and when
I have made your folly prisoner, I'll laugh at you.

 Scent. She shall expect you ; trust to me for knowledge.

 Lord. I'm for the present somewhere else engaged ;
Let me hear from you.   [*Exit.*

 Scent. So ! I am glad he's yet
So near conversion.

 Kick. I am for Aretina.

 Scent. No mention of my lord.

 Kick. Prepare his lady,
'Tis time he were reduced [1] to the old sport ;
One lord like him more would undo the court. [*Exeunt.*

SCENE II.—*A Room in* Sir THOMAS BORNWELL'S
      House.

Enter Lady BORNWELL *with a letter, and* DECOY.

 Dec. He is the ornament of your blood, madam ;
I am much bound to his lordship.

 Lady B. He gives you
A noble character,

 Dec. 'Tis his goodness, madam.

 Lady B. I wanted such an engine. My lord has
Done me a courtesy, to disclose her nature ;

     [1] *i.e.* Brought back.

I now know one to trust, and will employ her.— [*Aside.*
Touching my lord, for reasons which I shall
Offer to your ladyship hereafter, I
Desire you would be silent ; but, to show
How much I dare be confident in your secrecy,
I pour my bosom forth : I love a gentleman,
One whom there would not need much conjuration
To meet.—Your ear. [*Whispers her.*

Dec. I apprehend you, and I shall
Be happy to be serviceable. I am sorry
Your ladyship did not know me before now :
I have done offices : and not a few
Of the nobility but have done feats
Within my house, which is convenient
For situation, and artful chambers,
And pretty pictures to provoke the fancy.

Enter LITTLEWORTH.

Little. Madam, all pleasures languish in your absence.

Lady B. Your pardon a few minutes, sir.—You must
Contrive it thus. [*Walks aside with* DECOY.

Little. I attend, and shall account it
Honour to wait on your return.

Lady B. He must not
Have the least knowledge of my name or person.

Dec. I have practised that already for some great ones,
And dare again, to satisfy you, madam ;
I have a thousand ways to do sweet offices.

Little. If this Lady Aretina should be honest,
I have lost time : she's free as air ; I must
Have closer conference, and if I have art,
Make her affect me in revenge.

Dec. This evening ?
Leave me to manage things.

Lady B. You will oblige me.

Dec. You shall command my art, and thank me after,
[*Exit.*

Lady B. I hope the revels are maintained within?

Little. By Sir Thomas and his mistress.

Lady B. How? his mistress?

Little. The lady Celestina; I never saw
Eyes shoot more amorous interchange.

Lady B. Is't so?

Little. He wears her favour with more pride—

Lady B. Her favour?

Little. A feather that he ravished from her fan;
And is so full of courtship! which she smiles on.

Lady B. 'Tis well.

Little. And praises her beyond all poetry.

Lady B. I am glad he has so much wit.

Little. Not jealous!   [*Aside.*

Lady B. This secures me. What would make other
    ladies pale
With jealousy, gives but license to my wanderings.
Let him now tax me, if he dare; and yet
Her beauty's worth my envy, and I wish
Revenge upon it, not because he loves,
But that it shines above my own.   [*Aside.*

Enter KICKSHAW.

Kick. Dear madam!

Lady B. I have it.—You two gentlemen profess
Much service to me; if I have a way
To employ your wit and secrecy?—

Both. You'll honour us.

Lady B. You gave a high and worthy character
Of Celestina.

Kick. I remember, madam.

Lady B. Do either of you love her?

Kick. Not I, madam.

Little. I would not, if I might.

Lady B. She's now my guest,
And, by a trick, invited by my husband,
To disgrace me.—You, gentlemen, are held

Wits of the town, the consuls that do govern
The senate here, whose jeers are all authentic.
The taverns and the ordinaries are
Made academies, where you come, and all
Your sins and surfeits made the time's example.
Your very nods can quell a theatre,
No speech or poem good without your seal;
You can protect scurrility, and publish,
By your authority believed, no rapture
Ought to have honest meaning.

    Kick. Leave our characters.

    Little. And name the employment.

    Lady B. You must exercise
The strength of both your wits upon this lady,
And talk her into humbleness or anger,
Both which are equal, to my thought. If you
Dare undertake this slight thing for my sake,
My favour shall reward it; but be faithful,
And seem to let all spring from your own freedom.

    Kick. This all! We can defame her; if you please,
My friend shall call her whore, or any thing,
And never be endangered to a duel.

    Lady B. How's that?

    Kick. He can endure a cudgelling, and no man
Will fight after so fair a satisfaction:
But leave us to our art, and do not limit us.

    Lady B. They are here; begin not till I whisper
you.

Enter Sir THOMAS BORNWELL, CELESTINA, MARIANA,
and ISABELLA.

    Lady B. *Je vous prie, madame, d'excuser l'importunité
de mes affaires, qui m'ont fait offenser, par mon absence,
une dame de laquelle j'ai reçu tant d'obligations.*

    Cel. *Pardonnez moi, madame; vous me faites trop
d'honneur.*

    Lady B. *C'est bien de la douceur de votre naturel, que*

vous tenez cette langage; mais j'espère que mon mari n'a pas manqué de vous entretenir en mon absence.

Cel. *En vérité, monsieur nous a fort obligé.*

Lady B. *Il eut trop failli, s'il n'eut taché de tout son pouvoir à vous rendre toutes sortes de services.*

Cel. *C'est de sa bonté qu'il nous a tant favorisé.*

Lady B. *De la vôtre plutôt, madame, que vous fait donner d'interprétation si bénigne à ses efforts.*

Cel. *Je vois bien que la victoire sera toujours à madame, et de langage et de la courtesie.*

Lady B. *Vraiment, madame, que jamais personne a plus désiré l'honneur de votre compagnie que moi.*

Cel. *Laissons-en, je vous supplie, des complimens, et permettez à votre servante de vous baiser les mains.*

Lady B. *Vous m'obligez trop.*

Born. I have no more patience; let's be merry again
In our own language : madam, our mirth cools.
Our nephew!

Enter FREDERICK *intoxicated, and* Steward.

Lady B. Passion of my brain!

Fred. Save you, gentlemen! save you, ladies!

Lady B. I am undone.

Fred. I must salute; no matter at which end I begin.
[*Salutes* CELESTINA.

Lady B. There's a compliment!

Cel. Is this your nephew, madam?

Lady B. *Je vous prie, madame, d'excuser les habits et le rude comportement de mon cousin. Il est tout fraîchement venu de l'université, où on l'a tout gâté.*

Cel. *Excusez moi, madame, il est bien accompli.*

Fred. This language should be French by the motions of your heads, and the mirth of your faces.

Lady B. I am dishonoured.

Fred. 'Tis one of the finest tongues for ladies to show their teeth in : if you'll Latin it, I am for you, or Greek it ; my tailor has not put me into French yet. *Mille basia, basia mille.*

Cel. *Je ne vous entends pas, monsieur ;*
I understand you not, sir.

Fred. Why, so!
You and I then shall be in charity ;
For though we should be abusive, we have the benefit
Not to understand one another. Where's my aunt?
I did hear music somewhere ; and my brains,
Tuned with a bottle of your capering claret,
Made haste to show their dancing.

Little. Please you, madam,
       [*Offering his box of sweetmeats to* CELESTINA.
They are very comfortable.

Stew. Alas, madam,
How would you have me help it? I did use
All means I could, after he heard the music,
To make him drunk, in hope so to contain him ;
But the wine made him lighter, and his head
Flew hither, ere I missed his heels.

Kick. Nay, he
Spoke Latin to the lady.

Lady B. Oh, most unpardonable !
Get him off quickly, and discreetly too.
Or, if I live—

Stew. It is not in my power ; he swears I am
An absurd sober fellow ; and if you keep
A servant in his house to cross his humour,
When the rich sword and belt come home, he'll kill him.

Lady B. What shall I do? Try your skill, Master Littleworth.

Little. He has ne'er a sword.—Sweet master Frederick—

Born. 'Tis pity, madam, such a scion should
Be lost ; but you are clouded.

Cel. Not I, sir,
I never found myself more clear at heart.

Born. I could play with a feather ; your fan, lady.—
Gentlemen, Aretina, ta, ra, ra, ra ! Come, madam.

Fred. Why, my good tutor in election,
You might have been a scholar.

Little. But I thank
My friends, they brought me up a little better.
Give me the town wits, that deliver jests
Clean from the bow, that whistle in the air,
And cleave the pin at twelvescore ! Ladies do
But laugh at a gentleman that has any learning ;
'Tis sin enough to have your clothes suspected.
Leave us, and I will find a time to instruct you.
Come, here are sugar plums ; 'tis a good Frederick.

Fred. Why, is not this my aunt's house in the Strand?
The noble rendezvous? Who laughs at me ?
Go, I will root here if I list, and talk
Of rhetoric, logic, Latin, Greek, or any thing,
And understand 'em too ; who says the contrary ?
Yet, in a fair way, I contemn all learning,
And will be as ignorant as he, or he,
Or any taffata, satin, scarlet, plush,
Tissue, or cloth o' bodkin gentleman,
Whose manners are most gloriously infected.—
Did you laugh at me, lady ?

Cel. Not I, sir ;
But if I did show mirth upon your question,
I hope you would not beat me, little gentleman ?

Fred. How ! "little gentleman ?" you dare not say
These words to my new clothes, and fighting sword.

Lady B. Nephew Frederick !

Fred. "Little gentleman !"
'Tis an affront both to my blood and person.
I am a gentleman of as tall a birth
As any boast nobility ; though my clothes
Smell o' the lamp, my coat is honourable,
Right honourable, full of or and argent.—
A "little gentleman !"

Born. Coz, you must be patient;
My lady meant you no dishonour, and
You must remember she's a woman.

Fred. Is she a woman? that's another matter.—
Do you hear? my uncle tells me what you are.

Cel. So, sir.

Fred. You called me " little gentleman."

Cel. I did, sir.

Fred. A little pink [1] has made a lusty ship
Strike her top-sail; the crow may beard the elephant,
A whelp may tame the tiger, spite of all
False decks and murderers; [2] and a "little gentleman"
Be hard enough to grapple with your ladyship,
Top and top-gallant.—Will you go drink, uncle,
T' other enchanted bottle? you and I
Will tipple, and talk philosophy.

Born. Come, nephew.—
You will excuse a minute's absence, madam.—
Wait you on us.

Stew. My duty, sir.

[*Exeunt* Sir THOMAS BORNWELL, FREDERICK, *and*
Steward.

Lady B. Now, gentlemen.

Kick. Madam, I had rather you excuse my language
For speaking truth, than virtue suffer in
My further silence; and it is my wonder
That you, whose noble carriage hath deserved
All honour and opinion, should now
Be guilty of ill manners.

Cel. What was that
You told me, sir?

Little. Do you not blush, madam,
To ask that question?

Cel. You amaze rather
My cheek to paleness. What mean you by this?

---

[1] A small vessel.
[2] Cannon charged with grape-shot.

I am not troubled with the hickup, gentlemen,
You should bestow this fright upon me.
 Little. Then
Pride and ill memory go together.
 Cel. How, sir?
 Kick. The gentleman on whom you exercised
Your thin wit, was a nephew to the lady
Whose guest you are; and though her modesty
Look calm on the abuse of one so near
Her blood, the affront was impious.
 Little. I am ashamed on't.
You an ingenious lady, and well mannered!
I'll teach a bear as much civility.
 Cel. You may be master of the college, sir,
For aught I know.
 Little. What college?
 Cel. Of the bears.
Have you a plot upon me? Do you possess
Your wits, or know me, gentlemen?

   Re-enter Sir THOMAS BORNWELL *behind.*

 Born. How's this?
 Kick. Know you? yes; we do know you to an atom.
 Little. Madam, we know what stuff your soul is made on.
 Cel. But do not bark so like a mastiff, pray.—
Sure they are mad.—Let your brains stand awhile,
And settle, gentlemen; you know not me;
What am I?
 Little. Thou'rt a puppet, a thing made
Of clothes and painting, and not half so handsome
As that which played Susanna in the fair.
 Cel. I heard you visited those canvas tragedies,
One of their constant audience, and so taken
With Susan, that you wished yourself a rival
With the two wicked elders.
 Kick. You think this
Is wit now. Come, you are—

Cel. What, I beseech you?
Your character will be full of salt and satire,
No doubt. What am I?

Kick. Why, you are a woman——

Cel. And that's at least a bow wide of your knowledge.

Kick. Would be thought handsome, and might pass
    i' the country
Upon a market day; but so miserably
Forfeit to pride and fashions, that if Heaven
Were a new gown, you'd not stay in't a fortnight.

Cel. It must be miserably out of fashion then.
Have I no sin but pride?

Kick. Hast any virtue,
Or but a good face, to excuse that want?

Cel. You praised it yesterday.

Kick. That made you proud.

Cel. More pride!

Kick. You need not:—to close up the praise,
I have seen a better countenance in a sybil.

Cel. When you wore spectacles of sack, mistook
The painted cloth,[1] and kissed it for your mistress.

Kick. Let me ask you a question: how much
Have you consumed in expectation
That I would love you?

Cel. Why I think as much
As you have paid away in honest debts
This seven year. 'Tis a pretty impudence,
But cannot make me angry.

Little. Is there any
Man that will cast away his limbs upon her?

Kick. You do not sing so well as I imagined,
Nor dance; you reel in your coranto,[2] and pinch
Your petticoat too hard: you've no good ear
To the music, and incline too much one shoulder,

---

[1] Canvas or cloth, painted in imitation of tapestry, for which it
was a cheap substitute.

[2] A quick, lively dance.

As you were dancing on the rope, and falling.
You speak abominable French, and make
A curtsey like a dairy-maid.—Not mad!　　　*[Aside.*

 Little. Do we not sting her handsomely?

 Born. A conspiracy!

 Kick. Your state is not so much as 'tis reported,
When you confer notes, all your husband's debts,
And your own reconciled; but that's not it
Will so much spoil your marriage.

 Cel. As what, sir?
Let me know all my faults.

 Kick. Some men do whisper
You are not over honest.

 Cel. All this shall not
Move me to more than laughter, and some pity,
Because you have the shapes of gentlemen;
And though you have been insolent upon me,
I will engage no friend to kick or cudgel you,
To spoil your living and your limbs together:
I leave that to diseases that attend you,
And spare my curse, poor silken vermin! and
Hereafter shall distinguish men from monkeys.

 Born. Brave soul!—You brace of horse-leeches!
 [Coming forward.]—I have heard
Their barbarous language, madam; you are too merciful:
They shall be silent to your tongue; pray punish them.

 Cel. They are things not worth my character, nor
  mention
Of any clean breath; so lost in honesty,
They cannot satisfy for wrongs enough,
Though they should steal out of the world at Tyburn.

 Little. We are hanged already.

 Cel. Yet I will talk a little to the pilchards.—
You two, that have not 'twixt you both the hundred
Part of a soul, coarse woollen-witted fellows,
Without a nap, with bodies made for burdens!
You, that are only stuffings for apparel,

As you were made but engines for your tailors
To frame their clothes upon, and get them custom,
Until men see you move ; yet, then you dare not,
Out of your guilt of being the ignobler beast,
But give a horse the wall, whom you excel
Only in dancing of the brawls, because
The horse was not taught the French way. Your two
    faces,
One fat, like Christmas, t' other lean, like Candlemas,
And prologue to a Lent, both bound together,
Would figure Janus, and do many cures
On agues, and the green disease, by frighting
But neither can, with all the characters
And conjuring circles, charm a woman, though
She'd fourscore years upon her, and but one
Tooth in her head, to love, or think well of you :
And I were miserable, to be at cost
To court such a complexion, as your malice
Did impudently insinuate. But I waste time,
And stain my breath in talking to such tadpoles.
Go home, and wash your tongues in barley-water,
Drink clean tobacco,[1] be not hot i' the mouth,
And you may 'scape the beadle ; so I leave you
To shame, and your own garters !—Sir, I must
Entreat you, for my honour, do not penance them
They are not worth your anger. How shall I
Acquit your lady's silence ?

   Born. Madam, I
Am sorry to suspect, and dare revenge.

   Cel. No cause of mine.

   Born. It must become me to attend you home.

   Cel. You are noble.—Farewell, mushrooms.

               [*Exit with* Sir THOMAS BORNWELL.

   Lady B. Is she gone ?

   Little. I think we peppered her.

---

[1] The expression "drink tobacco," simply implied the smoking
of it.

Kick. I'm glad 'tis over;
But I repent no service for you, madam.—

Enter Servant, *with a letter and a jewel, which he delivers to* KICKSHAW.

To me? from whence?—a jewel! a good preface.
Be happy the conclusion!   *[Reads and smiles.*

   Lady B. Some love letter.

   Little. He has a hundred mistresses: you may
Be charitable, madam, I have none;
He surfeits, and I fall away i' the kidneys.

   Kick. I'll meet.—   *[Exit* Servant.
'Tis some great lady, questionless, that has
Taken notice, and would satisfy her appetite.   *[Aside.*

   Lady B. Now, Master Alexander, you look bright o'
    the sudden;
Another spirit's in your eye.

   Kick. Not mine, madam;
Only a summons to meet a friend.

   Lady B. What friend?

   Little. By this jewel, I know her not.

   Lady B. 'Tis a she-friend. I'll follow, gentlemen;
We may have a game at cent[1] before you go.

   Kick. I shall attend you, madam.

   Little. 'Tis our duty.
    [Exeunt KICKSHAW *and* LITTLEWORTH.

   Lady B. I blush while I converse with my own
    thoughts.
Some strange fate governs me, but I must on;
The ways are cast already, and we thrive
When our sin fears no eye nor perspective.   *[Exit.*

---

[1] A game at cards, supposed to have resembled piquet; a score of a hundred was the game.

ACT THE FOURTH.

SCENE I.—*A Room in* DECOY'S *House.*

Enter two men leading KICKSHAW *blinded, and go off suddenly.*

ICK. I am not hurt; my patience to obey them,
    Not without fear to have my throat cut else,
    Did me a courtesy. Whither have they brought me? [*Pulls off a bandage.*
'Tis devilish dark; the bottom of a well
At midnight, with but two stars on the top,
Were broad day to this darkness. I but think
How like a whirlwind the rogues caught me up,
And smothered my eyesight. Let me see,
These may be spirits, and, for aught I know,
Have brought me hither over twenty steeples.
Pray Heaven they were not bailiffs! that's more worth
My fear, and this a prison. All my debts
Reek in my nostril, and my bones begin
To ache with fear to be made dice ; and yet
This is too calm and quiet for a prison.—
What if the riddle prove I am robbed? and yet
I did not feel 'em search me. How now! music!
                        [*Music within.*

Enter DECOY, *disguised like an* old Woman, *with a light.*

And a light! What beldam's this? I cannot pray.—
What art?

Dec. A friend.   Fear not, young man, I am
No spirit.

Kick. Off !

Dec. Despise me not for age,
Or this coarse outside, which I wear not out
Of poverty : thy eyes be witness ; 'tis
No cave, or beggar's cell, thou'rt brought to ; let
That gold speak here's no want, which thou mayst spend,
And find a spring to tire even prodigality,
If thou be'st wise.   [*Gives him a purse.*

Kick. The devil was a coiner
From the beginning ; yet the gold looks current.

Dec. Thou'rt still in wonder : know, I am mistress of
This house, and of a fortune that shall serve
And feed thee with delights ; 'twas I sent for thee ;
The jewel and the letter came from me.
It was my art thus to contrive our meeting,
Because I would not trust thee with my fame,
Until I found thee worth a woman's honour.

Kick. Honour and fame ! the devil means to have
A care on's credit.   Though she sent for me,
I hope she has another customer
To do the trick withal ; I would not turn
Familiar to a witch.   [*Aside.*

Dec. What say'st ?   Canst thou
Dwell in my arms to-night ? shall we change kisses,
And entertain the silent hours with pleasure,
Such as old Time shall be delighted with,
And blame the too swift motion of his wings,
While we embrace ?

Kick. Embrace ! she has had no teeth
This twenty years, and the next violent cough
Brings up her tongue ; it cannot possibly
Be sound at root.   I do not think but one
Strong sneeze upon her, and well meant, would make
Her quarters fall away ; one kick would blow
Her up like gunpowder, and loose all her limbs.

She is so cold, an incubus would not heat her ;
Her phlegm would quench a furnace, and her breath
Would damp a musket bullet. [*Aside.*

    Dec. Have you, sir,
Considered ?

    Kick. What ?

    Dec. My proposition.
Canst love ?

    Kick. I could have done ; whom do you mean ?
I know you are pleased but to make sport.

    Dec. Thou art not
So dull of soul as thou appear'st.

    Kick. This is
But some device ; my grannam has some trick in't.—
Yes, I can love.

    Dec. But canst thou affect me ?

    Kick. Although to reverence so grave a matron
Were an ambitious word in me, yet since
You give me boldness, I do love you.

    Dec. Then
Thou art my own.

    Kick. Has she no cloven foot ?

    Dec. And I am thine, and all that I command,
Thy servants ; from this minute thou art happy,
And fate in thee will crown all my desires.
I grieved a proper man should be compelled
To bring his body to the common market.
My wealth shall make thee glorious ; and, the more
To encourage thee, howe'er this form may fright
Thy youthful eyes, yet thou wilt find, by light
Of thy own sense, for other light is banished
My chamber, when our arms tie lovers' knots,
And kisses seal the welcome of our lips,
I shall not there affright thee, nor seem old,
With rivelled veins ; my skin is smooth and soft
As ermines, with a spirit to meet thine,
Active, and equal to the queen of love's,
When she did court Adonis.

    Shir.   Y

Kick. This doth more
Confirm she is a devil, and I am
Within his own dominions. I must on,
Or else be torn o' pieces. I have heard
These succubæ must not be crossed.   [*Aside.*

Dec. We trifle
Too precious time away; I'll show you a prospect
Of the next chamber, and then out the candle.

Kick. Have you no sack i' the house? I would go
Upon this breach.   [*armed*

Dec. It shall not need.

Kick. One word,
Mother; have not you been a cat in your days?

Dec. I am glad you are so merry, sir. You observe
That bed?   [*Opens a door.*

Kick. A very brave one.

Dec. When you are
Disrobed, you can come thither in the dark.
You shall not stay for me? Come, as you wish
For happiness.   [*Exit.*

Kick. I am preferred, if I
Be modest and obey: she cannot have
The heart to do me harm, an she were Hecate,
Herself. I will have a strong faith, and think
I march upon a mistress, the less evil.
If I 'scape fire now, I defy the devil.   [*Exit*

SCENE II.—*A Room in* Sir THOMAS BORNWELL'S
House.

Enter FREDERICK *gaily dressed*, LITTLEWORTH, *and*
Steward.

Fred. And how do you like me now?

Stew. Most excellent.

Fred. Your opinion, Master Littleworth.

Little. Your French tailor
Has made you a perfect gentleman; I may
Converse now with you, and preserve my credit.
Do you find no alteration in your body
With these new clothes?

Fred. My body altered? No.

Little. You are not yet in fashion then? that must
Have a new motion, garb, and posture too,
Or all your pride is cast away; it is not
The cut of your apparel makes a gallant,
But the geometrical wearing of your clothes.

Stew. Master Littleworth tells you right; you wear
your hat
Too like a citizen.

Little. 'Tis like a midwife
Place it with best advantage of your hair.
Is half your feather moulted? This does make
No show; it should spread over, like a canopy ·
Your hot-reined monsieur wears it for a shade,
And cooler to his back. Your doublet must
Be more unbuttoned hereabouts; you'll not
Be a sloven else, a foul shirt is no blemish;
You must be confident, and outface clean linen.
Your doublet and your breeches must be allowed
No private meeting here; your cloak's too long,
It reaches to your buttock, and doth smell
Too much of Spanish gravity; the fashion
Is to wear nothing but a cape; a coat
May be allowed a covering for one elbow,
And some, to avoid the trouble choose to walk
In *querpo*,[1] thus.

Stew. Your coat and cloak's a brushing
In Long-lane, Lombard.   [*Aside.*

Fred. But what if it rain?

Little. Your belt about your shoulder is sufficient

---

[1] *i.e.* Cuerpo, stripped of the upper garment.

To keep off any storm; beside, a reed [1]
But waved discreetly, has so many pores,
It sucks up all the rain that falls about one.
With this defence, when other men have been
Wet to the skin through all their cloaks, I have
Defied a tempest, and walked by the taverns
Dry as a bone.

 Stew. Because he had no money
To call for wine.   [*Aside.*

 Fred. Why, do you walk enchanted?
Have you such pretty charms in town? But stay;
Who must I have to attend me?

 Little. Is not that
Yet thought upon?

 Stew. I have laid out for servants.

 Little. They are everywhere.

 Stew. I cannot yet be furnished
With such as I would put into his hands.

 Fred. Of what condition must they be, and how
Many in number, sir?

 Little. Beside your fencing,
Your singing, dancing, riding, and French master,
Two may serve domestic, to be constant waiters
Upon a gentleman; a fool, a pimp.

 Stew. For these two officers I have enquired,
And I am promised a convenient whiskin:
I could save charges, and employ the pie-wench,
That carries her intelligence in whitepots;
Or 'tis but taking order with the woman
That trolls the ballads, she could fit him with
A concubine to any tune; but I
Have a design to place a fellow with him
That has read all Sir Pandarus' works; a Trojan
That lies concealed, and is acquainted with
Both city and suburban fripperies,

---

[1] This is a Plymouth cloak, as our old dramatists called a
cudgel.

Can fetch 'em with a spell at midnight to him,
And warrant which are for his turn ; can, for
A need, supply the surgeon too.

Fred. I like thy providence ; such a one deserves
A livery twice a year.

Stew. It shall not need ; a cast suit of your worship's
Will serve ; he'll find a cloak to cover it,
Out of his share with those he brings to bed to you,

Fred. But must I call this fellow pimp ?

Little. It is
Not necessary ; Tom, or Jack, or Harry.
Or what he's known abroad by, will sound better,
That men may think he is a Christian.

Fred. But hear you, Master Littleworth : is there not
A method, and degrees of title in
Men of this art ?

Little. According to the honour
Of men that do employ 'em.   An emperor
May give this office to a duke ; a king
May have his viceroy to negociate for him ;
A duke may use a lord ; the lord a knight,
A knight may trust a gentleman ; and when
They are abroad, and merry, gentlemen
May pimp to one another.

Fred. Good, good fellowship !
But for the fool now, that should wait on me,
And break me jests ?

Little. A fool is necessary.

Stew. By any means.

Fred. But which of these two servants
Must now take place ?

Little. That question, Master Frederick,
The school of heraldry should conclude upon :
But if my judgment may be heard, the fool
Is your first man ; and it is known a point
Of state to have a fool.

Stew. But, sir, the other

Is held the finer servant; his employments
Are full of trust, his person clean and nimble,
And none so soon can leap into preferment,
Where fools are poor.

    Little. Not all; there's story for't;
Princes have been no wiser than they should be.
Would any nobleman, that were no fool,
Spend all in hope of the philosopher's stone,
To buy new lordships in another country?
Would knights build colleges, or gentlemen
Of good estates challenge the field, and fight,
Because a whore will not be honest? Come,
Fools are a family over all the world;
We do affect one naturally; indeed
The fool is leiger[1] with us.

    Stew. Then the pimp
Is extraordinary.

    Fred. Do not you fall out
About their places.—Here's my noble aunt!

Enter Lady BORNWELL.

    Little. How do you like your nephew, madam, now?

    Lady B. Well! turn about, Frederick. Very well!

    Fred. Am I not now a proper gentleman?
The virtue of rich clothes! Now could I take
The wall of Julius Cæsar, or affront
Great Pompey's upper lip, and defy the senate.
Nay, I can be as proud as your own heart, madam,
You may take that for your comfort; I put on
That virtue with my clothes, and I doubt not
But in a little time I shall be impudent
As any page, or player's boy. I am
Beholding to this gentleman's good discipline;

---

[1] "Leiger," in the language of diplomacy at this period, meant resident. In this sprightly scene, and particularly in this speech, there are several personal allusions, which seem to show that the censorship of the stage had now somewhat relaxed.—*Gifford.*

But I shall do him credit in my practice.
Your steward has some pretty notions too,
In moral mischief.

Lady B. Your desert in this
Exceeds all other service, and shall bind me
Both to acknowledge and reward.

Little. Sweet madam,
Think me but worth your favour ; I would creep
Upon my knees to honour you, and for every
Minute you lend to my reward, I'll pay
A year of serviceable tribute.

Lady B. You
Can compliment.

Little. Thus still she puts me off ; unless I speak
The downright word, she'll never understand me.
A man would think that creeping on one's knees
Were English to a lady.   [*Aside.*

Enter KICKSHAW.

Kick. How is't, Jack ?—Pleasures attend you, madam !
How does my plant of honour ?

Lady B. Who is this ?

Kick. 'Tis Alexander.

Lady B. Rich and glorious !

Little. 'Tis Alexander the Great.

Kick. And my Bucephalus
Waits at the door.

Lady B. Your case is altered, sir.

Kick. I cannot help these things, the Fates will
    have it ;
'Tis not my land does this.

Little. But thou hast a plough
That brings it in.

Lady B. Now he looks brave and lovely.

Fred. Welcome, my gallant Macedonian.

Kick. Madam, you gave your nephew for my pupil.
I read but in a tavern ; if you'll honour us,

The Bear at the Bridge foot[1] shall entertain you.
A drawer is my Ganymede, he shall skink[2]
Brisk nectar to us; we will only have
A dozen partridge in a dish; as many pheasants,
Quails, cocks, and godwits shall come marching up
Like the trained-band; a fort of sturgeon
Shall give most bold defiance to an army,
And triumph o'er the table.—

   Lady B. Sir, it will
But dull the appetite to hear more, and mine
Must be excused.   Another time I may be
Your guest.

   Kick. 'Tis grown in fashion now with ladies;
When you please, I'll attend you.   Littleworth.—
Come, Frederick.

   Fred. We'll have music; I love noise.
We will out-roar the Thames, and shake the bridge, boy.
                           [Exit with KICKSHAW.

   Little. Madam, I kiss your hand; would you would
     think
Of your poor servant; flesh and blood is frail,
And troublesome to carry, without help.

   Lady B. A coach will easily convey it, or
You may take water at Strand-bridge.

   Little. But I
Have taken fire.

   Lady B. The Thames will cool it, sir.

   Little. But never quench my heart; your charity
Can only do that.

   Lady B. I will keep it cold
Of purpose.

   Little. Now you bless me, and I dare
Be drunk in expectation.   *[Exit.*

---

[1] The Bear was a well-known tavern. The Strand-bridge crossed the Strand nearly opposite the present Catherine-street, where the collected waters from the high grounds were discharged into the Thames.   [2] Pour out.

Lady B. I am confident
He knows me not, and I were worse than mad
To be my own betrayer.—Here's my husband.

Enter Sir THOMAS BORNWELL.

Born. Why, how now, Aretina? What! alone?
The mystery of this solitude? My house
Turn desert o' the sudden! all the gamesters
Blown up! Why is the music put to silence?
Or have their instruments caught a cold, since we
Gave them the last heat? I must know thy ground
Of melancholy.

Lady B. You are merry, as
You came from kissing Celestina.

Born. I
Feel her yet warm upon my lip; she is
Most excellent company: I did not think
There was that sweetness in her sex. I must
Acknowledge, 'twas thy care to disenchant me
From a dull husband to an active lover.
With such a lady I could spend more years
Than since my birth my glass hath run soft minutes,
And yet be young; her presence has a spell
To keep off age; she has an eye would strike
Fire through an adamant.

Lady B. I have heard as much
Bestowed upon a dull-faced chambermaid,
Whom love and wit would thus commend. True beauty
Is mocked when we compare thus, itself being
Above what can be fetched to make it lovely;
Or, could our thoughts reach something to declare
The glories of a face, or body's elegance,
That touches but our sense; when beauty spreads
Over the soul, and calls up understanding
To look what thence is offered, and admire.
In both I must acknowledge Celestina
Most excellently fair, fair above all

The beauties I have seen, and one most worthy
Man's love and wonder.

Born. Do you speak, Aretina,
This with a pure sense to commend? or is't
The mockery of my praise?

Lady B. Although it shame
Myself, I must be just, and give her all
The excellency of women; and were I
A man—

Born. What then?

Lady B. I know not with what loss
I should attempt her love. She is a piece
So angelically moving, I should think
Frailty excused to dote upon her form,
And almost virtue to be wicked with her.   [*Exit.*

Born. What should this mean? This is no jealousy,
Or she believes I counterfeit. I feel
Something within me, like a heat, to give
Her cause, would Celestina but consent.
What a frail thing is man! It is not worth
Our glory to be chaste, while we deny
Mirth and converse with women. He is good
That dares the tempter, yet corrects his blood   [*Exit.*

SCENE III.—*A Room in* CELESTINA'S *House.*

Enter CELESTINA, MARIANA, *and* ISABELLA.

Cel. I have told you all my knowledge: since he is
    pleased
To invite himself, he shall be entertained,
And you shall be my witnesses.

Mar. Who comes with him?

Cel. Sir William Scentlove, that prepared me for
The honourable encounter. I expect
His lordship every minute.

Enter Sir WILLIAM SCENTLOVE.

Scent. My lord is come.

Cel. He has honoured me.

Enter Lord A. *and* HAIRCUT.

Scent. My lord, your periwig is awry.

Lord. You, sir—

> [*While* HAIRCUT *is busy about his hair,* Sir WIL-
> LIAM SCENTLOVE *goes to* CELESTINA.

Scent. You may guess at the gentleman that's with
him.

It is his barber, madam, do you observe?

An your ladyship wants a shaver.

Hair. She is here, sir.

I am betrayed.—Scentlove, your plot.   I may

Have opportunity to be revenged.   [*Exit.*

Scent. She is in the midst.

Lord. She's fair, I must confess;

But does she keep this distance out of state?

Cel. Though I am poor in language to express

How much your lordship honours me, my heart

Is rich and proud in such a guest.   I shall

Be out of love with every air abroad,

And for this grace done my unworthy house,

Be a fond prisoner, become anchorite,

And spend my hours in prayer, to reward

The blessing and the bounty of this presence.

Lord. Though you could turn each place you move
in to

A temple, rather than a wall should hide

So rich a beauty from the world, it were

Less want to lose our piety and your prayer.

A throne were fitter to present you to

Our wonder, whence your eyes, more worth than all

They look on, should chain every heart a prisoner.

Scent. 'Twas pretty well come off.

Lord. By your example
I shall know how to compliment; in this,
You more confirm my welcome.

 Cel. I shall love
My lips the better, if their silent language
Persuade your lordship but to think so truly.

 Lord. You make me smile, madam.

 Cel. I hope you came not
With fear that any sadness here should shake
One blossom from your eye. I should be miserable
To present any object should displease you.—

 Lord. You do not, madam.

 Cel. As I should account
It no less sorrow, if your lordship should
Lay too severe a censure on my freedom.
I will not court a prince against his justice,
Nor bribe him with a smile to think me honest.
Pardon, my lord, this boldness, and the mirth
That may flow from me. I believe my father
Thought of no winding-sheet when he begot me.

 Lord. She has a merry soul.—It will become
Me ask your pardon, madam, for my rude
Approach, so much a stranger to your knowledge.

 Cel. Not, my lord, so much stranger to my knowledge;
Though I have but seen your person afar off,
I am acquainted with your character,
Which I have heard so often, I can speak it.

 Lord. You shall do me an honour.

 Cel. If your lordship will
Be patient.

 Lord. And glad to hear my faults.

 Cel. That as your conscience can agree upon them:
However, if your lordship give me privilege,
I'll tell you what's the opinion of the world.

 Lord. You cannot please me better.

 Cel. You're a lord,

Born with as much nobility as would,
Divided, serve to make ten noblemen,
Without a herald ; but with so much spirit
And height of soul, as well might furnish twenty.
You are learned, a thing not compatible now
With native honour ; and are master of
A language that doth chain all ears, and charm
All hearts, where you persuade ; a wit so flowing,
And prudence to correct it, that all men
Believe they only meet in you, which, with
A spacious memory, make up the full wonders :
To these you have joined valour, and upon
A noble cause, know how to use a sword
To honour's best advantage, though you wear none.
You are as bountiful as the showers that fall
Into the spring's green bosom ; as you were
Created lord of Fortune, not her steward ;
So constant to the cause in which you make
Yourself an advocate, you dare all dangers ;
And men had rather you should be their friend,
Than justice or the bench bound up together.

   Lord. But did you hear all this ?

   Cel. And more, my lord.

   Lord. Pray let me have it, madam.

   Cel. To all these virtues there is added one,—
(Your lordship will remember, when I name it,
I speak but what I gather from the voice
Of others)—it is grown to a full fame
That you have loved a woman.

   Lord. But one, madam ?

   Cel. Yes, many ; give me leave to smile, my lord,
I shall not need to interpret in what sense ;
But you have showed yourself right honourable,
And, for your love to ladies, have deserved,
If their vote might prevail, a marble statue.
I make no comment on the people's text,—
My lord, I should be sorry to offend.

Lord. You cannot, madam; these are things we owe
To nature for.

Cel. And honest men will pay
Their debts.

Lord. If they be able, or compound.

Cel. She had a hard heart would be unmerciful,
And not give day to men so promising;
But you owed women nothing.

Lord. Yes, I am
Still in their debt, and I must owe them love,
It was part of my character.

Cel. With your lordship's
Pardon, I only said you had a fame
For loving women; but of late, men say
You have, against the imperial laws of love,
Restrained the active flowings of your blood,
And with a mistress buried all that is
Hoped for in love's succession, as all beauty
Had died with her, and left the world benighted!
In this you more dishonour all our sex
Than you did grace a part; when everywhere
Love tempts your eye to admire a glorious harvest,
And everywhere as full blown ears submit
Their golden heads, the laden trees bow down
Their willing fruit, and court your amorous tasting.

Lord. I see men would dissect me to a fibre;
But do you believe this?

Cel. It is my wonder,
I must confess, a man of nobler earth
Than goes to vulgar composition,
(Born and bred high, so unconfined, so rich
In fortunes, and so read in all that sum
Up human knowledge, to feed gloriously,
And live at court, the only sphere wherein
True beauty moves; nature's most wealthy garden,
Where every blossom is more worth than all
The Hesperian fruit by jealous dragon watched,

Where all delights do circle appetite,
And pleasures multiply by being tasted,)
Should be so lost with thought of one turned ashes.
There's nothing left, my lord, that can excuse you,
Unless you plead, what I am ashamed to prompt
Your wisdom to?

   Lord. What's that?

   Cel. That you have played
The surgeon with yourself.

   Lord. And am made eunuch?

   Cel. It were much pity.

   Lord. Trouble not yourself,
I could convince your fears with demonstration
That I am man enough, but knew not where,
Until this meeting, beauty dwelt. The court
You talk of must be where the queen of love is,
Which moves but with your person; in your eye
Her glory shines, and only at that flame
Her wanton boy doth light his quickening torch.

   Cel. Nay, now you compliment; I would it did,
My lord, for your own sake.

   Lord. You would be kind,
And love me then?

   Cel. My lord, I should be loving,
Where I found worth to invite it, and should cherish
A constant man.

   Lord. Then you should me, madam.

   Cel. But is the ice about your heart fallen off?
Can you return to do what love commands?—
Cupid, thou shalt have instant sacrifice,
And I dare be the priest.

   Lord. Your hand, your lip;   [*Kisses her.*
Now I am proof 'gainst all temptation.

   Cel. Your meaning, my good lord?

   Lord. I, that have strength
Against thy voice and beauty, after this
May dare the charms of womankind.—Thou art,

Bella Maria, unprofanèd yet ;
This magic has no power upon my blood.—
Farewell, madam ! if you durst be the example
Of chaste as well as fair, you were a brave one.

Cel. I hope your lordship means not this for earnest :
Be pleased to grace a banquet.

Lord. Pardon, madam.—
Will Scentlove, follow ; I must laugh at you.

Cel. My lord, I must beseech you stay, for honour,
For her whose memory you love best.

Lord. Your pleasure.

Cel. And by that virtue you have now professed,
I charge you to believe me too ; I can
Now glory that you have been worth my trial,
Which, I beseech you, pardon. Had not you
So valiantly recovered in this conflict,
You had been my triumph, without hope of more
Than my just scorn upon your wanton flame ;
Nor will I think these noble thoughts grew first
From melancholy, for some female loss,
As the fantastic world believes, but from
Truth, and your love of innocence, which shine
So bright in the two royal luminaries
At court, you cannot lose your way to chastity.[1]
Proceed, and speak of me as honour guides you.

                                        [*Exit* Lord A.

I am almost tired.—Come, ladies, we'll beguile
Dull time, and take the air another while.   [*Exeunt.*

---

[1] This tribute to the nuptial virtues of Charles and Henrietta was
not unmerited. The compliment, though frequent enough on the
stage, was not always paid at so small an expense of truth.—
Gifford.

ACT THE FIFTH.

SCENE I.—*A Room in* Sir THOMAS BORNWELL'S *House.*

Enter Lady BORNWELL, *and a* Servant *with a purse.*

ADY B. But hath Sir Thomas lost five
hundred pounds
Already?

    Serv. And five hundred more he bor-
        rowed.

The dice are notable devourers, madam;
    They make no more of pieces than of
But thrust their heaps together, to engender.   [pebbles,
" Two hundred more the caster!" cries this gentleman.
" I am with you.—I have that to nothing, sir."
Again; "'Tis covered!" and the table too,
With sums that frightened me. Here one sneaks out,
And with a martyr's patience smiles upon
His money's executioner, the dice;
Commands a pipe of good tobacco, and
I' the smoke on't vanishes. Another makes
The bones vault o'er his head, swears that ill-throwing
Has put his shoulder out of joint, calls for
A bone-setter. That looks to the box, to bid
His master send him some more hundred pounds,
Which lost, he takes tobacco, and is quiet.
Here a strong arm throws in and in, with which
He brushes all the table, pays the rooks

    Shir.   Z

That went their smelts a piece upon his hand,
Yet swears he has not drawn a stake this seven year.
But I was bid make haste ; my master may
Lose this five hundred pounds ere I come hither. [*Exit.*

   Lady B. If we both waste so fast, we shall soon find
Our state is not immortal.   Something in
His other ways appear not well already.

Enter Sir THOMAS BORNWELL, *and* Servants, *one with a
purse.*

   Born. Ye tortoises, why make ye no more haste ?
Go pay to the master of the house that money,
And tell the noble gamesters I have another
Superfluous thousand ; at night I'll visit 'em.
Do you hear?

   Serv. Yes, an please you.

   Born. Do't ye drudges.   [*Exeunt* Servants.
Ta, ra, ra !—Aretina !

   Lady B. You have a pleasant humour, sir.

   Born. What ! should a gentleman be sad?

   Lady B. You have lost—

   Born. A transitory sum ; as good that way
As another.

   Lady B. Do you not vex within for't ?

   Born. I had rather lose a thousand more, than one
Sad thought come near my heart for't.   Vex for trash !
Although it go from other men like drops
Of their life blood, we lose with the alacrity
We drink a cup of sack, or kiss a mistress.
No money is considerable with a gamester ;
They have souls more spacious than kings.   Did two
Gamesters divide the empire of the world,
They'd make one throw for't all, and he that lost
Be no more melancholy than to have played for
A morning's draught.   Vex a rich soul for dirt !
The quiet of whose every thought is worth
A province.

Lady B. But when dice have consumed all,
Your patience will not pawn for as much more.

Born. Hang pawning! sell outright, and the fear's
    over.

Lady B. Say you so? I'll have another coach to-
If there be rich above ground.   [morrow

Born. I forgot
To bid the fellow ask my jeweller
Whether the chain of diamonds be made up ;
I will present it to my Lady Bellamour,
Fair Celestina.

Lady B. This gown I have worn
Six days already; it looks dull, I'll give it
My waiting-woman, and have one of cloth
Of gold embroidered ; shoes and pantables [1]
Will show well of the same.

Born. I have invited
A covey of ladies, and as many gentlemen
To-morrow, to the Italian ordinary ;
I shall have rarities and regalias
To pay for, madam ; music, wanton songs,
And tunes of silken petticoats to dance to.

Lady B. And to-morrow have I invited half the court
To dine here. What misfortune 'tis your company
And our's should be divided ! After dinner
I entertain them with a play.

Born. By that time
Your play inclines to the epilogue, shall we
Quit our Italian host ; and whirl in coaches
To the Dutch magazine of sauce, the Stillyard,
Where deal, and backrag, [2] and what strange wine else
They dare but give a name to in the reckoning,
Shall flow into our room, and drown Westphalias,

---

[1] Slippers ; apparently a corruption of the French word *pantoufle.*
[2] *i.e.* Baccarach, a famous Rhine wine. There was a Rhenish
wine house in the Steelyard, which was at this epoch famous for
its Rhenish wines.

Tongues, and anchovies, like some little town
Endangered by a sluice, through whose fierce ebb
We wade, and wash ourselves, into a boat,
And bid our coachmen drive their leather tenements
By land, while we sail home, with a fresh tide,
To some new rendezvous.

 Lady B. If you have not
Pointed the place, pray bring your ladies hither;
I mean to have a ball to-morrow night,
And a rich banquet for 'em, where we'll dance
Till morning rise, and blush to interrupt us.

 Born. Have you no ladies i' the next room, to advance
A present mirth? What a dull house you govern!
Farewell! a wife's no company.—Arctina,
I've summed up my estate, and find we may have
A month good yet.

 Lady B. What mean you?

 Born. And I'd rather
Be lord one month of pleasures, to the height
And rapture of our senses, than be years
Consuming what we have in foolish temperance.
Live in the dark, and no fame wait upon us!
I will live so, posterity shall stand
At gaze when I am mentioned.

 Lady B. A month good!
And what shall be done then?

 Born. I'll over sea,
And trail a pike. With watching, marching, lying
In trenches, with enduring cold and hunger,
And taking here and there a musket-shot,
I can earn every week four shillings, madam;
And if the bullets favour me to snatch
Any superfluous limb, when I return,
With good friends, I despair not to be enrolled
Poor knight of Windsor. For your course, madam,
No doubt you may do well; your friends are great:
Or if your poverty, and their pride, cannot

Agree, you need not trouble much invention,
To find a trade to live by; there are customers.
Farewell, be frolic, madam! If I live,
I will feast all my senses, and not fall
Less than a Phaeton from my throne of pleasure,
Though my estate flame like the world about me. [*Exit.*

Lady B. 'Tis very pretty!—

Enter DECOY.

Madam Decoy!

Dec. What! melancholy,
After so sweet a night's work? Have not I
Showed myself mistress of my art?

Lady B. A lady.

Dec. That title makes the credit of the act
A story higher. You've not seen him yet?
I wonder what he'll say.

Lady B. He's here.

Enter KICKSHAW *and* FREDERICK.

Kick. Bear up,
My little myrmidon; does not Jack Littleworth
Follow?

Fred. Follow? he fell into the Thames
At landing.

Kick. The devil shall dive for him,
Ere I endanger my silk stockings for him:
Let the watermen alone, they have drags and engines.
When he has drunk his julep, I shall laugh
To see him come in pickled the next tide.

Fred. He'll never sink, he has such a cork brain.

Kick. Let him be hanged or drowned, all's one to me;
Yet he deserves to die by water, cannot
Bear his wine credibly.

Fred. Is not this my aunt?

Kick. And another handsome lady; I must know her.
[*Goes up to* DECOY.

Fred. My blood is rampant too, I must court some-
        body;
As good my aunt as any other body.
    Lady B. Where have you been, cousin?
    Fred. At the Bear
At the Bridge-foot, where our first health began
To the fair Aretina, whose sweet company
Was wished by all.   We could not get a lay,
A tumbler, a device, a *bona roba*,[1]
For any money; drawers were grown dull:
We wanted our true firks, and our vagaries.—
When were you in drink, aunt?
    Lady B. How?
    Fred. Do not ladies
Play the good fellows too?   There's no true mirth
Without 'em.   I have now such tickling fancies!
That doctor of the chair of wit has read
A precious lecture, how I should behave
Myself to ladies; as now, for example.
                    [*Goes up to* Lady BORNWELL.
    Lady B. Would you practise upon me?
    Fred. I first salute you,
You have a soft hand, madam; are you so
All over?
    Lady B. Nephew!
    Fred. Nay, you should but smile.
And then again I kiss you; and thus draw
Off your white glove, and start, to see your hand
More excellently white: I grace my own
Lip with this touch, and turning gently thus,
Prepare you for my skill in palmistry,
Which, out of curiosity, no lady
But easily applies to: the first line
I look with most ambition to find out,
Is Venus' girdle, a fair semicircle,
Enclosing both the mount of Sol and Saturn;

---

[1] Courtesan.

If that appear, she's for my turn ; a lady
Whom nature has prepared for the career ;
And, Cupid at my elbow, I put forward :
You have this very line, aunt.

Lady B. The boy's frantic !

Fred. You have a couch or pallet ; I can shut
The chamber door.   Enrich a stranger, when
Your nephew's coming into play !

Lady B. No more.

Fred. Are you so coy to your own flesh and blood ?

Kick. Here, take your playfellow ; I talk of sport,
And she would have me marry her.

Fred. Here's Littleworth.

Enter LITTLEWORTH, *wet.*

Why, how now, tutor?

Little. I have been fishing.

Fred. And what have you caught ?

Little. My belly full of water.

Kick. Ha, ha ! Where's thy rapier?

Little. My rapier is drowned,
And I am little better ; I was held up by the heels,
And out came a ton of water, beside wine.

Kick. It has made thee sober.

Little. Would you have me drunk
With water?

Lady B. I hope your fire is quenched by this time.

Fred. It is not now, as when " your worship walked
By all the taverns, Jack, dry as a bone."

Kick. You had store of fish under water, Jack.

Little. It has made a poor John of me.

Fred. I do not think but if we cast an angle
Into his belly, we might find some pilchards.

Little. And boiled, by this time.—Dear madam, a
bed.

Kick. Carry but the water-spaniel to a grass-plot,
Where he may roll himself ; let him but shake

His ears twice in the sun, and you may grind him
Into a posset.

Fred. Come, thou shalt to my bed,
Poor pickerel.

Dec. Alas, sweet gentleman!

Little. I have ill luck an I should smell by this time;
I am but new ta'en, I am sure.—Sweet gentlewoman!

Dec. Your servant.

Little. Pray do not pluck off my skin;
It is so wet, unless you have good eyes,
You'll hardly know it from a shirt.

Dec. Fear nothing.

   [*Exeunt all but* KICKSHAW *and* Lady BORNWELL.

Lady B. He has sack enough, and I may find his
humour.   [*Aside.*

Kick. And how is't with your ladyship? You look
Without a sunshine in your face.

Lady B. You are glorious
In mind and habit.

Kick. Ends of gold and silver!

Lady B. Your other clothes were not so rich. Who
   was
Your tailor, sir?

Kick. They were made for me long since;
They have known but two bright days upon my back.
I had a humour, madam, to lay things by;
They will serve two days more: I think I have gold
   enough
To go to the mercer. I'll now allow myself
A suit a week, as this, with necessary
Dependances, beaver, silk stockings, garters,
And roses, in their due conformity;
Boots are forbid a clean leg, but to ride in.
My linen every morning comes in new,
The old goes to great bellies.

Lady B. You are charitable.

Kick. I may dine with you sometime, or at the court,

To meet good company, not for the table.
My clerk o' the kitchen's here, a witty epicure,
A spirit, that, to please me with what's rare,
Can fly a hundred mile a day to market,
And make me lord of fish and fowl. I shall
Forget there is a butcher; and to make
My footman nimble, he shall feed on nothing
But wings of wild fowl.

   Lady B. These ways are costly.

   Kick. Therefore I'll have it so; I have sprung a
     mine.

   Lady B. You make me wonder, sir, to see this change
Of fortune: your revenue was not late
So plentiful.

   Kick. Hang dirty land, and lordships!
I would not change one lodging I have got,
For the Chamber of London.

   Lady B. Strange, of such a sudden,
To rise to this estate! No fortunate hand
At dice could lift you up so, for 'tis since
Last night: yesterday, you were no such monarch.

   Kick. There be more games than dice.

   Lady B. It cannot be
A mistress, though your person is worth love;
None possibly are rich enough to feed
As you have cast the method of your riots.
A princess, after all her jewels, must
Be forced to sell her provinces.

   Kick. Now you talk
Of jewels, what do you think of this?

   Lady B. A rich one.

   Kick. You'll honour me to wear't; this other toy
I had from you; this chain I borrowed of you,
A friend had it in keeping. [*Gives her the jewel and
     chain.*]—If your ladyship
Want any sum, you know your friend, and Alexander.

   Lady B. Dare you trust my security?

Kick. There's gold,
I shall have more to-morrow.

Lady B. You astonish me ;
Who can supply these?

Kick. A dear friend I have.
She promised we should meet again i' the morning.

Lady B. Not that I wish to know
More of your happiness than I have already
Heart to congratulate,—be pleased to lay
My wonder.

Kick. 'Tis a secret—

Lady B. Which I'll die
Ere I'll betray.

Kick. You have always wished me well ;
But you shall swear not to reveal the party.

Lady B. I'll lose the benefit of my tongue.

Kick. Nor be
Afraid at what I say.   What think you first
Of an old witch, a strange ill-favoured hag,
That, for my company last night, has wrought
This cure upon my fortune?   I do sweat
To think upon her name.

Lady B. How, sir! a witch?

Kick. I would not fright your ladyship too much
At first, but witches are akin to spirits.
The truth is—Nay, if you look pale already,
I have done.

Lady B. Sir, I beseech you.

Kick. If you have
But courage then to know the truth, I'll tell you
In one word ; my chief friend is—the devil !

Lady B. What devil? how I tremble !

Kick. Have a heart ;
'Twas a she-devil too, a most insatiate,
Abominable devil, with a tail
Thus long.

Lady B. Goodness defend me ! did you see her ?

Kick. No, 'twas i' the dark ; but she appeared first to
  me
I' the likeness of a beldam, and was brought,
I know not how, nor whither, by two goblins,
More hooded than a hawk.

Lady B. But would you venture
Upon a devil !

Kick. Ay, for means.

Lady B. How black
An impudence is this ! [*Aside.*]—But are you sure
It was the devil you enjoyed?

Kick. Say nothing ;
I did the best to please her ; but as sure
As you live, 'twas a hell-cat.

Lady B. Do you not quake ?

Kick. I found myself in the very room i' the morning,
Where two of her familiars had left me.

Enter Servant.

Serv. My lord is come to visit you.

Kick. No words,
As you respect my safety. I have told tales
Out of the devil's school ; if it be known,
I lose a friend. 'Tis now about the time
I promised her to meet again ; at my
Return I'll tell you wonders. Not a word. [*Exit.*

Lady B. 'Tis a false glass ; sure I am more deformed :
      [*Looks in her pocket mirror.*
What have I done?—my soul is miserable.

Enter Lord A.

Lord. I sent you a letter, madam.

Lady B. You expressed
Your noble care of me, my lord.

Re-enter Sir THOMAS BORNWELL *with* CELESTINA.

Born. Your lordship
Does me an honour.

Lord. Madam, I am glad
To see you here ; I meant to have kissed your hand,
Ere my return to court.

Cel. Sir Thomas has
Prevailed to bring me, to his trouble, hither.

Lord. You do him grace.

Born. Why, what's the matter, madam ?
Your eyes are tuning Lachrimæ.[1]

Lady B. As you
Do hope for Heaven, withdraw, and give me but
The patience of ten minutes.

Born. Wonderful !
I will not hear you above that proportion.
She talks of Heaven :—Come, where must we to counsel ?

Lady B. You shall conclude me when you please.

[*Exit.*

Born. I follow.

Lord. What alteration is this ? I, that so late
Stood the temptation of her eye and voice,
Boasted a heart 'bove all licentious flame,
At second view turn renegade, and think
I was too superstitious, and full
Of phlegm, not to reward her amorous courtship
With manly freedom.

Cel. I obey you, sir.

Born. I'll wait upon your lordship presently.   [*Exit.*

Lord. She could not want a cunning to seem honest
When I neglected her. I am resolved.—
You still look pleasant, madam.

Cel. I have cause,
My lord, the rather for your presence, which
Hath power to charm all trouble in my thoughts.

Lord. I must translate that compliment, and owe
All that is cheerful in myself to these
All-quick'ning smiles : and rather than such bright

---

[1] The name of a popular musical work by John Dowland, the lutenist.

Eyes should repent their influence upon me,
I would release the aspects, and quit the bounty
Of all the other stars.   Did you not think me
A strange and melancholy gentleman,
To use you so unkindly?
    Cel. Me, my lord?
    Lord. I hope you made no loud complaint; I would
        not
Be tried by a jury of ladies.
    Cel. For what, my lord?
    Lord. I did not meet that noble entertainment
You were late pleased to show me.
    Cel. I observed
No such defect in your lordship, but a brave
And noble fortitude.
    Lord. A noble folly;
I bring repentance for't.   I know you have,
Madam, a gentle faith, and will not ruin
What you have built to honour you.
    Cel. What's that?
    Lord. If you can love, I'll tell your ladyship.
    Cel. I have a stubborn soul else.
    Lord. You are all
Composed of harmony.
    Cel. What love do you mean?
    Lord. That which doth perfect both; madam, you have
        heard
I can be constant, and if you consent
To grace it so, there is a spacious dwelling
Prepared within my heart for such a mistress.
    Cel. Your mistress, my good lord?
    Lord. Why, my good lady,
Your sex doth hold it no dishonour
To become mistress to a noble servant
In the now court Platonic way.   Consider
Who 'tis that pleads to you; my birth, and present
Value, can be no stain to your embrace;

But these are shadows when my love appears,
Which shall, in his first miracle, return
Me in my bloom of youth, and thee a virgin;
When I, within some new Elysium,
Of purpose made and meant for us, shall be
In every thing Adonis, but in his
Contempt of love; and court thee from a Daphne
Hid in the cold rind of a bashful tree,
With such warm language and delight, till thou
Leap from that bays into the queen of love,
And pay my conquest with composing garlands
Of thy own myrtle for me.

    Cel. What's all this?

    Lord. Consent to be my mistress, Celestina,
And we will have it spring-time all the year;
Upon whose invitations, when we walk,
The winds shall play soft descant to our feet,
And breathe rich odours to re-pure the air:
Green bowers on every side shall tempt our stay,
And violets stoop to have us tread upon 'em.
The red rose shall grow pale, being near thy cheek,
And the white blush, o'ercome with such a forehead.
Here laid, and measuring with ourselves some bank,
A thousand birds shall from the woods repair,
And place themselves so cunningly behind
The leaves of every tree, that while they pay
Us tribute of their songs, thou shalt imagine
The very trees bear music, and sweet voices
Do grow in every arbour. Here can we
Embrace and kiss, tell tales, and kiss again,
And none but Heaven our rival.

    Cel. When we are
Weary of these, what if we shift our paradise,
And through a grove of tall and even pine,
Descend into a valley, that shall shame
All the delights of Tempe; upon whose
Green plush the Graces shall be called to dance,

To please us, and maintain their fairy revels,
To the harmonious murmurs of a stream
That gently falls upon a rock of pearl.
Here doth the nymph, forsaken Echo, dwell,
To whom we'll tell the story of our love,
Till at our surfeit and her want of joy,
We break her heart with envy.   Not far off,
A grove shall call us to a wanton river,
To see a dying swan give up the ghost,
The fishes shooting up their tears in bubbles,
That they must lost the genius of their waves—
And such love linsey woolsey, to no purpose.

Lord. You chide me handsomely ; pray tell me how
You like this language.

Cel. Good my lord, forbear.

Lord. You need not fly out of this circle, madam ;
These widows are so full of circumstance !
I'll undertake, in this time I have courted
Your ladyship for the toy, to have broken ten,
Nay, twenty colts, virgins I mean, and taught 'em
The amble, or what pace I most affected.

Cel. You're not, my lord, again, the lord I thought
    you ;
And I must tell you now, you do forget
Yourself and me.

Lord. You'll not be angry, madam ?

Cel. Nor rude, (though gay men have a privilege,)
It shall appear :—there is a man, my lord,
Within my acquaintance, rich in worldly fortunes,
But cannot boast any descent of blood,
Would buy a coat of arms.

Lord. He may, and legs
Booted and spurred, to ride into the country.

Cel. But these will want antiquity, my lord,
The seal of honour.   What's a coat cut out
But yesterday, to make a man a gentleman?
Your family, as old as the first virtue

That merited an escutcheon, doth owe[1]
A glorious coat of arms ; if you will sell now
All that your name doth challenge, in that ensign,
I'll help you to a chapman, that shall pay,
And pour down wealth enough for't.

Lord. Sell my arms !
I cannot, madam.

Cel. Give but your consent,
You know not how the state may be inclined
To dispensation ; we may prevail
Upon the Heralds' office afterward.

Lord. I'll sooner give these arms to the hangman's
        axe,
My head, my heart, to twenty executions,
Than sell one atom from my name.

Cel. Change that,
And answer him would buy my honour from me ;
Honour, that is not worn upon a flag,
Or pennon, that, without the owner's dangers,
An enemy may ravish, and bear from me ;
But that which grows and withers with my soul,
Beside the body's stain : think, think, my lord,
To what you would unworthily betray me,
If you would not, for price of gold, or pleasure,
(If that be more your idol,) lose the glory
And painted honour of your house.—I have done.

Lord. Enough to rectify a satyr's blood.
Obscure my blushes here.

Enter Sir WILLIAM SCENTLOVE *and* HAIRCUT *behind.*

Hair. Or this, or fight with me ;
It shall be no exception that I wait
Upon my lord ; I am a gentleman,
You may be less, and be a knight : the office
I do my lord is honest, sir.   How many
Such you have been guilty of Heaven knows.

[1] *i.e.* Own.

Scent. 'Tis no fear of your sword, but that I would not
Break the good laws established against duels.

Hair. Off with your periwig, and stand bare.

[Sir WILLIAM SCENTLOVE *takes off his periwig.*

Lord. From this
Minute I'll be a servant to your goodness ;
A mistress in the wanton sense is common,
I'll honour you with chaste thoughts, and call you so.

Cel. I'll study to be worth your fair opinion.

Lord. Scentlove, your head was used to a covering,
Beside a hat ; when went the hair away ?

Scent. I laid a wager, my lord, with Haircut,
Who thinks I shall catch cold, that I'll stand bare
This half hour.

Hair. Pardon my ambition,
Madam, I told you truth ; I am a gentleman,
And cannot fear that name is drowned in my
Relation to my lord.

Cel. I dare not think so.

Hair. From henceforth call my service duty, madam :
That pig's head, that betrayed me to your mirth,
Is doing penance for't.

Scent. Why may not I,
My lord, begin a fashion of no hair ?

Cel. Do you sweat, Sir William ?

Scent. Not with store of nightcaps.

Re-enter Sir THOMAS *and* Lady BORNWELL, *in
conversation.*

Lady B. Heaven has dissolved the clouds that hung
upon
My eyes, and if you can with mercy meet
A penitent, I throw my own will off,
And now in all things obey yours. My nephew
Send back again to the college, and myself
To what place you'll confine me.

Born. Dearer now

Shir.   A A

Than ever to my bosom, thou shalt please
Me best to live at thy own choice.   I did
But fright thee with a noise of my expenses ;
The sums are safe, and we have wealth enough,
If yet we use it nobly.   My lord—madam,
Pray honour us to-night,

   Lady B. I beg your presence,
And pardon.

   Born. I know not how my Aretina
May be disposed to-morrow for the country.

   Cel. You must not go before you have done
Me honour to accept an entertainment
Where I have power ; on those terms I'm your guest.

   Born. You grace us, madam.

   Lady B. Already
I feel a cure upon my soul, and promise
My after life to virtue.   Pardon, Heaven,
My shame, yet hid from the world's eye.   [*Aside.*

Re-enter DECOY *behind.*

   Dec. Sweet madam !

   Lady B. Not for the world be seen here ! we are lost.
I'll visit you at home. [*Exit* DECOY.]—But not to practise
What she expects : my counsel may recover her. [*Aside.*

Re-enter KICKSHAW.

   Kick. Where's madam ?—Pray lend me a little money,
My spirit has deceived me ; Proserpine
Has broke her word.

   Lady B. Do you expect to find
The devil true to you ?

   Kick. Not too loud.

   Lady B. I'll voice it
Louder, to all the world, your horrid sin,
Unless you promise me religiously,
To purge your foul blood by repentance, sir.

   Kick. Then I'm undone.

Lady B. Not while I have power
To encourage you to virtue ; I'll endeavour
To find you out some nobler way at court,
To thrive in.

Kick. Do't, and I'll forsake the devil,
And bring my flesh to obedience. You shall steer me.—
My lord, your servant.

Lord. You are brave again.

Kick. Madam, your pardon.

Born. Your offence requires
Humility.

Kick. Low as my heart.—Sir Thomas,
I'll sup with you, a part of satisfaction.

Born. Our pleasures cool. Music! and when our
ladies
Are tired with active motion, to give
Them rest, in some new rapture to advance
Full mirth, our souls shall leap into a dance. [*Exeunt.*

THE CARDINAL.

 IR HENRY HERBERT, Master of the
Revels, licensed the tragedy of *The
Cardinal* in 1641, and it was acted the
same year at the Blackfriars play-
house. It was first printed with five
other plays in an octavo volume in
1652. After the Restoration *The Cardinal* was revived, and Pepys saw it at the Cockpit in Drury Lane,
in 1662.

Dyce considers that in writing this play Shirley was
under the influence of Webster's *Duchess of Malfy*.

To my Worthily Honoured Friend,

G. B. ESQ.

SIR,

 DID suffer at the first some contention within me, and looking upon myself, was inclined to stifle my ambitious thoughts in this dedication ; but when some time, and a happy conversation, had preferred me to more acquaintance with you, (which was more argument to me than the fame I had heard of your reputation, with the most temperate and ingenious men,) I found you not only an excellent judge, but a good man : at this my modesty took full encouragement, to make this offering, which, as I conceive, to be the best of my flock, I knew not a better altar whereon to make it a sacrifice, with this protestation, that it comes (and that is it only which makes all devotions acceptable) from the heart ; and your candid acceptance will bind me with all my services and remembrance, to merit a reception with you in the quality and honour of,

Sir,
Your most humble devoted servant,

JAMES SHIRLEY.

PROLOGUE.

The CARDINAL! 'Cause we express no scene,
We do believe most of you, gentlemen,
Are at this hour in France, and busy there,
Though you vouchsafe to lend your bodies here;
But keep your fancy active, till you know,
By the progress of our play, 'tis nothing so.
A poet's art is to lead on your thought
Through subtle paths and workings of a plot;
And where your expectation does not thrive,
If things fall better, yet you may forgive.
I will say nothing positive; you may
Think what you please; we call it but a Play:
Whether the comic Muse, or ladies' love,
Romance, or direful tragedy it prove,
The bill determines not; and would you be
Persuaded, I would have't a Comedy,
For all the purple in the name, and state
Of him that owns it; but 'tis left to fate:
Yet I will tell you, ere you see it played,
What the author, and he blushed too, when he said,
Comparing with his own, (for't had been pride,
He thought, to build his wit a pyramid
Upon another's wounded fame,) this play
Might rival with his best, and dared to say—
Troth, I am out: he said no more. You, then,
When 'tis done, may say your pleasures, gentlemen.

DRAMATIS PERSONÆ.

King of NAVARRE.
The CARDINAL.
COLUMBO, the CARDINAL'S Nephew.
COUNT D'ALVAREZ.
HERNANDO, a Colonel.
ALPHONSO, a Captain.
Lords.
ANTONIO, Secretary to the Duchess.
Colonels.
ANTONELLI, the CARDINAL'S Servant.
Gentleman-Usher.
Surgeon.
JAQUES, PEDRO, and other Servants.
Guard.
Attendants, &c.

DUCHESS ROSAURA.
VALERIA, }
CELINDA, } Ladies.
PLACENTIA, the Duchess's Waiting-woman.

SCENE—The Capital of NAVARRE, and once on the
frontiers.

ACT THE FIRST.

SCENE I.—*An Apartment in the Palace.*

Enter at one door, two Lords; *at the other,* Antonio.

IRST LORD. Who is that?

    2nd Lord. The duchess' secretary.

    1st Lord. Signior!

    Ant. Your lordship's servant.

    1st Lord. How does her grace, since she left off her mourning
For the young Duke Mendoza, whose timeless death
At sea left her a virgin and a widow?

    2nd Lord. She's now inclining to a second bridegroom.
When is the day of mighty marriage
To our great Cardinal's nephew, Don Columbo?

    Ant. When they agree, they will not steal to church;
I guess the ceremonies will be loud and public.
Your lordships will excuse me.   [*Exit.*

    1st Lord. When they agree! Alas! poor lady, she
Dotes not upon Columbo, when she thinks
Of the young Count d'Alvarez, divorced from her
By the king's power.

    2nd Lord. And counsel of the Cardinal,
To advance his nephew to the duchess' bed;
It is not well.

    1st Lord. Take heed; the Cardinal holds
Intelligence with every bird i' the air.

2nd Lord. Death on his purple pride! he governs all;
And yet Columbo is a gallant gentleman.

1st Lord. The darling of the war, whom victory
Hath often courted; a man of daring,
And most exalted spirit.   Pride in him
Dwells like an ornament, where so much honour
Secures his praise.

2nd Lord. This is no argument
He should usurp, and wear Alvarez' title
To the fair duchess; men of coarser blood,
Would not so tamely give this treasure up.

1st Lord. Although Columbo's name is great in war,
Whose glorious art and practice is above
The greatness of Alvarez, yet he cannot
Want soul, in whom alone survives the virtue
Of many noble ancestors, being the last
Of his great family.

2nd Lord. 'Tis not safe, you'll say,
To wrestle with the king.

1st Lord. More danger if the Cardinal be displeased,
Who sits at helm of state.   Count d'Alvarez
Is wiser to obey the stream, than by
Insisting on his privilege to her love,
Put both their fates upon a storm.

2nd Lord. If wisdom,
Not inborn fear, make him compose, I like it.
How does the duchess bear herself?

1st Lord. She moves by the rapture [1] of another wheel
That must be obeyed; like some sad passenger,
That looks upon the coast his wishes fly to,
But is transported by an adverse wind,
Sometimes a churlish pilot.

2nd Lord. She has a sweet and noble nature.

1st Lord. That
Commends Alvarez; Hymen cannot tie
A knot of two more equal hearts and blood.

---

[1] *i.e.* Force.

Enter ALPHONSO.

2nd Lord. Alphonso!

Alph. My good lord.

1st Lord. What great affair

Hath brought you from the confines?

Alph. Such as will

Be worth your counsels, when the king hath read

My letters from the governor: the Arragonians,

Violating their confederate oath and league,

Are now in arms: they have not yet marched towards us;

But 'tis not safe to expect, if we may timely

Prevent invasion.

2nd Lord. Dare they be so insolent?

1st Lord. This storm I did foresee.

2nd Lord. What have they, but

The sweetness of the king, to make a crime?

1st Lord. But how appears the Cardinal at this news?

Alph. Not pale, although

He knows they have no cause to think him innocent,

As by whose counsel they were once surprised.

1st Lord. There is more

Than all our present art can fathom in

This story, and I fear I may conclude,

This flame has breath at home to cherish it;

There's treason in some hearts, whose faces are

Smooth to the state.

Alph. My lord, I take my leave.

2nd Lord. Your friends, good captain.   [*Exeunt.*

SCENE II.—*A Room in the* Duchess's *House.*

Enter Duchess, VALERIA, *and* CELINDA.

Val. Sweet madam, be less thoughtful; this obedience

To passion will destroy the noblest frame

Of beauty that this kingdom ever boasted.

Cel. This sadness might become your other habit,

And ceremonies black, for him that died.
The times of sorrow are expired ; and all
The joys that wait upon the court, your birth,
And a new Hymen, that is coming towards you
Invite a change.

   Duch. Ladies, I thank you both ;
I pray excuse a little melancholy
That is behind ; my year of mourning hath not
So cleared my account with sorrow, but there may
Some dark thoughts stay, with sad reflections,
Upon my heart, for him I lost. Even this
New dress, and smiling garment, meant to show
A peace concluded 'twixt my grief and me,
Is but a sad remembrance ; but I resolve
To entertain more pleasing thoughts ; and if
You wish me heartily to smile, you must
Not mention grief, not in advice to leave it.
Such counsels open but afresh the wounds
You would close up, and keep alive the cause,
Whose bleeding you would cure. Let's talk of some-
That may delight. You two are read in all   [thing
The histories of our court : tell me, Valeria,
Who has thy vote for the most handsome man?—
Thus I must counterfeit a peace, when all
Within me is at mutiny.   [*Aside.*

   Val. I have examined
All that are candidates for the praise of ladies,
But find—may I speak boldly to your grace?
And will you not return it in your mirth,
To make me blush ?

   Duch. No, no ; speak freely.

   Val. I will not rack your patience, madam ; but
Were I a princess, I should think the Count d'Alvarez
Had sweetness to deserve me from the world.

   Duch. Alvarez ! she's a spy upon my heart.   [*Aside.*

   Val. He's young and active, and composed most

   Duch. I have seen a face more tempting.   [sweetly.

Val. It had then
Too much of woman in't : his eyes speak movingly,
Which may excuse his voice, and lead away
All female pride his captive ; his hair, black,
Which, naturally falling into curls—
   Duch. Prithee, no more ; thou art in love with him.—
The man in your esteem, Celinda, now ?
   Cel. Alvarez is, I must confess, a gentleman
Of handsome composition ; but with
His mind, the greater excellence, I think
Another may delight a lady more,
If man be well considered, that's Columbo,
Now, madam, voted to be yours.
   Duch. My torment !   [*Aside.*
   Val. She affects him not.
   Cel. He has a person, and a bravery beyond
All men, that I observe.
   Val. He is a soldier,
A rough-hewn man, and may show well at distance
His talk will fright a lady ; War, and grim-
Faced Honour are his mistresses ; he raves
To hear a lute ; Love meant him not his priest.—
Again your pardon, madam.   We may talk,
But you have art to choose, and crown affection.
            [CELINDA *and* VALERIA *walk aside.*
   Duch. What is it to be born above these ladies,
And want their freedom ! they are not constrained,
Nor slaved by their own greatness, or the king's ;
But let their free hearts look abroad, and choose
By their own eyes to love.   I must repair
My poor afflicted bosom, and assume
The privilege I was born with, which now prompts me
To tell the king, he hath no power nor art
To steer a lover's soul.—

            Enter ANTONIO.

What says Count d'Alvarez ?

Ant. Madam, he'll attend you.

Duch. Wait you, as I directed. When he comes,
Acquaint me privately.

Ant. Madam, I have news;
'Tis now arrived the court; we shall have wars.

Duch. I find an army here of killing thoughts.

Ant. The king has chosen Don Columbo general,
Who is immediately to take his leave.

Duch. What flood is let into my heart! How far
Is he to go?

Ant. To Arragon.

Duch. That's well
At first; he should not want a pilgrimage
To the unknown world, if my thoughts might convey
          him.

Ant. 'Tis not impossible he may go thither.

Duch. How?

Ant. To the unknown world; he goes to fight,
That's in his way: such stories are in nature.

Duch. Conceal this news.

Ant. He will not be long absent;
The affair will make him shift
To kiss your grace's hand.

Duch. He cannot fly
With too much wing to take his leave.—I must
Be admitted to your conference; you have
Enlarged my spirits; they shall droop no more.

Cel. We are happy, if we may advance one thought
To your grace's pleasure.

Val. Your eye before was in eclipse; these smiles
Become you, madam.

Duch. I have not skill to contain myself.   [*Aside.*

Enter PLACENTIA.

Pla. The Cardinal's nephew, madam, Don Columbo.

Duch. Already! Attend him.   [*Exit* PLACENTIA.

Val. Shall we take our leave?

Duch. He shall not know, Celinda,[1] how you praised
him.

Cel. If he did, madam, I should have the confidence
To tell him my free thoughts.

Enter COLUMBO.

Duch. My lord, while I am in study to requite
The favour you have done me, you increase
My debt to such a sum, still by new honouring
Your servant, I despair of my own freedom.

Colum. Madam, he kisses your white hand, that must
Not surfeit in this happiness—and, ladies,
I take your smiles for my encouragement!
I have not long to practise these court tactics.

[*Kisses them.*

Cel. He has been taught to kiss.

Duch. There's something, sir,
Upon your brow I did not read before.

Colum. Does the character please you, madam?

Duch. More,
Because it speaks you cheerful.

Colum. 'Tis for such
Access of honour, as must make Columbo
Worth all your love; the king is pleased to think
Me fit to lead his army.

Duch. How! an army?

Colum. We must not use the priest, till I bring home
Another triumph, that now stays for me,
To reap it in the purple field of glory.

Duch. But do you mean to leave me, and expose
Yourself to the devouring war? No enemy
Should divide us; the king is not so cruel.

Colum. The king is honourable; and this grace

---

[1] The old copy reads, "Valeria;" but erroneously, as appears from
the dialogue, on p. 367, and the commencement of the third act.
In fact, the names of these two ladies are strangely confounded;
and in a subsequent part of this scene it has been found necessary
to make them everywhere change places.—*Gifford.*

Shir.   B B

More answers my ambition, than his gift
Of thee, and all thy beauty, which I can
Love, as becomes thy soldier, and fight
To come again, a conqueror of thee.   [*She weeps.*
Then I must chide this fondness.

Re-enter ANTONIO.

Ant. Madam, the king, and my lord Cardinal. [*Exit.*

Enter King, Cardinal, *and* Lords.

King. Madam, I come to call a servant from you,
And strengthen his excuse; the public cause
Will plead for your consent; at his return
Your marriage shall receive triumphant ceremonies;
Till then you must dispense.

Car. She appears sad
To part with him.—I like it fairly, nephew.

Cel. Is not the General a gallant man?
What lady would deny him a small courtesy?

Val. Thou hast converted me, and I begin
To wish it were no sin.

Cel. Leave that to narrow consciences.

Val. You are pleasant.

Cel. But he would please one better. Do such men
Lie with their pages?

Val. Wouldst thou make a shift?

Cel. He is going to a bloody business;
'Tis pity he should die without some heir:
That lady were hard-hearted now, that would
Not help posterity, for the mere good
Of the king and commonwealth.

Val. Thou art wild; we may be observed.

Duch. Your will must guide me; happiness and con-
          quest
Be ever waiting on his sword!

Colum. Farewell.

          [*Exeunt* King, COLUMBO, Cardinal, *and* Lords.

Duch. Pray give me leave to examine a few thoughts.—
Expect me in the garden.

    Cel. We attend.   [*Exeunt* CELINDA *and* VALERIA.

    Duch. This is above all expectation happy.
Forgive me, Virtue, that I have dissembled,
And witness with me, I have not a thought
To tempt or to betray him, but secure
The promise I first made, to love and honour.

Re-enter ANTONIO.

    Ant. The Count d'Alvarez, madam.

    Duch. Admit him,
And let none interrupt us. [*Exit* ANTONIO.]—How
    shall I
Behave my looks? The guilt of my neglect,
Which had no seal from hence, will call up blood
To write upon my cheeks the shame and story
In some red letter.

Enter ALVAREZ.

    Alv. Madam, I present
One that was glad to obey your grace, and come
To know what your commands are.

    Duch. Where I once
Did promise love, a love that had the power
And office of a priest to chain my heart
To yours, it were injustice to command.

    Alv. But I can look upon you, madam, as
Becomes a servant; with as much humility,
In tenderness of your honour and great fortune,
Give up, when you call back your bounty, all that
Was mine, as I had pride to think them favours.

    Duch. Hath love taught thee no more assurance in
Our mutual vows, thou canst suspect it possible
I should revoke a promise, made to heaven
And thee, so soon? This must arise from some
Distrust of thy own faith.

Alv. Your grace's pardon ;
To speak with freedom, I am not so old
In cunning to betray, nor young in time,
Not to see when and where I am at loss,
And how to bear my fortune, and my wounds,
Which, if I look for health, must still bleed inward,
A hard and desperate condition.
I am not ignorant your birth and greatness
Have placed you to grow up with the king's grace
And jealousy, which, to remove, his power
Hath chosen a fit object for your beauty
To shine upon, Columbo, his great favourite.
I am a man, on whom but late the king
Has pleased to cast a beam, which was not meant
To make me proud, but wisely to direct,
And light me to my safety. Oh, dear madam !
I will not call more witness of my love
(If you will let me still give it that name)
Than this, that I dare make myself a loser,
And to your will give all my blessings up.
Preserve your greatness, and forget a trifle,
That shall, at best, when you have drawn me up,
But hang about you like a cloud, and dim
The glories you are born to.

   Duch. Misery
Of birth and state ! That I could shift into
A meaner blood, or find some art to purge
That part which makes my veins unequal ! yet
Those nice distinctions have no place in us ;
There's but a shadow difference, a title :
Thy stock partakes as much of noble sap
As that which feeds the root of kings ; and he
That writes a lord hath all the essence of
Nobility.

   Alv. 'Tis not a name that makes
Our separation ; the king's displeasure
Hangs a portent to fright us, and the matter

That feeds this exhalation is the Cardinal's
Plot to advance his nephew; then Columbo,
A man made up for some prodigious act,
Is fit to be considered: in all three
There is no character you fix upon
But has a form of ruin to us both.

   Duch. Then you do look on these with fear?

   Alv. With eyes
That should think tears a duty, to lament
Your least unkind fate; but my youth dares boldly
Meet all the tyranny o' the stars, whose black
Malevolence but shoots my single tragedy.
You are above the value of many worlds,
Peopled with such as I am.

   Duch. What if Columbo,
Engaged to war, in his hot thirst of honour,
Find out the way to death?

   Alv. 'Tis possible.

   Duch. Or say, (no matter by what art or motive,)
He give his title up, and leave me to
My own election?

   Alv. If I then be happy
To have a name within your thought, there can
Be nothing left to crown me with new blessing;
But I dream thus of heaven, and wake to find
My amorous soul a mockery. When the priest
Shall tie you to another, and the joys
Of marriage leave no thought at leisure to
Look back upon Alvarez, that must wither
For loss of you; yet then I cannot lose
So much of what I was once in your favour,
But, in a sigh, pray still you may live happy.   [*Exit.*

   Duch. My heart is in a mist; some good star smile
Upon my resolution, and direct
Two lovers in their chaste embrace to meet!
Columbo's bed contains my winding sheet.   [*Exit.*

ACT THE SECOND.

SCENE I.—*Before the Walls of the frontier City.—*
Columbo's *Tent.*

Columbo, Hernando, *two* Colonels, Alphonso, *two*
Captains, *and other* Officers, *seated at a Council of War.*

COLUM. I see no face in all this council
  that
  Hath one pale fear upon't, though we
  arrived not
So timely to secure the town, which gives
  Our enemy such triumph.

1st Col. 'Twas betrayed.

Alph. The wealth of that one city
Will make the enemy glorious.

1st Col. They dare
Not plunder it.

Alph. They give fair quarter yet:
They only seal up men's estates, and keep
Possession for the city's use: they take up
No wares without security ; and he,
Whose single credit will not pass, puts in
Two lean comrades, upon whose bonds 'tis not
Religion to deny them.

Colum. To repair this
With honour, gentlemen ?

Her. My opinion is
To expect awhile.

Colum. Your reason ?

Her. Till their own
Surfeit betray them ; for their soldiers,
Bred up with coarse and common bread, will show
Such appetites on the rich cates they find,
They'll spare our swords a victory, when their own
Riot and luxury destroys them.

1st Col. That
Will show our patience too like a fear.
With favour of his excellence, I think
The spoil of cities takes not off the courage,
But doubles it on soldiers ; besides,
While we have tameness to expect, the noise
Of their success and plenty will increase
Their army.

Her. 'Tis considerable ; we do not
Exceed in foot or horse, our muster not
'Bove sixteen thousand both ; and the infantry
Raw, and not disciplined to act.

Alph. Their hearts,
But with a brave thought of their country's honour,
Will teach them how to fight, had they not seen
A sword. But we decline our own too much ;[1]
The men are forward in their arms, and take
The use with avarice of fame.   [*They rise, and talk aside.*

Colum. [*Staying* HERNANDO.]—Colonel,
I do suspect you are a coward.

Her. Sir !

Colum. Or else a traitor ; take your choice.   No more.
I called you to a council, sir, of war ;
Yet keep your place.

Her. I have worn other names.

Colum. Deserve them.   Such
Another were enough to unsoul an army.
Ignobly talk of patience, till they drink
And reel to death ! we came to fight, and force them

---

[1] *i.e.* Form too low an estimate of the military qualities of our
own troops.

To mend their pace : thou hast no honour in thee,
Not enough noble blood to make a blush
For thy tame eloquence.

Her. My lord, I know
My duty to a general : yet there are
Some that have known me here.   Sir, I desire
To quit my regiment.

Colum. You shall have license.—
Ink and paper !

Enter Attendant *with ink and paper, and exit.*

1st Col. The general's displeased.

2nd Col. How is't, Hernando ?

Her. The general has found out employment for me ;
He is writing letters back.

Alph. and Capt. To his mistress?

Her. Pray do not trouble me ; yet, prithee speak,
And flatter not thy friend.   Dost think I dare
Not draw my sword, and use it, when a cause,
With honour, calls to action ?

Alph. and 1st Col. With the most valiant man alive.

Her. You'll do me some displeasure in your loves :
Pray to your places.

Colum. So ; bear those letters to the king ;
They speak my resolution, before
Another sun decline, to charge the enemy.

Her. A pretty court way
Of dismissing an officer.—I obey ; success
Attend your counsels !   [*Exit.*

Colum. If here be any dare not look on danger,
And meet it like a man, with scorn of death,
I beg his absence ; and a coward's fear
Consume him to a ghost !

1st Col. None such are here.

Colum. Or, if in all your regiments you find
One man that does not ask to bleed with honour,
Give him a double pay to leave the army :

There's service to be done will call the spirits
And aid of men.

1st Col. You give us all new flame.

Colum. I am confirmed, and you must lose no time ;
The soldier that was took last night, to me
Discovered their whole strength, and that we have
A party in the town.   The river, that
Opens the city to the west, 's unguarded ;—
We must this night use art and resolution ;
We cannot fall ingloriously.

1st Capt. That voice
Is every man's.

Enter Soldier, *and* ANTONIO *with a letter.*

Colum. What now?

Sold. Letters.

Colum. Whence ?

Sold. From the duchess.

Colum. They are welcome.—   [*Takes the letter.*
Meet at my tent again this evening ;
Yet stay, some wine.—The duchess' health !   [*Drinks.*
See it go round.   [*Opens the letter.*

Ant. It will not please his excellence.

1st Col. The duchess' health.   [*Drinks.*

2nd Capt. To me ! more wine.

Ant. The clouds are gathering, and his eyes shoot fire ;
Observe what thunder follows.

2nd Capt. The general has but ill news.   I suspect
The duchess sick, or else the king.

1st Capt. May be
The Cardinal.

2nd Capt. His soul has long been looked for.

Colum. She dares not be so insolent.   It is
The duchess' hand.   How am I shrunk in fame
To be thus played withal !   She writes, and counsels,
Under my hand, to send her back a free
Resign of all my interest to her person,

Promise, or love ; that there's no other way,
With safety of my honour, to revisit her.
The woman is possessed with some bold devil,
And wants an exorcism ; or, I am grown
A cheap, dull, phlegmatic fool, a post, that's carved
I' the common street, and holding out my forehead
To every scurril wit to pin disgrace
And libels on't.—Did you bring this to me, sir?
My thanks shall warm your heart.   [*Draws a pistol.*

 Ant. Hold, hold ! my lord !
I know not what provokes this tempest, but
Her grace ne'er showed more freedom from a storm
When I received this paper.   If you have
A will to do an execution,
Your looks, without that engine, sir, may serve.—
I did not seek the employment.

 Colum. Ha ! had she
No symptom, in her eye or face, of anger,
When she gave this in charge ?

 Ant. Serene, as I
Have seen the morning rise upon the spring ;
No trouble in her breath, but such a wind
As came to kiss, and fan the smiling flowers.

 Colum. No poetry.

 Ant. By all the truth in prose,
By honesty, and your own honour, sir,
I never saw her look more calm and gentle.

 Colum. I am too passionate ; you must forgive me.
I have found it out ; the duchess loves me dearly ;
She expressed a trouble in her when I took
My leave, and chid me with a sullen eye :
'Tis a device to hasten my return ;
Love has a thousand arts.   I'll answer it
Beyond her expectation, and put
Her soul to a noble test.—Your patience, gentlemen ;
The king's health will deserve a sacrifice
Of wine.   [*Retires to the table and writes.*

Ant. I am glad to see this change, and thank my wit

For my redemption.   [*Aside.*

  1st Col. Sir, the soldier's curse

On him loves not our master!

  2nd Col.   And they curse

Loud enough to be heard.

  2nd Capt. Their curse has the nature of gunpowder.

  Ant. They do not pray with half the noise.

  1st Col. Our general is not well mixed;

He has too great a portion of fire.

  2nd Col. His mistress cool him, (her complexion

Carries some phlegm,) when they two meet in bed ;—

  2nd Capt. A third may follow.

  1st Capt.   'Tis much pity

The young duke lived not, to take the virgin off.

  1st Col. 'Twas the king's act, to match two rabbit-

  2nd Col. A common trick of state;[1]   [*suckers.*

The little great man marries, travels then

Till both grow up, and dies when he should do

The feat ; these things are still unlucky

On the male side.

  Colum. This to the duchess' fair hand.

                      [*Gives* ANTONIO *a letter.*

  Ant. She will think

Time hath no wing, till I return.   [*Exit.*

  Colum. Gentlemen,

Now each man to his quarter, and encourage

The soldier. I shall take a pride to know

Your diligence, when I visit all your several

Commands.

  All. We shall expect.

  2nd Col.   And move

By your directions.

  Colum. You are all noble.   [*Exeunt.*

---

1 Shirley was thinking of his own government here; he had seen more than one example of the marriages which he mentions, and their unlucky termination "on the male side."—*Gifford.*

SCENE II.—*A Room in the* Duchess's *House.*

Enter Cardinal, Duchess, *and* PLACENTIA.

Car. I shall perform a visit daily, madam,
In th' absence of my nephew, and be happy
If you accept my care.

Duch. You have honoured me ;
And if your entertainment have not been
Worthy your grace's person, 'tis because
Nothing can reach it in my power ; but where
There is no want of zeal, other defect
Is only a fault to exercise your mercy.

Car. You are bounteous in all.   I take my leave,
My fair niece, shortly, when Columbo has
Purchased more honours to prefer his name,
And value to your noble thoughts ; meantime,
Be confident you have a friend, whose office
And favour with the king shall be effectual
To serve your grace.

Duch. Your own good deeds reward you,
Till mine rise equal to deserve their benefit.—
                                                    [*Exit* Cardinal.
Leave me awhile.—   [*Exit* PLACENTIA.
Do not I walk upon the teeth of serpents,
And, as I had a charm against their poison,
Play with their stings ?   The Cardinal is subtle,
Whom 'tis not wisdom to incense, till I
Hear to what destiny Columbo leaves me :
May be the greatness of his soul will scorn
To own what comes with murmur ;—if he can
Interpret me so happily.—Art come ?

Enter ANTONIO *with a letter.*

Ant. His excellence salutes your grace.

Duch. Thou hast
A melancholy brow.   How did he take my letter

Ant. As he would take a blow ; with so much sense
Of anger, his whole soul boiled in his face ;
And such prodigious flame in both his eyes,
As they'd been the only seat of fire, and at
Each look a salamander leaping forth,
Not able to endure the furnace.

Duch. Ha! thou dost
Describe him with some horror.

Ant. Soon as he
Had read again, and understood your meaning,
His rage had shot me with a pistol, had not
I used some soft and penitential language,
To charm the bullet.

Duch. Wait at some more distance.—
My soul doth bathe itself in a cold dew ;
Imagine I am opening of a tomb ;   [*Opens the letter.*
Thus I throw off the marble, to discover
What antic posture death presents in this
Pale monument to fright me.—Ha!   [*Reads.*
My heart, that called my blood and spirits to
Defend it from the invasion of my fears,
Must keep a guard about it still, lest this
Strange and too mighty joy crush it to nothing.—
Antonio.

Ant. Madam.

Duch. Bid my steward give thee
Two thousand ducats.   Art sure I am awake?

Ant. I shall be able to resolve you, madam,
When he has paid the money.

Duch. Columbo now is noble.   [*Exit.*

Ant. This is better
Than I expected ; if my lady be
Not mad, and live to justify her bounty.   [*Exit.*

SCENE III.—*An Apartment in the Palace.*

Enter King, ALVAREZ, HERNANDO, *and* Lords.

King. The war is left to him; but we must have
You reconciled, if that be all your difference.
His rage flows like a torrent, when he meets
With opposition; leave to wrestle with him,
And his hot blood retreats into a calm,
And then he chides his passion. You shall back
With letters from us.

    Her. Your commands are not
To be disputed.

    King. Alvarez.   [*Takes him aside.*

    1st Lord. Lose not
Yourself by cool submission; he will find
His error, and the want of such a soldier.

    2nd Lord. Have you seen the Cardinal?

    Her. Not yet.

    1st Lord. He wants no plot—

    Her. The king I must obey:
But let the purple gownman place his engines
I' the dark, that wound me.

    2nd Lord. Be assured
Of what we can to friend you; and the king
Cannot forget your service.

    Her. I am sorry
For that poor gentleman.

    Alv. I must confess, sir,
The duchess has been pleased to think me worthy
Her favours, and in that degree of honour,
That has obliged my life to make the best
Return of service, which is not, with bold
Affiance in her love, to interpose
Against her happiness, and your election.
I love so much her honour, I have quitted
All my desires; yet would not shrink to bleed

Out my warm stock of life, so the last drop
Might benefit her wishes.

    King. I shall find
A compensation for this act, Alvarez;
It hath much pleased us.

               Enter Duchess *with a letter.*

    Duch. Sir, you are the king,
And in that sacred title it were sin
To doubt a justice: all that does concern
My essence in this world, and a great part
Of the other's bliss, lives in your breath.

    King. What intends the duchess?

    Duch. That will instruct you, sir. [*Gives the letter.*]—
      Columbo has,
Upon some better choice, or discontent,
Set my poor soul at freedom.

    King. 'Tis his character.   [*Reads.*
"Madam, I easily discharge all my pretensions to your
love and person; I leave you to your own choice;
and in what you have obliged yourself to me, resume a
power to cancel, if you please. Columbo."
This is strange!

    Duch. Now do an act to make
Your chronicle beloved and read for ever.

    King. Express yourself.

    Duch. Since by divine infusion,—
For 'tis no art could force the general to
This change, second this justice, and bestow
The heart you would have given from me, by
Your strict commands to love Columbo, where
'Twas meant by Heaven; and let your breath return
Whom you divorced, Alvarez, mine.

    Lords. This is
But justice, sir.

    King. It was decreed above;
And since Columbo has released his interest,

Which we had wrought him, not without some force
Upon your will, I give you your own wishes :
Receive your own Alvarez.   When you please
To celebrate your nuptial, I invite
Myself your guest.

    Duch. Eternal blessings crown you !

    All. And every joy your marriage !

        [*As the* King *is going out, he meets the* Cardinal ;
           they converse together.

    Alv. I know not whether I shall wonder most,
Or joy to meet this happiness.

    Duch. Now the king
Hath planted us, methinks we grow already,
And twist our loving souls, above the wrath
Of thunder to divide us.

    Alv. Ha ! the Cardinal
Has met the king ! I do not like this conference ;
He looks with anger this way.   I expect
A tempest.

    Duch. Take no notice of his presence ;
Leave me to meet, and answer it.   If the king
Be firm in's royal word, I fear no lightning.
Expect me in the garden.

    Alv. I obey ;
But fear a shipwreck on the coast.   [*Exit.*

    Car. Madam.

    Duch. My lord.

    Car. The king speaks of a letter that has brought
A riddle in't.

    Duch. 'Tis easy to interpret.

    Car. From my nephew ?   May I deserve the favour?
           [*The* Duchess *gives him the letter.*

    Duch. He looks as though his eyes would fire the
      paper.
They are a pair of burning glasses, and
His envious blood doth give them flame.

    Car. What lethargy

Could thus unspirit him ?   I am all wonder.   [*Aside.*
Do not believe, madam,
But that Columbo's love is yet more sacred
To honour and yourself, than thus to forfeit
What I have heard him call the glorious wreath
To all his merits, given him by the king,
From whom he took you with more pride than ever
He came from victory : his kisses hang
Yet panting on your lips ; and he but now
Exchanged religious farewell to return,
But with more triumph, to be yours.

   Duch. My lord,
You do believe your nephew's hand was not
Surprised or strained to this ?

   Car. Strange arts and windings in the world ! most
      dark
And subtle progresses !   Who brought this letter ?

   Duch. I enquired not his name ; I thought it not
Considerable[1] to take such narrow knowledge.

   Car. Desert and honour urged it here, nor can
I blame you to be angry ; yet his person
Obliged you should have given a nobler pause,
Before you made your faith and change so violent,
From his known worth, into the arms of one,
However fashioned to your amorous wish,
Not equal to his cheapest fame, with all
The gloss of blood and merit.

   Duch. This comparison,
My good lord Cardinal, I cannot think
Flows from an even justice ; it betrays
You partial where your blood runs.

   Car. I fear, madam,
Your own takes too much license, and will soon
Fall to the censure of unruly tongues.
Because Alvarez has a softer cheek,
Can, like a woman, trim his wanton hair,

---

[1] *i.e.* Of sufficient importance.

Shir.   C C

Spend half a day with looking in the glass,
To find a posture to present himself,
And bring more effeminacy than man,
Or honour, to your bed, must he supplant him?
Take heed, the common murmur, when it catches
The scent of a lost fame—

Duch. My fame, lord Cardinal?
It stands upon an innocence as clear
As the devotions you pay to Heaven.
I shall not urge, my lord, your soft indulgence
At my next shrift.

Car. You are a fine court lady!

Duch. And you should be a reverend churchman.

Car. One,
That if you have not thrown off modesty,
Would counsel you to leave Alvarez.

Duch. 'Cause
You dare do worse than marriage, must not I
Be admitted what the church and law allows me?

Car. Insolent! Then you dare marry him?

Duch. Dare!
Let your contracted flame and malice, with
Columbo's rage, higher than that, meet us
When we approach the holy place, clasped hand
In hand, we'll break through all your force, and fix
Our sacred vows together there.

Car. I knew
When, with as chaste a brow, you promised fair
To another. You are no dissembling lady!

Duch. Would all your actions had no false lights
About them!

Car. Ha!

Duch. The people would not talk, and curse so loud.

Car. I'll have you chid into a blush for this.

Duch. Begin at home, great man, there's cause
        enough:
You turn the wrong end of the perspective

Upon your crimes, to drive them to a far
And lesser sight; but let your eyes look right,
What giants would your pride and surfeit seem!
How gross your avarice, eating up whole families!
How vast are your corruptions and abuse
Of the king's ear! at which you hang a pendant,
Not to adorn, but ulcerate, while the honest
Nobility, like pictures in the arras,
Serve only for court ornament.   If they speak,
'Tis when you set their tongues, which you wind up,
Like clocks, to strike at the just hour you please.
Leave, leave, my lord, these usurpations,
And be what you were meant, a man to cure,
Not let in, agues to religion:
Look on the church's wounds.

   Car. You dare presume,
In your rude spleen to me, to abuse the church?

   Duch. Alas, you give false aim, my lord; 'tis your
Ambition and scarlet sins, that rob
Her altar of the glory, and leave wounds
Upon her brow; which fetches grief and paleness
Into her cheeks, making her troubled bosom
Pant with her groans, and shroud her holy blushes
Within your reverend purples.

   Car. Will you now take breath?

   Duch. In hope, my lord, you will behold yourself
In a true glass, and see those unjust acts
That so deform you, and by timely cure
Prevent a shame, before the short-haired men [1]
Do crowd and call for justice; I take leave.   [*Exit.*

   Car. This woman has a spirit, that may rise

---

[1] I am not sure that I understand this: but it seems as if the
poet was again thinking of England, and meant to warn the prelates
not to push their pretensions too far, lest they should exasperate the
Puritans (short-haired men), and unite them in a body against them.
In 1641 (when this play was written), this hint might not perhaps
be very generous or charitable; but it might, unfortunately, be
offered with impunity.—*Gifford.*

To tame the devil's: there's no dealing with
Her angry tongue; 'tis action and revenge
Must calm her fury. Were Columbo here,
I could resolve; but letters shall be sent
To th' army, which may wake him into sense
Of his rash folly, or direct his spirit
Some way to snatch his honour from this flame:
All great men know the soul of life is fame. [*Exit.*

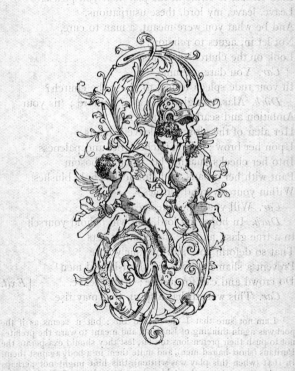

ACT THE THIRD.

SCENE I.—*An Apartment in the Palace.*

Enter VALERIA *and* CELINDA.

AL. I did not think, Celinda, when I
    praised
Alvarez to the duchess, that things thus
Would come about. What does your
    ladyship
Think of Columbo now? It staggers all
The court, he should forsake his mistress; I
Am lost with wonder yet.

    Cel. 'Tis very strange,
Without a spell; but there's a fate in love;—
I like him ne'er the worse.

Enter two Lords.

    1st Lord. Nothing but marriages and triumph now!
    Val. What new access of joy makes you, my lord,
So pleasant?
    1st Lord. There's a packet come to court
Makes the king merry; we are all concerned in't.
Columbo hath given the enemy a great
And glorious defeat, and is already
Preparing to march home.
    Cel. He thrived the better for my prayers.
    2nd Lord. You have been
His great admirer, madam.
    1st Lord. The king longs
To see him.

Val. This news exalts the Cardinal.

Enter Cardinal.

1st Lord. He's here !
He appears with discontent ; the marriage
With Count d'Alvarez hath a bitter taste,
And's not worn off his palate : but let us leave him.

Cel. and Val. We'll to the duchess.   [*Exeunt.*

Car. He has not won so much upon the Arragon
As he has lost at home ; and his neglect
Of what my studies had contrived, to add
More lustre to our family by the access
Of the great duchess' fortune, cools his triumph,
And makes me wild.

Enter HERNANDO.

Her. My good lord Cardinal !

Car. You made complaint to the king about your
      general ?

Her. Not a complaint, my lord ; I did but satisfy
Some questions o' the king's.

Car. You see he thrives
Without your personal valour or advice
Most grave and learned in the wars.

Her. My lord,
I envy not his fortune.

Car. 'Tis above
Your malice, and your noise not worth his anger ;
'Tis barking 'gainst the moon.

Her. More temper would
Become that habit.

Car. The military thing would show some spleen.
I'll blow an army of such wasps about
The world.—Go look your sting you left i' the camp, sir.

Enter King *and* Lords.

Her. The king !—This may be one day counted for.
                                          [*Exit.*

King. All things conspire, my lord, to make you
    fortunate.
Your nephew's glory—
    Car. 'Twas your cause and justice
Made him victorious ; had he been so valiant
At home he had had another conquest to
Invite, and bid her welcome to new wars.
    King. You must be reconciled to providence.
My lord,
I heard you had a controversy with
The duchess ; I will have you friends.
    Car. I am not angry.
    King. For my sake, then,
You shall be pleased, and with me grace the marriage,—
A churchman must show charity ; and shine
With first example : she's a woman.
    Car. You shall prescribe in all things, sir. You cannot
Accuse my love, if I still wish my nephew
Had been so happy, to be constant to
Your own, and my election ; yet my brain
Cannot reach how this comes about ; I know
My nephew loved her with a near affection.

        Re-enter HERNANDO.

    King. He'll give you fair account at his return.—
Colonel, your letters may be spared ; the general
Has finished, and is coming home.   [*Exit.*
    Her. I am glad on't, sir.—My good lord Cardinal,
'Tis not impossible but some man provoked,
May have a precious mind to cut your throat.
    Car. You shall command me, noble Colonel ;
I know you will not fail to be at the wedding.
    Her. 'Tis not Columbo that is married, sir.
    Car. Go teach the postures of the pike and musket ;
Then drill your myrmidons into a ditch,
Where starve, and stink in pickle.—You shall find
Me reasonable ; you see the king expects me.   [*Exit.*

Her. So does the devil.—
Some desperate hand may help you on your journey.

[*Exit.*

SCENE II.—*A Room in the* Duchess's *House.*

Enter ANTONIO *and four* Servants, *with masques, dresses, &c.*

Ant. Here, this; ay, this will fit your part: you shall wear the slashes, because you are a soldier. Here's for the blue mute.[1]

1st Serv. This doublet will never fit me; pox on't! are these breeches good enough for a prince too? Pedro plays but a lord, and he has two laces more in a seam.

Ant. You must consider Pedro is a foolish lord; he may wear what lace he please.

2nd Serv. Does my beard fit my clothes well, gentle-men?

Ant. Pox o' your beard!

3rd Serv. That will fright away the hair.

1st Serv. This fellow plays but a mute, and he is so troublesome, and talks.

3rd Serv. Master Secretary might have let Jaques play the soldier; he has a black patch already.

2nd Serv. By your favour, Master Secretary, I was asked who writ this play for us?

Ant. For us? Why, art thou any more than a blue mute?

2nd Serv. And, by my troth, I said, I thought it was all your own.

Ant. Away, you coxcomb!

4th Serv. Dost think he has no more wit than to write a comedy? My lady's chaplain made the play, though

---

[1] *i.e.* For the mute who was to take the servant's part, blue being the general colour of a servant's livery.

he is content, for the honour and trouble of the business,
to be seen in't.

Enter 5th *Servant.*

5th *Serv.* Did anybody see my head, gentlemen? 'twas
here but now.—I shall have never a head to play my
part in.

Ant. Is thy head gone? 'twas well thy part was not
in't. Look, look about; has not Jaques it?

4th *Serv.* His head? 'twill not come on upon my
shoulders. 　　　　　　　　　　　　[*Exit* 5th Servant.

Ant. Make haste, gentlemen, I'll see whether the king
has supped. Look every man to his wardrobe and his
part. 　　　　　　　　　　　　　　　　　[*Exit.*

2nd *Serv.* Is he gone? In my mind, a masque had
been fitter for a marriage.

4th *Serv.* Why, mute? There was no time for't, and
the scenes are troublesome.

2nd *Serv.* Half a score deal tacked together in the
clouds, what's that? a throne, to come down and dance;
all the properties have been paid forty times over, and
are in the court stock:—but the secretary must have a
play, to show his wit.

4th *Serv.* Did not I tell thee 'twas the chaplain's?
Hold your tongue, mute.

1st *Serv.* Under the rose, and would this cloth of silver
doublet might never come off again, if there be any more
plot than you see in the back of my hand.

2nd *Serv.* You talk of a plot! I'll not give this for the
best poet's plot in the world, an if it be not well carried.

4th *Serv.* Well said, mute.

3rd *Serv.* Ha, ha! Pedro, since he put on his doublet,
has repeated but three lines, and he has broke five
buttons.

2nd *Serv.* I know not; but by this false beard, and
here's hair enough to hang a reasonable honest man, I
do not remember, to say, a strong line indeed in the

whole comedy, but when the chambermaid kisses the captain.

3rd Serv. Excellent, mute!

Re-enter 5*th* Servant.

5th Serv. They have almost supped, and I cannot find my head yet.

4th Serv. Play in thine own.

5th Serv. Thank you for that! so I may have it made a property. If I have not a head found me, let Master Secretary play my part himself without it.

Re-enter ANTONIO.

Ant. Are you all ready, my masters? The king is coming through the gallery. Are the women dressed?

1st Serv. Rogero wants a head.

Ant. Here, with a pox to you! take mine. You a player! you a puppy-dog. Is the music ready?

Enter Gentleman-Usher.

Gent. Gentlemen, it is my lady's pleasure that you expect till she call for you. There are a company of cavaliers, in gallant equipage, newly alighted, have offered to present their Revels in honour of this Hymen; and 'tis her grace's command, that you be silent till their entertainment be over.

1st Serv. Gentlemen?

2nd Serv. Affronted?

5th Serv. Master Secretary, there's your head again; a man's a man. Have I broken my sleep, to study fifteen lines for an ambassador, and after that a constable, and is it come to this?

Ant. Patience, gentlemen, be not so hot; 'tis but deferred, and the play may do well enough cold.

4th Serv. If it be not presented, the chaplain will have the greatest loss; he loses his wits.   [*Hautbois play.*

Ant. This music speaks the king upon entrance. Retire, retire, and grumble not.   [*Exeunt all but* ANTONIO.

Enter King, Cardinal, ALVAREZ, Duchess, CELINDA,
VALERIA, PLACENTIA, Lords, *and* HERNANDO, *and
take their seats: then enter* COLUMBO *and five more, in
rich habits, vizarded; between every two a* Torch-
bearer: *they dance, and afterwards beckon to* ALVAREZ,
as if desirous to speak with him.

Alv. With me! [*They embrace and whisper, and exeunt.*
King. Do you know the masquers, madam?
Duch. Not I, sir.
Car. There's one,—but that my nephew is abroad,
And has more soul than thus to jig upon
Their hymeneal night, I should suspect
'Twere he. [*Aside.*
Duch. Where's my Lord Alvarez?
King. Call in the bridegroom.
[*Recorders* [1] *sound within.*

Re-enter COLUMBO, *followed by the five* Masquers, *bringing
in the dead body of* ALVAREZ *in one of their habits, and
having laid it down, exeunt, all but* COLUMBO.

Duch. What mystery is this?
Car. We want the bridegroom still.
King. Where is Alvarez?
[COLUMBO *points to the body; they take off the mask
and habit, and find* ALVAREZ *bleeding*
Duch. Oh, 'tis my lord! he's murdered!
King. Who durst commit this horrid act?
Colum. I, sir. [*Throws off his disguise.*
King. Columbo? Ha!
Colum. Yes; Columbo, that dares stay
To justify that act.
Her. Most barbarous!
Duch. Oh, my dearest lord!
King. Our guard!

[1] Flageolets.

Enter Guard.

Seize on them all :
This sight doth shake all that is man within me.
Poor Alvarez, is this thy wedding day ?

Duch. If you do think there is a Heaven, or pains
To punish such black crimes i' the other world,
Let me have swift, and such exemplar justice,
As shall become this great assassinate ;
You will take off our faith else : and, if here
Such innocence must bleed, and you look on,
Poor men, that call you gods on earth, will doubt
To obey your laws, nay, practise to be devils,
As fearing, if such monstrous sins go on,
The saints will not be safe in Heaven.

King. You shall,
You shall have justice.

Car. Now to come off were brave.   [*Aside.*

Enter Servant.

Serv. The masquers, sir, are fled ; their horse, prepared
At gate, expected to receive them, where
They quickly mounted : coming so like friends,
None could suspect their haste, which is secured
By advantage of the night.

Colum. I answer for them all ; 'tis stake enough
For many lives : but if that poniard
Had voice, it would convince they were but all
Spectators of my act.   And now, if you
Will give your judgments leave, though at the first
Face of this object your cool bloods were frighted,
I can excuse this deed, and call it justice ;
An act, your honours, and your office, sir,
Is bound to build a law upon, for others
To imitate.   I have but took his life,
And punished her with mercy, who had both
Conspired to kill the soul of all my fame.
Read there ; and read an injury as deep

In my dishonour, as the devil knew
A woman had capacity or malice
To execute : read there, how you were cozened, sir,

    [*Gives the* Duchess's *letter to the* King.

Your power affronted, and my faith ; her smiles,
A juggling witchcraft to betray, and make
My love her horse to stalk withal, and catch
Her curled minion.

 Car. Is it possible
The duchess could dissemble so, and forfeit
Her modesty with you, and to us all ?
Yet I must pity her.   My nephew has
Been too severe ; though this affront would call
A dying man from prayers, and turn him tiger ;
There being nothing dearer than our fame,
Which, if a common man, whose blood has no
Ingredient of honour, labour to
Preserve, a soldier (by his nearest tie
To glory) is, above all others, bound
To vindicate :—and yet it might have been
Less bloody.

 Her. Charitable devil !

 King. [*Reads.*] "I pray, my lord, release under your
hand, what you dare challenge in my love or person, as a
just forfeit to myself; this act will speak you honourable
to my thoughts ; and when you have conquered thus
yourself, you may proceed to many victories, and after,
with safety of your fame, visit again

        the lost Rosaura."

To this your answer was a free resign ?

 Colum. Flattered with great opinion of her faith,
And my desert of her (with thought that she,
Who seemed to weep and chide my easy will
To part with her, could not be guilty of
A treason, or apostasy so soon,
But rather meant this a device to make
Me expedite the affairs of war,) I sent

That paper, which her wickedness, not justice,
Applied (what I meant trial,) her divorce.
I loved her so, I dare call heaven to witness,
I knew not whether I loved most ; while she,
With him, whose crimson penitence I provoked,[1]
Conspired my everlasting infamy :
Examine but the circumstance.

   Car. 'Tis clear ;
This match was made at home, before she sent
That cunning writ, in hope to take him off,
As knowing his impatient soul would scorn
To own a blessing came on crutches to him.
It was not well to raise his expectation,
(Had you, sir, no affront ?) to ruin him
With so much scandal and contempt.

   King. We have
Too plentiful a circumstance, to accuse
You, madam, as the cause of your own sorrows ;
But not without an accessary more
Than young Alvarez.

   Car. Any other instrument ?

   King. Yes ; I am guilty, with herself, and Don
Columbo, though our acts looked several ways,
That thought a lover might so soon be ransomed ;
And did exceed the office of a king,
To exercise dominion over hearts,
That owe to the prerogative of Heaven
Their choice, or separation : you must, therefore,
When you do kneel for justice and revenge,
Madam, consider me a lateral agent
In poor Alvarez' tragedy.

   1st Lord. It was your love to Don Columbo, sir.

   Her. So, so ! the king is charmed. Do you observe,
How, to acquit Columbo, he would draw
Himself into the plot.   Heaven, is this justice ?

   Car. Your judgment is divine in this.

---

[1] *i.e.* Compelled.

King. And yet
Columbo cannot be secure, and we
Just in his pardon, that durst make so great
And insolent a breach of law and duty.

2nd Lord. Ha! will he turn again?

King. And should we leave
This guilt of blood to Heaven, which cries, and strikes
With loud appeals the palace of eternity;
Yet here is more to charge Columbo than
Alvarez' blood, and bids me punish it,
Or be no king.

Her. 'Tis come about, my lords.

King. And if I should forgive
His timeless death, I cannot the offence,
That with such boldness struck at me. Has my
Indulgence to your merits, which are great,
Made me so cheap, your rage could meet no time
Nor place for your revenge, but where my eyes
Must be affrighted, and affronted with
The bloody execution? This contempt
Of majesty transcends my power to pardon,
And you shall feel my anger, sir.

Her. Thou shalt
Have one short prayer more for that.

Colum. Have I,
I' the progress of my life,
No actions to plead me up deserving
Against this ceremony? [1]

Car. Contain yourself.

Colum. I must be dumb then. Where is honour,
And gratitude of kings, when they forget
Whose hand secured their greatness? Take my head off;
Examine then which of your silken lords,
As I have done, will throw himself on dangers;
Like to a floating island move in blood;
And where your great defence calls him to stand

---

[1] This and the preceding line are hopelessly corrupt.

A bulwark, upon his bold breast to take
In death, that you may live :—but soldiers are
Your valiant fools, whom, when your own securities
Are bleeding, you can cherish ; but when once
Your state and nerves are knit, not thinking when
To use their surgery again, you cast
Them off, and let them hang in dusty armories,
Or make it death to ask for pay.

    King. No more ;
We thought to have put your victory and merits
In balance with Alvarez' death, which, while
Our mercy was to judge, had been your safety ;
But the affront to us, made greater by
This boldness to upbraid our royal bounty,
Shall tame, or make you nothing.

    Lord. Excellent !

    Her. The Cardinal is not pleased.

    Car. Humble yourself
To the king.

    Colum. And beg my life ? Let cowards do't,
That dare not die ; I'll rather have no head,
Than owe it to his charity.

    King. To the castle with him !—

                [COLUMBO *is led off by the* Guard.
Madam, I leave you to your grief, and what
The king can recompense to your tears, or honour
Of your dead lord, expect.

    Duch. This shows like justice.   [*Exeunt severally.*

ACT THE FOURTH.

SCENE I.—*An Apartment in the Palace.*

Enter two Lords *and* HERNANDO.

IRST LORD. This is the age of wonders.

    2nd Lord. Wonderous mischiefs!

    Her. Among those guards, which some
        call tutelar angels,

    Whose office is to govern provinces,

    Is there not one will undertake Navarre?

    Hath Heaven forsook us quite?

  1st Lord. Columbo at large!

  2nd Lord. And graced now more than ever.

  1st Lord. He was not pardoned;

That word was prejudicial to his fame.

  Her. But, as the murder done had been a dream,

Vanished to memory, he's courted as

Preserver of his country. With what chains

Of magic, does this Cardinal hold the king?

  2nd Lord. What will you say, my lord, if they enchant

The duchess now, and by some impudent art,

Advance a marriage to Columbo yet?

  Her. Say!

I'll say no woman can be saved; nor is

It fit, indeed, any should pretend to Heaven,

After one such impiety in their sex:

And yet my faith has been so staggered, since

The king restored Columbo, I'll be now

Of no religion.

  1st Lord. 'Tis not possible

She can forgive the murder; I observed
Her tears.

 Her. Why, so did I, my lord;
And if they be not honest, 'tis to be
Half damned, to look upon a woman weeping.
When do you think the Cardinal said his prayers?

 2nd Lord. I know not.

 Her. Heaven forgive my want of charity!
But, if I were to kill him, he should have
No time to pray; his life could be no sacrifice,
Unless his soul went too.

 1st Lord. That were too much.

 Her. When you mean to dispatch him, you may give
Time for confession: they have injured me
After another rate.

 2nd Lord. You are too passionate, cousin.

COLUMBO, Colonels, ALPHONSO, *and* Courtiers, *pass over
the stage.*

 Her. How the gay men do flutter, to congratulate
His gaol delivery! There's one honest man:
What pity 'tis, a gallant fellow should
Depend on knaves for his preferment!

 1st Lord. Except this cruelty upon Alvarez,
Columbo has no mighty stain upon him;
But for his uncle—

 Her. If I had a son
Of twelve years old that would not fight with him,
And stake his soul against his cardinal's cap,
I would disinherit him. Time has took a lease
But for three lives, I hope; a fourth may see
Honesty walk without a crutch.

 2nd Lord. This is
But air and wildness.

 Her. I will see the duchess.

 1st Lord. You may do well to comfort her; we must
Attend the king.

 Her. Your pleasures.
           [*Exit.*

Enter King *and* Cardinal.

1st Lord. A man of a brave soul.

2nd Lord. The less his safety.—

The king and Cardinal in consult!

King. Commend us to the duchess, and employ
What language you think fit and powerful,
To reconcile her to some peace.—My lords.

Car. Sir, I possess all for your sacred uses. [*Exeunt.*

SCENE II.—*A Room in the* Duchess's *House.*

Enter ANTONIO *and* CELINDA.

Ant. Madam, you are the welcomest lady living.

Cel. To whom, Master Secretary?

Ant. If you have mercy
To pardon so much boldness, I durst say,
To me—I am a gentleman.

Cel. And handsome.

Ant. But my lady has
Much wanted you.

Cel. Why, Master Secretary?

Ant. You are the prettiest,—

Cel. So!

Ant. The wittiest,—

Cel. So!

Ant. The merriest lady i' the court.

Cel. And I was wished, to make the duchess pleasant?

Ant. She never had so deep a cause of sorrow ;
Her chamber's but a coffin of a larger
Volume, wherein she walks so like a ghost,
'Twould make you pale to see her.

Cel. Tell her grace
I attend here.

Ant. I shall most willingly.—
A spirited lady! would I had her in my closet!

She is excellent company among the lords.
Sure she has an admirable treble.—Madam.   [*Exit.*

Cel. I do suspect this fellow would be nibbling,
Like some, whose narrow fortunes will not rise
To wear things when the invention's rare and new:
But treading on the heel of pride, they hunt
The fashion when 'tis crippled, like fell tyrants.
I hope I am not old yet; I had the honour
To be saluted by our Cardinal's nephew
This morning: there's a man!

Re-enter ANTONIO.

Ant. I have prevailed.
Sweet madam, use what eloquence you can
Upon her; and if ever I be useful
To your ladyship's service, your least breath commands
          me.   [*Exit.*

Enter Duchess.

Duch. Madam, I come to ask you but one question:
If you were in my state, my state of grief,
I mean, an exile from all happiness
Of this world, and almost of Heaven, (for my
Affliction is finding out despair,)
What would you think of Don Columbo?

Cel. Madam?

Duch. Whose bloody hand wrought all this misery.
Would you not weep, as I do, and wish rather
An everlasting spring of tears to drown
Your sight, than let your eyes be cursed to see
The murderer again, and glorious?
So careless of his sin, that he is made
Fit for new parricide, even while his soul
Is purpled o'er, and reeks with innocent blood?
But do not, do not answer me; I know
You have so great a spirit, (which I want,
The horror of his fact surprising all
My faculties), you would not let him live:

But I, poor I, must suffer more.   There's not
One little star in Heaven will look on me,
Unless to choose me out the mark, on whom
It may shoot down some angry influence.

Enter PLACENTIA.

Pla. Madam, here's Don Columbo says he must
Speak with your grace.

Duch. But he must not, I charge you.

[*Exit* PLACENTIA.

None else wait ?—Is this well done,
To triumph in his tyranny ?—Speak, madam,
Speak but your conscience.

Enter COLUMBO *and* ANTONIO.

Ant. Sir, you must not see her.

Colum. Not see her ? Were she cabled up above
The search of bullet or of fire, were she
Within her grave, and that the toughest mine
That ever nature teemed and groaned withal,
I would force some way to see her.—Do not fear
I come to court you, madam ; you are not worth
The humblest of my kinder thoughts. I come
To show the man you have provoked, and lost,
And tell you what remains of my revenge.—
Live, but never presume again to marry ;
I'll kill the next at the altar, and quench all
The smiling tapers with his blood : if after,
You dare provoke the priest and Heaven so much,
To take another, in thy bed I'll cut him from
Thy warm embrace, and throw his heart to ravens.

Cel. This will appear an unexampled cruelty.

Colum. Your pardon, madam ; rage, and my revenge,
Not perfect, took away my eyes. You are
A noble lady, this not worth your eye-beam ;
One of so slight a making, and so thin,
An autumn leaf is of too great a value
To play, which shall be soonest lost i' the air.

Be pleased to own me by some name, in your
Assurance, I despise to be received
There; let her witness that I call you mistress;
Honour me to make these pearls your carkanet.

> *[Gives her a necklace.*

 Cel. My lord, you are too humble in your thoughts.
 Colum. There's no vexation too great to punish her.

> *[Aside, and exit.*

 Ant. Now, madam.
 Cel. Away, you saucy fellow!—Madam, I
Must be excused, if I do think more honourably
Than you have cause, of this great lord.
 Duch. Why, is not
All womankind concerned to hate what's impious?
 Cel. For my part—
 Duch. Antonio, is this a woman?
 Ant. I know not whether she be man or woman;
I should be nimble to find out the experiment.
She looked with less state when Columbo came.
 Duch. Let me entreat your absence. I am cozened
  in her.—   *[Aside.*
I took you for a modest, honest lady.
 Cel. Madam, I scorn any accuser; and
Deducting the great title of a duchess,
I shall not need one grain of your dear honour
To make me full weight: if your grace be jealous,
I can remove.   *[Exit.*
 Ant. She is gone.
 Duch. Prithee remove
My fears of her return [*Exit* ANT.]—She is not worth
Considering; my anger's mounted higher.
He need not put in caution for my next
Marriage.—Alvarez, I must come to thee,
Thy virgin wife, and widow; but not till
I have paid those tragic duties to thy hearse
Become my piety and love. But how?
Who shall instruct a way?

Enter PLACENTIA,

Pla. Madam, Don
Hernando much desires to speak with you.

Duch. Will not thy own discretion think I am
Unfit for visit?

Pla. Please your grace, he brings
Something, he says, imports your ear, and love
Of the dead lord, Alvarez.

Duch. Then admit him.   [*Exit* PLACENTIA.

Re-enter PLACENTIA *with* HERNANDO.

Her. I would speak, madam, to yourself.

Duch. Your absence.   [*Exit* PLACENTIA.

Her. I know not how your grace will censure so
Much boldness, when you know the affairs I come for.

Duch. My servant has prepared me to receive it,
If it concern my dead lord,

Her. Can you name
So much of your Alvarez in a breath,
Without one word of your revenge?   O, madam,
I come to chide you, and repent my great
Opinion of your virtue, that can walk,
And spend so many hours in naked solitude;
As if you thought that no arrears were due
To his death, when you had paid his funeral charges,
Made your eyes red, and wet a handkerchief—
I come to tell you, that I saw him bleed;
I, that can challenge nothing in his name
And honour, saw his murdered body warm,
And panting with the labour of his spirits,
Till my amazed soul shrunk and hid itself:
While barbarous Columbo grinning stood,
And mocked the weeping wounds.   It is too much,
That you should keep your heart alive so long
After this spectacle, and not revenge it.

Duch. You do not know the business of my heart,

That censure me so rashly; yet I thank you:
And, if you be Alvarez' friend, dare tell
Your confidence, that I despise my life,
But know not how to use it in a service,
To speak me his revenger: this will need
No other proof, than that you, who may
Be sent with cunning to betray me, I
Have made this bold confession. I so much
Desire to sacrifice to that hovering ghost
Columbo's life, that I am not ambitious
To keep my own two minutes after it.

 Her. If you will call me coward, which is equal
To think I am a traitor, I forgive it
For this brave resolution, which time
And all the destinies must aid. I beg
That I may kiss your hand for this; and may
The soul of angry honour guide it—

 Duch. Whither?

 Her. To Don Columbo's heart.

 Duch. It is too weak, I fear, alone.

 Her. Alone? are you in earnest? Why, will it
not
Be a dishonour to your justice, madam,
Another arm should interpose? But that
It were a saucy act to mingle with you,
I durst, nay, I am bound in the revenge
Of him that's dead, (since the whole world has interest
In every good man's loss,) to offer it:
Dare you command me, madam?

 Duch. Not command;
But I should more than honour such a truth
In man, that durst, against so mighty odds,
Appear Alvarez' friend, and mine. The Cardinal—

 Her. Is for the second course; Columbo must
Be first cut up; his ghost must lead the dance;
Let him die first.

 Duch. But how?

Her. How! with a sword; and, if I undertake it,
I will not lose so much of my own honour,
To kill him basely.

Duch. How shall I reward
This infinite service? 'Tis not modesty
While now my husband groans beneath his tomb,
And calls me to his marble bed, to promise,
What this great act might well deserve, myself,
If you survive the victor; but if thus
Alvarez' ashes be appeased, it must
Deserve an honourable memory;
And though Columbo (as he had all power,
And grasped the fates) has vowed to kill the man
That shall succeed Alvarez—

Her. Tyranny!

Duch. Yet, if ever
I entertain a thought of love hereafter,
Hernando from the world shall challenge it;
Till when, my prayers and fortune shall wait on you.

Her. This is too mighty recompense.

Duch. 'Tis all just.

Her. If I outlive Columbo, I must not
Expect security at home.

Duch. Thou canst
Not fly where all my fortunes, and my love
Shall not attend to guard thee.

Her. If I die—

Duch. Thy memory
Shall have a shrine, the next within my heart,
To my Alvarez.

Her. Once again your hand.
Your cause is so religious, you need not
Strengthen it with your prayers; trust it to me.

Re-enter PLACENTIA, *with the* Cardinal.

Pla. Madam, the Cardinal

Duch. Will you appear?

Her. An he had all the horror of the devil
In's face, I would not baulk him.

> [*He stares upon the* Cardinal *in his exit.*

Car. What makes Hernando here? I do not like
They should consult; I'll take no note. [*Aside.*]—The king
Fairly salutes your grace; by whose command
I am to tell you, though his will and actions
Illimited, stoop not to satisfy
The vulgar inquisition, he is
Yet willing to retain a just opinion
With those that are placed near him; and although
You look with nature's eye upon yourself,
Which needs no perspective to reach, nor art
Of any optic to make greater, what
Your narrow sense applies an injury,
(Ourselves still nearest to ourselves,) yet there's
Another eye that looks abroad, and walks
In search of reason, and the weight of things,
With which, if you look on him, you will find
His pardon to Columbo cannot be
So much against his justice, as your erring
Faith would persuade your anger.

Duch. Good my lord,
Your phrase has too much landscape, and I cannot
Distinguish, at this distance you present,
The figure perfect; but indeed my eyes
May pray your lordship find excuse, for tears
Have almost made them blind.

Car. Fair peace restore them!
To bring the object nearer, the king says,
He could not be severe to Don Columbo
Without injustice to his other merits,
Which call more loud for their reward and honour,
Than you for your revenge; the kingdom made
Happy by those; you only, by the last,
Unfortunate:—nor was it rational,
I speak the king's own language, he should die

For taking one man's breath, without whose valour
None now had been alive without dishonour.

   Duch. In my poor understanding, 'tis the crown
Of virtue to proceed in its own track,
Not deviate from honour. If you acquit
A man of murder, 'cause he has done brave
Things in the war, you will bring down his valour
To a crime, nay, to a bawd, if it secure
A rape, and but teach those that deserve well,
To sin with greater license: but dispute
Is now too late, my lord; 'tis done; and you,
By the good king, in tender of my sorrows,
Sent to persuade me 'tis unreasonable
That justice should repair me.

   Car. You mistake;
For if Columbo's death could make Alvarez
Alive, the king had given him up to law,
Your bleeding sacrifice; but when his life
Was but another treasure thrown away,
To obey a clamorous statute, it was wisdom
To himself, and common safety, to take off
This killing edge of law, and keep Columbo
To recompense the crime by noble acts,
And sorrow, that in time might draw your pity.

   Duch. This is a greater tyranny than that
Columbo exercised; he killed my lord;
And you have not the charity to let
Me think it worth a punishment.

   Car. To that,
In my own name, I answer: I condemn,
And urge the bloody guilt against my nephew;
'Tis violent and cruel, a black deed;
A deed, whose memory doth make me shudder;
An act, that did betray a tyrannous nature,
Which he took up in war, the school of vengeance;
And though the king's compassion spare him here,
Unless his heart
Weep itself out in penitent tears.—

Duch. This sounds
As you were now a good man.

Car. Does your grace
Think I have conscience to allow the murder!
Although, when it was done, I did obey
The stream of nature, as he was my kinsman,
To plead he might not pay his forfeit life,
Could I do less for one so near my blood?
Consider, madam, and be charitable;
Let not this wild injustice make me lose
The character I bear, and reverend habit.
To make you full acquainted with my innocence,
I challenge here my soul, and Heaven to witness,
If I had any thought, or knowledge with
My nephew's plot, or person, when he came,
Under the smooth pretence of friend, to violate
Your hospitable laws, and do that act,
Whose frequent mention draws this tear, a whirlwind
Snatch me to endless flames!

Duch. I must believe,
And ask your grace's pardon. I confess
I have not loved you since Alvarez' death,
Though we were reconciled.

Car. I do not blame
Your jealousy, nor any zeal you had
To prosecute revenge against me, madam,
As I then stood suspected, nor can yet
Implore your mercy to Columbo. All
I have to say is, to retain my first
Opinion and credit with your grace;
Which you may think I urge not out of fear,
Or ends upon you, (since, I thank the king,
I stand firm on the base of royal favour,)
But for your own sake, and to show I have
Compassion of your sufferings.

Duch. You have cleared
A doubt, my lord; and by this fair remonstrance,

Given my sorrow so much truce, to think
That we may meet again, and yet be friends.—
But be not angry, if I still remember
By whom Alvarez died, and weep, and wake
Another justice with my prayers.

   Car. All thoughts
That may advance a better peace dwell with you ! [*Exit.*

   Duch. How would this cozening statesman bribe my
        faith
With flatteries, to think him innocent !
No ; if his nephew die, this Cardinal must not
Be long-lived.   All the prayers of a wronged widow
Make firm Hernando's sword ! and my own hand
Shall have some glory in the next revenge.
I will pretend my brain with grief distracted,
It may gain easy credit ; and beside
The taking off examination
For great Columbo's death, it makes what act
I do in that believed want of my reason,
Appear no crime, but my defence.—Look down,
Soul of my lord, from thy eternal shade,
And unto all thy blest companions boast,
Thy duchess busy to revenge thy ghost !   [*Exit.*

SCENE III.—*A retired spot without the City.*

Enter on one side COLUMBO *and* ALPHONSO ; *on the other,*
    HERNANDO *and a* Colonel.

   Colum. Hernando, now I love thee, and do half
Repent the affront my passion threw upon thee.

   Her. You will not be too prodigal o' your penitence.

   Colum. This makes good thy nobility of birth ;
Thou may'st be worth my anger and my sword,
If thou dost execute as daringly

As thou provok'st a quarrel.   I did think
Thy soul a starveling, or asleep.

   Her. You'll find it
Active enough to keep your spirit waking ;
Which to exasperate, for yet I think
It is not high enough to meet my rage—
Do you smile ?

   Colum. This noise is worth it.—Gentlemen,
I'm sorry this great soldier has engaged
Your travail ; all his business is to talk.

   Her. A little of your lordship's patience,
You shall have other sport, and swords that will
Be as nimble 'bout your heart as you can wish.
Tis pity more than our two single lives
Should be at stake.

   Colum. Make that no scruple, sir.

   Her. To him then that survives, if fate allow
That difference, I speak, that he may tell
The world, I came not hither on slight anger,
But to revenge my honour, stained and trampled on
By this proud man ; when general, he commanded
My absence from the field.

   Colum. I do remember,
And I will give your soul now a discharge.

   Her. I come
To meet it, if your courage be so fortunate.
But there is more than my own injury
You must account for, sir, if my sword prosper ;
Whose point and every edge is made more keen
With young Alvarez' blood, in which I had
A noble interest.   Does not that sin benumb
Thy arteries, and turn the guilty flowings
To trembling jelly in thy veins ?   Canst hear
Me name that murder, and thy spirits not
Struck into air, as thou wert shot by some
Engine from Heaven ?

   Colum. You are the duchess' champion

Thou hast given me a quarrel now.   I grieve
It is determined all must fight, and I
Shall lose much honour in his fall.

   Her. That duchess,
(Whom but to mention with thy breath is sacrilege,
An orphan of thy making, and condemned
By thee to eternal solitude, I come
To vindicate ; and while I am killing thee,
By virtue of her prayers sent up for justice,
At the same time, in Heaven I am pardoned for't.

   Colum. I cannot hear the bravo.

   Her. Two words more,
And take your chance.   Before you all I must
Pronounce that noble lady without knowledge
Or thought of what I undertake for her.
Poor soul ! she's now at her devotions,
Busy with Heaven, and wearing out the earth
With her stiff knees, and bribing her good angel
With treasures of her eyes, to tell her lord
How much she longs to see him.   My attempt
Needs no commission from her : were I
A stranger in Navarre, the inborn right
Of every gentleman to Alvarez' loss
Is reason to engage their swords and lives
Against the common enemy of virtue.

   Colum. Now have you finished ? I have an instru
      ment
Shall cure this noise, and fly up to thy tongue,
To murder all thy words.

   Her. One little knot
Of phlegm, that clogs my stomach, and I have done :—
You have an uncle, called a Cardinal,
Would he were lurking now about thy heart,
That the same wounds might reach you both, and send
Your reeling souls together ! Now have at you.

   Alph. We must not, sir, be idle.

              [*They fight ;* ALPHONSO *is slain.*

Her. What think you now of praying?

Colum. Time enough. [*He kills* HERNANDO's *second.*
Commend me to my friend; the scales are even:
I would be merciful, and give you time
Now to consider of the other world;
You'll find your soul benighted presently.

Her. I'll find my way i' the dark.

[*They fight, and close;* COLUMBO *gets both the
swords, and* HERNANDO *takes up the second's
weapon.*

Colum. A stumble's dangerous.
Now ask thy life.—Ha!

Her. I despise to wear it,
A gift from any but the first bestower.

Colum. I scorn a base advantage.—[COLUMBO *throws
away one of the swords; they fight;* HERNANDO
wounds COLUMBO.]—Ha!

Her. I am now
Out of your debt.

Colum. Thou hast done't, and I forgive thee.
Give me thy hand; when shall we meet again?

Her. Never, I hope.

Colum. I feel life ebb apace: yet I'll look upwards,
And show my face to Heaven. [*Dies.*

Her. The matter's done;
I must not stay to bury him. [*Exit.*

ACT THE FIFTH.

SCENE I.—*A Garden.*

Enter two Lords.

IRST LORD. Columbo's death doth
much afflict the king.

    2nd Lord. I thought the Cardinal
would have lost his wits.

At first, for's nephew; it drowns all the
Of the others that were slain.   [talk

  1st Lord. We are friends.
I do suspect Hernando had some interest,
And knew how their wounds came.

  2nd Lord. His flight confirms it,
For whom the Cardinal has spread his nets.

  1st Lord. He is not so weak to trust himself at home
To his enemy's gripe.

  2nd Lord. All strikes not me so much,
As that the duchess, most oppressèd lady,
Should be distracted, and before Columbo
Was slain.

  1st Lord. But that the Cardinal should be made
Her guardian, is to me above that wonder.

  2nd Lord. So it pleased the king; and she, with that
Of reason left her, is so kind and smooth   [small stock
Upon him.

  1st Lord. She's turned a child again: a madness,
That would have made her brain and blood boil high,
In which distemper she might have wrought something,—

  2nd Lord. Had been to purpose.

Shir.   E E

1st Lord. The Cardinal is cunning; and howe'er
His brow does smile, he does suspect Hernando
Took fire from her, and waits a time to punish it.

2nd Lord. But what a subject of disgrace and mirth
Hath poor Celinda made herself by pride,
In her belief Columbo was her servant!
Her head hath stooped much since he died, and she
Almost ridiculous at court.

   Enter Cardinal, ANTONELLI, *and* Servant.

 1st Lord. The Cardinal
Is come into the garden, now—
 Car. Walk off.—   [*Exeunt* Lords.
It troubles me the duchess, by her loss
Of brain, is now beneath my great revenge.
She is not capable to feel my anger,
Which, like to unregarded thunder spent
In woods, and lightning aimed at senseless trees,
Must idly fall, and hurt her not, not to
That sense her guilt deserves: a fatal stroke,
Without the knowledge for what crime, to fright her,
When she takes leave, and make her tug with death,
Until her soul sweat, is a pigeon's torment,
And she is sent a babe to the other world.
Columbo's death will not be satisfied,
And I but wound her with a two-edged feather;
I must do more: I have all opportunity,
(She by the king now made my charge,) but she's
So much a turtle, I shall lose by killing her,
Perhaps do her a pleasure and preferment;
That must not be.

   Enter CELINDA *with a parchment.*

 Anton. [*Stopping her.*]—Is not this she, that would
be thought to have been
Columbo's mistress?—Madam, his grace is private,
And would not be disturbed; you may displease him.

Cel. What will your worship wager that he shall
Be pleased again before we part?

Anton. I'll lay this diamond, madam, 'gainst a kiss,
And trust yourself to keep the stakes.

Cel. 'Tis done.   [*Comes forward.*

Anton. I have long had an appetite to this lady;
But the lords keep her up so high—this toy
May bring her on.

Car. This interruption tastes not of good manners.

Cel. But where necessity, my lords, compel
The boldness may meet pardon, and when you
Have found my purpose, I may less appear
Unmannerly.

Car. To the business.

Cel. It did please
Your nephew, sir, before his death, to credit me
With so much honourable favour, I
Am come to tender to his near'st of blood,
Yourself, what does remain a debt to him.
Not to delay your grace with circumstance,
That deed, if you accept, makes you my heir
Of no contemptible estate.—This way   [*He reads.*
Is only left to tie up scurril tongues
And saucy men, that since Columbo's death
Venture to libel on my pride and folly;
His greatness and this gift, which I enjoy
Still for my life, (beyond which term a kingdom's
Nothing,) will curb the giddy spleens of men
That live on impudent rhyme, and railing at
Each wandering fame they catch.   [*Aside.*

Car. Madam, this bounty
Will bind my gratitude, and care to serve you.

Cel. I am your grace's servant.

Car. Antonelli!—   [*Whispers.*
And when this noble lady visits me,
Let her not wait.

Cel. What think you, my officious sir? His grace

Is pleased, you may conjecture : I may keep
Your gem ; the kiss was never yours.

Anton. Sweet madam—

Cel. Talk if you dare ; you know I must not wait ;
And so, farewell for this time.   [*Exit.*

Car. 'Tis in my brain already, and it forms
Apace—good, excellent, revenge, and pleasant !
She's now within my talons : 'tis too cheap
A satisfaction for Columbo's death,
Only to kill her by soft charm or force.
I'll rifle first her darling chastity ;
It will be after time enough to poison her,
And she to the world be thought her own destroyer.
As I will frame the circumstance, this night
All may be finished : for the colonel,
Her agent in my nephew's death, (whom I
Disturbed at counsel with her,) I may reach him
Hereafter, and be master of his fate.
We starve our conscience when we thrive in state.

[*Exeunt.*

SCENE II.—*A Room in the* Duchess's *House.*

Enter ANTONIO *and* PLACENTIA.

Ant. Placentia, we two are only left
Of all my lady's servants ; let us be true
To her, and one another ; and be sure,
When we are at prayers, to curse the Cardinal.

Pla. I pity my sweet lady.

Ant. I pity her too, but am a little angry ;
She might have found another time to lose
Her wits.

Pla. That I were a man !

Ant. What would'st thou do, Placentia ?

Pla. I would revenge my lady.

Ant. 'Tis better, being a woman ; thou may'st do

Things that may prosper better, and the fruit
Be thy own another day.

    Pla. Your wit still loves
To play the wanton.

    Ant. 'Tis a sad time, Placentia ;
Some pleasure would do well : the truth is, I
Am weary of my life, and I would have
One fit of mirth before I leave the world.

    Pla. Do not you blush to talk thus wildly ?

    Ant. 'Tis good manners
To be a little mad after my lady ;
But I have done. Who is with her now ?

    Pla. Madam Valeria.

    Ant. Not Celinda ? There's a lady for my humour !
A pretty book of flesh and blood, and well
Bound up, in a fair letter too. Would I
Had her with all the errata !

    Pla. She has not
An honourable fame.

    Ant. Her fame ! that's nothing ;
A little stain ;—her wealth will fetch again
The colour, and bring honour into her cheeks
As fresh ;—
If she were mine, and I had her exchequer,
I know the way to make her honest ;
Honest to the touch, the test, and the last trial.

    Pla. How, prithee ?

    Ant. Why,
First I would marry her, that's a verb material ;
Then I would print her with an *index*
Expurgatorius ; a table drawn
Of her court heresies ; and when she's read,
Cum privilegio, who dares call her whore ?

    Pla. I'll leave you, if you talk thus.

    Ant. I have done ;
Placentia, thou may'st be better company
After another progress : and now tell me,

Didst ever hear of such a patient madness
As my lady is possessed with? She has raved
But twice :—an she would fright the Cardinal,
Or at a supper if she did but poison him,
It were a frenzy I could bear withal.
She calls him her dear governor.—

Enter HERNANDO *disguised, with a letter.*

Pla. Who is this?

Her. Her secretary!—Sir,
Here is a letter, if it may have so
Much happiness to kiss her grace's hand.

Ant. From whom?

Her. That's not in your commission, sir,
To ask, or mine to satisfy; she will want
No understanding when she reads.

Ant. Alas!
Under your favour, sir, you are mistaken ;
Her grace did never more want understanding.

Her. How?

Ant. Have you not heard? her skull is broken, sir,
And many pieces taken out; she's mad.

Her. The sad fame of her distraction
Has too much truth, it seems,

Pla. If please you, sir,
To expect awhile, I will present the letter.

Her. Pray do.— [*Exit* PLACENTIA.
How long has she been thus distempered, sir?

Ant. Before the Cardinal came to govern here,
Who, for that reason, by the king was made
Her guardian. We are now at his devotion.

Her. A lamb given up to a tiger! May diseases
Soon eat him through his heart!

Ant. Your pardon, sir.
I love that voice ; I know it too a little.
Are not you—be not angry, noble sir,
I can with ease be ignorant again,

And think you are another man ; but if
You be that valiant gentleman they call—

Her. Whom ? what ?

Ant. That killed—I would not name him, if I thought
You were not pleased to be that very gentleman.

Her. Am I betrayed ?

Ant. The devil shall not
Betray you here : kill me, and I will take
My death you are the noble colonel.
We are all bound to you for the general's death,
Valiant Hernando ! When my lady knows
You are here, I hope 'twill fetch her wits again.
But do not talk too loud ; we are not all
Honest i' the house ; some are the Cardinal's creatures.

Her. Thou wert faithful to thy lady.   I am glad
'Tis night.   But tell me how the churchman uses
The duchess.

Enter ANTONELLI.

Ant. He carries angels in his tongue and face, but I
Suspect his heart : this is one of his spawns.—
Signior Antonelli.

Anton. Honest Antonio !

Ant. And how, and how—a friend of mine—where is
The Cardinal's grace ?

Her. That will be never answered.   [*Aside.*

Anton. He means to sup here with the duchess.

Ant. Will he ?

Anton. We'll have the charming bottles at my chamber.
Bring that gentleman ; we'll be mighty merry.

Her. I may disturb your jollity.   [*Aside.*

Anton. Farewell, sweet—   [*Exit.*

Ant. Dear Antonelli !—A round pox confound you !
This is court rhetoric at the back-stairs.

Enter PLACENTIA.

Pla. Do you know this gentleman ?

Ant. Not I.

Pla. My lady presently dismissed Valeria,
And bade me bring him to her bed-chamber.

Ant. The gentleman has an honest face.

Pla. Her words
Fell from her with some evenness and joy.—
Her grace desires your presence.

Her. I'll attend her.   [*Exit with* PLACENTIA.

Ant. I would this soldier had the Cardinal
Upon a promontory, with what a spring
The churchman would leap down! it were a spectacle
Most rare, to see him topple from the precipice,
And souse in the salt water with a noise
To stun the fishes; and if he fell into
A net, what wonder would the simple sea-gulls
Have, to draw up the o'ergrown lobster,
So ready boiled! He shall have my good wishes.
This colonel's coming may be lucky; I
Will be sure none shall interrupt them.

Enter CELINDA.

Cel. Is
Her grace at opportunity?

Ant. No, sweet madam;
She is asleep, her gentlewoman says.

Cel. My business is but a visit. I'll expect.

Ant. That must not be, although I like your company.

Cel. You are grown rich, Master Secretary.

Ant. I, madam? Alas!

Cel. I hear you are upon another purchase.

Ant. I upon a purchase!

Cel. If you want any sum—

Ant. If I could purchase your sweet favour, madam.

Cel. You shall command me, and my fortune, sir.

Ant. How's this?   [*Aside.*

Cel. I have observed you, sir, a staid
And prudent gentleman—and I shall want—

Ant. Not me?

Cel. A father for some infant: he has credit

I' the world.   I am not the first cast lady
Has married a secretary.   [*Aside.*

   Ant. Shall I wait upon you?
   Cel. Whither?
   Ant. Any whither.
   Cel. I may chance lead you then——
   Ant. I shall be honoured to obey.   My blood
Is up, and in this humour I'm for anything.
   Cel. Well, sir, I'll try your manhood.
   Ant. 'Tis my happiness;
You cannot please me better.
   Cel. This was struck
I' the opportunity.   [*Aside, and exit.*
   Ant. I am made for ever.   [*Exit, following her.*

SCENE III.—*Another Room in the same.*

Enter HERNANDO *and* Duchess.

   Her. Dear madam, do not weep.
   Duch. You're very welcome;
I have done; I will not shed a tear more
Till I meet Alvarez, then I'll weep for joy.
He was a fine young gentleman, and sung sweetly;
An you had heard him but the night before
We were married, you would have sworn he had been
A swan, and sung his own sad epitaph.
But we'll talk o' the Cardinal.
   Her. Would his death
Might ransom your fair sense! he should not live
To triumph in the loss.   Beshrew my manhood,
But I begin to melt.
   Duch. I pray, sir, tell me,
For I can understand, although they say
I have lost my wits; but they are safe enough,
And I shall have them when the Cardinal dies;

Who had a letter from his nephew, too,
Since he was slain.

 Her. From whence?

 Duch. I know not where he is. But in some bower
Within a garden he is making chaplets,
And means to send me one; but I'll not take it;
I have flowers enough, I thank him, while I live.

 Her. But do you love your governor?

 Duch. Yes, but I'll never marry him; I am promised
Already.

 Her. To whom, madam?

 Duch. Do not you
Blush when you ask me that? must not you be
My husband? I know why, but that's a secret.
Indeed, if you believe me, I do love
No man alive so well as you: the Cardinal
Shall never know't; he'll kill us both; and yet
He says he loves me dearly, and has promised
To make me well again; but I'm afraid,
One time or other, he will give me poison.

 Her. Prevent him, madam, and take nothing from
  him.

 Duch. Why, do you think 'twill hurt me?

 Her. It will kill you.

 Duch. I shall but die, and meet my dear-loved lord,
Whom, when I have kissed, I'll come again and work
A bracelet of my hair for you to carry him,
When you are going to Heaven; the posy shall
Be my own name, in little tears, that I
Will weep next winter, which congealed i' the frost,
Will show like seed-pearl. You'll deliver it?
I know he'll love, and wear it for my sake.

 Her. She is quite lost.

 Duch. Pray give me, sir, your pardon:
I know I talk not wisely; but if you had
The burthen of my sorrow, you would miss
Sometimes your better reason. Now I'm well;

What will you do when the Cardinal comes?
He must not see you for the world.

   Her. He shall not;
I'll take my leave before he come.

   Duch. Nay, stay;
I shall have no friend left me when you go.
He will but sup; he shall not stay to lie with me;
I have the picture of my lord abed;
Three are too much this weather.

Enter PLACENTIA.

   Pla. Madam, the Cardinal.

   Her. He shall sup with the devil.

   Duch. I dare not stay;
The red cock will be angry. I'll come again.

[Exeunt Duchess and PLACENTIA.

   Her. This sorrow is no fable. Now I find
My curiosity is sadly satisfied.—
Ha! if the duchess in her strangled wits
Let fall words to betray me to the Cardinal,
The panther will not leap more fierce to meet
His prey, when a long want of food hath parched
His starvèd maw, than he to print his rage,
And tear my heart-strings. Everything is fatal;
And yet she talked sometimes with chain of sense,
And said she loved me. Ha! they come not yet.
I have a sword about me, and I left
My own security to visit death.
Yet I may pause a little, and consider
Which way does lead me to't most honourably.
Does not the chamber that I walk in tremble?
What will become of her, and me, and all
The world in one small hour? I do not think
Ever to see the day again; the wings
Of night spread o'er me like a sable hearse-cloth;
The stars are all close mourners too; but I
Must not alone to the cold silent grave,

I must not.—If thou cans't, Alvarez, open
That ebon curtain, and behold the man,
When the world's justice fails, shall right thy ashes,
And feed their thirst with blood ! thy duchess is
Almost a ghost already, and doth wear
Her body like an useless upper garment,
The trim and fashion of it lost.—Ha !

Re-enter PLACENTIA.

Pla. You need not doubt me, sir.—My lady prays
You would not think it long ; she in my ear
Commanded me to tell you, that when last
She drank, she had happy wishes to your health.

Her. And did the Cardinal pledge it ?

Pla. He was not
Invited to't, nor must he know you are here.

Her. What do they talk of, prithee ?

Pla. His grace is very pleasant   [*A lute is heard.*
And kind to her ; but her returns are after
The sad condition of her sense, sometimes
Unjointed.

Her. They have music.

Pla. A lute, only,
His grace prepared ; they say, the best of Italy,
That waits upon my lord.

Her. He thinks the duchess
Is stung with a tarantula.

Pla. Your pardon ;
My duty is expected.   [*Exit.*

Her. Gentle lady !—A voice too ?

SONG *within.*

Strep. Come, my Daphne, come away,
        We do waste the crystal day ;
        'Tis Strephon calls. *Dap.* What would my love ?
Strep. Come, follow to the myrtle grove,
        Where Venus shall prepare
        New chaplets for thy hair.

Dap. Were I shut up within a tree,
    I rend my bark to follow thee.
Strep. My shepherdess, make haste,
    The minutes slide too fast.
Dap. In those cooler shades will I,
    Blind as Cupid, kiss thine eye.
Strep. In thy perfumèd bosom then I'll stray;
    In such warm snow who would not lose his
        way?
Chor. We'll laugh, and leave the world behind,
      And gods themselves that see,
      Shall envy thee and me,
            But never find
    Such joys, when they embrace a deity.

Her. If at this distance I distinguish, 'tis not
Church music; and the air's wanton, and no anthem
Sung to't, but some strange ode of love and kisses.
What should this mean?—Ha? he is coming hither.
                          [*Draws his sword.*
I am betrayed; he marches in her hand.
I'll trust a little more; mute as the arras,
My sword and I here.
            [*Conceals himself behind the arras.*

Enter Cardinal, Duchess, ANTONELLI, *and* Attendants.

Car. Wait you in the first chamber, and let none
Presume to interrupt us.
           [*Exeunt* ANTONELLI *and* Attendants.
    She is pleasant;
Now for some art, to poison all her innocence.
Duch. I do not like the Cardinal's humour; he
Little suspects what guest is in my chamber.
Car. Now, madam, you are safe.   [*Embraces her.*
Duch. How means your lordship?
Car. Safe in my arms, sweet duchess.
Duch. Do not hurt me.
Car. Not for the treasures of the world! You are

My pretty charge.   Had I as many lives
As I have careful thoughts to do you service,
I should think all a happy forfeit, to
Delight your grace one minute; 'tis a Heaven
To see you smile.

   Duch. What kindness call you this?

   Car. It cannot want a name while you preserve
So plentiful a sweetness; it is love.

   Duch. Of me?   How shall I know't, my lord?

   Car. By this, and this, swift messengers to whisper
Our hearts to one another.   [*Kisses her.*

   Duch. Pray do you come a wooing?

   Car. Yes, sweet madam;
You cannot be so cruel to deny me.

   Duch. What? my lord.

   Car. Another kiss.

   Duch. Can you
Dispense with this, my lord?—Alas, I fear
Hernando is asleep, or vanished from me   [*Aside.*

   Car. I have mocked my blood into a flame; and
My angry soul had formed for my revenge,   [what
Is now the object of my amorous sense.
I have took a strong enchantment from her lips,
And fear I shall forgive Columbo's death,
If she consent to my embrace. [*Aside.*]—Come, madam.

   Duch. Whither? my lord.

   Car. But to your bed or couch,
Where, if you will be kind, and but allow
Yourself a knowledge, love, whose shape and raptures
Wise poets have but glorified in dreams,
Shall make your chamber his eternal palace;
And with such active and essental streams
Of new delights glide o'er your bosom, you
Shall wonder to what unknown world you are
By some blest change translated.   Why do you pause,
And look so wild?   Will you deny your governor?

   Duch. How came you by that cloven foot?

Car. Your fancy
Would turn a traitor to your happiness.
I am your friend ; you must be kind.

Duch. Unhand me,
Or I'll cry out a rape.

Car. You will not, sure ?

Duch. I have been cozened with Hernando's shadow,
Here's none but Heaven to hear me.—Help ! a rape !

Car. Are you so good at understanding ? then,
I must use other argument.

    [*He seizes her.*   HERNANDO *rushes from the arras.*

Her. Go to, Cardinal.   [*Strikes him ; exit* Duchess.

Car. Hernando ? Murder ! treason ! help !

Her. An army shall not rescue thee.   Your blood
Is much inflamed ; I have brought a lancet with me
Shall open your hot veins, and cool your fever.—
To vex your parting soul, it was the same
Engine that pierced Columbo's heart.

Car. Help ! murder !   [*Stabs him.*

Enter ANTONELLI *and* Servants.

Anton. Some ring the bell, 'twill raise the court ;
My lord is murdered !   'Tis Hernando.   [*The bell rings.*

Her. I'll make you all some sport.—[*Stabs himself.*]
—So ; now we are even.
Where is the duchess ? I would take my leave
Of her, and then bequeath my curse among you.

    [*He falls.*

Enter King, Duchess, VALERIA, Lords, *and* Guard.

King. How come these bloody objects ?

Her. With a trick my sword found out.   I hope he's
    paid.

1st Lord. I hope so too.—A surgeon
For my lord Cardinal !

King. Hernando ?

Duch. Justice ! oh, justice, sir, against a ravisher !

Her. Sir, I have done you service.

King. A bloody service.

Her. 'Tis pure scarlet.

Enter Surgeon.

Car. After such care to perfect my revenge,
Thus bandied out of the world by a woman's plot !
                                                    [*Aside.*

Her. I have preserved the duchess from a rape.
Good night to me and all the world for ever !   [*Dies*

King. So impious !

Duch. 'Tis most true ; Alvarez' blood
Is now revenged ; I find my brain return,
And every straggling sense repairing home.

Car. I have deserved you should turn from me, sir,
My life hath been prodigiously wicked ;
My blood is now the kingdom's balm.   Oh, sir,
I have abused your ear, your trust, your people,
And my own sacred office ; my conscience
Feels now the sting.   Oh, show your charity,
And with your pardon, like a cool soft gale,
Fan my poor sweating soul, that wanders through
Unhabitable climes, and parchèd deserts.—
But I am lost, if the great world forgive me,
Unless I find your mercy for a crime
You know not, madam, yet, against your life,
I must confess, more than my black intents
Upon your honour ; you're already poisoned.

King. By whom ?

Car. By me,
In the revenge I owed Columbo's loss ;
With your last meat was mixed a poison, that
By subtle, and by sure degrees, must let
In death.

King. Look to the duchess, our physicians !

Car. Stay ;
I will deserve her mercy, though I cannot

Call back the deed.   In proof of my repentance,
If the last breath of a now dying man
May gain your charity and belief, receive
This ivory box; in it an antidote,
'Bove that they boast the great magistral medicine:
That powder, mixed with wine, by a most rare
And quick access to the heart, will fortify it
Against the rage of the most nimble poison.
I am not worthy to present her with it.
Oh, take it, and preserve her innocent life.

   1st Lord. Strange, he should have a good thing in such
readiness.

   Car. 'Tis that, which in my jealousy and state,
Trusting to false predictions of my birth,
That I should die by poison, I preserved
For my own safety ; wonder not, I made
That my companion was to be my refuge.

Enter Servant *with a bowl of wine.*

   1st Lord. Here is some touch of grace.

   Car. In greater proof of my pure thoughts, I take
This first, and with my dying breath confirm
My penitence; it may benefit her life,
But not my wounds.   [*He drinks.*]   Oh, hasten to pre
      serve her ;
And though I merit not her pardon, let not
Her fair soul be divorced.
                [*The* Duchess *takes the bowl and drinks.*

   King. This is some charity ; may it prosper, madam

   Val. How does your grace?

   Duch. And must I owe my life to him, whose death
Was my ambition?   Take this free acknowledgment ;
I had intent, this night, with my own hand
To be Alvarez' justicer.

   King. You were mad,
And thought past apprehension of revenge.

   Duch. That shape I did usurp, great sir, to give

   Shir.   F F

My heart more freedom and defence ; but when
Hernando came to visit me, I thought
I might defer my execution ;
Which his own rage supplied without my guilt,
And when his lust grew high, met with his blood.

1st Lord. The Cardinal smiles.

Car. Now my revenge has met
With you, my nimble duchess ! I have took
A shape[1] to give my act more freedom too,
And now I am sure she's poisoned with that dose
I gave her last.

King. Thou'rt not so horrid.

Duch. Ha ! some cordial.

Car. Alas, no preservative
Hath wings to overtake it ; were her heart
Locked in a quarry it would search, and kill
Before the aids can reach it. I am sure
You shall not now laugh at me.

King. How came you by that poison ?

Car. I prepared it,
Resolving, when I had enjoyed her, which
The colonel prevented, by some art
To make her take it, and by death conclude
My last revenge. You have the fatal story.

King. This is so great a wickedness, it will
Exceed belief.

Car. I knew I could not live.

Surg. Your wounds, sir, were not desperate.

Car. Not mortal ? Ha ! were they not mortal?

Surg. If I have skill in surgery.

Car. Then I have caught myself in my own engine.

2nd Lord. It was your fate, you said, to die by poison.

Car. That was my own prediction, to abuse
Your faith ; no human art can now resist it :
I feel it knocking at the seat of life ;
It must come in ; I have wrecked all my own,

---

[1] Shape is the technical word for a stage-dress, a disguise.

To try your charities : now it would be rare,—
If you but waft me with a little prayer ;
My wings that flag may catch the wind ; but 'tis
In vain, the mist is risen, and there's none
To steer my wandering bark.   [*Dies.*

    1st Lord. He's dead.

    King. With him
Die all deceivèd trust.

    2nd Lord. This was a strange impiety.

    King. When men
Of gifts and sacred function once decline
From virtue, their ill deeds transcend example.

    Duch. The minute's come that I must take my leave,
Your hand, great sir ; and though you be a king,   [too.
We may exchange forgiveness.   Heaven forgive you,
And all the world !   I come, I come, Alvarez.   [*Dies.*

    King. Dispose their bodies for becoming funeral.
How much are kings abused by those they take
To royal grace, whom, when they cherish most
By nice indulgence, they do often arm
Against themselves ! from whence this maxim springs :
None have more need of perspectives[1] than kings.
                            [*Exeunt.*

EPILOGUE.

    [*Within.*] Master Pollard ! where's Master Pollard, for
    the epilogue?
                  [*He is thrust upon the stage, and falls.*

    Epi. [*Rising.*]   I am coming to you, gentlemen ; the
    poet
Has helped me thus far on my way, but I'll
Be even with him : the play is a tragedy,

---

    [1] Telescopes.

The first that ever he composed for us,
Wherein he thinks he has done prettily,

Enter Servant.

And I am sensible.—I prithee look,
Is nothing out of joint? has he broke nothing?
  Serv. No, sir, I hope.
  Epi. Yes, he has broke his epilogue all to pieces.
Canst thou put it together again?
  Serv. Not I, sir.
  Epi. Nor I; prithee be gone. [*Exit* Serv.]—Hum!—
    Master poet,
I have a teeming mind to be revenged.—
You may assist, and not be seen in't now,
If you please, gentlemen, for I do know
He listens to the issue of his cause;
But blister not your hands in his applause;
Your private smile, your nod, or hem! to tell
My fellows that you like the business well;
And when, without a clap, you go away,
I'll drink a small-beer health to his second day;
And break his heart, or make him swear and rage,
He'll write no more for the unhappy stage.
But that's too much; so we should lose; faith, shew it,
And if you like his play, 'tis as well he knew it.

THE TRIUMPH OF PEACE.

*HE TRIUMPH OF PEACE*, which
Dyce calls " the most magnificent
pageant ever, perhaps, exhibited in
England," was presented to the King
and Queen early in February, 1633-4,
by the members of the four Inns of
Court. It originated in an avowed
intention to " confute " Prynne, who,
in his famous *Histriomastix* (pub-
lished in 1632) had attacked Interludes. The musical
department was assigned to Whitelock, who appointed
Simon Ives and William Lawes to compose the airs, and
called in the assistance of eminent English, French, Italian,
and German musicians. The scenes were prepared by
Inigo Jones at the lower end of the Banqueting House.

On the evening of the 3rd February the Masquers
assembled at Ely House, Holborn, and moved in solemn
procession down Chancery Lane to Whitehall, with torches
by the side of the chariots, while the streets were thronged
by multitudes who " seemed loath to part with so glorious
a spectacle." The Queen and her ladies joined in the
dances, and towards morning a stately banquet was served
up to the Gentlemen of the Inns of Court.

The expenses amounted to £21,000, or even a larger sum.
The Masque was printed, as " invented and written " by
Shirley, and reached a third edition in the same year.

To the Four Equal and Honourable Societies,

THE INNS OF COURT.

 WANT words to express your cheerful and active desires, to present your duties to their royal Majesties, in this Masque; to celebrate, by this humble tender of your hearts and services, the happiness of our Kingdom, so blest in the present government, and never so rich in the possession of so many and great pledges of their Parents' virtue, our native Princes.

Your clear devotions already offered and accepted, let not me want an altar for my oblation to you. This entertainment, which took life from your command, and wanted no motion or growth it could derive from my weak fancy, I sacrifice again to you, and under your smile to the world. Let it not repent you to look upon, what is the second time made your own, and with it, the heart of the sacrificer, infinitely bound to acknowledge your free, and noble souls, that have left no way for a poet to satisfy his ambition, how to thank you, but with thinking, he shall never be able to satisfy it.

I dare not rack my preface to a length. Proceed to be yourselves (the ornament of our nation), and when you have leisure to converse with imaginations of this kind, it shall be an addition to your many favours, to read these papers, and oblige beside the seals of your other encouragement,

The humblest of your honourers,

JAMES SHIRLEY.

SPEAKING CHARACTERS IN THE MASQUE.

OPINION.
CONFIDENCE.
FANCY.
JOLLITY.
LAUGHTER.
NOVELTY.
ADMIRATION.

IRENE.
EUNOMIA.
DICHE.
Genius.
AMPHILUCHE.
The Hours.
Chorus.

Carpenter.
Taylor.
Blackguard.
Painter.

Taylor's wife.
Property-man's wife
Feather-maker's wife.
Embroiderer's wife.

Guards.

THE TRIUMPH OF PEACE.

THE MASQUE OF THE GENTLEMEN

OF THE FOUR HONOURABLE SOCIETIES, OR INNS OF
COURT.

At Ely and Hatton Houses, the gentlemen and their assistants met, and in this manner prepared for the Court.

The Antimasquers *were ushered by a hornpipe, and a shawm;* [1] *riding in coats and caps of yellow taffeta, spotted with silver, their feathers red, their horses led by men in coats of blue taffeta, their wings red, and part of their sleeves yellow, caps and feathers; all the torchbearers in the same habit appointed to attend, and give plentiful light to the whole train.*

FANCY *in a suit of several-coloured feathers, hooded, a pair of bat's wings on his shoulders, riding alone, as sole presenter of the Antimasques.*

After him rode OPINION *and* CONFIDENCE *together:*

OPINION *in an old fashioned doublet of black velvet, and trunk hose, a short cloak of the same with an antique cape, a black velvet cap pinched up, with a white fall, and a staff in his hand;*

CONFIDENCE *in a slashed doublet parti-coloured, breeches suitable with points at knees, favours upon his breast and arm, a broad-brimmed hat, tied up on one side, banded with*

---

[1] The shawm resembled the clarionet or hautboy.

a feather, a long lock of hair, trimmed with several-coloured ribands, wide boots, and great spurs with bells for rowels.

Next rode JOLLITY *and* LAUGHTER :

JOLLITY *in a flame-coloured suit, but tricked like a morris dancer, with scarfs and napkins, his hat fashioned like a cone, with a little fall;*

LAUGHTER *in a long side coat of several colours, laughing, vizards on his breast and back, a cap with two grinning faces, and feathers between.*

Then followed variety of antic music; after which rode six Projectors, *one after another, their horses led by torch-bearers :*

The first,[1] *a* Jockey *with a bonnet on his head, upon the top of it a whip, he seeming much to observe and affect a bridle which he had in his hand;*

The second, a Country *fellow in a leather doublet and grey trunk hose, a wheel with a perpetual motion on his head, and in his hand a flail;*

The third a grim Philosophical-faced *fellow, in his gown, furred and girdled about him, a furnace upon his head, and in his hand a lamp;*

The fourth, in a case of black leather, vast to the middle, and round on the top, with glass eyes, and bellows under each arm;

---

[1] "First in this Antimasque, rode a fellow upon a little horse, with a great bit in his mouth, and upon the man's head was a bit, with headstall and reins fastened, and signified a Projector who begged a patent that none in the kingdom might ride their horses, but with such bits as they should buy of him. Then came another fellow with a bunch of carrots upon his head, and a capon upon his fist, describing a Projector who begged a patent of monopoly, as the first inventor of the art to feed capons fat with carrots, and that none but himself might make use of that invention, and have the privilege for fourteen years, according to the statute. Several other Projectors were in like manner personated in this Antimasque ; and it pleased the spectators the more, because by it an information was covertly given to the King of the unfitness and ridiculousness of these projects against the law ; and the Attorney Noy, who had most knowledge of them, had a great hand in this Antimasque of the Projectors."—Whitelock's *Memorials*, quoted by *Dyce.*

The fifth, a Physician, *on his head a hat with a bunch of carrots, a capon perched upon his fist;*

The sixth, like a Seaman, *a ship upon his head and holding a line and plummet in his hand.*

Next these, rode so many Beggars[1] *in timorous looks and gestures, as pursued by two* Mastiffs *that came barking after them.*

Here variety of other antic music, counterfeiting the voices of birds; and after these rode, a Magpie, *a* Crow, *a* Jay, *and a* Kite, *in a quadrangular figure, and in the midst an* Owl;[2] *these were followed by three* Satyrs, *two abreast, and one single, sided with torchbearers; then three* Dotterels *in the same manner and attendance.*

After these a Windmill, *against which a fantastic* Knight *with his lance, and his* Squire *armed, seemed to make their attempts.*

These moving forward in ridiculous show and postures, a Drummer *followed on horseback, in a crimson taffeta coat, a white hat and feather tipped with crimson, beating two kettle drums. Then fourteen* Trumpeters, *in crimson satin coats, white hats and feathers, and rich banners.*

The Marshal *followed these, bravely mounted; attended with ten horse and forty foot, in coats and hose of scarlet trimmed with silver lace, white hats and feathers, their truncheons tipped with silver; these upon every occasion moving to and fro, to preserve the order of their march, and restrain the rudeness of people, that in such triumphs, are wont to be insolent, and tumultuary.*

After these an hundred Gentlemen, *gloriously furnished and gallantly mounted, riding two and two abreast, every gentleman having his two pages richly attired, and a groom to attend him.*

[1] The Beggars, says Whitelock, "had their music of keys and tongs, and the like, snapping, and yet playing in a consort before them. These Beggars were also mounted, but on the poorest leanest jades that could be gotten out of the dirt-carts or elsewhere."

[2] "These," says Whitelock, "were little boys put into covers of the shapes of those birds, rarely fitted, and sitting on small horses," &c.

Next after these, a chariot drawn by four horses, two and two together, richly furnished and adorned with gold and silver, the charioteer in a Polonian coat of green cloth of silver. In this were advanced Musicians, *like Priests and Sybills, sons and daughters of harmony, some with coronets, others with wreaths of laurel and myrtle, playing upon their lutes, three footmen on each side in blue satin wrought with silver, and every one a flambeau in his hand.*

In the next chariot of equal glory, were placed on the lowest stairs four in sky-coloured taffeta robes seeded with stars, mantles ash-coloured, adorned with fringe and silver lace, coronets with stars upon their heads. In a seat a little more elevate sat Genius *and* Amphiluche.

On the highest seat of this chariot, sat the three Hours, *or heavenly sisters,* Irene, Diche, *and* Eunomia ; *all whose habits shall be described in their proper places : this chariot attended as the former.*

After these, came the four triumphals or magnificent chariots, in which were mounted the Grand Masquers, *one of the four houses in every chariot, seated within an half oval, with a glorious canopy over their heads, all bordered with silver fringe, and beautified with plumes of feathers on the top ;*

The first chariot, silver and orange,
The second, silver and watchet,[1]
The third, silver and crimson,
The fourth, silver and white ;

All after the Roman form, adorned with much embossed and carved works, and each of them wrought with silver, and his several colour ; they were mounted on carriages, the spring-trees, pole and axle-trees, the charioteer's seat, and standers, wheels, with the fellies, spokes, and naves, all wrought with silver, and their several colour.

They were all drawn with four horses afront, after the magnificent Roman triumphs, their furniture, harness, headstall, bits, reins, and traces, chamfron, cronet, petronel, and

[1] Pale blue.

barb of rich cloth of silver, of several works and colours, answerable to the linings of the chariots.

The charioteers in Polony coats of the same colour of the chariots, their caps, feathers, and buskins answerable.

The two out-horses of every chariot led by two men, in habits wrought with silver, and conformable to the colour of the other furniture, four footmen on either side of every chariot, in rich habits, also wrought with silver, answerable to the rest, every one carrying a flambeau in his hand.

Between every of these chariots, four musicians in their robes and garlands, were mounted, riding two abreast, attended with torchbearers.

The habit of the Masquers *gave infinite splendour to this solemnity ; which more aptly shall be expressed in its place.*

This Masque was presented in the Banquetting-house at Whitehall, before the King and Queen's Majesties, and a great assembly of lords and ladies, and other persons of quality, whose aspect, sitting on the degrees prepared for that purpose, gave a great grace to this spectacle, especially being all richly attired.

At the lower end of the room, opposite to the State,[1] was raised a stage with a descent of stairs in two branches landing into the room. This basement was painted in rustic work.

The border of the front and sides that enclosed all the scene, had first a ground of arbour-work, intermixed with loose branches and leaves ; and in this was two niches ; and in them two great figures standing in easy postures, in their natural colours, and much bigger than the life. The one, attired after the Grecian manner, held in one hand a sceptre, and in the other a scroll, and a picked antique crown on his head, his cuirass was of gold richly enchased, his robe blue and silver, his arms and thighs bare, with buskins enriched

---

[1] *i.e.* The raised platform on which were placed the royal seats under a canopy.

with ornaments of gold, his brown locks long and curled, his beard thick, but not long, and his face was of a grave and jovial aspect; this figure stood on a round pedestal, feigned of white marble, enriched with several carvings; above this in a compartment of gold was written MINOS. The figure on the other side was in a Roman habit, holding a table[1] in one hand, and a pen in the other, and a white bend or diadem about his head, his robe was crimson and gold, his mantle yellow and silver, his buskins watchet trimmed with silver, his hair and beard long and white, with a venerable aspect, standing likewise on a round pedestal answerable to the other; and in the compartment over him was written NUMA. Above all this, in a proportionate distance, hung two great festoons of fruits in colours, which served for finishing to these sides. The upper part, in manner of a large frieze, was adorned with several compartments with draperies hanging down, and the ends tied up in knots, with trophies proper to feasts and triumphs, composed of masking vizards and torches. In one of the lesser compartments, was figured a sharp-sighted eye, and in the other a golden yoke; in the midst was a more great and rich compartment, on the sides of which sat naked children in their natural colours, with silver wings, in action of sounding golden trumpets, and in this was figured a caduceus with an olive branch, all which are hieroglyphics of Peace, Justice, and Law.

A curtain being suddenly drawn up, the SCENE was discovered, representing a large street with sumptuous palaces, lodges, porticos, and other noble pieces of architecture, with pleasant trees and grounds; this going far from the eye, opens itself into a spacious place, adorned with public and private buildings seen afar off, representing the forum or piazza of Peace. Over all was a clear sky with transparent clouds, which enlightened all the scene.

The spectators having entertained their eyes awhile with the beauty and variety of this scene, from one of the sides of the streets

[1] Writing tablet.

Enter OPINION ; CONFIDENCE *meets him; they salute.*

Con. Most grave Opinion !

Opin. Confidence, most welcome !
Is Fancy come to court ?

Con. Breaking his way
Thorough the guard.

Opin. So violent ?

Con. With jests
Which they are less able to resist ;
He'll crack a halbert with his wit.

Opin. A most
Strong Fancy ! yet we have known a little engine
Break an ingenious head-piece. But your master—

Con. Companion, sir ; Fancy will keep no servants,
And Confidence scorns to wait.

Opin. Cry mercy, sir ;
But is this gentleman, this Signor Fancy,
So rare a thing, so subtle, as men speak him?

Con. He's a great prince of th' air, believe it, sir,
And yet a bird of night.

Opin. A bird !

Con. Between
An owl and bat, a quaint hermaphrodite,
Begot of Mercury and Venus, Wit and Love,
He's worth your entertainment.

Opin. I am most
Ambitious to see him ; he is not
So nimble as I wish him. Where's my wife,
My Lady Novelty?

Enter NOVELTY.

Nov. Your wife ! you might
Have framed a newer word ; they can but call
Us so i' the country.

Opin. No exception.
Dear Madam Novelty ; I must prepare you,

To entertain a gentleman.   Where's Admiration,
Our daughter?

Enter ADMIRATION.

Adm. Here, sir.   What gay man is this?
Opin. Please you honour us, and bring in your friend,
Con. I'll do't; but he prevents me.   [sir.

Enter FANCY, JOLLITY, *and* LAUGHTER.

Opin. Sir, I am ignorant
By what titles to salute you, but you're welcome
To court.
Fan. Save yourself, sir; your name's Opinion.
Opin. And your's Fancy.
Fan. Right.
Jol. Mine Jollity.
Laugh. Mine Laughter; ha, ha, ha!
Nov. Here's a strange shape!
Adm. I never saw the like.
Fan. I come to do you honour with my friends here,
And help the masque.
Opin. You'll do a special favour.
Fan. How many antimasques¹ have they? of what
        nature?
For these are fancies that take most; your dull
And phlegmatic inventions are exploded.
Give me a nimble antimasque.
Opin. They have none, sir.
Laugh. No antimasque! I'd laugh at that, i'faith.
Jol. What make we here?   No jollity!
Fan. No antimasque!
Bid 'em down with the scene, and sell the timber,
Send Jupiter to grass, and bid Apollo
Keep cows again; take all their gods and goddesses,
For these must farce up this night's entertainment,

¹ The antimasque was a direct contrast to the principal masque,
and admitted of the wildest extravagances. It was mostly performed by professional actors.

And pray the court may have some mercy on 'em,
They will be jeered to death else for their ignorance.
The soul of wit moves here; yet there be some,
If my intelligence fail not, mean to show
Themselves jeer majors; some tall [1] critics have
Planted artillery and wit murderers.
No antimasque! let 'em look to't.

   Opin. I have heard, sir;
Confidence made 'em trust, you'd furnish 'em:
I fear they should have made their address earlier
To your invention, but your brain's nimble.
Pray, for the expectation that's upon 'em,
Lend them some witty fancies, set some engines
In motion, that may conduce to the design.
I am their friend against the crowd that envy 'em,
And since they come with pure devotions
To sacrifice their duties to the king
And queen, I wish 'em prosper.

   Fan. You have charmed me:
I'll be their friend to-night; I have a fancy
Already.

   Laugh. Let it be ridiculous.

   Con. And confident.

   Jol. And jolly.

   Fan. The first antimasque
We will present ourselves in our own persons;
What think you on't? Most grave Opinion,
You shall do well to lead the dance, and give
Authority with your face; your lady may
Admire what she finds new.

   Nov. I shall applaud
The novelties.

   Adm. And I admire.

   Fan. They tumble;
My skull's too narrow.

   Laugh. Now his fancies caper.

---

[1] Great.

Shir.

                          G G

Fan. Confidence, wait you upon Opinion ;
Here Admiration, there Novelty ;
This is the place for Jollity and Laughter ;
Fancy will dance himself too.

The first Antimasque, the dance expressing the natures of the presenters.

Fan. How like you this device ?
Opin. 'Tis handsome, but—
Laugh. Opinion will like nothing.
Nov. It seems new.
Con. 'Twas bold.
Jol. 'Twas jocund.
Laugh. Did not I do the fool well ?
Ad. Most admirably.
Laugh. Nay, and the ladies do but take
My part, and laugh at me, I am made, ha, ha !
Opin. I could wish something, sir, of other nature,
To satisfy the present expectation.
Fan. I imagine ; nay, I'm not ignorant of proprieties
And persons ; 'tis a time of peace, I'll fit you,
And instantly make you a representation
Of the effects.
Opin. Of peace ? I like that well.
Fan. And since in nothing they are more expressed
Than in good fellowship, I'll present you with
A tavern.

The SCENE *is changed into a Tavern, with a flaming red lattice, several drinking-rooms, and a back door, but especially, a conceited sign, and an eminent bush.*

Nov. A spick and span new tavern !
Ad. Wonderful ! here was none within two minutes.
Laugh. No such wonder, lady : taverns are quickly up ;

it is but hanging out a bush at a nobleman's door, or an alderman's gate, and 'tis made instantly.

Con. Will't please you, ladies, to accept the wine?

Jol. Well said, Confidence.

Nov. It will be new for ladies
To go to th' tavern; but it may be a fashion.
Follow me, Admiration.

Laugh. And the fool;
I may supply the absence of your fiddlers.

Jol. If we can, let's leave Opinion behind us;
Fancy will make him drunk.

> [*Exeunt to the tavern,* CONFIDENCE, JOLLITY,
> LAUGHTER, NOVELTY, *and* ADMIRATION.

Another Antimasque of the Master *of the tavern, his* Wife, *and* Servants. *After these a* Maquerelle,[1] *two* Wenches, *two wanton* Gamesters. *These having danced and expressed their natures, go into the tavern. Then enter a* Gentleman, *and four* Beggars. *The* Gentleman *first danceth alone; to him the* Beggars; *he bestows his charity; the* Cripples, *upon his going off, throw away their legs, and dance.*

Opin. I am glad they are off:
Are these effects of peace?
Corruption rather.

Fan. Oh, the beggars show
The benefit of peace.

Opin. Their very breath
Hath stifled all the candles, poisoned the
Perfumes: beggars a fit presentment! how
They cleave still to my nostril! I must tell you,
I do not like such base and sordid persons,
And they become not here.

Fan. I apprehend.
If these distaste you, I can fit you with

---

[1] Old French meaning a bawd.

Persons more cleanly ;
What think you of projectors ?
  Opin. How, projectors ?
  Fan. Here's one already.

Enter a Jockey.

This is a jockey :
He is to advance a rare and cunning bridle,
Made hollow in the iron part, wherein
A vapour subtly conveyed, shall so
Cool and refresh a horse, he shall ne'er tire ;
And now he falls to his pace.   [*The* Jockey *dances.*

Enter a Country-Fellow.

  Opin. This other ?
  Fan. His habit speaks him ;
A country fellow, that hath sold his acres
To purchase him a flail, which, by the motion
Of a quaint wheel, shall, without help of hands,
Thresh corn all day ; and now he lays about him.
                [*The* Country-fellow *dances.*

Enter a third Projector.

This with a face philosophical and beard,
Hath with the study of twenty years found out
A lamp, which placed beneath a furnace, shall
Boil beef so thoroughly, that the very steam
Of the first vessel shall alone be able
To make another pot above seethe over.
  Opin. A most scholastic project ! his feet follow
                [*The third* Projector *dances.*
The motions of his brain.

Enter a fourth Projector.

But what thing's this ?
A chimera out of Rabelais ?
  Fan. A new project,
A case to walk you all day under water ;

So vast for the necessity of air,
Which, with an artificial bellows cooled,
Under each arm is kept still from corruption ;
With those glass eyes he sees, and can fetch up
Gold or whatever jewels have been lost,
In any river o' the world.

               [The fourth Projector *dances.*

    Opin. Strange water-rat !

Enter a fifth Projector.

    Fan. This grave man, some years past, was a physician,
A Galenist, and parcel Paracelsus ;[1]
Thrived by diseases, but quite lost his practice,
To study a new way to fatten poultry
With scrapings of a carrot, a great benefit
To th' commonwealth.   *[The fifth* Projector *dances.*

    Opin. He will deserve a monument.

Enter a sixth Projector.

    Fan. This is a kind of sea-gull too, that will
Compose a ship to sail against the winds ;
He'll undertake to build a most strong castle
On Goodwin sands, to melt huge rocks to jelly,
And cut 'em out like sweetmeats with his keel ;
And thus he sails.   *[The sixth* Projector *dances.*

All the Projectors *dance after their Antimasque. The*
    Maquerelle, Wenches, Gentlemen, *return, as from the*
    tavern ; they dance together ; the Gallants *are cheated ;*
    and left to dance in, with a drunken repentance.

    Opin. I know not, sir, how this may satisfy ;
But might we be beholding to your fancy
For some more quaint variety, some other
Than human shapes, would happily delight
And reach the expectation ; I have seen

---

[1] *i.e.* Partly a follower of Paracelsus.

Dainty devices in this kind, baboons
In quellios,[1] and so forth.
    Fan. I can furnish you.
    Opin. Fancy will much oblige us.
    Fan. If these objects
Please not, Fancy can present a change.
What see you now?

The Scene *becomes a woody Landscape, with low grounds
proper for hunting, the furthest part more desert, with
bushes and bye-ways representing a place fit for purse-
taking.*
*In the furthest part of the scene is seen an ivy-bush, out of
which comes an* Owl.

    Opin. A wood, a broad-faced owl,
An ivy-bush, and other birds about her!
    Fan. These can imagination create.
Silence, observe.

An Owl, *a* Crow, *a* Kite, *a* Jay, *a* Magpie. *The birds
dance and wonder at the* Owl. *When these are gone,
enter a* Merchant, *a' Horseback with his portmanteau;
two* Thieves, *set upon him and rob him: these by a* Constable *and* Officers *are apprehended and carried off.
Then four* Nymphs *enter dancing, with their javelins;
three* Satyrs *spy them and attempt their persons; one of
the* Nymphs *escapeth; a noise of hunters and their horns
within, as at the fall of a deer; then enter four* Hunts-
men *and one* Nymph; *these drive away the* Satyrs, *and
having rescued the* Nymphs, *dance with them.*

    Opin. This all you will present?
    Fan. You speak as if
Fancy could be exhaust; invention flows

---

[1] Ruffs: Span. *cuello.*

From an immortal spring; you shall taste other
Variety, nimble as thought. We change the scene.

The SCENE, *a Landscape; enter three* Dotterels, *and three*
Dotterel-catchers.

Opin. What are these?
Fan. Dotterels; be patient, and expect.

After the Dotterels *are caught by several imitations,*[1] *enter
a* Windmill, *a fantastic* Knight *and his* Squire *armed.
The fantastic adventurer with his lance makes many
attempts upon the* Windmill, *which his* Squire *imitates: to
them enter a* Country-gentleman *and his* Servant. *These
are assaulted by the* Knight *and his* Squire, *but are sent
off lame for their folly.   Then enter four* Bowlers, *who
show much variety of sport in their game and postures,
and conclude the Antimasque.*

Enter CONFIDENCE, JOLLITY, LAUGHTER, NOVELTY,
ADMIRATION.

Opin. Madam, accuse your absence—
Nov. Come, we know
All your devices, sir; but I will have
An antimasque of my own, in a new place too.
Opin. Hah, what's the matter?
Confidence, Jollity, Laughter, Admiration,
And Madam Novelty, all drunk! these are
Extremes indeed.
Adm. Admirable Opinion!
Con. Be confident.
Laugh. And foolish.

[1] These foolish birds were said to let themselves be taken in the
net of the fowler, while they were mimicking his gestures; if he
stretched out a leg, so did the dotterel, &c.—*Dyce.*

Jol. I am as light now!—

Fan. Let 'em enjoy their fancies.

Opin. What new change

Is this? these strains are heavenly.

　　　　　　　　　[FANCY *and the rest go off fearfully.*

　　The Antimasquers *being gone, there appears in the highest
and foremost part of the heaven, by little and little to break
forth, a whitish cloud, bearing a chariot feigned of goldsmith's work; and in it sat* IRENE, *or* PEACE, *in a flowery
vesture like the spring, a garland of olives on her head, a
branch of palm in her hand, buskins of green taffeta, great
puffs about her neck and shoulders.*

SONG I.

Irene. Hence, ye profane, far hence away!

Time hath sick feathers while you stay.

　　　　　　Is this delight

　　　　　For such a glorious night,

　　　　　　Wherein two skies

　　　　　　Are to be seen,

One starry, but an agèd sphere,

　　　　　　Another here,

Created new and brighter from the eyes

　　　　　　Of king and queen?

　　Cho. Hence, ye profane, far hence away!

Time hath sick feathers while you stay.

Song II.

Irene. Wherefore do my sisters stay?
Appear, appear Eunomia!
'Tis Irene calls to thee,
>Irene calls:
>Like dew that falls
>Into a stream,
>I'm lost with them
That know not how to order me.

Cho. See where she shines, oh see
In her celestial gaiety!
Crowned with a wreath of stars, to show
The evening's glory in her brow.

Here, out of the highest part of the opposite side, came softly descending another cloud, of an orient colour, bearing a silver chariot curiously wrought, and differing in all things from the first; in which sate EUNOMIA *or* LAW, *in a purple satin robe, adorned with golden stars, a mantle of carnation laced, and fringed with gold, a coronet of light upon her head, buskins of purple, drawn out with yellow. This chariot attended as the former.*

Song III.

Euno. Think not I could absent myself this night:
But Peace is gentle and doth still invite
Eunomia; yet shouldst thou silent be,
>The rose and lily which thou strowest
>All the cheerful way thou goest,
>Would direct to follow thee.
Irene. Thou dost beautify increase,
>And chain security with peace.
Euno. Irene fair, and first divine,
>All my blessings spring from thine.
Irene. I am but wild without thee, thou abhorrest
>What is rude, or apt to wound,
>Canst throw proud trees to the ground,
>And make a temple of a forest.

Euno. No more, no more, but join
      Thy voice and lute with mine.
Both. The world shall give prerogative to neither ;
      We cannot flourish but together.
Cho. Irene enters like a perfumed spring,
      Eunomia ripens everything,
      And in the golden harvest leaves
      To every sickle his own sheaves.

*At this, a third cloud of various colour from the other
two, begins to descend toward the middle of the scene with
sowewhat a more swifter motion ; and in it sat a person,
representing* DICHE *or* JUSTICE, *in the midst, in a white
robe and mantle of satin, a fair long hair circled with a
coronet of silver pikes, white wings and buskins, a crown
imperial in her hand.*

SONG IV.

Diche. Swiftly, oh, swiftly ! I do move too slow,
What holds my wing from making haste
When every cloud sails by so fast ?
I heard my sisters' voice and know
They have forsaken Heaven's bright gate,
To attend another state,
Of gods below.
Irene, chaste Eunomia !
  Irene and Euno. We,
Diche, have stayed expecting thee ;
Thou giv'st perfection to our glory,
And seal to this night's story ;
Astrea, shake the cold dew from thy wing.
  Euno. Descend.
  Irene. Descend.
  Euno. Descend, and help us sing
The triumph of Jove's upper court abated,
And all the deities translated.

  Cho. The triumph of Jove's upper court abated,
And all the deities translated.

Euno. Now gaze, and when thy wonder will allow,
Tell what thou hast beheld.

Diche. Never, till now,
Was poor Astrea blind; oh strange surprise,
That too much sight should take away my eyes!
Am I in earth or Heaven?

Irene. What throne is that,
On which so many stars do wait?

Dich. My eyes are blest again, and now I see
The parents of us three:
'Tis Jove and Themis; forward move,
And sing to Themis, and to Jove.

Then the whole train of Musicians *move in a comely figure towards the king and queen, and bowing to their State, this following ode is sung.*

SONG V.

To you, great king and queen, whose smile
Doth scatter blessings through this isle,
   To make it best
   And wonder of the rest
We pay the duty of our birth;
Proud to wait upon that earth
   Whereon you move,
   Which shall be named
And by your chaste embraces famed,
   The paradise of love.

Irene, plant thy olives here;
Thus warmed, at once they'll bloom and bear:
   Eunomia, pay thy light;
While Diche, covetous to stay,
Shall throw her silver wings away,
   To dwell within your sight.

The SCENE *is changed, and the* Masquers *appear sitting on the ascent of a hill, cut out like the degrees of a theatre; and over them a delicious arbour with terms of young men, their arms converted into scrolls, and under their waists a foliage with other carvings to cover the joining of the term from the naked, all feigned of silver; these bore up an architrave, from which was raised a light covering arched, and interwoven with branches through which the sky beyond was seen.*

The Masquers *were sixteen in number, the sons of* PEACE, LAW, *and* JUSTICE, *who sitting in a gracious but not set form, every part of the seats made a various composition, but all together tending to a pyramidal figure.*

Their habits were mixed, between the ancient and modern; their bodies carnation, the shoulders trimmed with knots of pure silver, and scallops of white and carnation, under them the labels of the same, the under sleeves white, and a puffed sleeve full of gathering, falling down to the elbow; about their waist was a small scallop, and a slender girdle; their under bases were carnation and white, with labels as at their shoulders, and all this in every part was richly embroidered with pure silver; their hats carnation low crowned, the brim double, and cut into several quarters lined with white, and all over richly embroidered, as the rest; about their hats were wreaths of olive, and plumes of white feathers with several falls, the longest toward the back; their long stockings were white, with white shoes and roses.

Beneath these a Genius *or angelical person, with wings of several coloured feathers, a carnation robe tucked up, yellow, long hair, bound with a silver coronet, a small white rod in his hand, white buskins; who descended to the stage speaketh.*

Gen. No foreign persons I make known,
But here present you with your own,
The children of your reign, not blood;
Of age, when they are understood,

Not seen by faction or owl's sight,
Whose trouble is the clearest light.
But treasures to their eye, and ear,
That love good for itself, not fear.
Oh, smile on what yourselves have made!
These have no form, no sun, no shade,
But what your virtue doth create;
Exalted by your glorious fate,
They'll tower to heaven, next which, they know,
And wish no blessedness but you.
That very look into each eye   [*The* Masquers *move.*
Hath shot a soul, I saw it fly.
Descend, move nimbly, and advance,
Your joyful tribute in a dance.

Here, with loud music, the Masquers *descend and dance
their entry to the violins; which ended, they retire to the
scene, and then the* Hours *and* Chori *again move toward
the State and sing.*

Song VI.

They that were never happy Hours
Till now, return to thank the powers
       That made them so.
       The Island doth rejoice,
And all her waves are echo to our voice,
Which, in no ages past, hath known
       Such treasures of her own.

Live, royal pair, and when your sands are spent
       With Heaven's and your consent,
       Though late, from your high bowers,
       Look down on what was yours;
For, till old Time his glass hath hurled,
And lost it in the ashes of the world,
We prophesy, you shall be read and seen,
In every branch, a king or queen.

The song ended, and the Musicians *returned, the* Masquers *dance their main dance ; after which they again retire to the scene ; at which they no sooner arrive, but there is heard a great noise, and confusion of voices within, some crying,* "We will come in," *others* "Knock 'em down, call the rest of the guard;" *then a crack is heard in the works, as if there were some danger by some piece of the machines falling ; this continued a little time, there rush in a* Carpenter, *a* Painter, *one of the* Black guard,[1] *a* Tailor, *the* Tailor's Wife, *an* Embroiderer's Wife, *a* Feather maker's Wife, *and a* Property man's Wife.

Carp. D'ye think to keep us out ?

1st Guard. Knock her down.

Tai. Knock down my wife ! I'd see the tallest beef-eater on you all but hold up his halberd in the way of knocking my wife down, and I'll bring him a button hole lower.

Tai. Wife. Nay, let 'em, let 'em, husband, at their peril.

2nd Guard. Complain to my lord chamberlain.

Property m. Wife. My husband is somewhere in the works; I'm sure I helped to make him an owl and a hobby horse, and I see no reason but his wife may be admitted in *forma paperis,*[2] to see as good a masque as this.

Bl. guard. I never saw one afore: I am one of the guard, though of another complexion, and I will see't, now I am here, though I be turned out of the kitchen to-morrow for't.

Paint. Ay, come, be resolute ; we know the worst, and let us challenge a privilege ; those stairs were of my painting.

Carp. And that timber I set up ; somebody is my witness.

Feath. Wife. I am sure my husband sold 'em most of the feathers ; somebody promised me a fall too, if I came to court, but let that pass.

---

[1] The meanest drudges in royal residences, who carried coals, &c.
[2] *i.e. Pauperis.*

Emb. Wife. And mine embroidered two of the best
habits: what though we be no ladies, we are Christians
in these clothes, and the king's subjects, God bless us.

Tai. Nay, now I am in, I will see a dance, though my
shop windows be shut up for't. Tell us?—hum? d'ye
hear? do not they laugh at us? what were we best to
do? The masquers will do no feats as long as we are
here: be ruled by me, hark every one; 'tis our best
course to dance a figary ourselves, and then they'll think
it a piece of the plot, and we may go off again with the
more credit; we may else kiss the porter's lodge [1] for't;
let's put a trick upon 'em in revenge, 'twill seem a new
device too.

All. Content.

Tai. And the musicians knew but our mind now?

[*The violins play.*

Hark, they are at it; now for a lively frisk. [*They dance.*
Now, let us go off cleanly, and somebody will think this
was meant for an antimasque.

They being gone, the Masquers *are encouraged by a song,
to their revels with the ladies.*

Song VII.

Why do you dwell so long in clouds,
    And smother your best graces?
'Tis time to cast away those shrouds,
    And clear your manly faces.

Do not behave yourselves like spies
    Upon the ladies here;
On even terms go meet their eyes,
    Beauty and love shine there.

You tread dul measures thus alone,
    Not satisfy delight;
Go kiss their hands, and make your own
    With every touch more white.

---

[1] Where servants were punished.

The Revels being passed, the SCENE *is changed into a plain champaign country, which terminates with the horizon, and above a darkish sky, with dusky clouds, through which appeared the new moon, but with a faint light by the approach of the morning; from the furthest part of this ground, arose by little and little a great vapour, which being come about the middle of the scene, it slackens its motion, and begins to fall downward to the earth from whence it came; and out of this rose another cloud of a strange shape and colour, on which sate a young maid, with a dim torch in her hand; her face was an olive colour, so was her arms and breast, on her head a curious dressing, and about her neck a string of great pearl; her garment was transparent, the ground dark blue, and sprinkled with silver spangles, her buskins white, trimmed with gold; by these marks she was known to be the forerunner of the morning, called by the ancients* AMPHILUCHE, *and is that glimpse of light, which is seen when the night is past, and the day not yet appearing.*

SONG VIII.

Amph. In envy to the Night,
That keeps such revels here,
With my unwelcome light,
Thus I invade her sphere;
  Proclaiming wars
To Cynthia, and all her stars,
That, like proud spangles, dress
  Her azure tress.
Because I cannot be a guest, I rise
To shame the Moon, and put out all her eyes.

AMPHILUCHE *ascending, the* Masquers *are called from their revels by other voices.*

SONG IX.

1st Voice. Come away, away, away,
See the dawning of the day,

Risen from the murmuring streams :
Some stars show with sickly beams,
What stock of flame they are allowed,
Each retiring to a cloud ;
Bid your active sports adieu,
The morning else will blush for you.

   2nd Voice. Ye feather-footed Hours run
To dress the chariot of the Sun ;
Harness the steeds, it quickly will
Be time to mount the eastern hill.

   3rd Voice. The lights grow pale with modest fears,
Lest you offend their sacred ears,
And eyes, that lent you all this grace ;
Retire, retire, to your own place.

   4th Voice. And as you move from that blest pair,
Let each heart kneel, and think a prayer,
That all, that can make up the glory
Of good and great may fill their story.

   AMPHILUCHE *hidden in the heavens, and the* Masquers
retired, the Scene closeth.

   And thus concluded this MASQUE, which was, for the variety of
the shows, and richness of the habits, the most magnificent that
hath been brought to court in our time.

   The scene and ornament, was the act of Inigo Jones, Esquire,
Surveyor of his Majesty's works.

   The composition of the music, was performed by Mr. William
Lawes, and Mr. Simon Ives, whose art gave an harmonious soul to
the otherwise languishing numbers.

A Speech to the King and Queen's Majesties, when they were pleased to honour the City with their presence, and gave a gracious command, the former Triumph should attend them.

Genius. Most great and glorious princes, once more, I
Present to your most sacred Majesty
The sons of Peace, who tender you, by me,
Their joy-exalted heart, and humble knee ;
Happy in their ambition to wait,
And pay this second duty to your state,
Acknowledging no triumph but in you :
The honour you have done them is so new,
And active in their souls, that it must grow
A part of them, and be immortal too.
These wonders you create, and every man
Receives as much joy as the island can ;
Which shows you nearest heaven, that can let fail
Unequal, yet a perfect bliss to all.
Dwell still within yourselves, for other place
Is straight, and cannot circumscribe your grace,
Whilst men grow old with prayers for your blest reign,
Yet with your smiles shall be restored again.

UNWIN BROTHERS, LIMITED, PRINTERS, WOKING AND LONDON.